PROPHETS <small>AND</small> MOGULS, RANGERS <small>AND</small> ROGUES, BISON <small>AND</small> BEARS

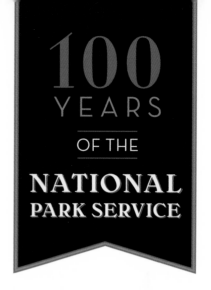

PROPHETS AND MOGULS, RANGERS AND ROGUES, BISON AND BEARS

Heather Hansen

Foreword by
Jonathan B. Jarvis, Director, National Park Service

MOUNTAINEERS
BOOKS

MOUNTAINEERS BOOKS

Mountaineers Books is the publishing division of The Mountaineers, an organization founded in 1906 and dedicated to the exploration, preservation, and enjoyment of outdoor and wilderness areas.

1001 SW Klickitat Way, Suite 201, Seattle, WA 98134
800-553-4453, www.mountaineersbooks.org

Printed in China
18 17 16 15   5 4 3 2 1

Copy editor: Kris Fulsaas
Design, layout, and cartography: John Barnett, www.4eyesdesign.com

Cover photographs (front, clockwise from upper left): *Stephen Mather in Glacier National Park, 1920s* (NPS Historic Photograph Collection, photo by T. J. Hileman); *St. Mary Lake, Glacier NP* (Library of Congress, Prints and Photographs Division, Carol M. Highsmith Archive, LC-DIG-highsm-14289); *bison in rut* (Creative Commons, photo by Neal Herbert); *a cannon captured from the French, Springfield Armory National Historic Site* (Library of Congress, Prints and Photographs Division, LC-DIG-det-4a12241); *Everglades aerial* (NPS Digital Image Archives); back: *driving through the Tunnel Log in 1957, Sequoia National Park* (Library of Congress, Prints and Photographs Division, LC-DIG-matpc-23254); *a proud new junior ranger in Joshua Tree National Park* (NPS Photo by Kurt Moses)

Frontispiece: *Theodore Roosevelt and John Muir on Overhanging Rock at Glacier Point, near where they camped in Yosemite in 1903. When imploring Muir to be his park guide, the president wrote, ". . . I want to drop politics absolutely for four days and just be out in the open with you."* (Library of Congress, Prints and Photographs Division, LC-USZ62-107389)

Excerpts from "The Wilderness Letter" from *The Sound of Mountain Water* by Wallace Stegner (on page 203) are copyright © 1969 by Wallace Stegner. Used by permission of Doubleday, an imprint of the Knopf Doubleday Publishing Group, a division of Penguin Random House LLC. All rights reserved.

National Park Foundation brand marks are registered trademarks of the National Park Foundation, and are used under license by Mountaineers Books.

Library of Congress Cataloging-in-Publication Data
Hansen, Heather.
  Prophets and moguls, rangers and rogues, bison and bears : 100 years of the National Park Service / Heather Hansen ; foreword by Jonathan Jarvis, director, National Park Service.
     pages cm
  Includes bibliographical references and index.
  ISBN 978-1-59485-888-8 (paperback)—ISBN 978-1-59485-889-5 (ebook)
1. United States. National Park Service—History. 2. National parks and reserves—United States—History. 3. United States. National Park Service—Officials and employees—Biography. I. Title.
  SB482.A4H34 2015
  363.6'80973—dc23
                       2015007674

ISBN (paperback): 978-1-59485-888-8
ISBN (ebook): 978-1-59485-889-5

This 1872 photograph of the lower basin of Mammoth Hot Springs was among the first images of Yellowstone National Park seen by average Americans.

CONTENTS

A trail beckons visitors into the cool recesses of Muir Woods.

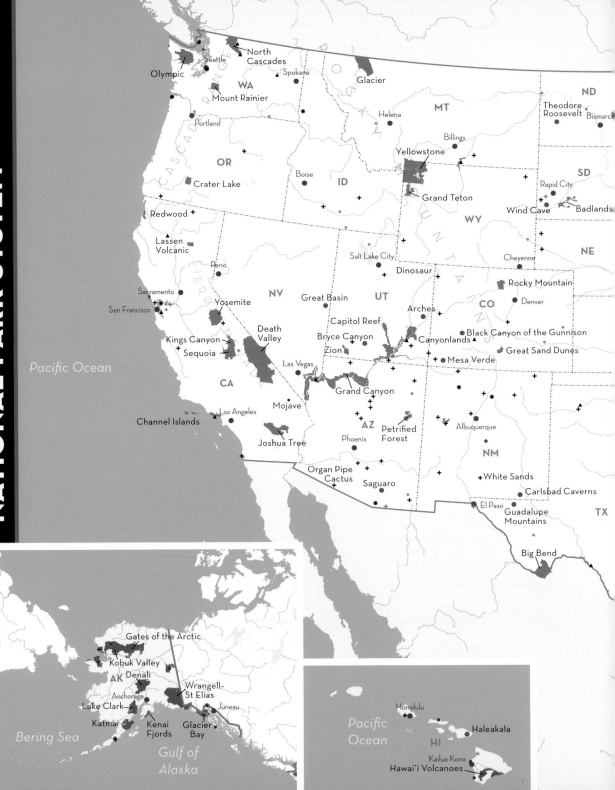

NATIONAL PARK SYSTEM

WA
Seattle
Olympic
North Cascades
Mount Rainier
Spokane
Glacier
Portland
OR
Crater Lake
Redwood
Lassen Volcanic
Reno
Sacramento
San Francisco
Yosemite
Kings Canyon
Sequoia
Death Valley
Las Vegas
Mojave
NV
Great Basin
CA
Channel Islands
Los Angeles
Joshua Tree
Organ Pipe Cactus
Saguaro
Phoenix
AZ
Petrified Forest

Pacific Ocean

Helena
Billings
MT
Yellowstone
Grand Teton
Boise
ID
WY
Salt Lake City
Dinosaur
Cheyenne
UT
Arches
Capitol Reef
Bryce Canyon
Zion
Canyonlands
Grand Canyon
Mesa Verde
CO
Rocky Mountain
Denver
Black Canyon of the Gunnison
Great Sand Dunes
Albuquerque
NM
White Sands
Carlsbad Caverns
El Paso
Guadalupe Mountains
Big Bend

ND
Theodore Roosevelt
Bismarck
SD
Rapid City
Wind Cave
Badlands
NE
TX

Gates of the Arctic
Kobuk Valley
Denali
Wrangell-St Elias
Anchorage
Lake Clark
AK
Katmai
Kenai Fjords
Glacier Bay
Juneau

Bering Sea
Gulf of Alaska

Honolulu
Pacific Ocean
HI
Haleakala
Kailua Kona
Hawai'i Volcanoes

Spring meltwater thunders down countless tributaries at Mount Rainier National Park.

PROTECT
YOUR PARKS

FOREWORD

MANY THINGS SEEM to divide us as a nation: socioeconomic status, political leanings, religion, ethnicity, or income. But the theme behind the National Park Service, "America's best idea," can surely unite Americans with a sense of wonder and pride. Our mission at NPS is unique among government agencies. As the stewards of the national experience, the keepers of cultural memory, and the guardians of world-renowned landscapes, for us not only is it an honor to serve but an awesome responsibility. Former Supreme Court Justice Sandra Day O'Connor wrote, "There's no better route to civic understanding than visiting our national parks. They're who we are and where we've been." The social challenges and ecological shifts we continually face as a nation require the actions of informed, engaged, open-minded individuals who can look to national parks—our most underutilized classrooms—for guidance and inspiration.

Above: Government-sponsored messages, such as this one, promoted conservation during the Great Depression.

The park system is the biggest real-world science laboratory on the planet, and an eyewitness to American history. The parks have no equal in their ability to teach about past and present. They provide endless opportunities to explore subjects like human rights, labor, immigration, climate change, and a host of other topics that are relevant today.

This book—written by a journalist looking from the outside in—gives us a better understanding of what the NPS offers society as a whole, as well as insight into a century of the agency's foresight, tribulations, and triumphs. It underscores the social identity, economic impacts, and quality of life that parks and monuments afford the public. It reminds readers that we all have access to secret and incredible places that can be life-changing. And it presents a vision of our work that speaks to the legacy of the NPS and its ongoing relevance to our lives.

National parks must be, in the minds of coming generations, as treasured and vital as they were to the generations that have sustained them. And the work of the National Park Service must continue to touch communities and improve people's lives— our success during the next century depends on it and, in a way, the success of our country depends on the NPS achieving this higher calling.

Since its creation in 1916, the National Park Service has grown, learned, adapted, and become even more important to civil society. In 1970, Congress reaffirmed this mission by stating that the national parks are *cumulative expressions of a single national heritage.* I fear at times that this heritage has become frayed and realize that the NPS is needed more now than ever before. For the first century, citizens worked hard to save the parks from people who saw them only as a commercial commodity. Now perhaps the national parks will save us by reminding each American that we are citizens of a country with high ideals, who have a history of respect and restraint and the ability to be inspired through contact with nature in wild places.

Like this book, we tell stories through place, places where this nation and its ambitions were forged in the hottest fires, places where people acted upon their convictions for conservation, for civil rights, for the future of their children's children. At the dawn of the park system's second century, let these stories and places inspire us all to rise to new challenges with purpose and pride inspired by our national parks.

Jonathan B. Jarvis
Director, National Park Service

ACKNOWLEDGMENTS

THANKS FIRST to my favorite travel companion (who also happens to be my mother) for encouraging her kids to pitch in and to make discoveries that last a lifetime. Love and gratitude to other family and friends who are ceaseless supporters of this nomadic spirit—a year on the road would not have been possible without your meals, couches, and encouragement.

To the crew at Mountaineers Books, my sincere thanks, especially Kate Rogers, Kirsten Colton, Laura Shauger, and Kris Fulsaas, who skillfully guided this book from idea to reality.

To the past, present, and future women and men of the NPS: after examining a century's worth of your work, I hold you in high esteem. To Brianne Cassetta at Fairsted (Frederick Law Olmsted), Michael Haynie at Guadalupe Mountains, Tim Karle at Klondike Gold Rush (Seattle unit), Peter Dessauer at Harpers Ferry, Reneel Langdon at the Statue of Liberty, Carol Quinn on the Natchez Trace, Masyih Ford at North Cascades, and Wade Myers at the Harpers Ferry Center—and many more mentioned within these pages: each of you is an asset to the Park Service. Your enthusiastic stewardship and belief that the future can be positively impacted by understanding past and present are energizing and inspiring, often making it tough to tear myself away! With special thanks to Yosemite National Park, where I spent days in conversation and on trails with some truly remarkable rangers; David Dahlen and Katrina Fritts at the Mather Training Center; Chris Robinson at the Historic Preservation Training Center; and Bob Sonderman and his dedicated staff at the Museum Resource Center. With particular appreciation to Ann Foster at Yellowstone for the insight and assistance of the skilled archivists there who brought the Bannock Trail to life.

Finally, to visionaries with the courage to defend foresight, you are rare but critical to conservation and preservation. The national park system and Park Service would not exist if not for your recognition of shifting conditions and finite resources. This book celebrates you at a time when we need your guidance more than ever.

INTRODUCTION

BEYOND THE SUBWAY RUMBLE and taxi horns of New York City, there's a surprisingly peaceful alcove just off Broadway in Lower Manhattan. From above, the park is shaped like an old keyhole, with grass and trees lining its perimeter. A sweep of black granite panels with elegant symbols carved in white express themes like humility, strength, diversity, and life. They surround a map of the world, centered on West Africa, etched into the ground. Those walls lead to stairs that ascend into an A-frame memorial, also dark granite, straddled by twin reflecting pools. The landscaped garden includes several mounds marking the burial sites of seven wooden crypts containing the remains of 419 enslaved and free Africans. Those remains were discovered in 1991 when this land was excavated for a federal building.

What is now the African Burial Ground National Monument is but one small portion of the 6.6-acre burial site that serves as the final resting place of an estimated 15,000 people of African descent from the seventeenth and eighteenth

16

centuries. Back then this place was still called New Amsterdam, and many European Americans brought kidnapped Africans here and sold them into lives of brutal servitude in the "New" World. It is one of the most important archaeological finds of the twentieth century: a portal to days now seldom evoked but eternally relevant, where the image of the visitors themselves is reflected back off of every polished surface. The entry panel reads "For all those who were lost / For all those who were stolen / For all those who were left behind / For all those who are not forgotten."

The monument is one of the newest additions to the network of more than 400 parks administered by the National Park Service. It's a microcosm of the types of resources the NPS is entrusted with nationwide—it is a critical cultural landmark, a historical powerhouse, and an open green space amid a stronghold of steel and concrete. In fact, if you look at the national park units in just New York you get a sense of the enormous breadth of NPS responsibilities.

Not far from the African Burial Ground are Castle Clinton National Monument and the Statue of Liberty National Monument, including Ellis Island, through which millions of immigrants passed seeking better futures. Mere blocks away also lies the birthplace of one of the country's greatest conservationists: President Theodore Roosevelt. Not much farther afoot is Gateway National Recreation Area, home to an astonishing array of wildlife in several ecosystems. Nearby, off of Long Island, are the protected wetlands and sand flats of Fire Island National Seashore. Travel up the Hudson River, and you intercept the Appalachian Trail, which covers 88 miles in New York State (out of its total 2200 miles from Maine to Georgia). Venture farther north and find places steeped in the history of the

Civil War, the Revolutionary War, women's rights, and industrialization. *All* are national park units.

Pick any state in the United States, the District of Columbia, and the US islands of the Caribbean and Pacific, and you will find places under the care of the Park Service. These places connected to history, culture, and nature are protected, owing to the foresight of early conservationists and the commitment of their current guardians in green and gray. The Park Service is known best, of course, for protecting iconic parks (Yellowstone, Yosemite, Grand Canyon, and Great Smoky Mountains), but the existence of these parks and a bureau dedicated to protecting them was not a foregone conclusion—far from it. It took years of debate and persuasion to establish the national park system and Park Service, which are now known and emulated worldwide. To advance the idea, early park boosters had to banish the doubt, avarice, and fear characteristic of their contemporaries. The concept of conservation of public land for the use and enjoyment of everyone was entirely new, an idea that President Theodore Roosevelt called "essentially democratic in spirit, purpose, and method."

Since its founding in 1916, the NPS has been unique in its history and challenges. At the time, utilitarian land management, which focused on the *use* of trees, water, grasses, and minerals, was well represented by the US Geological Survey (established in 1879), the US Forest Service (1905), and the Reclamation Service (1907). The NPS, however, began as a bureau tasked with preserving wilderness and a handful of cultural sites largely in the West. When the Park Service was born, there were thirty-six national park units encompassing roughly 6 million acres. Throughout the twentieth

WHAT'S IN A NAME?

There are more than 400 *units* in the national park system. Only 59 are national *parks*. The others are divided among two dozen or so other categories, including national monument, preserve, recreation area, seashore, lakeshore, scenic trail or riverway, and national historic site, memorial, historical park, or battlefield. In this book, the term "national park" is used to describe all these types of units.

The NPS also supports more than just national park units. It maintains the National Register of Historic Places and provides and facilitates grants for states, municipalities, tribes, and others to protect cultural artifacts and outdoor recreation areas and facilities.

century, the NPS evolved to include natural and cultural areas in remote locales and in cities, from the Arctic to the tropics. The NPS also took on historic sites, including birthplaces and battlefields, monuments and missions. It remains the only federal land management agency with the legal responsibility to protect entire environments, including some of the last true wilderness tracts in the nation.

As of the second decade of the twenty-first century, hundreds of national park units cover 84 million acres and have roughly 290 million visitors annually. The NPS safeguards sites as diverse as Cape Cod National Seashore, Gettysburg National Military Park, Blue Ridge Parkway, Indiana Dunes National Lakeshore, El Malpais National Monument, Lake Mead National Recreation Area, Big Cypress National Preserve, the Lincoln Memorial, and the White House. National park units have white sands, fall color, cooling waters, glinting glaciers, volcanoes, dinosaur bones, endangered species, wild and scenic rivers, and coral reefs, all offering countless recreational opportunities. Park units protect hallowed ground, living history and culture, and ideals such as freedom and justice,

conservation and equality. They are places of great drama, captivating characters, endless superlatives, and fathomless discoveries.

The mandate of the NPS remains "to conserve the scenery and the natural and historic objects and the wild life therein and to provide for the enjoyment of the same in such manner and by such means as will leave them unimpaired for the enjoyment of future generations." It's a short directive for a big idea, and each generation has interpreted the inherent paradoxes of this mandate in its own way. Amid big personalities and agendas—writer and conservationist Wallace Stegner called the environment the NPS operates in a "political alligatorhole"—missteps have been taken. But the fact remains that the Park Service has shielded national treasures through world wars, the Great Depression (and others to rival it), legions of schemes to exploit their fragile abundance, and disasters both natural and human-made. What was born as a bureau to protect scenery and "playgrounds" has evolved into one that looks after some of this continent's cleanest water and its remaining refuges of biodiversity.

The roughly 22,000 women and men who constitute the NPS these days are still easily recognizable in their stiff-brimmed hats and under-stated garb emblazoned with an arrowhead logo. Their responsibilities remain immense. Just as the NPS founders were the architects of family vacations that imprinted icons like Yosemite upon the world's psyche, contemporary Park Service employees are the protectors of these sources of education, inspiration, exploration, preservation, perspiration, integration, revelation, and—increasingly—adaptation. Parks are a stepping-off point, a catalyst, for adventures of mind and body, of ideology and identity. At a time when much divides humankind, national parks are rallying points, reminders of shared values and conditions and of human errors that should not be repeated. At times of uncertainty and cynicism, they are sources of pride, reflection, and conviction, places to refill the drained reservoirs of the soul.

What the Park Service protects has never been more valuable, or more at risk. In many ways the nation is in the same position it was a century ago when the Park Service was created. While a vast majority of Americans support national parks and the work of the NPS, parks' viability is threatened by slashed budgets, staggering maintenance backlogs, and unprecedented stresses both within and beyond their borders. Picture for a moment our nation without its parks—no Great Smokies, no Everglades, no Constitution Hall. Certainly no Acadia or Denali. No wolves or grizzlies, trumpeter swans or California condors. In their places are more big-box retail stores, sites of energy extraction, bland housing developments, fluorescent fast-food signs, and pavement. Would we be the poorer for it? Economically speaking, yes. For every tax dollar invested in the NPS, $10 is returned to the US economy via spending in gateway communities, to the tune of nearly $27 billion generated and hundreds of thousands of jobs supported annually.

Why else should Americans of all spots and stripes steward parks and fully fund the Park Service? Because by caring for parks we care for *ourselves*. Because we want to watch burly bison graze verdant meadows; to relive Dr. Martin Luther King Jr.'s electrifying "I Have a Dream" speech in the spot where he delivered it; to stand

AN EMBLEM SPEAKS A THOUSAND WORDS

What's now the official symbol of the NPS was authorized in 1951. The design includes three prongs of NPS protection: the arrowhead represents historic and archaeological resources, the mountains and water stand for the scenic and recreational aspects of parks, and the bison and sequoia tree symbolize natural resources.

The Ancestral Chamber as seen from the Circle of the Diaspora and Ancestral Libation Court
at the African Burial Ground National Monument

in the room where the Declaration of Independence was *signed*. Because we want to summit icy peaks and discover strengths we never knew we harbored; to gather with family and friends and create enduring memories; to log off, power down, and be turned on to incomparable riches. Because we want to know that when we return to our national parks next year, or our great-grandchildren visit them after a century more, there will still be something remarkable there to prolong gazes and propel adventures charged with astonishment. Because they remind us who we are and who we want to be. National parks are merely on loan from one generation to the next, and the NPS is responsible for passing that baton. As it strives to do that, one of its most profound wishes for its hundredth birthday is the interest and support of every American.

Efforts to preserve the African Burial Ground in New York City were guided by the West African concept of *sankofa*—symbolized with a stylized heart shape in which two equal parts meet head to head—which urges us to "learn from the past and prepare for the future." This principle must guide the NPS—and every American citizen—in the next century, if national parks are to endure. In looking at the concepts and people who have molded and safeguarded parks, it's clear that present conditions mix ideals (parks untouched by development, climate change, and budget woes) and reality (parks endangered by all three). If the future is a path across that lumpy landscape, signs at the trailhead might warn users about toting too much hubris, remind them to tread lightly and pick up after themselves, urge them to consider that this common ground would not exist and will not persist without attention paid and investment made in its needs. Although this is an uphill path, it transects a map on which national parks still lie at the center of a landscape of epic possibilities.

PROTECTED BY THE NPS

- Land area: 84 million acres
- Ocean, lake, and reservoir area: 4.5 million acres
- Miles of shoreline: 43,162
- Miles of rivers and streams: 85,000
- Wild and Scenic Rivers: 60
- Trail miles: 12,250
- Scenic and national historic trails: 23
- Road miles: 8,500
- Museum objects: more than 121 million
- Archaeological sites: nearly 69,000
- Historic structures: 27,000
- Highest and coldest spot in North America: 20,320-foot Mount McKinley (a.k.a. Denali) in Denali National Park; reached minus 118.1 degrees Fahrenheit in 2003
- Lowest and hottest point in North America: 282 feet below sea level in Death Valley National Park; reached 134 degrees Fahrenheit in 1913

CHAPTER 1

Whose Idea Was It?

CROSSING NORTH-CENTRAL Wyoming are the remnants of a centuries-old passage called the Bannock Trail. The roughly 200-mile path ran northeast from Idaho's Camas Meadows, overtaking the Continental Divide at Targhee Pass, then entering what is now Yellowstone National Park. From there it wove among the park's rugged western peaks, wildflower-studded meadows, blistering geyser basins, and spirited waterways. After dropping steeply into the Grand Canyon of the Yellowstone, the trail traversed that relentless river via a small island. That so-called Bannock Ford, which divides the flow of the Yellowstone River not far from Tower Falls, remains a powerful place for visitors to imagine those original pathfinders. From that juncture, the trail drives east through the Lamar Valley (dubbed "America's Serengeti" for its abundant wildlife) and onto the "buffalo" plains east of the park.

The once-great aboriginal highway was used heavily from 1838 to 1878 to reach the cool-in-summer high-country air, obsidian collection sites, and bison hunting grounds. It was named for the seminomadic Bannock Indians, who frequented the Upper Yellowstone country centuries before European Americans laid wide eyes upon the place. When white men did eventually venture into Yellowstone—indomitable trappers and traders chasing beaver pelts in the early nineteenth century—many of them traced those ancient trailways and brought home dubious tales of hissing, trembling earth marked by sky-high waterfalls, sundry wildlife, a fathomless canyon, and a gleaming inland sea.

John Colter, who left the Lewis and Clark Expedition in 1806 to seek a fortune in fur trapping, is believed to be the first non-Indian to traverse the Yellowstone region. After slogging over several hundred miles, he trotted into camp spouting off about smoking pits and noxious steam, and his compatriots just shook their heads in disbelief; surely all that time alone had addled the poor man's brain. Jim Bridger, another trapper and explorer, followed in Colter's footsteps decades later. Known for spinning yarns, he described the hot springs and geysers of Yellowstone as "Hell bubbling up" where swift rivers sizzled. Since mountain men had a reputation for hyperbole, Bridger's tales were also treated as suspect.

But as decades passed and similar accounts of Yellowstone began to corroborate what Colter and Bridger had described, one newspaper decided to chance introducing those wilds to the world. The first written impressions of the area's fairytale features appeared in eastern newspapers in 1827. From trapper Daniel Potts's letters to his brother, the *Gazette of the United States & Daily Advertiser* (Philadelphia) printed, "The Yellow Stone has a large fresh water lake near its head on the very top of the mountain, which is . . . as clear as crystal.

On the south border of this lake is a number of hot and boiling springs. One of our men visited one of these whilst taking his recreation—there at an instant the earth began a tremendous trembling, and he with difficulty made his escape, when an explosion took place resembling that of thunder."

Despite the uncloaking of Yellowstone in the press, a waning number of trappers crossed that northwest corner of Wyoming as beaver were hunted nearly to extinction in the West. Gold prospectors poked and prodded Yellowstone country but left empty-handed. Without something tangible to exploit there, the region remained terra incognita to most Americans through the 1830s. It was still "out there," thousands of miles from so-called civilization, a remote wasteland.

For decades after Yellowstone's debut in the press, tribes continued to pass along the rugged, winding Bannock Trail relatively unimpeded by European Americans. The Arapaho, Assiniboine, Blackfeet, Nez Perce, Northern Cheyenne, and Crow frequented the area, as did the Flathead, Gros Ventre, Kiowa, Sioux, and Shoshone. Some of their territories abutted or overlapped future park borders. The Tukudeka, a band of the Shoshone (called the "Sheep Eaters"), were the only permanent residents of what became the first national park.

But westward expansion changed all that; by 1842 pioneers were surging along the Oregon Trail, and in 1848 gold was discovered in California, drawing throngs of people west into wildernesses unknown. Ultimately, curiosity and necessity drew a succession of explorers into Yellowstone, starting with Captain William Raynolds's expedition in 1860, guided by Jim Bridger (by then in his midfifties) and documented by geologist Ferdinand Hayden. The group explored the future park's perimeter but failed to penetrate the

The well-equipped US Geological and Geographical Survey pack train at Mirror Lake en route to the East Fork of the Yellowstone River, 1871

heart of Yellowstone. Nevertheless the expedition produced a map that marked features of the Upper Yellowstone Valley, based on Bridger's descriptions, including the lake and falls. In his report Raynolds concluded that Bridger's descriptions must be true because "as he is uneducated, and had probably never heard of the existence of such natural marvels elsewhere, I have little doubt that he spoke of that which he had actually seen." When their exploration ended without seeing the area's interior, to the captain's dismay, he remarked prophetically, "At no very distant day the mysteries of this region will be fully revealed."

Within a year of his expedition, Raynolds, along with most of the rest of nation, was mired in the Civil War. Despite national turmoil, President Abraham Lincoln remarkably put preservation on the map in the summer of 1864. In June, the same month in which both the North and South were suffering tremendous losses at Cold Harbor,

Virginia, California Senator John Conness sponsored legislation to protect Yosemite Valley and nearby Mariposa Grove. As federal lands, they were open to claim-staking, so Conness proposed putting them under the jurisdiction of California, which could preserve them as parks—since there was no federal park system yet to do that. His constituents, including those Conness called "gentlemen of fortune, of taste, and of refinement," wanted the area protected; an act of Congress, signed by Lincoln, granted that historic request. The legislation required that the conserved land would "be held for public use, resort, and recreation . . . inalienable for all time."

A handful of years later, a gutsy trio pulled off the first real exploration of Yellowstone by European Americans for which there is a lasting record. Montanans David Folsom, Charles Cook, and William Peterson were due to join a larger party, but when their military detail fell through and fear of Indian hostility hung over the effort, all but those three men skipped the trip. With trepidation, they set out in September 1869 equipped with five horses, cooking utensils, fishing tackle, an ax, a field glass, a compass, blankets, buffalo robes, a pick and pan, a thermometer, six weeks' worth of provisions, and a veritable arsenal that included repeating rifles, Colt six-shooters, sheath knives, and a double-barreled shotgun. For all the odd and unfamiliar landscape—the gasp and gurgle of gaseous subterranean belches surfacing; soaring waterfalls thundering loud enough to drown out a man's yell; the sulfurous stench of steaming geothermal pools—they may as well have been exploring the surface of the moon. However harrowing it was, the explorers did not regret their thirty-six-day trek. In his journal Cook wrote, "Language is entirely inadequate to convey a just conception of the awful grandeur and sublimity of this masterpiece of nature's handiwork."

Upon the party's return, Cook figured the media would reject his journals as what he called the "too vivid imagination of a typical Rocky Mountain liar." The *New York Tribune* and *Scribner's Monthly* did decline to publish them, calling Cook's accounts unreliable and improbable, but *Western Monthly Magazine* took him at his word. In that article, Cook reflected on his time in the Valley of the Upper Yellowstone: "We felt glad to have looked upon it before its primeval solitude should be broken by the crowds of pleasure seekers which at no distant day will throng its shores." It would

be a while before Yellowstone would be beset by throngs of visitors, but the Cook-Folsom-Peterson Expedition certainly kicked open that door.

However incredible the accounts seemed to some people, they whetted others' appetites. Another privately sponsored expedition followed on Cook's heels, less than a year later. That one, which included government officials and prominent citizens of the Territory of Montana, warranted a military escort. The much larger thirty-four-day expedition—whose members named a now-famous geyser "Old Faithful" for its consistent eruptions—included General Henry Washburn, Lieutenant Gustavus Doane, and explorer and businessman Nathaniel Langford. For five weeks, the party picked its way through vast geothermal minefields. They encountered countless strange features: boiling mud vats, petrified trees, hissing steam vents, growling geysers spewing water toward the sun without warning, and streams colored green, orange, and blue by bacteria.

Unlike earlier forays into Yellowstone, Washburn's party was media fodder upon its return. Langford recounted his adventures to a sold-out Lincoln Hall in Washington, DC, in January 1871. Patrons paid fifty cents each to hear his lecture. A lengthy, detailed account with extraordinary illustrations, written by Langford and published in *Scribner's* in June 1871, extolled "The Wonders of the Yellowstone." On looking at the great gash of the Grand Canyon of the Yellowstone, Langford wrote, "The brain reels as we gaze into this profound and solemn solitude."

A surprisingly poetic account of the expedition came from Doane, whose official report to Secretary of War William Belknap was instrumental in establishing Yellowstone as the country's first national park. The young lieutenant made geographic,

IF YOU LIKE WILLIAM HENRY JACKSON, YOU'LL LOVE JOSHUA CRISSMAN

Joshua Crissman was an assistant to renowned photographer William Henry Jackson. Historians now know he should have gotten credit for at least some of Jackson's famous photos.

geologic, and meteorological observations, but it was his unabashed astonishment at what he saw that formed a powerful commentary. Remarking on three of the area's major waterfalls along the Firehole River, Doane wrote, "These pretty little falls, if located on an eastern stream, would be celebrated in history and song; here, amid objects so grand as to strain conception and stagger belief, they were passed without a halt." On Yellowstone's overall attributes, he wrote, "As a country for sightseers, it is without parallel; as a field for scientific research, it promises great results; in the branches of geology, mineralogy, botany, zoology, and ornithology, it is probably the greatest laboratory that nature furnishes on the surface of the globe."

With the nation's curiosity piqued, the first government-sponsored expedition was dispatched to confirm or refute, once and for all, Yellowstone's wild wonders. The old trappers Colter and Bridger were finally vindicated when the $40,000 (more than $750,000 today), thirty-man Hayden Expedition launched in late July 1871. Hayden (who'd been the geologist on the Raynolds Expedition a decade earlier), head of what would become the US Geological Survey, brought back to Washington, DC, what no one had up to that point: proof.

Artist Thomas Moran, who had illustrated Langford's *Scribner's* article (and then longed to see Yellowstone for himself), and photographer William Henry Jackson accompanied Hayden. While Moran's sketchbook was highly portable, Jackson's equipment included glass-plate negatives as big as 20 feet by 24 feet, but both men produced stunning images that put Yellowstone right in front of skeptical eyes. Their work circulated around Congress and gave decision-makers, at long last, a compelling look at the distant land. For the first time Americans could see images of the distant West in color, and Congress could see what budding conservationists meant when they insisted these were treasures to be owned by all Americans. Hayden's large collection of specimens, including rocks and plants, was on exhibition in Washington while Congress was in session.

For his part, Moran gained the nickname "Father of the Park System" because of the impact his work had on Congress in passing park legislation. It didn't take long for official talk of preserving Yellowstone to echo in the halls of Congress. Senator Samuel Pomeroy, a Republican from Kansas, got the ball rolling on an otherwise ordinary Monday in December 1871 when he addressed his colleagues, saying, "I ask leave to introduce a bill to set apart a certain tract of land lying near the headwaters of the Yellowstone as a public park. It has been ascertained within the last year or two that there are very valuable reservations at the headwaters of the Yellowstone, and it is thought they ought to be set apart for public purposes rather than to have private preemption or homestead claims attached to them." The big idea was known simply as Senate Bill 392.

In his *Scribner's* article, published in January 1872, Hayden rallied support for the bill by posing the question, "Why will not Congress at once pass a law setting it apart as a great public park for all time to come as has been done with that far inferior wonder, the Yosemite Valley?" Setting apart "this wonderland as a great National Park for all time," Hayden wrote in an article published in the *American Journal of Science and Arts*, "will prevent squatters from taking possession of the springs and destroying the beautiful decorations." SB 392 passed the Senate on January 30, 1872, and the House less than a month later. The Forty-Second US Congress passed the legislation with a Republican majority in both chambers. A precedent, with federal protection far exceeding the preservation enacted for Yosemite, had been set.

The Yellowstone Act of 1872 created the world's first national park. It withdrew more than 2 million acres from sale, settlement, or occupation to be "dedicated and set apart as a public park or pleasuring-ground for the benefit and enjoyment of the people." Unlike Yosemite, the bill put Yellowstone under federal control because ceding it to either Montana or Wyoming as newly minted states would have likely prompted a high-noon-style duel. The legislation placed the park under the control of the Secretary of the Interior to "provide for the preservation, from injury or spoliation, of all timber, mineral deposits, natural curiosities, or wonders within said park, and their retention in their natural condition."

❧   ❧   ❧

Who do we have to thank, ultimately, for the national park concept? Enduring NPS lore gave credit to members of the Washburn Expedition who, huddled around a campfire in Yellowstone's interior in September 1870, reportedly talked about setting aside that region as the nation's park. But time has unraveled that yarn. Of course the Washburn, Cook, and Hayden expeditions that risked life and limb to establish Yellowstone's legitimacy warrant some credit, as do members of Congress who sponsored and passed the national park bill. The influential railroad industry also deserves some credit for bringing early tourists to those far-flung nature reserves and pressuring policy makers to protect them.

But preservation on the national level is a notion that grew over generations, beginning with tribes that trod gently in the Yellowstone area out of reverence (not fear, as many European Americans would later suggest) for its strange character and bountiful resources. Artist George Catlin, famous for his paintings of American Indians, actually made the first written mention of the concept of federal protection. While traveling in

As seen here in *American Pasturage-Prairies of the Platte*, painter George Catlin depicted the still-sizeable but shrinking herds of bison that he observed on his journey west in the mid-nineteenth century.

the Dakotas in 1832, he worried about wilderness being despoiled and wrote that it could be preserved "by some great protecting policy of government . . . in a magnificent park . . . a nation's park, containing man and beast, in all the wild and freshness of their nature's beauty!" Throughout the nineteenth century, the work of other artists, philosophers, and writers, including Ralph Waldo Emerson, Henry David Thoreau, James Fenimore Cooper, and Albert Bierstadt, helped shift thinking about wilderness from a thing to be tamed or feared to something to be celebrated. Nature activists, including John Muir, also wielded prose and personality that raised consciousness by elevating in the mainstream media the profile and purpose of uncultivated places.

People such as landscape architect Frederick Law Olmsted (famous for planning New York City's Central Park and many other public and private green spaces) recognized this pivotal moment, in which America still had stretches of unclaimed

IF YOU LIKE JOHN MUIR, YOU'LL LOVE CLARENCE DUTTON

In 1875 Captain Clarence Dutton reluctantly joined legendary explorer John Wesley Powell on a US Geological Survey expedition of the Colorado Plateau in Utah. Surveying of western territories had ground to a halt during the Civil War but began again in earnest afterward. Dutton, Powell, and others ventured into the last area of the continental United States to be surveyed, including lands now known as Grand Canyon, Bryce Canyon, Zion, and Capitol Reef national parks and Grand Staircase–Escalante and Cedar Breaks national monuments. Dutton was hired to record, interpret, and sketch the geologic features on which to base more elaborate topographical maps and illustrations—which he did exceedingly well.

But Dutton (both a field geologist and a pioneering seismologist) also, apologetically and in spite of his scientific mind, conveyed lyrically what he saw. He was hypnotized by the alternating hues of the plateau's cliffs and canyons, writing that, unlike eastern landscapes with their "gentle tints" of blue and green, this area of the West had "belts of fierce staring red, yellow and toned white, which are intensified rather than alleviated by alternating belts of dark iron grey." While on the Aquarius Plateau, the soldier-scientist wrote, "The explorer who sits upon the brink of its parapet looking off into the southern and eastern haze, who skirts its lava-cap or clambers up and down its vast ravines, who builds his campfire by the borders of its snow-fed lake or stretches himself beneath its giant pines and spruces, forgets that he is a geologist and feels himself a poet."

IF YOU LIKE ANSEL ADAMS, YOU'LL LOVE CARLETON WATKINS

Carleton Watkins began photographing Yosemite in 1861 and became internationally renowned for his striking landscape images. That's forty years before Ansel Adams was born.

Carleton Watkins made this image of Mirror Lake in Yosemite with an extra large, custom-built camera and a "mammoth" glass-plate negative that he developed on-site in a portable darkroom.

land, mainly out West. It occurred to him and a handful of others that the nascent country, struggling to compete with Europe's rich cultural offerings, could distinguish itself with unmatched scenery.

Olmsted also perceived the need for natural retreats in a country recovering from the exhaustion of civil war and adjusting to the sights, sounds, and speed of industrialization. Growth was exponential and the pace of life in cities was stressful. When eastern urbanites fled the chaos for the relative calm of the natural world, many went to Niagara Falls. But the East's premier natural tourist attraction had devolved into a garish, overcrowded spectacle. It became clear to anyone who valued unique features that they must be protected from Niagara's fate.

Armed with this consciousness, Olmsted was instrumental in the protection of the Yosemite Valley. As one of the first commissioners of the area that eventually became Yosemite National Park, he wrote a report in 1865 that was astonishing in its foresight. In it Olmsted outlined the management of that

park—and ultimately described an ethos that would drive the future NPS: "To simply reserve [public parks] from monopoly by individuals, however, it will be obvious, is not all that is necessary. It is necessary that they should be laid open to the use of the body of the people. The establishment by government of great public grounds for the free enjoyment of the people under certain circumstances, is thus justified and enforced as a political duty," he wrote.

Regardless of who gets credit for the concept that began with Yellowstone and Yosemite and grew into a varied system protecting hundreds of natural, cultural, and historical sites, ultimately it required the vision and persistence of many. The national park "idea" was the untried notion of conservation, a powerful tool that continues to shape the United States. And while only remnants of the once-teeming Bannock Trail across Yellowstone can be glimpsed today, the traces of that bygone path remain symbolic of perils endured to reach a goal—of matchless wonders to be guarded for generations to come.

From loosely sketched field studies, painter Thomas Moran ultimately created huge, intricately detailed works like this one of Yellowstone.

CHAPTER 2

Prophets of Outdoordom

A FEW HOURS NORTH of New York City, a cadre of peaks contain in their ancient folds both a bit of wild America and the tale of how modern conservation came to be. The Catskill Mountains are 6000 square miles of streams and waterfalls, forests and farmlands, among heaving hillocks. The Mohican Indians (or, as they called themselves, the Muh-he-con-neok or "the People of the waters that are never still") once thrived in these abundant woodlands but were wary of malevolent spirits thought to be skulking among the trees.

Later, German and Dutch immigrants shared that sentiment; they said the devil had crafted the dark, mysterious Catskills and had carved out the countless valleys with heavy swipes of his tail.

One man with a very different sense of the place brought his carefully crafted vision into the mainstream, ultimately changing how Americans viewed their landscapes and natural resources. John Burroughs, who would become a famous naturalist and writer, was born in 1837 on his family's farmstead, Woodchuck Lodge, on a hushed hillside

John Muir and John Burroughs, dubbed "John o' Mountains" and "John o' Birds", respectively, by their friends

in the central Catskills. There the nature writer took root, as he described it, and though he traveled far and broad, he always returned to those fragrant, pulsing woods to observe the wild world and write about it; he was buried there in 1921. Nature is, he wrote, "an inexhaustible storehouse of that which moves the heart, appeals to the mind and fires the imagination."

On a midautumn day, fallen leaves coat a trail in layers of vermilion and pale yellow near Burroughs's rough-hewn log cabin called Slabsides, another of the author's Catskills retreats. Here, ample stands of maple, birch, spruce, and hemlock filter sunlight into lazy pools around his quiet sanctuary. At Slabsides in West Park and at Woodchuck Lodge, Burroughs welcomed many confidants and influential people, including Henry Ford, Walt Whitman, Theodore Roosevelt, Thomas Edison, and John Muir, who were all reportedly greatly influenced by his way of seeing. Burroughs, dubbed by mainstream media as the "Prophet of Outdoordom," gained widespread fame in his lifetime for reflecting on a world that was buckling under the weight of urbanization and industrialization. Close by his mountain refuges, the 315-mile-long Hudson River was lined with fuming factories and a tangle of railroad lines. Hundreds of belching steamboats plied the river carrying passengers and other commerce, including countless logs from the Catskills' clear-cut valleys.

Burroughs witnessed this and turned his gaze instead toward the wholesome soul of the Catskills—finches and falcons, timothy and clover—which was in stark contrast to cities choked by smog and disease. "To find the universal elements enough; to find the air and the water exhilarating; to be refreshed by a morning walk or an evening saunter . . . to be thrilled by the stars at night; to be elated over a bird's nest or a wildflower in spring—these are some of the rewards of the simple life," he wrote. With the ear of some of the country's main decision-makers bent in his direction, Burroughs also didn't shy from warning of the dangers of progress. "We can use our scientific knowledge to poison the air, corrupt the water, blacken the face of the country," he wrote at the end of the nineteenth century, "or we can use it to mitigate and abolish these things. One cannot but reflect what a sucked orange the earth will be in the course of a few more centuries."

Burroughs had borrowed that stark imagery from nature philosopher Ralph Waldo Emerson, who had already written extensively about the spirituality of nature and the dangers of exploitation. While Thoreau, Emerson's protégé, witnessed urban sprawl and deforestation advancing toward his hometown near Boston, he exalted nature and its critical role in the quality of human life: "Our village life would stagnate if it were not for the unexplored forests and meadows which surround it," he wrote. "We need the tonic of wildness." Though the Catskills were idealized in paintings and literature, many nineteenth-century visitors felt they had found in those mountains a therapeutic antidote to foul industries. There was a magnetism to those ancient Catskills and to the wide, powerful flow of the Hudson River that drew in other artists and writers with inclinations similar to Burroughs's.

By the time Burroughs had his first essay published in 1860, the writing of three others had cast a romantic light on the natural world, which, up to that point, had been seen as something nefarious. Washington Irving wrote of "wild solitudes" untouched by the outside world in his Catskills-set stories "The Legend of Sleepy Hollow" and "Rip Van Winkle" (both 1820). James Fenimore Cooper's *Leatherstocking Tales* (published between 1823 and 1841) emphasized a respect for land and envisioned civilized life coexisting with nature. In 1825 poet William Cullen Bryant wrote in "A Forest Hymn," "The groves were God's first temples" that were a "Fit shrine for [a] humble worshipper to hold Communion with his Maker."

Also in 1825, coinciding with the completion of the Erie Canal—which linked the East Coast to the country's interior—a promising painter visited the Hudson Valley from New York City. Thomas Cole, then twenty-four, was captivated by the area's untamed core characterized by dramatic light, thick woodlands, and rushing water, and he devoted himself completely to capturing it. His style, evident in works such as *Falls of the Kaaterskill* (1826) and *The Clove, Catskills* (1827), envisioned the American landscape as something sublime, as a new Garden of Eden. "None know how often

President Theodore Roosevelt with naturalist John Burroughs and others, at Fort Yellowstone, Yellowstone National Park

FORGOTTEN NO MORE

Lesser-known but no less talented artists who painted in the Hudson River School tradition had been relegated to the margins because of race or gender, but their

work has emerged in recent years and has begun to take its place alongside the masters. Among these rediscovered artists are Susie Barstow and Edith Cook, who were also leading members of the Appalachian Mountain Club. African American Robert Duncanson painted still lifes until being exposed to Thomas Cole's landscapes-with-moral-messages. No doubt the freedom those artists felt when stepping away from societal confines was part of the beauty inherent in the natural world.

Edith Cook's sylvan landscapes are typical of the Hudson River School style.

the hand of God is seen in a wilderness but them that rove it for a man's life," Cole wrote. Nature, he said, awakened humans to a "keener perception of the beauty of our existence."

In the following years and decades, many painters emulated Cole's technique and interpretation, and in doing so, they developed America's first real art movement, the Hudson River School. Artists in this new genre created landscapes (instead of portraits of people, de rigueur in that day) that aimed to transform viewers spiritually and morally. The works of Hudson River School painters were displayed upon the walls of collectors who sought to bring the "moral effects" of wilderness under their roofs. By elevating untrammeled nature to something sacred and

noble, the movement succeeded in shifting how Americans thought about their environment: from something to tame and exploit to a resource with which to live in harmony.

Cole didn't rely simply on the subtle symbols of destruction (a belching train, fallen trees, an ax-wielding woodsman) in his paintings but wrote essays warning about unbridled materialism. "I cannot but express my sorrow that the beauty of such landscapes are quickly passing away," he wrote. "The ravages of the ax are daily increasing. They cut down the forest with a wantonness for which there is no excuse, and leave the herbless rocks to glimmer in the burning sun." He used his art to teach regular Americans how to value the wild. And it worked; the concepts of the sanctity of

George Perkins Marsh was a diplomat, philologist, and groundbreaking conservationist.

nature and of human stewardship of the environment had hatched.

It's likely that George Perkins Marsh, born in Vermont in 1801, had been influenced by the Hudson Valley visionaries. In the 1860s Marsh's own work marked another turning point in the way people interacted with their surroundings. Throughout his life, Marsh had witnessed the devastation of the state's native forests firsthand; by the 1830s only 20 percent of Vermont's forests remained, and Marsh was making connections between deforestation, erosion, and the destruction of fish and wildlife habitats. He deduced that changes made to one aspect of an ecosystem tended to have a deleterious domino effect; such ecological insight was unheard of at the time. People believed that Earth was plentiful and its resources inexhaustible, and though humans might affect their surroundings, their impacts were minimal, inconsequential.

Marsh's 1864 work *Man and Nature* began to change all of that. In it he wrote, "But man is everywhere a disturbing agent. Wherever he plants his foot, the harmonies of nature are turned to discords. The proportions and accommodations which insured the stability of existing arrangements are overthrown." Marsh also argued that, ultimately, environmental destruction caused social and economic distress, which weakened the mainstays of a civilized society. By pointing to missteps made in other parts of the world that were suffering the effects of environmental abuse, he suggested a different path of stewardship and social reform for the United States to restore its natural fabric. He told his readers that the power to do this was completely in their hands, and they listened. While industrialization was moving at breakneck speed, Marsh convinced policy makers to put the brakes on the gutting of ecosystems, to approach resource extraction with sustainability in mind, and to work toward the restoration of exhausted natural areas.

Within a decade of the publication of his ground-shaking work, trees were being planted on lawns from Nebraska to the White House. But Marsh's influence was broader still. The forestry movement took root when Franklin Hough, a medical doctor whose hobby was trees, gave a paper called *On the Duty of Governments in the Preservation of Forests* to the American Association for the Advancement of Science in 1873, which led to his appointment as the first special forestry agent in the United States.

Inspired greatly by Marsh's ideas, Hough outlined regulations for the sale and use of US

ONE NATIONAL PARK, THREE CONSERVATION TITANS

On a brisk autumn day, the view from the sprawling porch of the mansion at the center of the Marsh-Billings-Rockefeller National Historical Park in Woodstock, Vermont, is of ancient, rolling hills flush with the changing seasons. Sugar maples flare red, beeches are butter-yellow, and centuries-old hemlocks hold fast to thick green canopies. Today the park includes the oldest sustainably managed woodland in North America. It's hard to imagine, given the current fullness of the landscape, that this 550-acre park east of the Green Mountains was once a burned-out, tilled-over, flood-ridden shadow of its present self.

The park also celebrates three famous families who made this place home, each contributing in its own way to the history of conservation and the evolution of land stewardship. Frederick Billings, who was born in nearby Royalton, emulated George Marsh and bought the estate in 1869. Billings had made a fortune as a lawyer and real estate developer out West, running the Northern Pacific Railway; Billings, Montana, was named in his honor. After seeing Yosemite as one of its first tourists, he agitated for national parks throughout the West, including Yellowstone, Glacier, and Mount Rainier. One of Billings's daughters, Mary, had a daughter also named Mary, who married Laurance Spelman Rockefeller in Woodstock in 1934. Rockefeller was the fourth child of Abby Aldrich and conservationist-philanthropist John D. Rockefeller Jr. (who contributed immeasurably to the founding and financing of several national parks). Mary and Laurance came together over a love of the outdoors, and the estate that Mary inherited from her mother came to hold a special place in Laurance's heart. What he saw and learned and felt there—along the paths where his wife rode her pony endlessly as a child—no doubt contributed to his conservation philosophy and philanthropy. Out of this modest patch of east-central Vermont grew some of the most cutting-edge thinking about both human influence on the environment and balance in the natural world.

The park's meticulously maintained two-story brick mansion features works from master Hudson River School painters. Romantic, gauzy scenes of Yosemite and the Grand Tetons beckon the traveler, and the Park Service is improving nesting sites for wood thrushes, ovenbirds, and at least four types of warblers. Current park superintendent Mike Creasey sees a clear link between the past conservationists who lived there and the present. "Marsh seemed to belong to a worn-out planet," he says. And yet, "In that house on the hill, in this place in a Vermont valley, those three changed our understanding of our relationship to nature and our obligation to the present and beyond."

forests and suggested that some of them remain in the public domain for protection. Hough later became the first chief of the Division of Forestry, the precursor to the US Forest Service. The passage of the Forest Reserve Act of 1891, which protected the nation's remaining timber stands, can be credited in large part to his efforts. Holistic legislation that both Hough and Marsh would

SEE AMERICA

VISIT THE NATIONAL PARKS

UNITED STATES TRAVEL BUREAU

MADE BY NYC ART PROJECT, WORK PROJECTS ADMINISTRATION

have approved of, the act was intended to safeguard not only trees but the role they play in ecosystems. Healthy forests, Marsh and Hough had come to understand, were crucial to a consistent water supply, flood mitigation, wildlife protection, recreation, and education.

John Muir was very familiar with Marsh's work and made reference to it in his journals. In his most popular book, *My First Summer in the Sierra*, published in 1911, Muir alludes to the interconnectedness in nature that Marsh had so firmly established. "When we try to pick out anything by itself, we find it hitched to everything else in the Universe," wrote Muir. President Theodore Roosevelt—the progressive young naturalist leader, born in New York City, who lived on a ranch in the Badlands of the Dakota Territory—also wrote in his memoir about the impact of Marsh's observations, which no doubt contributed to Roosevelt's great legacy as a conservation titan. Roosevelt and Muir camped together near Yosemite's Glacier Point in 1903, during which time Muir made the case for adding Yosemite Valley and the Mariposa Grove to the national park. In 1906, it was done.

As the nation galloped headlong toward a landscape of total exploitation, Burroughs, Marsh, and their like gave the reins of that runaway horse a firm tug. Their work cried "whoa!" and awakened the apathetic to the conservation cause. Their nature appreciation, in all its forms, highlighted

A VISIONARY TOOL FOR CONSERVATION

A movement began in the 1880s to protect prehistoric pueblos, missions, and cliff dwellings in the Southwest that were being ruthlessly looted or vandalized. An "antiquities act" was first proposed in 1882, but it wasn't until the Progressive Era a couple of decades later that the concept of conserving cultural resources and preserving history on a large scale began to gain traction. Around the country, as the economy was gaining strength in its shift from rural to urban, agricultural to industrial, progressives were facing truths about their surroundings. Prominent among those was the recognition that the nation's resources were finite; once they had been siphoned off or stolen, they were gone.

Taking advantage of the realization that runaway capitalism could have adverse effects, the Archaeological Institute of America lobbied Congress for protection of those priceless places. Further outcry from academics and the public got the attention of President Theodore Roosevelt. The landmark Antiquities Act of 1906 was signed that summer.

The short act is nevertheless long on presidential prerogative and ideals, allowing the president to create national monuments without congressional approval, and Roosevelt wasted no time in wielding the new conservation tool. "Very early on, President Roosevelt looked at where he could use the law, and much to the chagrin of Congress and maybe others, he realized it was not very restrictive," says Robert Sutton, present NPS chief historian. Roosevelt made liberal use of the fledgling law, single-handedly proclaiming a whopping eighteen national monuments during his administration.

the divide between industrial forces that *took*, consuming resources in great gulps, and natural ones that *gave*, rejuvenating the human spirit. It invited every onlooker to derive purpose and meaning from nature's fathomless font.

For decades, American artistry became synonymous with the natural world, igniting a fire in the belly of policy makers, philanthropists, and, importantly, average citizens. They were inspired to take a second look at how the riches of their still-new nation might be better utilized. Without the work of these Prophets of Outdoordom who discovered and publicized natural wonders from Yosemite to the Hudson Valley, there likely would not have been a national park system or a Park Service to accompany it. Their way of seeing helped mold the national park idea into an entirely new American ideal.

CHAPTER 3

All Aboard!

"**JUST IMAGINE THOSE PEOPLE** in San Francisco telling us that we could see the Valley (*do the Valley* is the correct expression) in two days, but that three would be ample!" wrote Lady Constance Gordon-Cumming on April 30, 1878. "Three days of jolting over the roughest roads—three days of hard work rushing from point to point in this wonderland, and then the weary journey to be done over again, shaking all impressions of calm beauty from our exhausted minds!" It was California's Yosemite Valley she was loath to rush through, and she resolved, instead, to stay for three months.

For travelers to the beguiling Yosemite Valley in the mid- to late nineteenth century, the days-long journey was largely something to be endured. Scottish noblewoman Gordon-Cumming carefully logged her own progress: First, she took a steamboat across the bay from San Francisco to Oakland, then boarded a train (which had become possible only recently) for the 150-mile ride through "monotonous wheat-fields" of the San Joaquin Valley to the town of Merced. Then the adventure truly began; after overnighting in a hotel, the travelers squeezed into a large but "supremely uncomfortable" six-horse-powered open coach. After hours of "violent shaking and jolting over loose stones" through rolling hills of lupine and larkspur, Gordon-Cumming's party stopped briefly for lunch. They resumed their twelve-hour ride into a wooded belt of cedars, firs, and pines with air "scented with the breath of the forests" to overnight at Galen Clark's rest stop.

Clark had settled in those meadowlands in Wawona more than two decades earlier, and during his fifty years or so in the area, he was instrumental in securing federal protection for the big trees and the Yosemite Valley. During that time he was a ceaseless explorer, vigilant guard, and enthusiastic guide and friend to many, including John Muir, Ralph Waldo Emerson, and early wealthy travelers like Gordon-Cumming. Clark (who only partially retired in his eighties) guided her party to the Mariposa Grove of Giant Sequoias. Though bruised and cut from the coach ride, they "spent a long day of delight in the most magnificent forest that it is possible to imagine." They wandered among the massive midriffs of these largest living things known to humans, some reaching close to 300 feet high, which had already been there a millennium or more.

From Clark's ranch they zigzagged more than 27 miles across the faces of steep hills, through dense forests, and past snowy upland valleys. At last they caught first sight of "an abrupt chasm in the great rolling expanse of billowy granite ridges," as Gordon-Cumming described the gaping expanse of the Yosemite Valley. "It is so indescribably lovely that I altogether despair of conveying any notion of it in words," she wrote. During her months in the valley, Gordon-Cumming saw, and painted, its many moods as light and water and time continued to refine it.

While the scenery exceeded expectations, the accommodations did not, though the noblewoman tried to put a positive spin on it. "All arrangements here are of the simplest—quite comfortable, but nothing fine" is the way the lady described her setup at Barnard's Hotel. "It must be confessed that the rooms are rough-and-ready; and the partitions apparently consist of sheets of brown paper, so that every word spoken in one room is heard in all the others!" she wrote. But there were some creature comforts to be had in the bustling valley: she indulged in hot baths and cold drinks, including mint juleps and something potently dubbed the "corpse reviver." Fresh strawberries and blackberries were served with rich cream. Billiards and a barber were available. She passed time in the cozy, quirky Big Tree Room, a public sitting room built around a huge red cedar, and thumbed through the Grand Register, which was the pride and joy of the bathhouse-keeper.

That foot-thick morocco-leather-bound guest book with a silver clasp sat on a grand wooden pedestal to record Yosemite's growing number of tourists. The 800-page, 100-pound book ultimately absorbed the experiences of thousands of intrepid travelers into its pages, including a handful of presidents, John Muir, William Randolph Hearst, General William Sherman, William "Buffalo Bill" Cody, and Rudyard Kipling. (It still vividly recounts their impressions from its perch at the Yosemite Museum.) The comments range widely but many commonalities surface: reflections on the great waterfalls and rock features figure prominently, as do the complaints by road- and nature-weary souls. "Why is there no mention

Turn-of-the-twentieth-century tourists explore a geothermal feature in Yellowstone's Upper Geyser Basin—perhaps too closely by current safety standards.

of the dust in the guide books?" asked one Scottish visitor. "Never room next to a man that snores" advised a visiting Californian. "All bitten up with Ants. Suffering awfully" complained a Bostonian.

By the time Gordon-Cumming and her contemporaries rolled into the valley, Yosemite had been in the tourist trade for nearly three decades. It was considerably rougher going for those earlier explorers who rode on mule or horseback 40 miles over precipitous trails from where the nearest stagecoach terminated. Such was the lot of some daring writers, artists, and tourism entrepreneurs looking to hitch their wagon to California's rising star.

The conditions were rugged, especially for those who were unaccustomed to "roughing it"—paradoxically, they were most of the people who could afford the time and expense of getting there. Yet most early descriptions of Yosemite

tourism balance the ugly with the splendid. Traveling into the Yosemite area around the same time Muir did in 1868, London parson Harry Jones described two hotels "as they call themselves" in the valley and the "rooms," which were just crudely partitioned stalls in a windowless shed. "But we could see the stars through the roof," he wrote, presumably looking on the bright side. Reverend J. M. Buckley, a Brooklyn pastor and editor of the influential periodical *The Christian Advocate,* visited for three weeks in 1871. While his accounts include hard floors, copious fleas, and a "lusty snorer," he also made this observation: "The Yosemite is more sublime than any cathedral, and the voices of its many waters more musical than the most magnificent orchestra."

While tourists braved dust and high water to get to Yosemite, the options for getting to Yellowstone, the nation's first national park, were few. Like the first Yosemite travelers, early Yellowstone tourists lurched and bumped in stagecoaches, guzzling great mouthfuls of dust. Travelers would take a stage either from Bismarck, Dakota Territory, where the Northern Pacific Railway terminated, or from Corrine, Utah, where the Union Pacific Railroad ended. Or they could travel by steamboat—3100 miles from St. Louis, Missouri, to Fort Benton, Montana Territory—and only then board a stagecoach to Yellowstone.

The days-long trip into the park was arduous enough that fewer than 500 tourists per year tried it in the park's first five years. The ones who did venture there, to soak in its purportedly healing waters, to view its august canyon, and to stir at the sight of its bubbling mud pots, were more or less on their own, with scant options for dining and sleeping. But there were some trailblazers. The ink from President Ulysses S. Grant's signature on the Yellowstone Act of 1872 was hardly dry when a fifty-strong tourist party rolled into the Mammoth Hot Springs area. One "hotel" run by Harry Horr and James McCartney was actually a one-story 25-foot-by-35-foot sod-covered log building. What they called a "bathhouse" was a euphemism for a row of flimsy tents covering warm-water hollows for customers to soak in. Visiting a few years later, the Irish Earl of Dunraven called the accommodations a "little shanty which is dignified by the name of 'hotel.'"

Still, Yellowstone's popularity grew steadily, and in 1879 its visitors numbered more than 1000. Most were from neighboring states and brought with them the equivalent of modern-day motorhomes to ensure self-sufficiency. McCartney's establishment changed hands a number of times over the next several years, with only modest improvements, but it endured as the only hotel in the area for nearly a decade. A *Bozeman Avant Courier* article from that decade predicted that "five years from this date these springs will achieve a world-wide reputation, and two years succeeding will make the greatest inland resort in the world." While talk of the parks spanned the nation and traveled over oceans, most people who dreamed of seeing the fabled locales would have to wait for a powerful partner to emerge. They had to cool their heels until the mighty railroads could give them a lift.

Rail travel was new west of the Missouri River in 1870, but there were already upwards of 45,000 miles of track in the East. It was there the unlikely relationship between railroads and landscape preservation was sparked as shrewd railroad boosters recognized there were profits to be made by shuttling "back-to-nature" people from cities into the country, especially wealthy patrons who demanded first-class service. The Bar Harbor Express, for example, brought the rich and famous to posh summer resorts on Mount Desert Island in Maine as early as 1884.

It was to the railroads' advantage to have any journey for pleasure-seekers be a scenic one, and this desire prompted companies' interest in preserving landscapes in corridors through which they traveled. Through the southern Appalachian Mountains, an area railroads advertised as the "Land of the Sky," picturesque vistas were of utmost importance. While they likely didn't know it at the time, the railroads played a major part in selling preservation of views to the American people. The areas that would become Acadia, Shenandoah, and Great Smoky Mountains national parks and the Blue Ridge Parkway were all promoted initially by the railroads. The railroads also supported what were, at the time, War Department historical parks. By the 1890s, survivors of the Civil War were returning in droves to battlefields on railroad excursions.

The success of rail tourism in the East fueled entrepreneur Jay Cooke's passion to corner the market on Yellowstone travelers. In the early 1870s, the Northern Pacific Railway planned a narrow-gauge rail line linking its main line to the park's Gardiner, Montana, entrance, along with spur lines

1001. The Magnificent New Virginia Canyon Road and Virginia Falls, Yellowstone National Park.
Copyrighted, 1905, by T. W. Ingersoll.

Tourists bump along past Yellowstone's Virginia Cascades on what was called the "magnificent new Virginia Canyon Road."

That number included several large parties of VIPs consisting of President Chester Arthur, railroad officials, potential investors, and their substantial entourages. One observer at the time wrote, "The Park is full of notables and one cannot go ten rods in any direction without rubbing against a lord, a duke, a senator, a government guide or some other gentleman of high degree."

Disembarking from the train in Montana, travelers would board stagecoaches—generally as part of a railroad package deal costing the equivalent of about $2000 today—that would wind their way up the Gardner River Canyon to Mammoth Hot Springs. Donning the preferred western wear of the "dude," as early tourists were called, including straw hats, long linen "duster" jackets, and petticoats for the women, they would see the park for four or five days on the Grand Tour. Coaches pulled by four-horse teams and designed to carry eleven passengers would be lorded over, more often than not, by well-intentioned but foul-mouthed drivers. Guides were plentiful in Yellowstone but they often spouted spurious "facts" to ignorant, captivated audiences. If they were interested in knowing more about Mammoth's terraces of chalky white travertine, tourists could consult a guidebook. When one such visitor in 1889 did, he commented disapprovingly about the features' names, "which some lurid hotel keeper has christened Cleopatra's Pitcher or Mark Anthony's Whiskey Jug, or something equally poetical." That sharp-tongued traveler was Rudyard Kipling.

Most of the middle-class people who could afford an expensive railroad journey wouldn't settle for—and, worse yet for the railroads, wouldn't recommend—a trip that included the likes of James

running into the park—although that notion was less popular among park protectors. All was going according to Cooke's plan until the Panic of 1873 struck and the bottom fell out of railroad financing. Tracks halted hundreds of miles short of their target. Geologist Ferdinand Hayden commented in 1878 that the Northern Pacific collapse "retarded the development of the Park for years."

Later reorganized and infused with cash, the railroad pushed ahead. In 1883 former President Grant, drove in the final spike at Gold Creek, Montana, for a line that now stretched from St. Paul, Minnesota, to the northwest Pacific coast. Soon thereafter, a multimillion-dollar branch—the Yellowstone Line—from Livingston, Montana, to Cinnabar, just a few miles from Yellowstone's Gardiner entrance, was completed. In that year, visitation jumped fivefold from the year before.

RIDING THE RAILS TO PARKS

Contemporary travelers can journey to national parks like people did a century ago, combining carefree train rides with epic scenery, with a little nostalgia tossed in. Amtrak's Empire Builder, Southwest Chief, and California Zephyr lines still offer access to many western parks. (Amtrak also still runs to Merced, where visitors finish the trip into Yosemite by bus.) Alaska's Denali Star and Coastal Classic hit Denali and Kenai Fjords national parks. On the American Orient Express, riders see Yellowstone, Grand Teton, and Glacier. The Coast Starlight chugs from Los Angeles to Seattle, passing the Santa Monica Mountains National Recreation Area and Crater Lake and Mount Rainier national parks along the way. And Grand Canyon Railway riders travel in style to the park's South Rim.

McCartney's "shanty" hotel. In the 1880s a growing variety of accommodations included Wylie Permanent Camps and Shaw & Powell Camps, which catered to a crowd that liked to eat with silver and china but didn't mind "roughing it" on cots in canvas-walled bedrooms. Next up were the mediocre but tolerable National Hotel and Cottage Hotel. Far superior was the 141-bed Fountain Hotel featuring hot water for bathing and electric lights, built in 1891, and the roomy Lake Hotel (still standing), which combined design and comfort.

Catering to choosy clientele, the Fountain and Lake hotels had been built by the Yellowstone Park Association, formed by the Northern Pacific Railway, which sank millions of dollars into construction at national parks in the West. A jewel in that concessionaire's crown is Yellowstone's Old Faithful Inn, finished in 1903, at a cost of $165,000 for construction and furnishings. With those improvements made to park accommodations, an early Northern Pacific Railway guide to Yellowstone declared, "Hitherto it has been closed to all but the most adventurous spirits; but now, not only has it been made easy of access, but it may

be visited as comfortably, yea, as luxuriously, as any of the older resorts of the pleasure seeker."

Trains and tourists continued to explore the wilderness in larger numbers into the twentieth century. By 1900, five transcontinental railroad lines connected eastern states to the Pacific coast. Dozens of spur lines ran north and south off of those east–west routes, and eventually there were more than 200,000 miles of railroad tracks pitching and winding among lands of opportunity and discovery. Several of those branch lines were built specifically for access to national parks.

When Yosemite became a national park in 1890, the Santa Fe and the Southern Pacific railways extended lines to the town of Merced, which, while greatly reducing travel time, still meant a two-day stagecoach slog into the park. Travel time was slashed when the Yosemite Valley Railroad commenced operations in 1907, transporting travelers to El Portal on the park boundary. Just under 100 miles of rail line had cost $3.4 million to lay, so confident were the investors in its profit-making ability. In that year, more than 7000 people visited Yosemite, and the park experience would

PEERLESS PARK LODGES

These early accommodations, listed in order by the date they opened, all still welcome park goers.

- **1891:** Lake Hotel, Yellowstone
- **1903:** Old Faithful Inn, Yellowstone
- **1905:** El Tovar Hotel, Grand Canyon
- **1913:** Glacier Park Lodge, Glacier
- **1914:** Sperry Chalet, Glacier
- **1915:** Crater Lake Lodge, Crater Lake
- **1915:** Many Glacier Hotel, Glacier
- **1917:** Paradise Inn, Mount Rainier

- **1925:** The Lodge at Bryce Canyon, Bryce Canyon
- **1927:** The Ahwahnee Hotel, Yosemite
- **1927:** The Inn at Furnace Creek, Death Valley
- **1934:** The Chateau at the Oregon Caves, Oregon Caves
- **1937 rebuild:** Grand Canyon Lodge at the North Rim, Grand Canyon
- **1941:** Volcano House, Hawai'i Volcanoes

never be the same as when Gordon-Cumming, Muir, Emerson, and Galen Clark plumbed its charms. Catering to well-heeled guests, the Yosemite Valley Railroad supplemented a tent camp with the well-appointed Del Portal Hotel in 1909.

The railroads' influence continued to expand elsewhere. On the South Rim of the Grand Canyon, the Atchison, Topeka and Santa Fe Railway opened the elegant El Tovar Hotel in 1905. Later, at Bryce Canyon and Zion national parks, Union Pacific (operating as the Utah Parks Company) poured money into refined lodges and cabins.

Railroads also sunk energy and funds into expanding the national park system, particularly when proposed park areas were convenient to one

of their whistle-stops. Of the railroad's role in securing federal protection for Yosemite, John Muir said, "Even the soulless Southern Pacific R.R. Co., never counted on for anything good, helped nobly in pushing the bill for this park through Congress." In addition to lobbying on behalf of Yosemite, the Southern Pacific influenced legislation on Sequoia, General Grant (now part of Kings Canyon), and Crater Lake national parks. The Northern Pacific, too, reached beyond its influence in Yellowstone and was instrumental in the creation of Mount Rainier National Park.

But perhaps the truest railroad-park symbiosis existed between Glacier National Park and the Great Northern Railway. Leading into the turn of the nineteenth century, there had been two unsuccessful bids by conservationists (including Audubon Society founder George Bird Grinnell) to add a chunk of northwest Montana to the national park system. Congress seemed poised to

Climbers examine a crevasse on the Paradise Glacier in Mount Rainier National Park.

The Ahwahnee Hotel in Yosemite Valley is a key example of National Park Service rustic architecture.

sink a third attempt when Great Northern president Louis Hill barreled into the fray. Encouraged by Grinnell, he envisioned the area as the "Playground of the Northwest" and set about bringing politicians around to his way of thinking. He fired off telegrams to influential committee members urging their support of the legislation. Reflecting on that time, Grinnell later wrote, "Important men in control of the Great Northern Railroad were made to see the possibilities of the region and after nearly twenty years of effort, a bill setting aside the park was passed."

In 1910, 60 miles of the Great Northern line in Montana became the southern border of the nation's tenth national park. Along that Empire Builder route from St. Paul, Minnesota, to Seattle, Washington, the Great Northern Railway had planted seeds that bloomed into towns strung across the prairie. With similar confidence, Hill saw the potential of Glacier's alpine setting to draw in wealthy tourists who would otherwise have spent millions on trips to the Canadian Rockies and on trans-Atlantic voyages to Europe. His vision took the shape of Swiss-style chalets and grand lodges built among a celebrated concentration of serrated arêtes, cerulean lakes, and glacial ice.

Hill masterminded an advertising campaign that was powerful in its simplicity: *See America First*. The sentimental, sometimes boastful ads were omnipresent in the mainstream media; posters tempted would-be travelers in thousands of railroad stations around the country. One persuaded travelers to "Freshen Up" in Glacier, where the air is "laden with the fragrance of pine and hemlock." Ultimately, Great Northern's efforts paid off: in the summer of 1913, 12,000 tourists saw Glacier, twice as many as the previous year. Visitation climbed in that vein, and the railroads dominated for decades.

The flurry of visitors surely thrilled the railroad tycoons and other park boosters, but it also tested the patience and power of the few on-the-ground park protectors. As visitor numbers grew, it was clear that something had to be done to educate people about the value of those resources and to allow early park guardians to throw the book at those visitors who did as they pleased.

These bison heads were likely confiscated from poacher Ed Howell by the military guard in Yellowstone in 1894.

CHAPTER 4

Who's in Charge?

BETWEEN YELLOWSTONE'S founding in 1872 and the creation of the National Park Service in 1916 was an uncertain and often lawless period in all national parks. The Yellowstone Act of 1872 required the secretary of the interior to prevent the "wanton destruction" and commercial taking of fish and game, but in those early years, that was nearly impossible to enforce. Just as there was no precedent for the establishment of the park, there was no blueprint for how it would be managed, protected, or maintained. The country was poor after the Civil War, and money for administering the national park "experiment" was virtually nil. With no enforcement mechanism, the landmark park legislation had no teeth.

Still, people were committed to Yellowstone's protection. First up was explorer Nathaniel Langford, a famous member of the 1870 Washburn Expedition, whose animated descriptions of the area had ignited the nation's imagination. Appointed as superintendent of Yellowstone by the secretary of the interior just two months after the park's establishment, Langford was essentially a volunteer charged with the Sisyphean task of securing an isolated and rugged region the size of Rhode Island and Delaware combined. This did not bode well for either Langford or the park.

The demands of his day job as a federal bank examiner for western states and territories allowed Langford to venture into the Yellowstone area only a handful of times in the five years he was superintendent. What he likely didn't know was that Congress had passed the Yellowstone Act on the condition that no appropriations to manage it would be requested for "at least several years" after its founding. Nevertheless, Langford repeatedly appealed for money to make the park safe, navigable, and truly public.

However, feelings about the park concept had hardened locally, and support for settlers in the Montana and Wyoming territories was emphatic. A *Rocky Mountain Weekly Gazette* (Helena) editorial in 1872 said, "We are opposed to any scheme which will have a tendency to remand [Yellowstone] into perpetual solitude, by shutting out private enterprise and by preventing individual energy from opening the country to the general traveling public." One such entrepreneur was Matthew McGuirk, who had built an unsanctioned settlement near the Boiling River, which in actuality is a large hot spring flowing into the Gardner River not far from Mammoth. Like others in the area, McGuirk felt the park should not exclude private business ventures. At his Medicinal Springs, rheumatism sufferers partook of "healing waters." Though he'd been there for several months before

the Yellowstone Act was passed, he'd laid claim to the plot a week *after* it became part of the park.

As Superintendent Langford quickly realized when faced with characters like McGuirk, congressional protection was only good in theory. In practice, vandals, squatters, poachers, and outlaws easily found their way across Yellowstone's porous borders and into its sparsely policed interior.

In 1875 an astute observer and pioneer naturalist, Colonel William Ludlow, was dispatched to patrol the park. He was outraged by the unruly atmosphere and what he called "the rude hand of man" and didn't keep it to himself. In a report published by the War Department, Ludlow lamented, "Miracles of art . . . can be ruined in five minutes by vandals armed with an axe, and nearly all the craters

DESECRATION OF OUR NATIONAL PARKS.

Men vie to persuade a tourist arriving near Yellowstone to ride in their companies' carriages in this 1883 cartoon, which illustrates early conservationists' anxiety about protecting park resources.

show signs of hopeless and unrestrained barbarity." He also talked about the "reckless destruction of animals" and said that, in the winter prior to his writing, hunters killed 3000 elk (for their skins and occasionally only their tongues) in one narrow segment of the Yellowstone Valley. Ludlow suggested in his report that such brazen takings could be prevented by troops already stationed nearby the park and argued that, lacking a bureau to administer national parks, the War Department should take control of Yellowstone. Not long after, in 1877, Langford was ousted from his position, thankless as it was, because of his perceived neglect of the park.

Langford's replacement, Philetus Norris, had two things his predecessor did not: a salary and the park's first congressional appropriations—$10,000—issued in June 1878. While a substantial sum, it was far less than estimates said would be necessary to make Yellowstone a secure public park. Norris set to work more than doubling the mileage of the park's trails and "roads" (a generous description of the 90-odd miles' worth of wagon ruts) while agonizing over both the safety and security of often-prominent visitors and the destruction some caused.

Not all wildlife had the same value to park visitors or managers at that time. In his 1880 report to Secretary of the Interior Samuel Kirkwood, Norris called bison, moose, elk, deer, antelope, and bighorn sheep the "noble" animals of the park. They were traditionally known as "game" animals until it was illegal to take them from national parks. The death of predators, however, was encouraged. Norris's comments provide a glimpse of the enmity humans felt for the park's most powerful carnivores.

Of the grizzly, Norris reported, "Indeed, it may truly be said to be the mountaineer's most dreaded foe." He described other bears also as having an "audacious ferocity." The wolverine has a "rapacious greed and pugnacity," according to Norris. Mountain lions, once "numerous and troublesome," wrote the superintendent, had been the target of people who wielded "rifle, trap, and poison to exterminate them, and so successful have their efforts proved that now the comparatively few survivors usually content themselves with slaughter of deer, antelope, and perhaps elk, at a respectful distance from camp." But Norris's most eager loathing was reserved for "sneaking, snarling" coyotes and "large, ferocious" wolves: "[T]he value of their hides and their easy slaughter with strychnine-poisoned carcasses have nearly led to their extermination," he said.

To protect the park's "noble" stock, Norris also hired Yellowstone's first game warden, in 1880—the first national park ranger, though he wasn't called that. Harry Yount had worked as a wrangler for a Ferdinand Hayden survey two years earlier and knew his way around Yellowstone. But nearly 3500 square miles was too immense an area for one person to patrol, so Norris tasked Yount with protecting herds of ungulates, specifically in the teeming Lamar Valley of northeastern Yellowstone. Yount shared his cabin at the confluence of Soda Butte Creek and the Lamar River with no one, spending harsh winters battling subzero temperatures, 150 inches or more of snow, and cutting winds.

But when he quit the next year, it wasn't due to punishing conditions. Besides the job requiring at least ten of him, Yount complained about the lack of consequences for lawbreakers. While the game warden could kick out offenders and confiscate their spoils, they weren't sanctioned for wrongdoing. They simply snuck in time and again, making the park boundary no more effective than a revolving door.

In a report on his time in the Lamar Valley, Yount vented his frustrations while echoing naturalist Colonel Ludlow's concept of law enforcement, which predated army protection and later NPS law enforcement rangers: "I do not think that any one man appointed by the honorable Secretary, and specifically designated as a gamekeeper, is what is needed . . . but a small and reliable police force of men, employed when needed . . . is what is really the most practicable way of seeing that the game is protected from wanton slaughter, the forests from careless use of fire, and the enforcement

Harry Yount was Yellowstone's first game warden tasked with preventing "market hunters" from laying waste, in particular, to its elk population.

of all the other laws, rules, and regulations for the protection and improvement of the park," he said. Yount suggested these men be stationed strategically throughout the park near game-heavy spots and natural curiosities.

It took years for the seeds of the idea of sending troops to the park to sprout. During that time, tourists threw trash into geysers and souvenir-seekers cracked off chunks of travertine terraces. Monopolists assumed exclusive rights over popular sights and tourist accommodations. Vandals set forests ablaze, and poachers continued their lucrative culling of park wildlife; one bison scalp could fetch $300.

In the face of these problems, some in Congress considered the national park concept a lost cause and voted against additional appropriations. Powerful locals interested in mining and real estate, and opposed to the national park concept in general, eagerly perpetuated the idea that trying to protect Yellowstone was pointless. Their agenda included either shrinking or eliminating the park altogether, or at least running a railroad across it. This opposition made it particularly challenging for conservationists to introduce and pass legislation focused on legally enforcing Yellowstone's national park mandate and truly protecting its odd and awesome treasures. A resolution to that effect was introduced in the Senate in 1882 and then in the House, but it was blasted by those prevailing winds of greed. However, the groundwork was laid, even though it would not come to fruition for nearly a dozen years.

In the meantime, in a last-ditch effort, Yellowstone turned to the military for help. In 1883 Congress authorized Secretary of the Interior Henry Teller to ask the War Department for help securing the park—yet three more vulnerable years passed, with two superintendents who were largely ineffective political appointees, before the cavalry arrived. In 1886, fifty soldiers from Company M, First US Cavalry, in Fort Custer, Montana Territory, led by Captain Moses Harris, rode into Mammoth Hot Springs. The men arrived late on a still August night, and what was left of the civilian administration was relieved of their duties. The by-the-book captain—a fellow officer called him "a terror to evil doers"—became the acting superintendent and immediately declared war on those who flouted the rules. The park was, he said, "surrounded by a class of old frontiersmen, hunters and trappers, and squaw-men" who had no respect for regulations.

Harris quickly put in place eight regulations addressing vandalism, campfires, alcohol consumption, wood removal, hunting and trapping, and grazing, among other activities. His orders added that "it is enjoined upon all soldiers . . . to be vigilant and attentive in the enforcement of the foregoing regulations, and to see that the stage drivers and other employees of the hotels do not use abusive language to, or otherwise maltreat, the visitors to the Park . . . They will in the enforcement of their orders conduct themselves in a courteous and polite, but firm and decided, manner." From then on, soldiers ventured into Yellowstone's wild recesses to battle vandalism, poaching, thievery, and more.

Yellowstone's wildlands must have seemed liked another planet for Harris's charges, who came from placid plains and pancake-flat deserts. Many had never trod any land higher than a molehill, yet found themselves patrolling mountainsides and traversing hundreds of miles of terrain, some booby-trapped by nature, often in subzero temperatures. Despite the sweat equity invested by

THAT'S A FACT

The Harry Yount Award is given to exceptional rangers, though present-day rangers don't have to provide meat for other park employees, as Yount did.

Captain Harris and his troops, they were often at a disadvantage, at least initially, compared to locals who could duck into and out of the park undetected. When poachers were captured, they could be forced out-of-bounds and discouraged from returning by the taking of their tools, as Yount had done. However, much as the soldiers would have liked to keep poachers, vandals, or fire starters on lockdown, they could not.

Amid growing criticism of the army's inability to prevent park crimes, Harris pled with his higher-ups to put in place some legal mechanism that allowed prosecution. A rule was useless without a deterring consequence, he told them. Harris got an earful from inside the government and from the mainstream media. Former civilian park superintendent David Wear told the *St. Paul Pioneer Press* that "the troops in charge are not taking proper care of the Park, [they are] allowing the indiscriminate killing of game and the desecration of the formations about the mineral springs, and, unless some change is made soon, great damage will result." Harris defended his men—who nevertheless took the attacks somewhat personally because many had learned to love this land they were defending—and continued to demand legal backup, which came slower than a Yellowstone springtime.

BUFFALO SOLDIERS: ON THE FRONT LINE OF PARK PROTECTION

In 1890 when Sequoia, Yosemite, and General Grant (later incorporated into Kings Canyon) earned federal park status, they also received military protection. Lacking large game, these parks didn't have Yellowstone's poaching problem but were instead troubled by timber interests, overfished lakes, and domestic sheep and cattle grazing. Back then, the acting superintendent at Sequoia and General Grant was Captain Charles Young, the first African American to hold that position in a national park.

In 1903 Young confidently led a regiment ordered to guard Sequoia National Park. They were "Buffalo Soldiers," a nickname given by Cheyenne and other Plains Indians who thought the soldiers' curly dark hair resembled the coat of a buffalo, a revered being. Roughly 500 Buffalo Soldiers from four black regiments served in Yosemite and Sequoia–Kings Canyon, driving out poachers and timber thieves, putting out fires, creating maps, keeping an eye on tourists, and sending illegal grazers packing.

Young and his men brought law and order to the wild while building—with astonishing efficiency—roads, trails, and other park infrastructure. This task included completing several engineering feats, such as building a wagon road to the Giant Forest that is still in use. Buffalo Soldiers also cut the first trail to the top of 14,494-foot Mount Whitney, a peak now summited by more than 20,000 people annually. When public interest grew in naming a tree in the Giant Forest in recognition of Young's service in parks, he insisted the sequoia be named instead for Booker T. Washington, who Young described as "that great and good American." Young himself went on to rise to the rank of full colonel, the highest rank held by an African American up to that time. The Charles Young Buffalo Soldiers National Monument in Ohio was established in 2013 to protect and celebrate his inspirational, trailblazing legacy.

Above: Buffalo soldiers of the Twenty-Fifth Infantry, some keeping warm in buffalo robes, at Fort Keogh, Montana. *Right:* Stationed at Sequoia, Captain Charles Young of the Ninth Cavalry was the first African American superintendent of a national park.

While criminal activity did decline somewhat with army officers on the job (despite what the critics said), their efforts were offset by the growth of towns around the park and by increased visitation. Captain George Anderson, who served as military superintendent of Yellowstone from 1891 to 1897, was sometimes comically exasperated by the poor behavior of tourists. One of his reports complains about the "propensities of women to gather 'specimens,' and of men to advertise their folly by writing their names on everything beautiful within their reach." Soldiers were stationed at every major geyser basin, and anyone found stealing objects or scrawling graffiti was taken into custody. Accused offenders were forced to face Captain Anderson, who gave them a booming scolding and told them that recidivists would be forcibly ejected from the park. Whether the temptation to do harm was too great or the threatened punishment too lenient, it would require the outrage of a nation to finally get Congress into the business of seriously protecting park resources.

In March 1894, one high-profile crime at last sparked meaningful reform in park policing. Amid pelting snow and wicked wind, an army patrol snuck up on infamous poacher Edgar Howell and nabbed him while he was skinning bison near Pelican Creek. While hauling him back to their guardhouse, the officers crossed paths with a journalist and a photographer who detailed the event in gory detail; Howell's "blood-stained hands" and dirty deeds were splashed across the pages of *Forest and Stream* (precursor to *Field and Stream*). How could a poacher skin roughly a dozen bison (by this time

sharply declining in number) within the nation's park and not be held to task? According to the magazine, "This was due to the laxness of Congress in failing to provide any law by which such depredations can be punished."

An outcry emerged from conservationists, including George Bird Grinnell, the magazine's editor at the time (later a founder of the Audubon Society and advisor to President Theodore Roosevelt). It wasn't long before indignation rippled through the general public far beyond the borders of Yellowstone about the exploitation of "their" national resources. That prompted Iowa Representative John Lacey, who had been held up in a stagecoach robbery in Gardiner, Montana, to sponsor a bill that would allow prosecution of acts prohibited by the national park legislation. The Lacey Act of 1894, or National Park Protection Act, was passed "to protect the birds and animals in Yellowstone National [P]ark, and to punish

Like many troops who protected national parks for decades, this cavalryman at Midway Geyser basin in Yellowstone likely grew fond of his unusual post.

EVER VIGILANT

Judge Mark Carman's sunny office has an enviable view of the bustling expanse of former Fort Yellowstone. Outside the magistrate's headquarters at the US District Court in the Mammoth Hot Springs area of Yellowstone National Park, elk mill around on grassy patches like guests at a garden party. Slack-jawed tourists fumble for cameras as elk occasionally lower their massive, shaggy heads to grab tufts of green. A tinge of sulfur permeates the air.

Taking office 119 years after John Meldrum, Magistrate Judge Carman is only the fifth person to hold the position; each justice who came before him averaged decades in the role. (The Federal Magistrate Act of 1968 abolished the office of US commissioner, putting in its place the office of US magistrate, later referred to as magistrate judge.) While misdeeds in the park no longer include stagecoach robberies, but still occasionally involve damaging or stealing treasures, the magistrate's position remains unique. Like his predecessors, Carman upholds the law while protecting Yellowstone's natural resources, as professed in the nearby carved basalt of the Roosevelt Arch: "for the benefit and enjoyment of the people."

Looking back to Meldrum's era, Carman says, "The sincerity of the response to crimes in Yellowstone was incredible for that time." The system of enforcement now in all national parks took root in Yellowstone, showing a commitment to order while serving another purpose entirely innovative in those times: conservation. "I think that's pretty cool," says Carman. Yosemite is the only other national park with a federal magistrate judge, though now base jumpers and drunk drivers are more likely to be prosecuted than cattle ranchers in that distinct US District Court near the base of Yosemite Falls.

crimes in said park." Finally, law enforcement had some recourse in responding to park crimes.

Two months later, John Meldrum—Wyoming Civil War veteran and jack-of-all-trades—was appointed as Yellowstone's first commissioner, to help crack down on criminal behavior. He hadn't been a judge or lawyer but had served ably as clerk for John Riner, influential US attorney for the Wyoming Territory (promoted to serve as the first US District Court judge when Wyoming became a state in 1890). Meldrum had never seen Yellowstone before he applied for the job (the position was formally renamed US commissioner and given additional authority by Congress in 1896),

though many years before, he'd heard about its uniqueness and longed to see it. In his request to Riner, who was hiring for the Yellowstone position, Meldrum said simply, "Judge, you know my capabilities. I would like to go to Yellowstone Park."

From his office in the Mammoth Hot Springs area of Yellowstone National Park, US Commissioner Meldrum witnessed the growth of Fort Yellowstone—a complex of clapboard and sandstone officers' quarters and barracks, headquarters, stables, and a chapel. It's not a long trip there from the northern border of the park along the winding Gardner River Canyon, where bighorn sheep

Soldiers capture poacher Ed Howell (far right). The resulting media firestorm and public outcry led to meaningful reform of the laws protecting national park resources.

brave passage along walls of crumbling sandstone. Perching eagles, ospreys, and kingfishers lord over Rocky Mountain juniper, and cottonwoods and willows are crammed together along the river's edge. Steam puffs and water flows from nearby travertine terraces like so many pots boiling over on a stove. The fantastical scene was being marred, however, by those tourists tossing coins or soap into geysers. Plenty of poachers were also culling the backcountry, and no doubt dreaded by everyone were the outlaws committing the all-too-common stickups.

Meldrum's enthusiasm for justice and the protection of park resources notwithstanding, he was hard-pressed on his own to interrupt the thrumming volume of chaos in the park. As Meldrum reflected later, "In the old days, there were many deliberate law violators. Stagecoach holdups were not infrequent. The craze for gold turned many adventurous and carefree individuals into gun-toting bad

men. Poaching was so common that many of those who had practiced it for years looked upon it pretty much like the steady drinker did the days of [P]rohibition—a necessity perhaps for others, but a nuisance law to be studiously broken by him."

During his forty-one-year tenure—which lasted until his retirement at age ninety-one—Meldrum was a somewhat controversial figure, as anyone wielding a new disciplinary tool might have been. But as word got out that prosecutions were on the rise and fines were being collected as often as illegal specimens once were, crime began to decline. However, neither the presence of Meldrum nor the army troops was a significant enough deterrent for some ruffians who were determined to make a living off of Yellowstone's wealthy tourists.

One infamous holdup occurred in August 1897 when six stagecoaches packed with tourists, followed by an army ambulance, on their way to the Canyon Hotel were halted by two masked bandits. The men had blackened their hands and faces, pulled gunnysacks over their shoes, and carried a small arsenal of guns. As the nervous desperados moved from coach to coach, some travelers successfully hid their valuables, and one army officer tossed into the bushes a satchel containing several hundred dollars. Nevertheless, the two masked men tore off on horseback with $630, a small fortune.

Weeks passed as evidence was gathered and the duo eluded capture. Commissioner Meldrum, assuming that "it takes one to know one," asked poacher Howell to help with the manhunt. While Meldrum was criticized for the move, Howell was instrumental in tracking and taking into custody "Little Gus" Smitzer and George Reeb, a.k.a. Morphine Charley. Thanks to some impressive nineteenth-century forensics work, the pair was convicted of highway robbery, and after doing their time, both men returned to society as productive members. Reeb, having kicked his morphine dependency in jail, returned to Yellowstone to thank the big-hearted commissioner, who later found him legitimate work on a nearby ranch. Justice had prevailed, but the crime encouraged the concept that an agency whose focus was safeguarding the nation's collective resources was needed. Many more seasons of discontent for park protectors would have to pass before that became a reality.

Meldrum and the cavalry were pleased with the punitive nature of the Lacey Act of 1894, but it earned them few fans. The Lacey Act essentially gave the Yellowstone Act of 1872 teeth; significantly, the Lacey Act said that activities prohibited in the legislation establishing the first national park were federal offenses and should be prosecuted as such, on the spot. Since the park was so far from any existing courts, Meldrum was empowered to try and to sentence offenders (nowadays, first appearances on felony charges are made in Yellowstone and then sent to a federal court elsewhere in Wyoming). That didn't go over well with some offenders, at least one of whom was himself a prominent judge, nor did the fact that the arresting superintendents—sometimes accused of being "draconian" and "overzealous"—received half the amount the offenders were fined. Infractions such as collecting obsidian chips or failing to thoroughly extinguish a campfire were subject to a $1000 fine and two years' imprisonment. The

punishment was impressively severe, an indication of the value Americans were beginning to put on their national parks.

While game species were finally getting a reprieve under the Lacey Act, such protection did not apply to predators. They were still considered public enemy number one. When bison were threatened by waning numbers (fewer than a hundred bison remained by the time Yellowstone celebrated its twentieth birthday), Congress allocated $15,000 to buy and relocate bison from domesticated supplies. Park management encouraged the interbreeding of wild and domesticated bison and eventually released their progeny into the backcountry. Groups of bison, elk, deer, and bighorn sheep were all penned and guarded from time to time to boost their numbers. Haying operations began in Yellowstone in 1904 (and in Grand Teton in 1912). During particularly rough winters in which forage within the park was limited, game animals were fed hay—some young deer were even bottle-fed—to encourage them to stay within park boundaries, since once they left, opportunistic hunters eliminated them by the thousands. Later a fence was erected on Yellowstone's northern boundary as an additional deterrent to seasonal migration. These de facto ranching techniques continued for decades.

Despite a massive manhunt, the robber sought in this wanted poster (who netted nearly $1400 in cash and more than $700 in jewelry) simply removed his shoes and disappeared into the woods.

$1.000.00 REWARD

For the arrest and conviction of the man who held up and robbed the stages of the Transportation Companies in the Yellowstone Park, near Keppler Cascades, on Aug. 24, 1908, $1000.00 will be paid.

Description of the robber. About 5 ft. 8 in. tall, blue gray eyes, bristly gray whiskers, acted either as a man badly out of breath or a consumptive, weight about 135-150 pounds, understood german. Had on bluish brown overalls, brown shirt, soft felt hat and carried an automatic rifle.

Y. N. P. TRANS. CO.   M-Y STAGE CO.   WYLIE CAMP. CO.

The US Fourth Cavalry Regiment, I Troop commanded by Captain James R. Lockett, poses with a fallen giant in Sequoia National Park, 1897.

Protecting favored species had nothing to do with the role those species played in their ecosystems and everything to do with aesthetics. Travelers to national parks at the turn of the twentieth century had been promised large herds of ungulates roaming wild spaces and huge flocks of birds taking flight, so park managers manipulated wildlife for the visitors' enjoyment.

The treatment of bears, specifically in Yellowstone, was another spectacle. Once public perception of bears shifted from fear to amusement, they were hand-fed for the benefit of paying customers and sometimes chained to trees so that tourists could be guaranteed a close-up look. Since the 1880s in Yellowstone, garbage dumps behind park hotels had at first inadvertently drawn grizzlies, but when the congregated bruins started drawing hordes of humans, park management encouraged the viewings.

Stocking waterways with fish had been a popular practice at Yellowstone since the park's beginning, and the practice spread to Crater Lake,

Yosemite, Glacier, and Sequoia national parks. No particular attention was paid to which species of fish belonged in which watershed. If they could survive in waterways chosen by management and would delight pole-toting tourists, they were released there.

Foreign flora and fauna were routinely introduced into parks in the early days without thought or fear of the consequences. Trees, grasses, shrubs, and even some mammals were put where original ecosystems had not intended them to be. Early on, concessionaires were allowed to hunt and fish park resources to feed tourists in Yellowstone. Farmers could tend garden plots on parkland if they sold the produce to park outfitters; the army had its own huge vegetable garden north of Mammoth Springs in Yellowstone. Beef and dairy cows and a multitude of horses grazed on park grasses. Hotel owners cut and sold wildflowers and did laundry near hot springs and geysers. There was even a meat processing plant within the park.

Still, by the turn of the twentieth century, a clearer conservation vision was coming into focus and national parks policy regarding resources, concessions, camping, and transportation was beginning to take shape. Another Lacey Act, passed in 1900, safeguarded plants and wildlife by establishing civil and criminal penalties for a wide range of violations. Slowly, surely, Yellowstone became more secure under US Commissioner Meldrum, the army, and the Lacey acts. Yellowstone soldiers continued to troll wagon roads for bandits and the backwater for poachers during summertime. In the winter, they roamed the isolated hinterlands and huddled in "snowshoe cabins," a system still used today. So important were their duties to the fledgling park system that, at the height of their presence in 1910, 324 soldiers were stationed throughout Yellowstone.

As order slowly began to displace lawlessness, the troops focused on park development. They designed and built hundreds of miles of roads and trails, as well as many historic structures. The army's temporary assignment grew into a tour of duty of more than thirty years. During that time, the military also collected scientific data, planted sequoia seedlings in California, and made the first proposal for interpretive programs, suggesting that educating people about the value of the resources might get them to follow the rules. Without the decades of labor and commitment of those early crime-busters, the view from where Meldrum's office stood in Yellowstone would likely look very different—if the park existed at all.

CHAPTER 5

Dam Hetch Hetchy!

ROUGHLY 15 MILES northwest of the mega-famous Yosemite Valley is another grand gorge within the national park: Hetch Hetchy is an understudy upon which little attention is lavished, but it is no less a star on nature's stage. Pine-studded green-gray slopes angle precipitously skyward, and sheer stone walls jutting toward the moon are companions of time. Manzanita snags emit a red glow; the scent of incense cedar spices warm breezes. In springtime, two of the continent's highest waterfalls take roaring flight over 1000-foot-high granite cliffs at Hetch Hetchy. The valley has other heady features to rival the idolized El Capitan and Half Dome: Kolana Rock and Hetch Hetchy Dome.

Naturalist John Muir considered this quieter northern recess to be Yosemite Valley's doppelgänger—and just as spectacular. He wagered that if everyone who had visited the famed valley were to see Hetch Hetchy, few would know the difference. "If this multitude were to be gathered again, and set down in Hetch Hetchy perhaps less than one percent of the whole number would doubt their being in Yosemite," Muir wrote in 1873. "They would see rocks and waterfalls, meadows and groves, of Yosemite size and kind, and grouped in Yosemite style. Amid so vast an assemblage of sublime mountain forms, only the more calm and careful observers would be able to fix upon special differences." In 1890, the year Yosemite became a national park—including Hetch Hetchy Valley— Muir wrote, "It is a flood of singing air, water, and sunlight woven into cloth that spirits might wear."

At least since 1882, Hetch Hetchy Valley had been mulled as a potential reservoir site. The growing population of San Francisco, 160 miles distant, demanded more potable water, so local officials sought alternatives to their partnership with the Spring Valley Water Company, a private entity that had been delivering water to the city since 1858. San Francisco Mayor James Phelan first proposed using Hetch Hetchy as a water catchment the year Yosemite became a national park. It was the cheapest option on the table because it didn't require buying any private land. Muir's writing about the park in national mainstream publications galvanized conservationists, and the suggestion was rebuffed. Undaunted, Phelan applied for water rights to the valley in 1901 and again in 1905, and for water storage rights in 1903; all requests were roundly denied.

But the landscape of debate shifted dramatically in April 1906 when a violent earthquake knocked San Francisco to its knees. Subsequent fires devastated the city, and blame was laid on a lack of water and pressure to deliver it. A city rebuilding from tragedy and desiring reliable sources of water and power garnered sympathy nationwide. If damming the Tuolumne River had been seen as a fringe

scheme before the earthquake, it was now game-on in the high-stakes competition for Hetch Hetchy Valley. The battle would illustrate the widening gap between two conservation camps: the preservation ideal embraced by Muir and the Sierra Club, and the long-standing utilitarian model championed by independently wealthy Chief Forester Gifford Pinchot of the US Forest Service.

The utilitarian conservationists looked at public lands as board-feet of lumber and acre-feet of water, as growth and security; the conservation purists had wilderness on the brain. While there were few places even then, especially in and around Yosemite Valley, that could be considered truly untrammeled

On a hillside overlooking San Francisco, spectators watch as fires consume the city after the devastating 1906 earthquake.

by humans, it was a concept Muir cultivated. "In God's wildness lies the hope of the world—the great fresh unblighted, unredeemed wilderness," he wrote. "The galling harness of civilization drops off, and wounds heal ere we are aware." Muir spawned a proto-environmentalism that embraced the wild while drawing on the radical philosophies of writers, artists, and naturalists who'd come before him. The clash between the Muir and Pinchot camps shook the very existence, purpose, and meaning of national parks—and, ultimately, led to the founding of the National Park Service.

Soon after the 1906 earthquake, Hetch Hetchy dam advocates got a break when pro-dam James Garfield, the former president's son, replaced park protector Ethan Hitchcock as secretary of the interior. San Francisco city officials immediately began lobbying Garfield for water and reservoir rights to the "Little Yosemite" and to nearby Lake Eleanor, vowing to develop the smaller Eleanor before approaching Hetch Hetchy. In the first move along a slick slope, Garfield gave San Francisco rights to Lake Eleanor alone in 1908. A heated congressional hearing before the Committee on Public Lands in the waning days of that year revealed that the city was surely renewing its bid for Hetch Hetchy—and it had the full support of Garfield.

In his early testimony, Garfield acknowledged that there was "serious opposition on the part of a number of citizens, not only of California, but throughout the country, to any action by me that would, as they stated, abandon the Hetch Hetchy as a valley and destroy, as they felt, one of the great and wonderful natural beauties of that section of the country." After regarding the conservationists' concerns, Garfield quickly dashed their hopes: "On the other hand, in weighing the two sides of this question, I felt that there could be no doubt but that it should be resolved in favor of the citizens of San Francisco, because this use of the valley would not destroy it as one of the most beautiful spots in the West. It would simply change the floor of the valley from a meadow to a beautiful lake." How Garfield knew that, having never been to Hetch Hetchy, was a mystery to those who had.

The conservationists who attended the committee hearing were likely shaking their heads, and then their fists, as Garfield spoke. They soon took the floor and vociferously fought for Hetch Hetchy's riches to remain in the nation's treasure chest. They included the well-known head of the American Civic Association, J. Horace McFarland; the secretary of the Sierra Club, William Colby; prominent journalist Robert Underwood Johnson, editor of *The Century Magazine*; and the insightful Allen Chamberlain of the Appalachian Mountain Club, among others.

Muir was not there in person, though his name was invoked many times, and the obvious fury present in his written statements was a guiding light for his allies: "Every national park is besieged by thieves and robbers and beggars with all sorts of plans and pleas for possession of some coveted treasure of water, timber, pasture, rights-of-way, etc. Nothing dollarable is safe, however guarded," he had written. McFarland added, "The United States has now all too few reservations of a public nature, supposedly to be held as public parks . . . the Yosemite National Park is unique and . . . no portion of it can be spared to any use unless that use benefits the whole public." They believed that damming the picturesque valley meant sacrificing it for the interests of a relative few.

In the vicious fight for public opinion and political sway, the preservationists had been labeled by the utilitarians as sentimentalists and poets, terminology meant to disparage their opinions. It was a characterization angrily disputed by McFarland at the committee hearing. "Cant of this sort on the part of people who have not developed beyond the pseudo-'practical' stage is one of the retarding influences of American civilization," he said.

Eventually rising above the name-calling, dam opponents demanded proof that Hetch Hetchy was its only option for reliable water, as the city had claimed. A statement submitted to the congressional committee from *Century* argued, "This involves a new principle and a dangerous precedent, and is a tremendous price for the nation to pay for San Francisco's water, and the burden of proof that it is necessary is upon those who advocated the grant." Editor Johnson added, "Satan himself would never have dared play such tricks with the Garden of Eden." He said damming the Tuolumne River would be like diverting the waters before they reached Niagara Falls. "The mind revolts at such a calamity," he said.

Though Garfield clearly grasped the crux of the anti-dam camp, he simply disputed the purpose of national parks as they saw them. "If we look at it from the point of view of those gentlemen, then everything should be made subservient to their single desire to retain the park as it is," he said.

In that same year, the first Governors' Conference on Conservation propelled such issues into the public consciousness. The meeting was financed mostly by Pinchot, who was well-known as a "conservation" advocate—meaning, by his definition, actively managing natural resources for sustainable exploitation. In his 1910 book *The Fight for Conservation*, Pinchot wrote, "Conservation means the greatest good to the greatest number for the longest time. It demands the complete and orderly development of all our resources for the benefit of all the people." The key to conservation for Pinchot was balance, while the core for Muir and many others was preservation. Muir's thinking, well understood nowadays but revolutionary at the turn of the twentieth century, was that certain places should be protected and maintained as they stood.

Pinchot's conference wasn't attended only by state officials but also by cabinet members, Supreme Court justices, and members of Congress, a wide-ranging and influential audience for the chief forester's agenda. Pinchot and his ideas were popular in Washington, DC, charting an uphill course for the protection and expansion of the national park system—and spelling disaster for Hetch Hetchy.

In the years following Pinchot's conservation conference, a special commission looked into the Hetch Hetchy morass, and San Francisco's right-of-way permit was rescinded. The Department of the Interior also asked for more information on other water resources available to the city and on what would be sacrificed at Hetch Hetchy should a dam be built. It seemed a reprieve might be forthcoming for Yosemite Valley's twin.

But the setback for the utilitarians only fed their fire, and both camps continued dispatching heated rhetoric. Pinchot's people began to position themselves as practical and masculine while trying to characterize Muir and his followers as weak and effeminate. One acerbic cartoon published at the time depicted Muir as a woman in a dress and apron attempting to sweep water out of Hetch Hetchy Valley with a straw broom. The purists didn't stoop to respond to such low blows, but Muir's tongue and pen nevertheless sharpened considerably during that time. In 1912 he thundered, "These temple destroyers, devotees of ravaging commercialism, seem to have a perfect contempt for Nature, and, instead of lifting their eyes to the God of the mountains, lift them to the Almighty Dollar. Dam Hetch Hetchy! As well dam for water-tanks the people's cathedrals and churches, for no

holier temple has ever been consecrated by the heart of man."

So cutting were the arguments over Hetch Hetchy that even Muir's treasured Sierra Club was torn apart, prompting him to found another organization through which to lobby Congress. The new Society for the Preservation of the National Parks included many of his old confidants, many of whom happily embraced one group his opponents wanted little to do with: women. One of Hetch Hetchy's most eloquent defenders was editor and scholar Harriet Monroe. She left a deep impression while testifying in front of the Senate on the issue: "It is for you to keep this treasure intact for the future, to pass it on like a crown jewel to the generations who shall know and love it," she said.

But at that point, the dam scheme had just as many friends as enemies, and some of those friends were close to home. California Congressman John Raker called Hetch Hetchy Valley a place of "old barren rocks"; Congressman William Kent, also of the Golden State, supported the dam. He had once been Muir's friend, but when Kent was among his congressional colleagues, he was dismissive of Muir. "I hope you will not take my friend Muir seriously, for he is a man entirely without social sense," he said. "With him it is me and God and the rock where God put it, and that is the end of the story. I know him well, and so far as this proposition is concerned, he is mistaken."

Perhaps least surprising but no doubt hurtful was the impotence of Muir's wealthy and politically influential friends, many of whom he'd towed around Yosemite during his half century there. The megarich steel magnate (and fellow Scot) Andrew Carnegie said of his friend during that time, "It is too foolish to say that the imperative needs of a city to a full and pure water supply should be thwarted

The charismatic and wealthy Gifford Pinchot was appointed the nation's first chief forester by his friend President Teddy Roosevelt, both complex but pioneering conservationists.

for the sake of a few trees or for scenery, no matter how beautiful it might be."

Much of the mainstream media boldly opposed the dam plan. A 1913 *New York Times* editorial hinted at the slippery slope the Hetch Hetchy dam legislation created. It said, "The only time to set aside national parks is before the bustling needs of civilization have crept upon them. Legal walls must be built about them for defense, for every park will be attacked. Men and municipalities who wish something for nothing will encroach upon them if permitted. The Hetch Hetchy Valley in the Yosemite National Park is an illustration of this universal struggle."

Mere months after that editorial appeal appeared, a fierce presidential race ended with the election of Woodrow Wilson. The former president, William Howard Taft, had seen Yosemite with Muir as his guide and had deflected advances on Hetch Hetchy, but as would soon become clear, wilderness purists had lost the Oval Office. Wilson chose as his secretary of the interior Franklin Lane, a former San Francisco city attorney who was good friends with Mayor Phelan. Though Lane had never seen the area, he was very much in favor of a reservoir at Hetch Hetchy.

A second and even more animated congressional hearing on Hetch Hetchy was held on two steamy June days in 1913. Dam boosters described a dire water shortage in San Francisco and characterized the valley as a mosquito-infested swamp. During his testimony, Secretary Lane admitted to having partisan interest in the dam but insisted the project would improve on

what Hetch Hetchy had to offer. "I think that I have as much appreciation of natural beauty as anyone and as much of a desire to conserve the natural beauties of my own home state as anyone," he said, "and my conclusion, after thinking of this thing a long while, has been that to turn that valley into a lake would add to the beauty of the whole thing rather than to detract from it in any way; but, of course, in matters of taste we all differ." Muir, who wasn't present at the hearing, later mocked the notion that a lake where the living glacial valley lay would improve its scenic quality: "As well say damming New York's Central Park would enhance its beauty."

Chief Forester Pinchot spoke at the hearing, reiterating his support and promoting his particular ethic: "Now, the fundamental principle of the whole conservation policy is that of use, to take every part of the land and its resources and put it to that use in which it will best serve the most people, and I think there can be no question at all but that in this case we have an instance in which all weighty considerations demand the passage of the bill," he said.

Since the hearing was held with little advance public notice, the only preservationist to attend in person was Edmund Whitman, who represented the Appalachian Mountain Club. He began his exhaustive statement by furiously discounting Secretary Lane's testimony. "He is hardly in the position of an impartial protector of the rights of the public," he said. Whitman said that, sure, the people of San Francisco need water; the only problem is that they are too stingy to pay for it.

A powerful letter from *Century* editor Johnson also was read: "I am aware that in certain quarters one who contends for the practical value of natural beauty is considered a 'crank,' and yet the love of beauty is the most dominant trait in mankind," he said. "The moment anyone of intelligence gets enough to satisfy the primal needs of the physical man, he begins to plan for something beautiful— house, grounds, or a view of nature. Could this be capitalized in dollars, could some alchemy reveal its value, we should not hear materialists deriding lovers of nature, with any effect upon legislators. Without this touch of idealism, this sense of beauty, life would only be a race for the trough."

Muir's Society for the Preservation of the National Parks also sent correspondence indicting the "Park invaders" for trying to rush through a Hetch Hetchy vote at a special session cloaked as "an emergency measure . . . before it can be brought to the attention of the ninety millions of people who own this park," they said.

But the dam opponents had done all they could. In the end, the newly minted notions of scenery for its own sake, of preservation for recreation, aesthetics, or spiritual renewal, proved too foreign to a nation accustomed to use and exploitation. The Raker Act passed the House by a landslide. In the Senate, the vote was much closer: 43 yeas, 25 nays, and more than 24 abstentions. President Wilson signed the bill into law in December 1913. The American people would lose their ancient valley, but San Francisco would get its lucrative dam.

Following the passage of the dam legislation, the *New York Times* editorialized, "Ever since the business of nation-making began, it has been the unwritten law of conquest that people who are too lazy, too indolent, or too parsimonious to defend their heritages will lose them to the hosts that know how to fight and to finance campaigns. The American people have been whipped in the Hetch Hetchy fight." It tasted of bitterness, but the sentiment was indicative of a consciousness that had been raised. Muir and his lot had popularized the idea of stewardship and of putting human existence in the context of the wider natural world; people may be on par with the birds, trees, and bees, but our physical needs are not superior.

Muir wrote to friends about the staggering loss: "[I]t goes to my very heart. But in spite of Satan & Co. some sort of compensation must surely come out of even this dark damn-dam-damnation," he said. His prediction was right: while the guardian of Yosemite would not live to see it—he died just a year after the valley was sacrificed—the legacy

UNDAM HETCH HETCHY!

Hetch Hetchy's O'Shaughnessy Dam, which cost sixty-eight lives and $100 million to build, was completed in 1923 (though water was not delivered from it until 1934), then was raised to its current height in 1938. And for at least the past fifty years, rumblings have been made for its removal. Most recently, during President Ronald Reagan's administration, Secretary of the Interior Donald Hodel proposed to restore Hetch Hetchy Valley. A 1988 report done by the Bureau of Reclamation (formerly the Reclamation Service) at the request of the National Park Service details the feasibility of dismantling the dam: "Such restoration would renew the national commitment to maintaining the integrity of the national park system and keep in perpetual conservation an irreplaceable and unique natural area," it says.

While nothing substantial came of that assessment or several other scientific studies conducted since (all concluding that dam removal would have little to no impact on the San Francisco Bay Area's current power supply or water supply, which is fed by eight other reservoirs), the general trend of dam removal in scenic areas is a positive one, says Spreck Rosekrans, executive director of the nonprofit Restore Hetch Hetchy. His organization feels it's time to eliminate Yosemite's role as the state's most beautiful water tank and renew the soul of that lost valley with the unhurried river and unmatched bioriches. "It would heal the greatest blemish in our national park history. It would make Yosemite whole," says Rosekrans.

Biologists project that within a decade of draining the valley, Hetch Hetchy would host native flora; within fifty years, well-established oaks and conifers would populate the valley floor and bears, deer, and other wildlife would live there year-round. "It would be spectacular almost right away," says Rosekrans. There might also be an opportunity to alleviate some of the stress on the heavily loved Yosemite Valley, a chance to limit development and to get it right.

Three former superintendents of Yosemite, writing on the hundredth anniversary of the passage of the Raker Act, ardently supported dam removal. In an editorial in the *San Jose Mercury News*, they wrote, "A century ago, our nation sought to tame the wilderness with large-scale engineering projects, occasionally with destructive results. Today we should commit to undoing one of the worst examples of that destruction. And tomorrow, we can watch a magnificent valley emerge from the depths."

of that fight endured. It ultimately fueled future opposition to similar schemes and stirred legislation for an agency to protect the parks. Many people had fought alongside Muir not because they'd seen the contested valley for themselves, but because the national park ideal had been violated. Without the existence of an agency whose specific job it was to safeguard resources being held in the public trust—not for the benefit of one city or one state, but for the entire nation—they toiled over which sacrificial lamb would follow Yosemite's Hetch Hetchy to the slaughter.

As the O'Shaughnessy Dam rose, Hetch Hetchy Valley became a memory.

And so Hetch Hetchy's name—most likely from the Miwok word *hatchhatchie*, meaning "edible grasses"—has not been accurate in nearly a century. The lush meadows for which it was named have been submerged under 300 feet of water since 1923, when the O'Shaughnessy Dam was completed and began impounding water from the Tuolumne River. Where one of the most diverse ecosystems in the country used to lie, with groves of towering oak, pine, and fir and riotous crowds of grass and azalea, now an 8-mile-long reservoir stretches. The silver thread of the Tuolumne River (as Muir described it), which once coursed through thousands of acres of meadow lilies, larkspurs, and lupine, is a historic footnote. Snowmelt from more than 450 square miles of Yosemite National Park is now sequestered behind a concrete dam taller than a high-rise building and delivered via an aqueduct to San Francisco and neighboring municipalities.

In the years before the valley was a reservoir, Muir wrote: "Imagine yourself in Hetch Hetchy. It is a sunny day in June, the pines sway dreamily, and you are shoulder-deep in grass and flowers. Looking across the valley through beautiful open groves you see a bare granite wall 1800 feet high rising abruptly out of the green and yellow vegetation and glowing with sunshine, and in front of it the fall, waving like a downy scarf, silver bright, burning with white sun-fire in every fiber."

Only time will tell if Hetch Hetchy will ever look that way again.

A guide leads climbers toward the 14,411-foot summit of Mount Rainier.

CHAPTER 6

Stephen Mather Goes to Washington

SEVERAL MONTHS BEFORE President Woodrow Wilson signed the legislation allowing Hetch Hetchy Valley to be dammed, an eager law school student from the University of California–Berkeley waited in Oakland to board a train. It was late spring 1913; the dogwood had bloomed in colorful canopies, and the wisteria hung heavy and sweet from their vines. Horace Albright, twenty-four, was anxious about embarking on his first cross-country trip and about the uncertainty of leaving school and family for a unique job in Washington, DC. He may have paced the platform wondering what lay ahead. But what seemed to be foremost in his mind was leaving behind, for an unknown time, the classmate for whom he'd recently fallen head over heels.

As Albright's train thundered east, he was astonished daily at the immensity and diversity of the expanse of America. He described the journey to Grace Noble, the woman with the most beautiful brown eyes he'd ever seen, penning a postcard to her from Ogden, Utah, and another from

Chicago. When he arrived in the nation's capital six days later, he wrote her a sixteen-page letter.

Despite his growing homesickness—or maybe because of it—Albright wasted no time in his new city, going from the train station to the Department of the Interior, stopping only to get his one suit cleaned. Compared to the rambling, leafy Berkeley campus, Washington must have seemed stark and riotous with its rumbling electric streetcars, horses and buggies, and growing number of Henry Ford's Model Ts. Here, as in most of the developed world, art, travel, music, prosperity, and peace were in abundant supply. Everyone was blissfully, if temporarily, ignorant of the world war that would erupt a year later.

Not long after he'd arrived at his new offices in the Old Patent Office Building, Albright was sworn in as confidential clerk to Secretary of the Interior Franklin Lane. At the time the Interior Department was small, and it fell to Albright to do any manner of tasks, some of which revolved around national park units. The Hetch Hetchy dam was being passionately debated on the national stage, and Albright was tagged to answer some of the thousands of angry letters opposing the proposed reservoir, which his boss supported. "I hated this job, for I was in sympathy with the protests," Albright later wrote.

The quiet, conscientious young man had been recommended for the position by William Colby, an attorney, a confidant of John Muir's, and a prominent figure in conservation circles. Albright had met Muir in San Francisco shortly before the older man's death. The conservation titan, disheveled by the battle over damming the Tuolumne River in Yosemite, "made an enormous impression on me with his discussion of the Hetch Hetchy problem in Yosemite," said Albright in his memoir, *The Missing Years*.

Another hot-button issue when Albright arrived in Washington, DC, involved crime in Yellowstone. After a convoy of fifteen stagecoaches traveling near Shoshone Point in the park was robbed, Albright learned all he could about the park in order to try to solve the problem. He discovered that the parks were in no way united save for the eight overwhelmed inspectors who traveled among them troubleshooting. And, in addition to having to coordinate with the War Department regarding park security, each park unit received separate, meager appropriations from Congress. While the national forests with their multiple-use mandate had robust representation, the national parks had no such oversight or defense.

Fueled by youthful idealism, Albright spent countless hours on Capitol Hill trying to sell distracted congressmen on legislation creating a dedicated bureau to oversee this growing group of public lands. Around that time J. Horace McFarland, who had testified so passionately against the Hetch Hetchy reservoir, also presented Congress with the idea of a service to administer national parks. But, Albright said, "National parks didn't arouse much enthusiasm."

Although the idea was premature, the seed for the National Park Service had been planted.

As the sticky summer days of 1913 retreated with cool air on their heels, Lane received a furious letter from a Chicago businessman who had recently been on a Tahoe-to-Mount Whitney outing that took in national parks and forests along the way. Stephen Mather, a decades-long member of the Sierra Club, had spent summers as a student working near and camping in the Sierra Nevada. When Mather met John Muir is a matter of debate, but it's clear the older man's work inspired the young entrepreneur toward conservationist thinking. Later, Mather made his fortune promoting the mineral borax for use as a household cleaner. When he reached his late forties, he was thinking about retirement. He began to spend more time in the backcountry, where he retreated whenever time allowed, because it alone provided him solace.

By the time of his letter, Mather had summited Mount Rainier and countless peaks throughout Yosemite, Sequoia, and what later became Kings Canyon. He was also a supporter of former President Theodore Roosevelt's "new nationalism," which professed that for a democracy to truly serve the greatest number of citizens it must be based on programs run by federal agencies. During the battle over Hetch Hetchy, and as threats to the fledgling park system were mounting, Mather also began to support the idea of a park service to safeguard the nation's natural and cultural resources.

On his Tahoe-to-Mount Whitney trip, Mather was appalled by the encroachment of mining and logging interests, as well as by what he called the theft of public land by private entities. In the lengthy polemic he sent to Lane in the fall of 1914, Mather also went into gruesome detail about the dodgy state of food and lodging offered to national park tourists. If the integrity of the parks was to be restored, he said, something must be done. According to Albright, Mather took umbrage at the "attitude of the government—the Department of the Interior in particular—in

First NPS Director Stephen Mather poses at Yellowstone's North Entrance (a.k.a. Antler Gate) in 1928.

ignoring, actually abandoning, its sacred trust to protect [parks]."

A popular myth goes that since Lane and Mather were friends from UC Berkeley, Lane responded to the irate letter by challenging the millionaire mountain man to come to Washington, DC, to run the parks if he thought he could do better. In truth, the two hadn't known each other, but when Lane asked around about Mather, he liked what he heard. The secretary of the interior was looking to replace his assistant who oversaw national parks, and he thought the entrepreneur's popularity and marketing prowess, not to mention his personal wealth (which made public service more realistic), made him the ideal candidate.

Why Lane, a strong advocate for the Hetch Hetchy dam and a champion of the utilitarian philosophy of natural resources, would pursue a Muir disciple such as Mather to work closely with him is a mystery. Some have speculated that regret over having sacrificed a beloved piece of national park wore on Lane, and he sought redemption by strengthening the park system in other ways. Still others contend that Lane truly believed in preservation through developing a robust park system but that Hetch Hetchy was a complex issue at a difficult moment in time. Whatever Lane's reasoning, in a meeting with Mather at Chicago's Blackstone Hotel in late 1914, the interior secretary broached the topic of Mather joining his ranks.

What Lane didn't know is that Mather may have already been persuaded to become a Washington insider when, after the Hetch Hetchy defeat, there was pressure to secure the High Sierra from future indignities. A year earlier, Robert Marshall, chief geographer of the US Geological Survey, was speculating behind the scenes with western conservationists about establishing a park to bridge the gap between Yosemite and Sequoia national parks. Marshall had written to Mather, "Muir and the Sierra Club are doing all they can for the cause at long distance, but it needs some real live man on the ground here to handle the matter personally. I wish it were possible for you to shoulder the task." Up until then, the conservation movement had been shepherded by shaggy, white-bearded, sagelike characters with walking sticks and an avuncular air. While Mather did have a shock of white hair, he was sun-kissed and sharp-dressed— more John Barrymore than John Muir. His eyes were pale, alpine-glacier blue, and he could charm a bear out of a berry patch if the occasion warranted. His crackling enthusiasm for wildlands drew even steely Capitol Hill types.

In December 1914, Mather arrived in DC and talked at length with Lane in the secretary's spacious corner office. The problem Lane presented was that the national parks were orphans whose care was divided among the Interior, War, and Agriculture departments. They needed to be united in a strong new bureau, and more Americans had to be made aware of their value and allure. "Just get out in the country, size up the park problems, and do a broad public relations job, so that you can convince the Congress of establishing an independent park service bureau," said Lane. "Besides that, this is a real opportunity for you to do a great public service."

In fact, Lane wanted Mather to apply his business know-how to the parks, which had plenty of spiritual and emotional appeal but little practical purpose, as Congress saw it. Lane knew that like-minded congressmen were more likely to be persuaded by economics than sentiment. Lane explained it this way: "A wilderness, no matter how impressive and beautiful, does not satisfy this soul of mine (if I have that kind of thing). It is a challenge to man. It says, 'Master me! Put me to use! Make something more than I am!'" It would take someone with financial sensibilities to persuade Congress that national parks could stimulate regional and national economies with the proper leadership, such as a National Park Service. It would also take someone who appealed to the John Muir faction, someone they believed truly understood the pull of the parks. Many saw Mather as the man to bridge that gap.

While Mather was nearly sold on the idea, he was repelled by the thought of being tangled in red tape on Capitol Hill. He was concerned that, with his big personality and passion for the parks, he might step on toes and imperil the very mission he was there to accomplish.

That's when Lane brought in Horace Albright, who had, since leaving California, finished his law degree at Georgetown University. Lane told the two to take a seat on the brown leather couch near the fireplace and talk about the future. Albright described that memorable meeting, in which Mather peppered him with questions, as one that began a lasting friendship. "He riveted his attention on my answers, interrupting frequently to pose new questions, jabbing his finger to make a point, restlessly moving head, body, and hands as he talked," wrote Albright. "His was a lightning fast brain with an electric nervous energy to go with it."

After several hours in deep conversation with Albright, Mather was ready to accept the year-long job, provided Albright agreed to be his right-hand man "to keep him out of jail," said Mather. But Albright confessed he was preparing to leave Washington for a promising legal career and, more importantly, his fiancée in California. Upon leaving Lane's office, Mather put an arm around the young man's shoulders and said, "Albright, you and I would do well together. Keep your mind open. Let's think about it for a while." Besides, he said, it would be only a year. Despite Albright's protests, the two could already sense destiny taking shape.

When Mather returned to Washington, DC, in January 1915, he repeated that having Albright, with his knowledge of the national parks and Capitol Hill, as his second in command was a condition of his accepting Lane's offer. Since their last meeting, Albright had agonized over delaying his life on the West Coast, but he had already begun to see Mather as a kindred spirit and father figure. He hadn't broached the topic with his future wife, and yet he felt his hesitation evaporating in the heat of Mather's enthusiasm. "I really hadn't asked for time to consider the proposal or even ask Grace. That was the power of the man," Albright later wrote. The young lawyer relented, promising only one more year of service in Washington, to help Mather settle into the political fray and to focus on the Organic Act, the legislation intended to create a National Park Service.

After Mather took his oath as a government servant in late January, the two got to work knocking on doors and shaking hands on Capitol Hill. Their first stop was the office of Congressman Raker, who had vigorously supported damming Hetch Hetchy (the legislation—the Raker Act—had his name on it) and was now also cosponsor of the NPS bill—an irony lost on few. Mather and Raker discovered they shared mutual friends and a love of the Sierra Nevada. Upon parting, Raker handed Albright copies of the bill to talk it up and start building a coalition of like minds. The bill was either off the radar of or unpopular with most elected officials, and it was clear to all three that

THAT'S A FACT

Sequoias and redwoods are often confused, but the two are quite different. While redwoods (*Sequoia sempervirens*) grow mainly on the cool, moisture-rich Northern California coast, sequoias (*Sequoiadendron giganteum*) prefer the higher elevations of the western Sierra and require periodic heat to thrive. Sequoias generally have a greater mass than redwoods, whereas the latter get taller but tend not to live as long.

MAKING HER-STORY

There are, of course, women who have worked tirelessly for the National Park Service prior to and since its founding. Foremost among them was Isabelle Story, a skilled writer poached from the US Geological Survey. From 1916 until 1954, she wrote annual reports, press releases, radio scripts, visitor guides, and articles. With a poetic pen, Story introduced many people to distant landscapes and likely did more to sell the American public on national parks than history will ever account for.

they were standing at the foot of a cliff looking up. But maybe, just maybe, together they could get to the top.

Even in 1915, the idea of a department dedicated to park protection and administration was not a new one. Legislation had been floated since the turn of the twentieth century. While those proposals had sunk, some influential lawmakers had gotten on board along the way. During William Taft's 1909–1913 presidency, sandwiched in between the conservation-minded administrations of Theodore Roosevelt and Woodrow Wilson (who, despite the thrashing he took over Hetch Hetchy, did establish fourteen national park units), Taft threw his weight behind a parks department. In a message to Congress in 1912, he said, "I earnestly recommend the establishment of a bureau of national parks. Such legislation is essential to the proper management of those wondrous manifestations of nature, so startling and so beautiful that everyone recognizes the obligations of the Government to preserve them for the edification and recreation of the people."

Yet when Mather and Albright began to work together, the concept was still a controversial one in need of champions. Secretary Lane wasn't the only

one who thought Mather was born for that role. William Colby, who had recommended Albright to Lane and whom Mather had befriended through the Sierra Club, expressed his happiness and relief over Mather's appointment in Washington. "When I heard that Mr. Mather had been appointed Assistant to the Secretary of the Interior, I had a feeling come over me of more genuine pleasure than any information that has come to me in a long while . . . I knew he was thoroughly in sympathy with everything that appertained to the welfare of our national parks. I knew that the star of the national-park idea was in the ascendancy."

To many, Mather seemed the savior of the embryonic park system. Mark Daniels, the first general superintendent of national parks, said, "When it was announced that Mr. Stephen T. Mather had been appointed Assistant to the Secretary, I think a sigh of relief went up from every man who has any interest in the national parks. In the short time that Secretary Mather has been connected with the parks, I have begun to see that the clouds are opening." Marshall, of the USGS, was even more enthusiastic. "My joy was beyond control," he said. Secretary Lane had selected "the one best man in the whole country" to lead the parks.

Mather had learned firsthand experiences were powerful drivers of the protection sentiment, and he believed that bringing influential people to parks would lead them to pursue his agenda. Mather had been on pack trips many times into Yosemite, Sequoia, and what is now Kings Canyon, and he felt those places had persuasive powers that exceeded even his own. It's no wonder, then, that he chose the High Sierra, soothing to his own spirit, for his First Mountain Party in the summer of 1915.

For those trips, Mather spared no expense in outfitting his charges with the latest gear—including sleeping bags and state-of-the-art air mattresses, Stetson hats, boots, and Levi's. His guests ate gourmet meals served on ironed white linen, with china, napkins, and silverware, as well as Japanese paper lanterns strung overhead. Their private chef served fresh fruit and eggs, fried chicken and venison, freshly baked bread and apple pie, and more. Mather invited along diverse characters, including Bob Marshall (later the general superintendent of the national parks), who was in charge of logistics, and Frank Ewing, a Sequoia ranger who was lead packer.

Mather cherry-picked other attendees based on their spheres of influence: Gilbert Grosvenor, director of the National Geographic Society and editor of its magazine. Congressman Frederick Gillett of Massachusetts, the ranking Republican on the House Appropriations Committee. Ernest McCormick, vice president of the Southern Pacific Railroad. Henry Fairfield Osborn (a boyhood friend of Theodore Roosevelt and nephew of financier J. P. Morgan), then president of the American Museum of Natural History and the New York Zoological Society. Wilbur McClure,

the California state engineer who was, during that time, plotting the route of the 211-mile John Muir Trail along the crest of the Sierra Nevada.

The thirty-strong group spent its first evening in Sequoia National Park, dining opulently and sleeping on pine needles beside behemoth trees that had witnessed prior millennia. Before selecting the mules or horses that would be their constant companions for nearly two weeks, the party stopped to take a memorable photo in the Giant Forest. With arms outstretched, the travelers encircled the General Sherman Tree: at more than 103 feet wide and 275 feet tall, it is, by volume, the world's largest tree. It was an act, engineered in typical Mather style, to build esprit de corps. Mather hoped that, by the end of their time on the trail, this group would become a fraternity that would remain linked in the fight for parks.

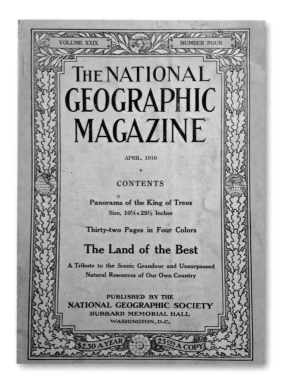

The April 1916 issue of *National Geographic*, devoted to America's "Land of the Best," urges readers to support the founding of a park service.

In the following days the group crossed Franklin Pass and dropped down into Kern Canyon, and toward the end of June, most of the party summited 14,495-foot Mount Whitney, the highest peak in the continental United States. During that time, they christened themselves in unnamed hot springs, lazily fished teeming rivers, dared one another to plunge into icy streams and pools of snowmelt, nursed strained muscles by the fireside, and ate sumptuous box lunches while they decried the shame of logging and grazing these hills. More than once they were struck silent by the scene of peaks and canyons crowding their way to the horizon, and they vowed to safeguard it.

It came as no surprise, but near the end of the trip Mather announced, "Well, men, we've had a glorious ten days together, and we'll have a few more before we part in Yosemite. I think the time has come, though, that I confess why I wanted you to come along with me on this adventure. Not only for your interesting company, but to hope you'd see the significance of these mountains in the whole picture of what we are trying to do. Hopefully, you will take this message and spread it throughout the land in your own avenue and style. These valleys and heights of the Sierra Nevada are just one small part of the majesty of

America . . . Try to save them for, and share them with, future generations."

Mather's plan was as successful as he'd hoped. Upon their return, his mountaineers released a torrent of publicity for national parks in mainstream newspapers and magazines and on the lecture circuit. The *Saturday Evening Post*, *Scribner's*, and many other publications introduced Americans to their parks. Grosvenor, the *National Geographic* editor (nicknamed "Tenderfoot" by the other members of the Mather Mountain Party), was ignited most by what he had seen. The entire April 1916 issue of the magazine was focused on the "The Land of the Best." The twenty-four-page spread showcased parklands from the craggy coast of Maine and the red-rock arches of Utah to the wildflowered meadows of Washington's Mount Rainier and glacier-draped flanks of Alaska's Mount McKinley. Grosvenor gushed,

A 20-mule Borax team (actually 18 mules and 2 horses) hauls the mineral from the mine to the railroad in Mojave, California. This mode of transportation inspired the advertising campaign that, in turn, made it a household (cleaner) name and made Stephen Mather a millionaire.

"Our country is the treasure-house of nature's scenic jewels, containing so many and such an infinite variety of marvels that thousands of our matchless treasures cannot even be mentioned in this brief article."

He also addressed the popularity of Europe as a tourist destination for Americans. Sure, the Old World had art, literature, and architecture, but consider what lies in your own backyards, he urged. "[I]n that architecture which is voiced in the glorious temples of the sequoia grove and in the castles of the Grand Canyon, in that art which is mirrored in American lakes, which is painted in geyser basins and frescoed upon the side walls of the mightiest canyons, there is a majesty and an appeal that the mere handiwork of man, splendid though it may be, can never rival," he wrote. In the piece Grosvenor also mentions Secretary Lane and Mather, remarking that they "realize that as playgrounds for recreation and instruction, our national parks are without rivals on any continent." In case they had missed his "Land of the Best" issue, the "Tenderfoot" of the Sierra made sure every member of Congress received a copy.

Because of its widespread influence in the public arena, that Sierra pack trip was, according to Albright, the "final catalyst" to the creation of the National Park Service.

Mather, of course, could not have done it alone and relied on a cadre of "Mather Men" who hailed from all corners of interest and influence—and also, in fact, included many women. Ultimately, his alliance with Albright formed an epic partnership that would shape, define, and direct the park system that has been enjoyed by billions of people over the past century. But first Albright, the shy young Californian who'd stepped off a train alone in Washington, DC, uncertain of his future, would have to find his voice and speak up for the parks. The bid for a National Park Service—the desire to embed and to expand that democratic ideal in the hearts of all Americans— was about to go mainstream.

The US Capitol, a timeless symbol of tenacity and ingenuity, as it appeared during Mather's tenure

The first automobile to enter Sequoia National Park along what would eventually be extended and named the Generals Highway, famous for its nail-biting switchbacks

25 H.P. Hudson' owned by H.T. Mayo, Visalia Cal. First auto to enter
Sequoia National Park - July 14.'10

CHAPTER 7

Playing Monopoly

AFTER A SHORT, bumpy ferry ride from the East Bay, attendees of the 1915 National Park Conference met at the bustling Fillmore Street entrance of San Francisco's Panama–Pacific International Exposition. Ultimately millions of people would flock to that world's fair, which spanned a 3-mile stretch. What now encompasses the Marina District and Presidio waterfront was transformed with dramatic displays of human ingenuity. Visitors toured dozens of exhibition halls and stood enthralled at the sight of massive courtyards, palaces, and sculptures. The expo celebrated the completion of the Panama Canal and the return to glory of a city that, less than a decade prior, had been leveled by earthquake and fire.

The fair highlighted the historic role the railroads had played in pushing the American empire west, and those captains of industry spared no expense in crafting some of the largest and most elaborate exhibits. While still plugging away inside the political machinery to get the Organic Act passed in Congress, Stephen Mather

Bird's-eye view of the sprawling Panama–Pacific International Exposition grounds in San Francisco where the big railroads spent millions of dollars enticing people to ride the rails to national parks

and Horace Albright took a day's diversion at the expo. Through the Fillmore Street entrance, the would-be National Park Service director and assistant director herded national park superintendents, supervisors, custodians, and concessionaires down jammed thoroughfares.

It was National Park Day at the fair, and the group was met by railroad officials and a full brass band, all marching noisily to the Union Pacific exhibition pavilion. Past a narrow enclosure flanked by "rock" outcroppings, the 5-acre exhibit opened to a scaled 50,000-square-foot version of Yellowstone National Park (1 inch equaled 4 miles), including waterfalls, hot springs, and working geysers that erupted at regular intervals. Fabricated rock faces made of lumber covered in burlap and plaster represented the Tetons, blocking from view San Francisco Bay and Alcatraz Island. At the north end of the circular exhibit was a full-scale replica of the huge Old Faithful Inn; it served as a concert hall and a 2000-seat restaurant at the fair. The Union Pacific spent $500,000 on the immense, intricate display.

Rivaling the Yellowstone exhibit was the "Grand Canyon of Arizona" pavilion, built on 5 acres for $350,000 by the Atchison, Topeka and Santa Fe Railway and the Fred Harvey Company, developer of successful hotels and restaurants along the railway route. The great chasm was replicated to scale, and for twenty-five cents visitors could ride in touring cars along its rim. There was also an Indian pueblo village, constructed with materials from actual pueblos including adobe bricks and pinyon logs. It was staffed by American Indians who lived *within* the exhibit and passed their days simulating aspects of pueblo life. For its contribution to the spectacle, the Great Northern Railway hired a group of actual Blackfeet Indians from Glacier National Park who brought along buffalo-hide tepees.

The railroads had brought the pueblo and tepees, canyon and geysers, to urban San Francisco to whet adventure appetites for visiting the real natural wonders. At the Pan–Pacific expo, national parks were elevated to the world stage, where a relatively new American endeavor—the creation of national parks and an economy to accompany them—could be shown off.

It was exactly the kind of exposure Mather wanted. How to attract people to the parks had

READING, WRITING, AND ROCKS

A century ago, Mary Belle Sherman understood the importance of national parks to all people. As the head of the General Federation of Women's Clubs, she influenced the formation of six national parks and was a vocal supporter of establishing a park service.

At the 1915 National Park Conference in Berkeley, Sherman spoke about having recruited 2 million women to work on behalf of parks. "The club women have undertaken this work because they recognize the growing and imperative need for more recreation places out of doors," she said. "A nation progresses largely according to the use that is made of the leisure time of its people."

Parks are the antidote to "a civilization that has become too complex to be wholly sane and wholly safe," Sherman continued. "Outside of home influences, the intimate acquaintance with nature is one of the strongest and greatest that can be brought into the life of a child. It has an influence that lasts all through life." She believed that children should learn about parks in school and that parks themselves should be used as classrooms. To this day, education is a core mission of the National Park Service.

been a topic of discussion in the prior days of the conference, which had been held at the University of California–Berkeley. Bob Marshall of the US Geological Survey said, "That is the object of this conference—to bring us together so that we may unite in the endeavor to get just as many of the people as we possibly can to visit the parks."

Mather also had implored the participants to work together to boost the national park idea. He went so far as to ask members of the Sigma Chi fraternity to clear out of their house to make room for the conference attendees, in an attempt to foster a collegial bond among them. "The parks must be, of course, much better known than they are today if they are going to be the true playgrounds of the people that we want them to be," said Mather. "There is much that can be done in making them better known. There are many ways in which they can be brought home to the great mass of eastern people." The moment was right; with World War I

raging overseas, travelers who would have otherwise crossed the Atlantic to vacation in Europe were ripe to spend their vacation money in their own backyards.

Whether or not national park visitors would rely on the railroad to get them there remained to be seen. Just as the railroads were pouring money into the expo, asserting their dominance on the national park playing field, a plucky start-up was waiting in the wings to usurp that power. Perhaps the railroads, whiffing change on the breeze carried off the bay, invested royally in the expo as a last-ditch effort to maintain their status. Or it may have been an indication that even the mighty railroads could not have predicted the factor that would revolutionize the national park experience, and American life entirely: the automobile.

At the dedication of Rocky Mountain National Park, which took place the same year as the national parks conference in Berkeley, revelers arrived on foot, on horseback, in carriages, on motorcycles, and—for the first time in large numbers—in cars. Among the other VIPs there, waving mini American flags as they sang "The Star-Spangled Banner," was F. O. Stanley, an entrepreneur and owner of the massive Stanley Hotel, still prominent in Estes Park, Colorado. He and his twin brother had invented a steam-powered automobile, and as they tweaked their design, the Stanley Steamer rivaled fossil-fuel–powered cars.

The railroad had never conveniently served the area before it officially became a national park, but determined visitors had braved wagon rides over precipitous terrain. Already, increasing numbers of vacationers had found their way to Rocky Mountain National Park to hike, fish, and restore themselves in the mountain air. Stanley's new eleven-person vehicle transported visitors from far-flung whistle stops in record time; what used to take days now took only hours. And Henry Ford's simple, affordable car, the $575 Model T, was rolling off assembly lines by the thousands. The popularity of both demanded better road conditions to and within national parks, a cause that was being advanced by a growing political base of auto-touring folks.

At the dawn of the automobile, the official position of the Department of the Interior was that no cars were allowed in national parks. This was largely due to safety concerns over conflicts between animals and machines. But as cars became more affordable and more prevalent, pressure to admit America's latest obsession mounted. Though their use was strictly limited, cars had first entered a national park unit at Hot Springs, Arkansas (then a federal reserve), in 1907. A year later, automobile clubs in Seattle and Tacoma persuaded park officials to let their members steer their shiny metal boxes into Mount Rainier National Park, making it the first national park to allow cars. General Grant (now part of Kings Canyon) was next, in 1910; Crater Lake, in 1911; Glacier, in 1912. Following these victories for car enthusiasts, a fledgling organization—the American Automobile Association—lobbied intensely for cars to be admitted to Yellowstone and Yosemite. Time and again, they were refused.

The automobile issue had been debated (ad nauseam, according to John Muir) at the National Park Conference in Yosemite in 1912. It was mid-October in the valley, and the black oaks, Pacific dogwoods, and big-leaf maples were showy in gold and auburn. Then-Secretary of the Interior Walter Fisher expressed skepticism at the prospect of successfully incorporating cars into park operations: "If all the automobiles were of certain types and if automobilists operated that type of machine in a way that some operate their automobiles, it would be a tame animal and we could introduce it into the parks with impunity," he said. "Unfortunately, in the process of evolution we have not got that far." Fisher's objection increased in intensity: "We do know that some automobiles make a great deal of noise; that they emit very obnoxious odors; that they drop their oil and gasoline all over the face of the earth wherever they go."

Fisher was considered part of the Interior Department's conservative faction, and his comments would have come as no surprise to conference attendees. But what was likely revelatory was the opinion of the Sierra Club, represented by William Colby and the august John Muir. While Muir didn't speak at length at the conference (at least on the record), he wrote to the secretary of the American Alpine Club later about the meeting. Regarding the discussion about cars in parks,

Muir said, "A prodigious lot of gaseous commercial eloquence was spent upon it by auto-club delegates from near and far." But instead of joining Fisher's anti-auto campaign, Muir sensed the relentlessness of the car's advance: "All signs indicate automobile victory, and doubtless, under certain precautionary restrictions, these useful, progressive, blunt-nosed mechanical beetles will hereafter be allowed to puff their way into all the parks and mingle their gas-breath with the breath of the pines and waterfalls, and, from the mountaineer's standpoint, with but little harm or good," he said.

Muir wasn't throwing in the towel, as modern-day preservationists might think. He was no wilderness purist and appreciated the complexity of modernity. Muir accepted, if reluctantly, the automobile as a necessary evil because he believed that once Americans had seen places like Yosemite, they might unite against activities like the damming of that park's Hetch Hetchy Valley (which was becoming a major issue, see chapter 5). Cars would also bring people to nature, to admire it and to be restored by it, and this was Muir's ultimate goal. Less than a year later, in the summer of 1913, cars were officially allowed to enter Yosemite. While only 127 cars maneuvered beneath the stone sentinels and stately sequoias the next year, the floodgates had opened. The way people experienced national parks was forever changed.

To many, cars were democratizing, a leveling tool. With them, parks were transformed from playgrounds for those who could afford big-ticket train fare, stagecoach tours, and concessionaires' fees to places where the middle class could go. Private vehicles also let visitors go where they wanted and encouraged an individuality that very much appealed to average Americans. But others felt the Faustian bargain sacrificed wilderness characteristics to common use. Foremost among them were The Mountaineers, a climbing and conservation group based in Seattle, Washington. They were cautiously supportive of early park road development in Mount Rainier because roads facilitated access to the backcountry for hikers and climbers. But as the scale of planned roads—around still lakes, across tranquil meadows, over mountain passes—became clearer, they withdrew their backing. While The Mountaineers may not have predicted tour buses, campers, and millions of cars eventually snaking along park roads, they saw Pandora's box being flung open and fought consistently for limits to auto use.

Tea time during the 1915 ceremony dedicating Rocky Mountain National Park (left to right): Stephen T. Mather (holding coat), Robert Sterling Yard, (acting supervisor of the park), Herford T. Cowling (future official NPS photographer), and Horace M. Albright

The automobile debate centered around what purpose national parks had and what expectations people had of them. Early-twentieth-century leadership stood on contradictory platforms: there were car-shunning park purists like Interior Secretary Fisher, but others would have been in favor of admitting spaceships, as long as they got people into parks. With Franklin Lane as head of the Interior Department and Stephen Mather as his deputy, auto enthusiasts gained allies at the top. As a consummate salesman, Mather knew that improving access to parks through better roads would sell more people on them. Advocates for a park service were grasping for a practical justification for parks, and they took hold of the thought that tourism to parks could increase the nation's economic strength. Capitalizing on the car craze could sell Congress on supporting existing parks and on creating new ones. In his memoir Albright reflected: "We recognized that the introduction of automobiles would vastly increase the visitation to the parks and their use. However, we also knew the Congress would count tourist visitation to decide how much money our bureau would get to operate the park system. Dollars would be doled out according to the number of visitors."

The car's momentum proved powerful. In August 1915, Yellowstone was officially opened to automobiles. Nearly 1000 tourists gleefully motored past its gushing geysers and surging cataracts that month. While attendance was still low in many national parks, the handful of busy parks were outgrowing their existing facilities. In 1914, for example, Yosemite had 15,145 visitors (concentrated, as they are these days, in the late spring and summer months) who swarmed its one medium-sized, expensive hotel, three private camps, and two public campgrounds. The valley also had a delicatessen and a meat market, several photography studios, and a curio shop.

Park Supervisor Gabriel Sovulewski, acting in the absence of a superintendent, warned of stress on the park staff and on the resources themselves. In his annual report, he described skyrocketing costs of policing and sanitation at campgrounds alone. The tourism influx required dozens of new and improved "water closets" (totaling eighty in the camping areas alone), which required regular "scrubbing and care." Garbage collection was an added headache. Maintenance of campgrounds that season cost the modern equivalent of around $150,000—a fortune for parks with only meager congressional allocations. The next year, in 1915, the number of Yosemite tourists more than doubled, to 33,452. Visitation in nearby Sequoia and General Grant parks also jumped from 1914 to 1915, from 8402 to 18,170. The story was the same in Yellowstone, which had 20,250 visitors in 1914 and 51,895 in 1915.

Once Mather and his men got people to the parks, where would they stay? What would they eat? How would they tour, and where could they buy supplies and services? Officials at the 1915 Berkeley National Park Conference were faced with the urgent need for infrastructure. The conference crowd chuckled when Mather said, "Scenery is a splendid thing when it is viewed by a man who is in a contented frame of mind. Give him a poor breakfast after he has had a bad night's sleep, and he will not care how fine your scenery is. He is not going to enjoy it." They guffawed but they knew it was true.

By 1915 national parks had a handful of high-end hotels built by railroads, which sold package

DESTINATION DRIVES

Blue Ridge Parkway—The road itself is a park unit (and a popular one at that), but it's really a series of parks with tremendous mountain views, drawn out over 469 miles from Shenandoah NP to Great Smoky Mountains NP. Though its plan was approved in 1933, local battles, world wars, and inconsistent funding intervened, and the road wasn't opened until 1987.

Going-to-the-Sun Road, Glacier NP—This engineering marvel completed in 1932 stretches east–west for nearly 50 miles, overtaking the Continental Divide at Logan Pass and offering heart-stopping views of peaks, forests, and, yes, glaciers.

Grand Loop Road, Yellowstone NP—The first 100 miles of this 140-mile route were passable by 1883, but it took many more decades for the figure-eight–shaped road, which offers access to most major park features, to be widened, paved, and improved.

Natchez Trace Parkway—This scenic byway is a 444-mile journey back in time. It winds lazily through Tennessee, Alabama, and Mississippi, revealing fascinating stories of people who traveled on or near it, through swamps and rolling hills, for thousands of years.

Newfound Gap Road, Great Smoky Mountains NP—The staggering variety of forest ecosystems experienced along this 32-mile route completed in 1936, which climbs roughly 3000 feet, has been equated to driving from Maine to Georgia. Cove hardwood, pine-oak, and northern hardwood forests dominate the lowlands, while evergreen spruce-fir forest grows at higher elevations.

Skyline Drive, Shenandoah NP—Sweeping views of the Blue Ridge Mountains and Shenandoah Valley are highlights along this 97-mile stretch, which reportedly cost $47,000 per mile (roughly $800,000 per mile today) to build. It was completed in 1939.

Trail Ridge Road, Rocky Mountain NP—This highest continuous US highway travels for 8 miles above 11,000 feet and reaches 12,183 feet, following the general route Ute and Arapaho tribes once took over the range. Snowdrifts on the 48-mile road, which is generally open from late May through mid-October, can average 20 feet high, and it has taken as many as 55 days to plow the road in springtime.

deals including meals and guided excursions. But Yellowstone's lofty Old Faithful Inn and the luxurious El Tovar Hotel at the Grand Canyon were beyond the fiscal means of most Americans. More economical camp alternatives had cropped up, but their quality was spotty. They were designed to meet only immediate needs, with no thought for how they impacted park resources. The threat of a hodgepodge of private interests setting up haphazard camps in parks and charging tourists for foul food, flea-infested beds, and guileful guides incensed Mather. It was one of the main issues, after all, that had drawn him to DC to work for the parks.

But where to start? The general sense among the Berkeley conference participants was that accommodations needed to be plentiful and of different cost categories, to democratize park appeal. As Charles Fee, passenger traffic manager for Southern Pacific Railroad, eloquently put it, "You must have a place to eat and sleep for people of all classes at prices that will suit their own pocketbooks."

Mark Daniels, then the general superintendent and landscape engineer of national parks, agreed. At the conference he described a plan taking shape for developing accommodations in parks. He said there should be four types: the hotel, the permanent camp, the supported public camp, and the nonsupported public camp. Daniels talked about a recent trip to Glacier, where a pilot program of tepees rented to tourists for fifty cents per night

was initially successful. A nearby camp store sold coffee, bread, and bacon at the going rate. "Every one of these camps was filled—every one of them," he said. Daniels was excited about advertising back East such reasonably priced outings. "The schoolteacher of the Atlantic coast, whose dream for years and years of a visit to Yellowstone National Park, the Yosemite Valley, Mount Rainier, or Crater Lake, would be able to come out here at a cost of eighty-five cents a day, which would be cheaper than she could live at home."

But these oases could not spring from relative deserts without infrastructure, including a water supply, sanitation, electricity, telephones, and policing. Daniels mentioned the tourist hordes in Yosemite Valley, saying, "That community ceases to be a camp; it becomes a village . . . It has municipal problems . . . There is no instance in the United States of any village that grew to any size without some forethought, without some planning, that did not turn out to be an ugly, repellant object. For that reason, if for no other, it is absolutely essential that we take care of the villages in these various parks." Mather seized upon the term "village," and since Yosemite was his pet park, he was determined to use it as an example of how the concept should be carried out.

But not everyone was in favor of the village concept or of large-scale development in general.

Tourists and their guides of the Shaw & Powell Camping Co. picnic in Yellowstone. In 1916, their six-day tour with accommodations and meals cost $35 per person, or roughly $500 today.

While the would-be NPS leadership stated time and again that key to building was the careful integration of structures into the natural environment, it experienced a pushback against development that endures. Original opponents argued a game of want versus need was being played in Yosemite that threatened to distract visitors from the virtues of parks. Did tourists to the valley really need postcards, candy, and liquor?

Vocal protest against development in parks came first from The Mountaineers, then from the Sierra Club and National Parks Conservation Association. But Mather rejected wilderness purists, agreeing instead with Marshall of the USGS. At the Berkeley conference, Marshall said, "One of the reasons why we can not get [NPS] legislation in Washington is that to the majority of the members of Congress the parks are practically unknown." In the predawn days of the nascent park service, Mather fussed, "Our national parks are practically lying fallow and only await proper development to bring them into their own." This reinforced his belief that "scenery is a hollow enjoyment to a tourist who sets out in the morning after an indigestible breakfast and a fitful sleep on an impossible bed."

As national parks struggled merely to keep their outhouses clean, park leadership turned to concessionaires with the capital to invest in park hospitality infrastructure. From the start, Mather and his small staff also looked to certain existing private agents in parks as role models. One of these was Ford Harvey, son of Fred Harvey and head of the Fred Harvey Company after his father's death. Speaking in Berkeley in 1915, Ford Harvey said, "In my opinion the hotels in each national park should be in one man's hands; he should not be there simply with a license to get as much money as possible, but should have a definite obligation and

responsibility in the way of satisfactory service. It is no small undertaking to do this properly." While under the watchful eye of the government, Harvey said, the agent operating in a national park "must be afforded protection from competition. I firmly believe that this service, to be satisfactory or successful, must be a regulated monopoly." Mather took hold of Harvey's terminology and, from that day on, pursued that structure for the entire national park system.

No doubt there were many heads nodding in agreement in California Hall that day on the Berkeley campus—but not all. David Curry, who had established Curry Camp in Yosemite Valley in 1899 with his wife, Jennie, was agitated. He didn't oppose the concept of a monopoly, as long as the management of different types of accommodations remained segregated (meaning a hotel franchisee would not run camps as well). He also questioned the logic of a concessionaire entering a park with no prior history in it. "What we want in our parks are businessmen who will go into the business and stay in the business and will be willing to put the last dollar they make into the business," he said.

Curry and his wife, both former schoolteachers from Indiana, ran what amounted to the first large-scale, affordable accommodations in Yosemite—a somewhat crude but clean and comfortable tent camp in the shadow of Half Dome. Supplies to build and then to sustain their camp had to be bumped and dragged over 100 miles of rough wagon roads. Their popular camp had grown steadily over the sixteen years leading up to the parks conference in Berkeley, and no doubt Curry felt threatened by the goliaths in his midst. The people who should operate in national parks, he said, must "take up that work as their life's work." It was clear he did not feel he was surrounded by such people. The comment stirred a dislike of Curry in Mather, who during those conference days told Albright, "I don't like David Curry. If we follow Harvey's idea, we could eliminate him from the Yosemite."

While Albright didn't say it at the time, he was concerned about the legality of the monopoly idea and, moreover, about Mather's intent to invest in it at Yosemite. During the conference, Mather asked his subordinate to set up a dinner party with some of the wealthiest men in the state. At the event Mather convinced his guests to form and fund a start-up concessionaire—the Desmond Park Service Company—with an initial $250,000 investment. Mather himself would, of course, contribute. The company would be allowed to build new accommodations in the park, some in direct competition with the Curry Camp, and would be given a twenty-year lease. The clear conflict of interest turned Albright's stomach, but he mentioned none of this to his chief at the time.

❧   ❧   ❧   ❧

National Park Conference attendees discussed more than the what and the where; they debated the who, too. Protecting hard-won parks and facilitating the public's enjoyment of them came down to, in part, who their custodians would be.

Naturally, most everybody at the 1915 conference had an opinion about what would make a good ranger. Colonel L. M. Brett, then acting superintendent of Yellowstone, raised the subject of what were called "rangers" in some parks and "scouts" in others. He announced the guidelines by which a ranger should be chosen, offered by the secretary of the interior. Even then, the criteria and expectations of that person were many and varied: "An applicant for the position of ranger must be between twenty-one and forty years of age, of good character and correct habits, of sound physique and capable of enduring hardships; tactful in handling people; possess a common-school education; able to ride and care for horses; know how to cook simple food; have had experience in outdoor life; be a good shot with rifle and pistol; and have some knowledge of trail construction and fighting forest fires." But that

Henry Klamer's curio shop (the second general store in Yellowstone) built in 1897 near Old Faithful

wasn't all; much emphasis was also put on the rangers' role as public servant: "[M]en who will not arise to the full realization of the fact that they are engaged upon a grand work for the public good have no place in this service and should be eliminated."

A week after the conference, parks general superintendent Daniels talked to the *Denver Post* about employing two Coloradans as rangers in the newly created Rocky Mountain National Park. He took his cue from the secretary of the interior's guidelines but added his own rigorous criteria: "The men who get into the national park ranger service must be competent horsemen," Daniels said. "They must be skilled in woodcraft. They must know about animals and birds and trees. They must be capable of caring for a lost baby or giving first aid to the wounded tourist. They must be sober men, absolutely healthy. They must be courteous and good tempered. The national park ranger service must be their ambition and their life." The sum of these various expectations ensured that if any superheroes were looking for work, surely they would have been hired. But then, as now, rangers were overworked and underpaid. In 1915 the standard ranger was paid $900 per year, the modern equivalent of less than $23,000 annually (and not much less than the entry-level salary of a ranger today).

Hotel guests surround an open campfire in the Glacier Park Hotel lobby (note the American Indian in full Native attire on the left).

What the ultimate ranger would look like or what the infrastructure of parks, relationships with concessionaires, and policy on cars would be were conversations to be continued. What parks needed most now was a bureau dedicated to sorting out all of these issues, a centralized place of decision-making, an advocate for the survival and growth of parks. Convincing Congress of the need for national parks had been a prickly pursuit; winning over legislators to the notion that a National Park Service must be created to accompany the parks would test the resolve of everyone involved.

CHAPTER 8

Mr. Albright, Telephone

THE SUMMER OF 1916 was sweltering in Washington, DC. Horace Albright and his new bride, Grace, lived in a fourth-floor walk-up not far from Capitol Hill. After a quick dinner at the Occidental Hotel, they returned to their stuffy flat; Grace, couch cushions in hand, retreated to the fire escape to sleep. Albright stripped down to his skivvies and lay down on the floor. Try as he might to rest, he was waiting anxiously for a phone call.

For Albright, it had been a busy few months scrambling to gain support for the Organic Act,

the bill to create the National Park Service. The bill would be the culmination of a five-year effort by California representatives John Raker and William Kent, ironically the same two congressmen who had led the effort to flood Hetch Hetchy Valley. Raker had introduced versions of a bill establishing a park agency twice before, and despite bad blood between him and the Muir-inspired conservationists, Raker pressed on. The juxtaposition struck more than one person as odd. Reflecting on it later, Albright wrote, "[Raker] always felt badly about his part

90

in promoting Hetch Hetchy and hoped he could redeem himself by pushing through a National Park Service bill with his name attached." James Mann, an Illinois congressman and political opponent of Raker's, was unable to reconcile Raker's two opposing efforts: "What was this?" he puzzled. "A fellow who helped destroy part of Yosemite is now mothering a national parks bureau?"

Kent was nearing the end of his third term in Congress and his time in political life, and he no doubt felt that establishing the NPS would be part of his legacy. Up to this point, he'd had an impassioned, if complex, history in conservation issues. A decade earlier, Kent and his wife had bought a 611-acre plot of wild forest on Mount Tamalpais, north of San Francisco, to preserve the mammoth redwoods there. In the thrust of development that followed the great San Francisco earthquake and fire in 1906, the area was in jeopardy of being claimed by eminent domain. Staying true to his preservation ideal, Kent mailed the deed to 295 acres of his parcel to the secretary of the interior. He asked President Teddy Roosevelt to use his authority under the ten-year-old Antiquities Act to protect the area as a national monument. Kent suggested it be named Muir Woods for the preservationist he greatly admired. In a letter to Muir about the designation, Kent wrote, "I know the dreams we have will come true and that men will learn to love nature. All I fear is that it may be too late."

His statement was a prophetic one. Not long after, the two men parted ways over Hetch Hetchy. Kent's support both for drowning Hetch Hetchy and for a National Park Service that would prevent such an event from being repeated may have confused those from Muir's camp, including Mather and Albright, but they took all the help they could get.

Resistance persisted where ignorance held tight. Those against the Organic Act clung to a lack of understanding about the purpose of national parks and how they differed from national forests. A hearing before the House Committee on the Public Lands in early April 1916 illuminated some of that confusion and prejudice. Henry S. Graves, head of the US Forest Service, no doubt trying to sell the idea of his bureau taking over management of national parks, portrayed his domain of national forests as public playgrounds: "The Forest Service is protecting the scenic value of the forests, and . . . the use of the forests for recreation and health is growing at a tremendous rate," he said.

But J. Horace McFarland of the American Civic Association refuted that claim. One of the earliest proponents of a park bureau, McFarland famously broke his alliance with USFS chief Gifford Pinchot after the loss of Hetch Hetchy. "The forests are the nation's wood lots," McFarland said. "There may be some places in which the two run parallel, but the fundamental thought behind the Forest Service is to grow as much wood for use as possible, and the fundamental thought behind the National Park Service . . . is to provide spots for recreation for the people of this great nation."

Later, Albright reflected on that conflict, writing, "We couldn't openly state it, but we felt that the perpetual defeat of a park service was due to the unrelenting pressure of Gifford Pinchot and his influence on the Forest Service. Pinchot always believed the Forest Service should take over the national park areas." Enos Mills, the "father" of the newly established Rocky Mountain National Park, was deeply suspicious of the Forest Service, which he dubbed an "enemy of human liberty." Years earlier, Mills had written to McFarland, "As you know their fight is largely undercover and while

President Woodrow Wilson addresses Congress in May 1916; he signed the Organic Act forming the NPS three months later.

one knows it is vicious it would be difficult to absolutely prove: they realize this and are going [to] the limit of unfairness." The animosity between the two camps would endure for decades.

In defining the purpose of national parks versus national forests, McFarland explained something to Congress about the newfangled concept of the national park: "I think sometimes we fall into a misapprehension, because the word 'park' in the minds of most of us suggests a place in which there are a number of flower beds, and probably stone dogs, and iron fountains, and things of that kind, and a road over which an automobile may travel," he said. "We forget that the park has passed out of that category in the United States."

His colleague, Richard Watrous, told Congress that a park service was needed to make the growing system more cohesive, accessible, and recognizable to average Americans. "You gentlemen would be surprised to know how little the people really know about our national park system," he said. "I have been out around the country recently and have asked different audiences if any gentlemen or lady in the audience could stand up and name four of our national parks, and it was on very, very rare occasions that I found that they could."

When Stephen Mather came forward to make his statement at that same hearing, he talked about the strain that overseeing the parks had had on the tight core of Department of the Interior employees dedicated to the task up to that point: "There is a little group of three or four persons who are handling the whole burden of this park work," he said. When Raker had his say, he spoke eloquently of how personal the fight to protect this uniquely American venture with a National Park Service had been: "My whole soul is wrapped up in this legislation," he said.

The committee meeting went smoothly, and the NPS promoters found that, among the two dozen or so members of the Public Lands committee, they had decent support. A few powerful congressmen were gravely opposed to expanding the federal government, however, and expressed deep reservations about spending any money on a parks-related venture. Over the spring of 1916 the bill boosters met often, all over Washington, attempting to home in on a bill that might remain standing when put before the 531 members of the Sixty-Fourth Congress.

Members who weren't directly opposed to a national parks bureau were distracted by other events: the upcoming presidential election, the Mexican revolution straddling the US border, Europe's entrenchment in World War I. Turning their attention toward a singular and somewhat abstract goal would not be easy. The stage was set for what Albright called the "summer of controversy."

While Mather did what he did best—got out of Washington and hit the trail—Albright continued to change minds in Washington. In the unrelenting heat, he crisscrossed the city, chasing down members of Congress in their homes, offices, clubs, and even at Union Station on their way to catch a train out of town. Tucked in his pocket he kept a little black book cataloging names and schedules so he'd have the best chance of intercepting elusive lawmakers. When Albright did track them down,

he pitched them on the importance of establishing a park service. The low-key, unseasoned law student surprised himself with his growing powers of persuasion and ability to keep his cool in the face of cantankerous congressmen.

It was an election year and focusing incumbents on anything but their own fate was maddening. In his memoir describing this historic time, Albright recalls it as a do-or-die moment: if the legislation didn't pass then, he could not imagine enduring such exhaustion again. "I was getting more and more worried that if this bill couldn't be passed in this Congress," he wrote, "we'd have to start all over. What if the administration changed from Democratic to Republican? What about a new batch of congressmen, a new president, a new secretary of the interior? All would have to be courted and placated.

What should have been a yearlong post turned into a 20-year career for Horace Albright, who ascended from confidential clerk in the Secretary of the Interior's office to director of the NPS.

It was too gruesome to dwell on. A decision for action had to be made now."

Albright's task was to align the House and Senate versions of the NPS bill into a final act that both chambers would vote to enact. Intensive fighting over grazing allotments within parks and funding for the NPS Washington headquarters dominated the debate. With Representative Scott Ferris, the Public Lands committee chair, Albright hammered out a general agreement. It was so hot in the Capitol Hill office where they worked, wrote Albright, "Even with four electric fans blowing on us, it was like a Turkish bath."

While Albright was sweating it out in DC, Mather was out in the field drumming up support. The group on his Second Mather Mountain Party trekked from Yosemite to Sequoia National Park along the new John Muir Trail, first taking in the iconic landmarks of Vernal Fall, Nevada Fall, Half Dome, and Cathedral Peak, then the lesser-known, towering basalt columns of Devil's Postpile and nearby prism-casting Rainbow Falls. Hiking through Evolution Basin along Kings River, a landscape bejeweled with lakes and dominated by snow-veiled peaks, they ate well, traded stories around a radiant campfire, stargazed, and slept soundly.

As on his First Mountain Party a year earlier, Mather brought along some influential figures, including his friend and media maven Robert Sterling Yard and popular and prolific photographer Edward S. Curtis. As always on his guided mountain outings, Mather pursued his agenda to popularize, protect, and expand parklands while spending as little time as possible in Washington, DC. The charismatic marketing genius—turned—civil servant often spoke of the way the city wore him down but how, once back in the wilderness, he became

reacquainted with his soul. Whether in a park or on pavement, Mather turned on the charm, wooing people and bringing them around to his viewpoint.

A few days after Albright's meeting with Congressman Ferris, he met with a group of men who were driven to get the legislation passed by hashing out the House and Senate versions of the bill at the F Street home of Congressman Kent. The task now came down to Albright and what he could accomplish against all accumulated odds in Washington. The group was a sundry one, given recent events. In addition to Kent there was Raker, as well as two members of the influential American

Frederick Law Olmsted Jr., here photographing at Yellowstone's Lake Landing in 1921, took up the mantle of park protection from his conservationist father.

Civic Association, McFarland and Watrous. The four men hadn't agreed on much in regard to conservation over the past few years, yet here they all sat with Albright, aligned to pass the Organic Act.

Landscape architect Frederick Law Olmsted Jr. was also there. He was as committed to conservation and the careful planning of national parks as his father had been. McFarland had approached Olmsted Jr. as early as 1910 for his input on creating a new bureau of national parks. For years they refined the concept, and the correspondence culminated in Olmsted's famous verbiage that would ultimately define the mission of the NPS and guide conservation for generations: "To conserve the scenery and the natural and historic objects and the wild life therein and to provide for the enjoyment of the same in such manner and by such means as will leave them unimpaired for the enjoyment of future generations." Albright later recalled Olmsted's trying to revise the now-famous paragraph —the "one example of lofty English in our organic act"—to boisterous objections that night. "Poor man. Everyone jumped on him at once," wrote Albright. "McFarland said, 'Don't you dare change a thing, Olmsted. Your one paragraph sells the whole bill.'" And so it remained.

After the writing session, it was up to Albright to continue swaying members of Congress so that the legislation would arrive in front of both chambers with enough support. It was a thankless task requiring a placating persistence that Albright, luckily, embodied. It took a toll on him, however, and he arrived back in his apartment at the end of those historically hot days frustrated and exhausted. "Grace used to laugh so hard at home at night when I'd blow off steam, calling some of our noble legislators every name I could use in front of a lady," he later wrote.

But everyone's efforts paid off when, on August 15, 1916, the Senate easily passed the compromise bill. It passed the House on August 22. With several hurdles cleared, there was still work to be done. The legislation had to be signed by President Woodrow Wilson.

Leaving nothing to chance, Albright went up to Capitol Hill to find out when the president would get the bill. The clerk he spoke to didn't know, but Albright happened to overhear an aide on a call to the White House talking about getting an army appropriations bill to Wilson immediately. Albright managed to smooth-talk the man into stuffing the National Park Service Organic Act into the same envelope. A messenger then set out for the White House with both bills in hand.

Again, determined to see it through to the bitter end, Albright hopped on a streetcar, taking it as close to the White House as he could get, then running the rest of the way. He arrived there

THAT'S A FACT

After the establishment of the National Park Service in 1916, the National Geographic Society donated $80,000—the equivalent of about $1.6 million today—to the agency, which was legal in those days. The society went on to also deed private land near Sequoia and Shenandoah national parks to the NPS. The partnership remains, to this day, a strong one.

breathless and soaked with sweat, managing to beat the messenger. Luckily, the legislative clerk who would field the bill, Maurice Latta, was someone Albright knew socially. Albright asked Latta to call him when the deed was done and to save the pen with which Wilson signed the Organic Act so that he could give it to Mather. Since Albright and his wife couldn't afford a phone, he gave the clerk the number for the public phone in the lobby of his apartment building.

That evening, fitfully trying to rest in his steaming flat while Grace slept out on the fire escape, Albright awaited the call from Latta. He hadn't lingered long before he heard a cry up the stairwell: "Mr. Albright, telephone." He struggled hurriedly back into his pants and ran down the four flights of stairs. To his exasperation, it was a friend inviting the couple to a birthday party. Disappointed, he climbed back up. Twice more the phone rang, and down Albright went, only to discover it was not the White House either time. It wasn't until the fourth phone call that he got the news he was waiting for: the president had signed the bill. Finally, the national parks had an agency devoted to their protection.

Albright wired the news to Mather, who had emerged from the High Sierra but was still in California. "Park Service bill signed nine o'clock last night," the message read. "Have pen President used in signing for you." Instead of reveling in their hard-won success, Albright next reminded his boss of the rugged terrain that lay ahead. "Appear before members Senate Subcommittee on deficiency bill today. Also Chairman Fitzgerald of House Subcommittee [sic]. Wire instructions regarding matters you wish me to handle before leaving. Horace."

Congressman William Kent worked tirelessly over several years to help found the NPS.

The nation now had national parks and an agency to run them, yet still scant cash with which to do that. The new National Park Service needed money—there were salaries to be paid, infrastructure to be laid, and projects in limbo, including a power plant in Yosemite. Albright would have to face his nemesis, House Committee on Appropriations chair and famous tightwad Representative John Fitzgerald, on the issue. The congressman was ruthless and dismissive in his questioning; spending money on parks was outrageous to him. "Albright, that power plant can stay rusting in that valley until Gabriel blows his horn, an everlasting monument to bureaucratic waste," he roared.

Albright was worried about how the fledgling bureau would make it off the ground, but he also had one foot out the door on his honeymoon. "I left town the next day without knowing what

The trip was so strenuous that on their last leg, to Glacier Park Hotel, the party (including Mather) accepted a car ride gratefully.

Overnight, the storm blew itself to pieces and the party members, who had arrived at Sperry Chalet alive, gave thanks to just about everything they could think of. The next morning the sun shone off myriad icy pinnacles. The air had been scrubbed clean—and apparently so had Mather's memory of the day before. While taking in the view of Gunsight Mountain and the Little Matterhorn, Mather said, "Horace, what God-given opportunity has come our way to preserve wonders like these before us? We must never forget or abandon our gift."

No doubt thrilled to have escaped their stuffy apartment in Washington, the Albrights traveled on to Yellowstone, leaving behind Glacier's snow to tour blistering thermal features instead. At the country's first national park, Albright had a revolutionary change in park management to oversee. Since 1886 the US Cavalry had been in charge of protecting park resources, but it was time for the newborn NPS to take over. Albright ironed out the details of the transfer from military control to the civilian hands of national park rangers, which went into effect that October of 1916. Among the park's first rangers were some of the finest soldiers, now discharged, from the corps that had defended Yellowstone for more than three decades. With that, the NPS began addressing the first part of its mandate: to protect parks. The second piece—providing for the enjoyment of people visiting them without impairing park resources for future generations—would prove to be an equal challenge for Albright and his chief.

this fearful ogre would do," wrote Albright, "and, frankly, not caring except to wish him a quick and horrible death." Finally, Albright was setting out to see more of the parks he had been killing himself to protect.

Grace and Horace Albright's honeymoon was, in part, a working one. In Glacier National Park, the couple met Mather and yet another of his mountain parties assembled to attract money and attention to the park system. It was early September, and hail and snow threatened to interrupt their escapade on horseback. For a stretch over some of the roughest terrain in the park, Mather rebuffed the offer to go by car, despite protests from packers and rangers. "On your horses! We need a little adventure!" he reportedly commanded. Such was the enthusiastic influence of the man that everyone obeyed. The party (including Grace, who'd never before been on a horse) endured 26 hellish miles. "The weather was merciless, a mixture of sleet, hail, and snow, hard-driven by a brutal wind," Albright recalled.

PART II
1916–1939

CHAPTER 9

Spare No Expense, But Keep It Simple

FROM DESERT VIEW POINT in Grand Canyon National Park, on the brink of that great gash, you can see for 100 miles on a clear day. To the east lies the radiant face of the Painted Desert; the lofty San Francisco Peaks dominate in the south. If you climb the wide stairs to the second level of the 70-foot-high Indian Watchtower, the scale of the Colorado River's grand excavation begins to take shape. The panorama from west to east brims with geological curiosities, from the speckled-green ramparts of Wotans Throne to the deep red and

burnt-orange cliffs of Chuar Butte. The serpentine, olive-tinted band of the Colorado flows ceaselessly a mile below.

The cork-shaped Indian Watchtower, the highest point on the South Rim, lies on the eastern end of the Grand Canyon. It was built in the early twentieth century to mimic lookouts constructed by the Ancestral Puebloans (once referred to as the Anasazi) who dominated the American Southwest several hundred years ago. The watchtower's bands of weathered rock, coarse at the base and smoother

This 1920s editorial cartoon depicts the United States as an automobile with Uncle Sam as the driver. The message: America has hit the road in large numbers to tour parks.

up top, blend with the time-eroded walls of the canyon itself. Striking murals by Native artist Fred Kabotie adorn the interior surfaces, representing a Hopi Snake Dance in shades of cinnamon, buff, and ochre. Large windows are portals to tens of millions of years of Earth's history. The watchtower's architect, Mary Colter, modeled it on authentic structures she'd studied in Mesa Verde National Park and at Hovenweep National Monument. It was painstakingly constructed with local materials, each stone hand-selected and hand-placed. Colter intended to create a simple, authentic-feeling space for visitors to spend time contemplating the canyon while also considering the human history linked to the area.

The tower straddles an important period in the National Park Service's development: the creation of parks that appeal to visitors both viscerally, with structures that blend with the natural world, and practically, with infrastructure that make parks feel hospitable and accessible. By the time the NPS was formed on that muggy August evening in 1916, hospitality was its preordained mission, as is clearly evident in the Organic Act that established the Park Service. A good portion of the otherwise brief legislation, while making no provision for trails, roads, rangers, or restrooms for that matter, specifically addressed concessions. Section 3 says, "[The Secretary of the Interior] may also grant privileges, leases, and permits for the use of land for the accommodation of visitors in the various parks, monuments, or other reservations herein provided for, but for periods not exceeding twenty years; and no natural curiosities, wonders, or objects of interest shall be leased, rented, or granted to anyone on such terms as to interfere with free access to them by the public." It was part

of the NPS's mandate, and Stephen Mather and his cohorts pursued it zealously by luring investors as well as visitors.

Because of the substantial cash they infused parks with, railroads worked closely with the NPS once the Organic Act passed. Some conservationists saw a partnership with the barons of transportation as a deal with the devil, but others, including the top brass of the new NPS, viewed it as anything from a necessary evil to a boon. Mather, now the first NPS director, was thrilled with the railroads' commitment to raising park profiles and launched an advertising blitz to complement their efforts. He hired a longtime friend, *The Century Magazine* editor Robert Sterling Yard, as his publicity chief. Yard held the position for four years, and his substantial salary was largely paid out of Mather's own pocket.

Between 1917 and 1919, Yard's energetic efforts led to more than 1000 articles about national parks being published. But perhaps his greatest triumph was the *National Parks Portfolio,* which was distributed in three editions from 1916 to 1921 to 350,000 opinion-makers, including every member of Congress. The volume focused on nine parks, with lavish descriptions and nearly 250 photographs. The $48,000 project was funded by Mather and seventeen railroad companies. The first edition, published in June, helped influence Congress to pass the Organic Act only months later; subsequent editions sought to boost both the reputation of parks among regular Americans and the allocations Congress gave to the fledgling agency. The park hype paid off, at least in terms of reaching potential visitors: droves of tourists answered the call.

While the Park Service's shiny new mandate had given NPS founders some direction about visitor use and concessionaires, it shed little light on issues that resulted from this boom, particularly those involving automobiles. While the agency was charged with conserving scenery unimpaired for future generations, it was also supposed to provide for the enjoyment of the parks by people. If that enjoyment of the parks relied on cars, and if conserving parks relied on people being in the parks (only then would Congress fund them), then cars and parks were a natural pairing. As auto enthusiasts wrote to their congressional representatives in large numbers about wanting road development, park planning expanded to meet that desire.

During that time, the American Automobile Association (AAA) was instrumental in securing funds for highway construction—the Federal Aid Road Act of 1916 allocated $10 million (more than $200 million today)—and promoted building highways to connect parks. AAA chair A. G.

Batchelder wrote that the network would allow access to multiple parks, a system unmatched in the world: "Surely the day has arrived when the American will truly begin to get acquainted with his own country," he said.

With equal fervor, the outcry against automobiles expanded as The Mountaineers were joined by other watchdog groups, including the National Parks Conservation Association (NPCA) and, in a reversal of its earlier position, the Sierra Club. That organization, in particular, decried the immense popularity of Yosemite Valley: campfire smoke was thick, gasoline fumes hung overhead, and cars kicked up so much dust that cherished views were obscured. Wilderness hard-liners didn't believe that a tree in the woods ceased to be valuable if there was no carload of people there to snap photos of it. The national park–minded conservationists had already split from the logging, damming, and mining utilitarians, who argued for sustainable exploitation of all natural resources. Now another philosophical divide had formed: those who believed wilderness was a scenic trait versus those who felt it was a physical one.

Despite managing to boost the number of people in parks and increasing their ease in moving around once there, Mather must have been troubled by this criticism from his friends at the Sierra Club and NPCA (which he had helped found). Using what Albright called his "mesmerizing power of enthusiasm and persuasion" also did not come cheap for Mather. Early on, he admitted that the work took a toll on him. At a House Committee on the Public Lands hearing in 1916, he had commented, "I must say it has been a rather strenuous proposition—a good deal heavier than I ever had in my own business by two or three times over, but I hope we are accomplishing something already in what we are

Rangers and tourists are lined up to enter Mesa Verde National Park in 1929; this traffic jam indicates the surge in system-wide park visitation, which more than tripled in the 1920s.

trying to do." A *Washington Times* article from 1922 reported, "Uncle Sam has an employee who is so enthusiastic over his work that he has donated many times his salary to the furtherance of his ideas." In addition to footing the bill for elaborate outings and doling out numerous salaries, Mather sometimes bought land, roads, and equipment and donated them to the federal government. Among these were a sequoia grove, a car for a superintendent, a ranger station, and a road that crosses Yosemite. Mather also spent myriad hours brokering land deals and convincing his wealthy friends and associates to invest in national parks.

All the while, he was trying to prevent the Desmond Park Service Company from going bankrupt, an ethical tightrope walk over the abyss of the concessionaires issue for growing parks. The only other person at the Department of the Interior who seemed aware of it was Secretary Lane, who had warned Mather sternly about the friction inherent in using his own money in government affairs. Rumors of Mather's involvement in engineering concessions swirled around Yosemite Valley, but none were confirmed. As Mather advanced the Desmond Company, his assistant, Horace Albright, knew little of the details. "He kept me out of them except for a bare sketch of his decisions," Albright wrote. "I felt he really didn't want me to be involved or even to know too much of the inner workings of that outfit. This was probably because he knew I was concerned and suspicious."

A few months prior to the founding of the NPS, Mather's nemesis in Yosemite, David Curry,

had died of gangrene, but despite the passing of Curry, things turned south for Mather and other investors. The company head, Joseph Desmond, was a supplier for construction camps (including for the despised Hetch Hetchy reservoir), but he was bad with money and a worse manager. As the outfit hemorrhaged cash and creditors were pounding fists over payments, he resigned. The Desmond Company went bankrupt in 1917 amid suspicious fires in its Yosemite hotels.

At this point, Mather approached Albright about the debacle. Mather said he was invested in the doomed company and planned to spend more to bail it out. Albright was alarmed. Reflecting on that time, he wrote, "I honored this man, and in his present condition I was fearful that he could bring disgrace on himself, his partners, and the new National Park Service." Albright pressed his boss for details, and his concern became evident. "He suddenly clammed up," wrote Albright. "He instructed me to forget our meeting and everything that we had talked about."

Soon after that conversation, Mather and Albright presided over the first national park conference since the NPS had been formed. Mather's attendance at the conference was inexplicably

MATHER'S LEGACY

Stephen Mather was, by most accounts, mercurial. He was creator and destroyer, adored and abhorred. The colleague who knew him best, his devoted second in command Horace Albright, described him as ebullient and gregarious yet prone to volatile mood changes. He also wrote that "Mather was one of the most thoughtful, kindly, and generous men I ever knew." In retrospect, what ailed Mather was likely bipolar disorder. Both despite and because of that turmoil, Mather ultimately boosted parks to new heights.

During Mather's dozen years as the first director of the National Park Service, the size of the national park system nearly doubled. Grand Canyon, Acadia, Bryce Canyon, Zion, Lassen Volcanic, Hawai'i Volcanoes, and Denali national parks were established on his watch. His gift for lobbying also secured key legislation for the future founding of parks including Mammoth Cave, Great Smoky Mountains, and Shenandoah national parks.

Though Mather could be all four seasons in one day (in one conversation, even), his steadfastness toward national parks never wavered. What he wrote poetically in his fourth annual NPS report nearly a century ago still rings true: "Who will gainsay that the parks contain the highest potentialities of national pride, national contentment, and national health? A visit inspires love of country; begets contentment; engenders pride of possession; contains the antidote for national restlessness. It teaches love of nature, of the trees and flowers, the rippling brook, the crystal lakes, the snow-clad mountain peaks, the wild life encountered everywhere amid native surrounding. He is a better citizen with a keener appreciation of the privilege of living here who has toured the national parks."

In a congressional eulogy to Mather, Representative Louis Cramton of Michigan summed up the NPS director's labors this way: "He sacrificed his money, his health, his time, his opportunities for wealth, in order that he might promote that which will mean so much to the people of this country in the future." At Logan Pass, the highest point along the Going-to-the-Sun Road across Glacier National Park, a bronze plaque has Mather's image on it. That memorial (and identical ones installed at parks across the country) was commissioned by a group of friends after the director's death. Alongside Mather's distinctive profile, those memorials recall a portion of the congressman's tribute: "There will never come an end to the good that he has done."

sporadic, and when he did show up, he was generally sullen and detached. Even when conference participants heaped praise upon Mather for the "miraculous" changes that had taken place in the administration of the park system, Mather was unmoved. Distressed, Albright asked what he could do to help. Mather responded, "There isn't anything else for you to do, and there really isn't much use for me either." When Mather nearly revealed his connection to the Desmond concessionaire quagmire—to a packed auditorium of politicians, journalists, conservationists, and scientists—Albright practically leapt from his chair to stop him.

Because of the Desmond mess, Mather felt he had failed in his position. His attitude deteriorated, and as the conference came to a close, he became completely unwound. During a dinner with friends at the Cosmos Club, he dropped his head onto the table and began to weep. After being led to a private room, Mather began rocking in his chair and raving incoherently. When he threatened suicide and ran from the room, his friends and colleagues restrained him and called a doctor. Mather became unresponsive and was committed to a sanatorium where he'd been once before. The Desmond concession misstep not only cost Mather hundreds of thousands of dollars, it nearly lost him his position—and his life.

Albright reassured Lane that Mather would return to his position and, until then, the twenty-seven-year-old would keep things moving at the fledgling NPS. That he did, as acting director, for the next eighteen months. At that time, and during several similar episodes until Mather's resignation in 1929, Albright protected his boss's reputation and their shared interests. While his chief recovered, young Albright organized the new NPS, framed some of its initial policies, and lobbied Congress to fund it. With Albright's capable intervention and the input of scores of others—who were as devoted to Mather as to the conservation cause—the bureau continued to grow until Mather returned.

Likely because of Mather's mistakes, foremost on the NPS's agenda was writing a concise, airtight concessions policy to be administered across the board. The two major tenets that emerged were that concessions would be under strict government control and that competition within parks would be restricted. The rates franchises could charge for rooms, meals, tours, and trinkets would be regulated, as would any changes to structures and operations. Competition was curtailed to maintain quality and to ensure that concessionaires, who injected substantial capital into the ventures, could have time to recoup those investments. For this reason, the concept of lengthy leases (an idea first suggested in Yellowstone in the 1880s) was also floated during this time. The NPS believed that the regulated monopoly structure would restore order—in a park like Yellowstone, where politics were paramount and services were chaotic—and establish a standard of quality, conduct, and courtesy.

Despite the allure and prestige of operating in a national park, capable concessionaires were not breaking down the NPS's door at first. Among their many challenges were raising initial capital; adhering to strict rules about construction, service, and

Visitors can tour the Cliff Palace at Mesa Verde, which is believed to have been a living and gathering place for Ancient Puebloans with 150 rooms and 23 kivas.

CONCESSIONAIRES IN THE TWENTY-FIRST CENTURY

The National Park Service's concessions policy, which dawned a century ago, has endured the test of time, despite some ups and downs and plenty of uneasiness. In 1925 the Park Service quit calling it a regulated monopoly, but its essence remains. Legislation in the 1960s and '90s refined the original policies and offered some of the first substantial changes to the public-private partnerships. A 1998 law requires a competitive bidding process and increases oversight and accountability.

Concessionaires now contract with the NPS for ten to twenty years. Today the NPS administers more than 500 concession contracts, including some with several large companies that have leases in multiple parks.

maintenance; and importing all the necessary supplies to often remote locations. Some of these places, such as deserts and mountainsides, had abbreviated tourist seasons, which meant all costs would have to be recouped in three or four months—never mind the droughts, storms, floods, and fires to consider. Hoping to deliver on the promise of bringing essential visitor services to all parks, the NPS forced a number of existing concessionaires to merge. One such arrangement in the troubled California valley forced the Curry Company to join forces with the Yosemite National Park Company (formerly Desmond Park Service Company). If Curry himself were to comment from the grave, he might have resisted—or perhaps been gratified that his once-small camp had persevered to become the park's main concessionaire. Mather's thoughts on the matter were never recorded.

Attracting capital for Mather's plan for a Park-to-Park Highway connecting a dozen western parks in eight states was more successful. The circuit was dedicated in 1920 as the postwar economy was roaring. An article syndicated in newspapers around the country proclaimed, "Twelve major federal playgrounds in the west, as well as many national monuments and forests, have been lassoed by a scenic running noose, in the master motor road of the country known as the National Park-to-Park Highway." The loop, which covered several thousand miles, took months to traverse. In the ceremony dedicating the route, Mather said it was "like a thread of gold connecting jewels of the rarest beauty." Echoing the famous railroad slogan—ironically, since the car had displaced the train—he added, "More than ever before there exists a real inclination among our people to see America first. Where for years the lure of Europe has caught their fancy, the eyes of all those countries are now directed to the most spectacular world aggregation of scenic wonders."

Ever the salesman, Mather failed to mention that World War I had virtually closed off Europe to travelers from 1914 to 1918, greatly aiding the US tourism market. But no matter: the car had been given the green light in national parks nationwide, and as roads were built, people got in gear to drive on them.

Visitation of national parks surpassed 1 million for the first time in 1920, as the popularity of auto camping tours rose. The phenomenon was popularized by Henry Ford, along with a group of famous friends who called themselves the Vagabonds. The well-engineered publicity stunt, which launched a tradition, began in 1914 when Ford met Thomas Edison in Florida for a tour of the Everglades. While the "river of grass" would not become a national park for another three decades, the pair did something to raise public awareness of its pulsing waters and abundant wildlife. During the next decade, Ford and Edison were joined on their excursions by noted naturalist writer John Burroughs, tire magnate Harvey Firestone, and, once, by sitting President Warren G. Harding.

The unlikely camping club wasn't exactly roughing it: they had generator-powered lighting and a custom-made kitchen car. That precursor to the recreational vehicle (dubbed the "Waldorf-Astoria on wheels" by Burroughs) included a large gas stove and a refrigerator. In his book *Our Vacation Days of 1918*, which chronicled an outing to the Great Smoky Mountains, Burroughs described their mobile accommodations as a "luxurious outfit calculated to be proof against any form of discomfort." He talked about the purpose of the trip for each member: "Mr. Edison . . . is always in need of an outing and of a shaking up as an antidote to his concentrated life," wrote Burroughs. After a decade, the Vagabonds reluctantly put an end to their outings when their caravan of high-profile and wealthy campers became too recognizable. But the car camping craze continued.

Members of the Vagabonds on the road, sometime after original member John Burroughs died in 1921 (left to right: Henry Ford, Thomas Edison, sitting US President Warren Harding, and Harvey Firestone).

For cars in parks, there was no U-turn in sight. The NPS pressed the gas pedal on park development, treading a fine line between preservation and exploitation. The same conservationists who had fought the car cried foul. The NPS argued that roads led to only a fraction of the land area in parks, leaving the rest essentially untouched by the masses. Besides, careful development could blend seamlessly with the wild, the Park Service said.

In an apparent response to criticism from the anti-auto camp, the NPS released a Resolution on Overdevelopment at the 1922 National Park Conference in Yosemite. It sought to reassure those who feared the paving of paradise, but at the same time, the agency reasserted its dual mandate to protect parks while opening them to the people who owned them. "It is not desirable to fully develop all portions of the park," the resolution said. "Some portions should be made easily accessible to motorists, by means of good roads; other regions should attract parties on horseback, by means of good trails; still other areas should be accessible only to those who journey on foot," reasoned the resolution. But it made clear the direction in which the NPS was steering. "If there were no development, no roads or trails, no hotels or camps, a national park would be merely a wilderness, not serving the purpose for what it was set aside, not benefitting the general public," it said. "No one is selfish enough to wish to withhold development." Apparently Congress agreed and, in 1924, it handed the NPS $7.5 million to be spent over three years to build 360 new miles of road and to improve 1000 miles more. Two years later, the NPS and the Bureau of Public Roads joined forces to build park thoroughfares.

In 1925 visitation to national parks topped 2 million for the first time. Driving across the country became the American pilgrimage, the rite-of-passage road trip. New and improved roads quickly became arteries into the heart of parks and into America's natural, historic, and cultural legacies. Roads became an integral part of the national park experience, and with engineering feats like Glacier's Going-to-the-Sun Road and the Blue Ridge Parkway, some roads became destinations themselves (see the Destination Drives sidebar in chapter 7, Playing Monopoly).

Meanwhile, infrastructure springing up along these roads attempted to serve the public, as the Indian Watchtower still does, without distracting from natural surroundings. This vision relies on fitting in utilitarian structures that inspire and educate without being intrusive. She didn't know it when she designed structures along the South Rim of the Grand Canyon from 1905 to 1937, but Mary Colter was setting a standard for what would later be known colloquially as "parkitecture": a general idea that each structure in a park would be suited to its setting. Structures would set a specific tone for visitors and guide them to certain places for a view or other experience chosen for them. The genre, eventually adopted and adapted by the National Park Service into its signature style, national park rustic, influenced construction in parks for decades. From entrance gates to roads, signs, bridges, overlooks, hotels and lodges, trail markers, campgrounds, visitor centers, and even water fountains, maintenance buildings, and restrooms, everything was to be in keeping with its environment.

It's difficult to pinpoint exactly when and where parkitecture first took hold, because like the national park idea itself, it grew over time with input from many parties. But one of the earliest references to minimizing the visual and physical impact of built structures in parks came from Frederick Law Olmsted Sr. In his 1865 report on the management of Yosemite, he said, "The first point to be kept in mind then is the preservation and maintenance as exactly as is possible of the natural scenery; the restriction, that is to say, within the narrowest limits consistent with the necessary accommodations of visitors, of all artificial constructions and the prevention of all constructions markedly inharmonious with the scenery or which would unnecessarily obscure, distort, or detract from the dignity of the scenery." Olmsted believed built features in the wild should *subtly* influence the feelings of the people who experience them. He wanted inhabitants of a space he designed to be submerged in and psychologically restored by it.

Architect Robert Reamer was only 29 when he was hired to design the Old Faithful Inn; it took his hearty crew of 45 men nearly a year straight (through Yellowstone's famous cold and snow) to build the western architectural icon.

Railroads contributed to parkitecture as well by crafting destination resorts that were regionally varied to blend with their environments, such as the immense log-frame Old Faithful Inn. Its hand-hewn gables, shingles, and woodwork are intentionally asymmetrical and chaotic, as architect Robert Reamer perceived nature to be. It was intended to have a rough western feel, one it retains today. Several years before the Grand Canyon joined the national park system, architect Charles Whittlessey used colors and textures when designing the posh El Tovar Hotel on the South Rim, achieving a scale that, according to a 1910 guidebook, "harmonized perfectly with the gray-green of its unique surroundings."

When it was just a fledgling agency, the NPS established a landscape division to guide both landscape and structural architecture while withstanding societal and political whims. The concept of working with nature instead of against it, and the tradition of rustic architecture, were both in full swing when the Department of the Interior put out its *Letter on National Park Management* in 1918, written by Albright for Secretary Lane. It said, "In the construction of roads, trails, buildings, and other improvements, particular attention must be devoted always to the harmonizing of these improvements with the landscape. This is the most important item in our program of development." The policy also required comprehensive development plans for each park and insisted that concessionaire construction "be confined to tracts no larger than absolutely necessary for the purposes of their business enterprises." In addition, the policy forbade private summer homes, saying they would "destroy the very basis upon which this national playground system is being constructed."

At the time the bureau was getting its legs underneath it, the Interior Department oversaw seventeen national parks and twenty-two national monuments. The NPS had the unenviable task of surveying a grab bag of roads and trails, camps and hotels, and everything in between to determine what would stay, what would go, and—most urgently—what would be added. That job went to Charles Punchard, the agency's first landscape engineer. He was blessed and cursed to inspect many parks, at a punishing pace, his first year: Yellowstone, of course, then on to Yosemite, Grand Canyon, Rocky Mountain, Mount Rainier, Crater Lake, General Grant, Sequoia, and Hawai'i Volcanoes national parks. Since few of the early NPS staff knew instinctively what should go where, they learned by studying each place. Did a Victorian-era hotel really suit Yosemite Valley? Where would visitors have the best view of Yellowstone Falls? In which directions, and to where, should trails in Mount Rainier National Park go? What's the best location for Crater Lake's privies?

The Desert View Point Indian Watchtower, designed by Mary Colter in 1932 and financed by the Santa Fe Railroad, offers unparalleled views of the Grand Canyon.

Punchard described his job as "a small fine arts commission [unto] himself." He consulted with architects, including Mary Colter, whose designs were considered exemplary by the NPS. Punchard spent most of his time in Yosemite, Mather's pet park. Mather had a vision of rustic style—"an expression of the romanticism of pioneer America," as NPS historian William Tweed put it—that would mold Yosemite into a showcase for national park values. Punchard built the framework upon which much park development was based for decades. Punchard felt his job was to prevent the inclination to desecrate a place and, when needed, to develop parks in a way that was subordinate to nature. Just as influential were his contemporaries, including Daniel Hull, who designed park villages based on a concept introduced by Mark Daniels (the first general superintendent of national parks) and conceived in response to the needs of a civilized society.

The tradition of nonintrusive design was upheld and matured under the direction of Thomas Vint. He began in 1923 as a draftsman for private architect Gilbert Stanley Underwood, whose interpretations of Mather's rustic ideal include Yosemite's triumphant Ahwahnee Hotel as well as whole village developments in Bryce Canyon, in Zion, and on the Grand Canyon's North Rim. Just four years later, Vint was promoted to chief landscape architect of the NPS and spent nearly forty years putting his mark on parks, following his main edict that each structure should match its specific site. He had a saying that characterizes the philosophy of this period in park construction and its generous funding during President Herbert Hoover's administration: "Spare no expense, but keep it simple." His work, and that of his predecessors, grew into a legacy that has landed many of those early buildings on the National Register of Historic Places; some have become national historic landmarks.

Despite making it up as they went along, early park developers crafted a distinctive national park look and feel—a brand as familiar to twenty-first century park goers as the iconic sites themselves. The rustic structures still in use are distinctive, priceless pieces of national heritage. The villages in Yosemite and Yellowstone now host millions each year who admire vistas at carefully chosen locations, pitch tents in campgrounds, and share adventure stories around grand lodge fireplaces. When exploring attractions on foot or by car— whether at Colter's Desert View Point Indian Watchtower, an impressive entrance gate, or a trailside shelter—travelers move in step with early visionaries.

CHAPTER 10

Parks During World War I: "Don't Let the Bastards Graze!"

NEARLY A MILE above sea level, Many Glacier Hotel wraps around the eastern shore of turquoise-tinged, glacier-fed Swiftcurrent Lake. Across the huge loch, clouds congregate near the imposing rock face of Grinnell Point and on the perfect pyramidal peak of Mount Wilbur. You may see moose foraging on the water's edge and bighorn sheep confidently navigating steep slopes nearby. Lumbering grizzly bears also ply these rugged, forested hillsides.

Construction was just finishing on the hotel when war erupted in Europe in 1914. It wouldn't

be long before the United States joined the Allies and the National Park Service got its first taste of what it was like defending sought-after natural riches in Glacier and other parks during wartime. The NPS headquarters in Washington, DC, officially opened on April 17, 1917, just eleven days after US troops went to Europe. More than 2 million American soldiers served in World War I. The NPS, which had been whittled down to a skeleton crew for protection and administration, almost immediately faced scores of commercial pressures.

The Department of the Interior was inundated with demands to put park resources to work for the war and for the homeland.

Hunting topped the list—the nearly extinct bison in Yellowstone were in the crosshairs, as were the park's elk herds. Advocates argued the meat could be used to supplement food shortages at home and canned meat could be sent to troops. Those who made a request did so "excusing it as patriotism but, in reality, attempting to open [parks] once and for all for commercial and money-making projects alien to the Park Service's Organic Act," according to Horace Albright. "This harassment had never let up," he wrote. The harder the NPS resisted, the more abrasive the attacks on it became. One western newspaper editorialized, "Soldiers need meat to eat, not wild flowers!"

As the pressure intensified, the NPS turned to the US Food Administration for help. In its head, Herbert Hoover (later the thirty-first president), the Park Service found a friend. His response to game-hungry profiteers was farsighted and remarkably level-headed for the times, a landmark moment in the history of wildlife protection. Hoover argued that ensuring a long-range food supply would be more successful by allowing wild game to multiply, rather than hunting it to extinction. He appreciated what an undertaking establishing parklands and the NPS had been. "Any effort to weaken the present laws or in any way relax them in one locality," he said, "would immediately lead to a demand for such relaxation of laws in all other localities, insuring a rapid breakdown of the whole legal structure of present game protection erected after efforts extending over numerous years." Without decimating park wildlife, Hoover launched a campaign asserting that saving food was patriotic. "Food Will Win

the War. Waste Nothing," advised omnipresent posters. In the end, the USFA succeeded in avoiding rationing at home while also sending much-needed food to allies abroad.

At the same time, the NPS had no such vocal champion against large-scale grazing. In an effort to prove his patriotism, Secretary of the Interior Franklin Lane sided with western cattle and sheep ranchers in their desire to use parks to feed their herds. "The minute war was declared, [Lane] assumed his bulldog psyche and searched for ways he and Interior could contribute to winning the conflict," Albright later wrote. In opposition, a sign hanging in the NPS Washington office declared, "Eternal vigilance is the price of don't let the bastards graze!" By law, Yellowstone was off-limits to grazing, but that was not true of any other park in the system. The Organic Act did not specifically prevent grazing, and anyway, didn't President Woodrow Wilson himself have sheep munching the White House lawn? Weren't wool and mutton worth more to troops than pansies?

During World War I, national parks were also making headlines, such as this story about Acting NPS Director Horace Albright's visit to Crater Lake during which he announced that a new trail to the lake would be built.

The Evening Herald

KLAMATH FALLS, OREGON, SATURDAY, JULY 28, 1917

Women on Both Sides Fight in World War

Improvement Promised for Crater Lake

Big Railroad Strike Starts at Chicago

Nineteen Roads Entering Switching District of Chicago are Directly Affected. Embargo On All Perishable Goods Declared. May Delay National Traffic

NEW TRAIL TO LAKE FROM RIM WILL BE BUILT

When Lane suggested allowing 50,000 sheep to graze in Yosemite Valley, Albright, who was then acting director of the NPS, offered his resignation. Lane wouldn't accept it and instead demanded that a compromise be reached. As conservation organizations, specifically the Sierra Club, caught wind of the scheme, they waged war in the press. Ultimately, sheep grazing in national parks was banned, but a group of hand-picked cattlemen were allowed to graze their herds in strategic areas.

A chance meeting in Glacier, where grazing pressure was exceptional, limited the destruction there. While in the park on a visit, Albright had mentioned to a gathered group of vocal park admirers that the flower-studded meadows they so admired might soon be devoured by livestock. One member of that group was Walter Hansen, a powerful local meat packer. After hearing about the plan to admit thousands of sheep ("hoofed locusts" as John Muir had dubbed them), Hansen suggested the NPS grant him a permit to graze cattle in order to control the number and location of domestic animals. Albright took a chance that Hansen could be both cattleman and park protector —and it paid off. A carload of Hansen's cattle was released in the southern end of the park, and when the war ended a few months later, they were removed, leaving few detectable traces.

At Mount Rainier, the grazing battle was at its fiercest. While the NPS was trying to stall action there, rumblings among conservationists again erupted. Influential outdoor organization The Mountaineers sent a letter of protest to the Interior Department, making a dramatic suggestion. The club offered their members' private flower gardens and lawns, and golf courses all over the Puget Sound area, as alternatives to opening the park to grazing. Again, the opportunists appealed to Hoover at the USFA, and he responded, Albright recalled, with an "entire lack of sympathy with all propositions of this kind." The Mountaineers would not have to sacrifice their lawns, and grazing would not happen at Mount Rainier.

Water, power, and lumber interests also wanted access to national park units where opportunities to dam and to log were plentiful. In the Northwest, in particular, lumber companies saw the war as the perfect opportunity to get what they had

long wanted: the Olympic Peninsula's ancient forests. President Theodore Roosevelt had established Mount Olympus National Monument in Washington in 1909, protecting 610,000 acres of Sitka spruce, Douglas fir, western red cedar, and western hemlock, as well as a unique elk herd later named for him. In a startling move less than a decade later, President Wilson divided the monument, which was still under the purview of the "utilitarian" US Forest Service, opening half of it to logging and mining. On the northern flank of what used to be the monument, loggers loaded up railroad cars with felled spruce, a desirable material for airplane fuselage parts. It didn't take long for the whole area to be decimated in what Albright remembered someone calling the "rape of Olympus."

National parks were not advertised during the war (though the NPS public relations campaign never really let up), railroad travel was greatly restricted, and

Massive crowds line the streets in Buffalo, New York, to watch soldiers return from World War I. The national parks offered veterans opportunities for healing after their traumatic service.

many park concessions were shuttered, yet people continued to visit the parks in large numbers. During the height of US involvement in the Great War from April 1917 to November 1918 (during which 116,516 American soldiers died and another 204,002 were wounded), park visitation hovered around a half million annually. This was also during the sweep of the 1918–1919 global influenza pandemic, which killed 675,000 Americans. The NPS hoped that in the aftermath of those horrific events, people would use their parks to aid recovery. In the annual Park Service report, drafted as the war was coming to a close in 1918, Director Stephen Mather promised that "the parks will be ready with their calm

A quiet stretch along the Hall of Mosses Trail in Olympic National Park

In the face of unprecedented world events, the NPS had deflected destructive advances on parklands as best it could. In its first postwar report, the agency summarized that time under the headlines "A New and Insidious Peril," "Food Administration's Far-Sighted Attitude," "Mountain Clubs to the Rescue," and "Determined Sheep Raids Defeated." And, as predicted, people were drawn to parklands to salve their postwar emotional and physical wounds. In 1919 annual visits to all parks nearly doubled, to more than 800,000, and in the next year visitation topped 1 million for the first time. After the ravages of World War I and the flu pandemic, the nation retreated to rivers and trees, to mountains and meadows, in part to grapple with those losses. Visitation in Glacier in 1919 was the highest the park had ever seen; records from its tourist season running June 15 to September 15 show that nearly 19,000 people entered

and glorious beauty, their inspiration, and their marvelous recuperative gifts. There the tired war workers may give themselves without stint to the business of restoring minds and bodies in preparation for the great era of peace and reconstruction to follow."

the park during that time, an increase of about 25 percent from its previous all-time high. Whether the war-weary sought refuge or predictability among the ancient peaks at the Crown of the Continent in Glacier or the primeval forests of Mount Olympus, they arrived.

Grizzly bears, like this one in Denali, are characterized by a dished face and prominent, muscular shoulder hump.

CHAPTER 11

If a Bear Is in a Hotel, Send a Ranger

FROM THE EASTERN END of Yosemite Valley, hikers aiming for Washburn Lake keep company with one of the country's most dynamic waterways: the Merced River. The National Park Service manages 81 miles of that national Wild and Scenic River flowing through the park. To reach Washburn Lake, you climb thousands of feet along the Giant Staircase, where the river alternates like Dr. Jekyll and Mr. Hyde, from lazy pools to death-defying plunges. The trail flattens out a bit through the Little Yosemite Valley, where

wildflowers seasonally thumb their noses at sentinel fir and pine. The Merced riffles and pools and the quaking aspen, their pale bark harmonizing with distant white granite walls, dominate the riverbanks on this stretch of the trail toward Merced Lake. Past that, the path turns south to Washburn Lake (elevation 7612 feet); on the way, water flows in sheets down canyon walls to join the coursing Merced River.

Continue on the trail, and soon you'll reach the spot where the Lyell Fork and Triple Peak Fork,

116

flowing from various headwater peaks both north and south, come together to feed the Merced. It is such a powerful sight that, despite its being encased in remote wilderness, roughly 20 miles on foot from Yosemite Valley, Gabriel Sovulewski saw fit to build a trail to it a century ago. In his 1914 seasonal report he wrote—characteristically downplaying his effort and achievement—that the new trail "opens beautiful country."

Sovulewski first saw Yosemite in 1895 as a member of the Fourth Cavalry tasked with guarding the park. He wrote of that time, "No one who has not participated in those strenuous years of hard riding and incessant fighting of natural and human obstacles can ever realize the need for indomitable spirit and unselfish devotion to a cause that existed during those first years in Yosemite National Park." Sovulewski had to leave the park for a far different fight, the Spanish American War of 1898, though clearly he had tucked away the High Sierra in his mind. He returned to Yosemite as a civilian in 1901, working first as a guide and packer, then as supervisor and acting superintendent. In all, Sovulewski spent the better part of four decades filling various ranger roles. But the thing he liked best was mapping out trails and physically carving them into the landscape; many are still followed by Yosemite visitors.

Comments Sovulewski made at the National Park Conference in Berkeley in 1915 give some insight into the joy of discovery and the

pride in accomplishment many early park protectors had: "It is my experience that exploring for trail building is the first and most important of all and, I may say, the hardest," he said. "It requires strength, determination, a natural instinct for direction, love for the work, love of nature, and an ability to forget everything for the time except the object in view and to be able to sit in the saddle for twelve or fourteen hours, or walk the same number of hours if required. The work is very interesting and delightful in spite of its hardships and dangers . . . on many days I do not return to headquarters until nine or ten o'clock at night." Many years later his granddaughter, Charlotte Ewing, who grew up in Yosemite (her father and brother were also rangers there) said of her grandfather, "He was dedicated in teaching all of us . . . how to treat the land, to take care of it, and to leave it for other people."

Before there was an official NPS, Stephen Mather and Horace Albright had been acting as a national park service unto themselves, with tremendous

Sergeant Gabriel Sovulewski of the Fourth US Cavalry in Yosemite in the mid-1890s. He later became its civilian supervisor, beginning 30 years of distinguished service in the park.

THE STORY BEHIND *THAT HAT*

The regulation straw "flat hat" with the wide, stiff brim that is now standard issue for all National Park Service rangers evolved over decades. The Montana Peak style—four pinches at the top—was likely introduced into park culture by the Buffalo Soldiers, many of whom had been stationed in more tropical climes during the Spanish American War of 1898 before they patrolled western parks. They had creased their hats to make them more useful in the rain, and the look stuck. The color, material, and style have been tweaked over the years, but the result is a symbol now recognizable throughout the country. The leather hatband has for a century been branded with the letters "USNPS" and embellished with sequoia cone ornaments (once sterling silver, they are now made of brass).

support from field personnel including superintendents, civilian custodians, and, of course, military patrols. Once the Organic Act of 1916 was passed, they started hiring new superintendents and staff at parks and bringing others into the fold to create a holistic system under the new bureau. Crowds definitely were *seeing America first*; park visitation took a tenfold jump from 1916 to 1923. All of those new visitors needed services to enhance their park trips, and key to that experience was rangers.

The newly minted NPS hit the ground running, particularly regarding the crucial ranger factor. When Albright oversaw the handoff from military to NPS control in Yellowstone in October 1916, he talked to the soldiers who enlisted as park rangers after their army discharge. In his memoir, Albright commented, "They were quite a group, tough as nails, but experienced, honest, and excited about their future work. I was very impressed. I always felt they set the standard for our future corps of rangers."

From the military the NPS had inherited a decent concept of what made a good ranger: a competent, knowledgeable, dedicated person with reasonable people skills—basically, part army scout, part boy scout. Since Harry Yount's tenure as Yellowstone's first game warden and park ranger, the rangers had grown in responsibility and mystique; their wilderness survival skills were legendary and enviable. A loose ranger corps had members in nine parks when the NPS got rolling, but each corps had different masters, all with different rules. Mather and Albright wanted to harness that lore and expertise while standardizing the operation. What should rangers do each day? Where should they be stationed? What relationship should they have to wildlife? What rules should they enforce? Mather also wanted education standards put in place for hiring and wanted to allow rangers to transfer between parks.

More than anything, Mather wanted "ranger" to be their identity. In his 1916 NPS report, he wrote, "I think a ranger should enter the service with the desire of making it his life's work." It was not something that would happen instantaneously, and to encourage esprit de corps, the former reporter began publishing the monthly *National Park Service News*. It kept rangers at various parks

DEPARTMENT OF THE INTERIOR, NATIONAL PARK SERVICE

THE NATIONAL PARKS
PRESERVE WILD LIFE

This poster promoting travel to national parks also illustrates one of the main responsibilities of "gun" and "fun" rangers alike—safeguarding indigenous species.

aware of what others were up to and what was going on in Washington, DC.

Whatever park Mather went to—and he pretty much hit them all—he wore the green and gray uniform and consistently reminded rangers they were part of an elite corps. Understanding the constant pressures of the job, in 1920 Mather had a Rangers Club built in Yosemite costing nearly $40,000—paid out of his own coffers. (Whenever he returned to the park, he stayed there, among the rangers; these days it is home to seasonal rangers.) At the well-attended dedication ceremony for the Rangers Club in late September 1920, Mather was beaming. Alongside

him were chief ranger Forest Townsley and the park's first chief naturalist, Ansel Hall. Their prominent presence was representative of the intentional branching off—which was then being put in motion—of what we know today as interpretive rangers from law enforcement rangers.

Education and interpretation became a more integral part of the NPS as the bureau began to mature. It's a practice that began with zoologist Harold Bryant. When talking to crowds of Lake Tahoe tourists about that environment, he was spotted by Mather. After seeing the scientist in action, Mather wanted to offer the popular programs in national parks. With scant funds available for experimental endeavors, Mather privately funded Bryant's work in Yosemite. For nearly a decade before being hired as a seasonal ranger at the park, Bryant lived out of a tent and organized nature programs from a small table in the chief ranger's office. During that time he put legs beneath the concept of natural interpretation for the NPS. The naturalists, whose division housed wildlife research into the 1960s, were often referred to as "posie pickers," but their work ultimately brought ecological thinking into park management. Bryant and Hall went on to serve at various western parks and to inspire generations of rangers.

Mather also established an educational division in 1917 and appointed journalist Robert Sterling Yard as its chief. Early visitor information booklets had focused on directions, accommodations, and general points of interest, but later efforts under Yard included checklists for birds, mammals, and fish; maps; writings about the

As a seasonal ranger, Clare Marie Hodges rode mounted patrol in Yosemite Valley in 1918.

she said, "Probably you'll laugh at me, but what I want to be is a ranger." Lewis's reply must have surprised her: "I beat you to it, young lady. It's been on my mind for some time to put a woman on one of these patrols," he said.

Many other adept, convention-breaking women fought discrimination in the boys' club that long characterized the NPS ranger corps, following in the footsteps of Wilson and Hodges. Siblings Elizabeth and Esther Burnell were popular licensed guides at Rocky Mountain National Park from 1917 on for many years. Elizabeth became the first female guide on Longs Peak (14,259 feet) despite efforts to limit women to day hikes below tree line. Margaret Fuller Boos ran Rocky Mountain's interpretive program in 1928 and 1929 and wrote a comprehensive geological guide to the park.

Marguerite Lindsley was Yellowstone's first female naturalist, hired in 1916, and on her heels was Herma Baggley, who in 1931 became one of the first permanent female naturalist rangers in the NPS. After laying out a trail at Old Faithful, she led hundreds of visitors on interpretive talks while shouting into a megaphone. Baggley's guide to Yellowstone wildflowers is still used. Maggie Howard, a Paiute who passed much of her life in Yosemite Valley, was a pioneer of cultural demonstration in that park. Since 1940, women also have been NPS park superintendents, regional directors, and directors (though only two out of eighteen in a century). Many more women, some named and others

parks; and suggested further reading. Around the same time, an outside educational committee made up of leading teachers and conservationists was formed to guide those efforts at the NPS. The group eventually merged with the National Parks Conservation Association (of which Mather was a founder and early funder), and Yard left the NPS to lead it. "The educational, as well as the recreational, use of the national parks should be encouraged in every practicable way," read Secretary of the Interior Franklin Lane's *Letter on National Park Management* in 1918.

When the first female rangers were hired, it was to fill a gap left by men enlisted in World War I. Because of the overall lack of personnel, those "rangerettes," as they were called, were both protection and interpretation rangers. The rangerettes included Helene Wilson, who left her home in Los Angeles to patrol Mount Rainier National Park, and Clare Marie Hodges, a Yosemite Valley schoolteacher turned park guardian. When Hodges, eighteen, applied to Superintendent W. B. Lewis,

unrecorded, welcomed visitors, protected archaeological resources, illuminated botanical and biological wonders, and guarded life and limb—and still do.

In the foreword to the 1928 book *Oh, Ranger!* written by Albright and Frank Taylor, Mather was full of praise for NPS rangers: "They are a fine, earnest, intelligent, and public-spirited body of men, the rangers. Though small in number, their influence is large. Many and long are the duties heaped upon their shoulders. If a trail is to be blazed, it is 'send a ranger.' If an animal is floundering in the snow, a ranger is sent to pull him out; if a bear is in the hotel, if a fire threatens a forest, if someone is to be saved, it is 'send a ranger.' If a Dude wants to know the why of Nature's ways, if a Sagebrusher is puzzled about a road, his first thought is, 'ask a ranger.' Everything the ranger knows, he will tell you, except about himself." The image of the national park ranger became synonymous with people who would drag themselves out of bed in the middle of the night to search for an overdue hiker, reunite him with his relieved family, and then, though weary, cheerfully greet visitors and dispatch park information the next morning.

Top: A ranger in Rocky Mountain National Park trades a horse for horsepower in the 1930s. *Bottom:* Pioneering ranger-naturalist Herma Baggley at Yellowstone's Mammoth Hot Springs in 1929

If a Bear Is in a Hotel, Send a Ranger **121**

THEIR PERSONAL KINGDOMS

The Upper Liberty Cap Trail bisects Colorado National Monument, which protects more than 30 square miles of western Colorado's deep, lush canyons; red-orange sandstone cliffs and rock spires; and desert bighorn sheep, mule deer, mountain lions, and coyote. The trail across Monument Mesa wends among rolling hills of pinyon-juniper woodlands; a golden eagle, peregrine falcon, or turkey vulture might ride thermals above this high-desert ecosystem 2000 feet above the Grand Valley of the Colorado River. The monument, though on a more accessible scale than its geological cousins Arches, Bryce Canyon, and Grand Canyon national parks, reveals as much about Earth's geological past as they do.

The 40-some-odd miles of trails in the monument also reveal a lot about the park's early caretakers. The footfalls of the monument's founding father, John Otto, can still be detected on the Corkscrew Trail in particular. Otto's enthusiasm and industriousness so inspired local

A ranger surveys the terrain along Going-to-the-Sun Road (under construction here in 1932) in Glacier National Park.

newspaper subscribers that they raised $154 for trail construction, which nearly covered the cost of tools and blasting powder. For all his hard work—ledges carved, steps etched, iron climbing rungs installed—Otto earned $1 per month, not even enough to keep him fed, but it was the going rate for national monument custodians a century ago.

Unlike the national parks, which were the early focus of promotion efforts, national monuments were relative orphans. Part of the problem was a lack of understanding about their purpose and whose responsibility they were. National monuments, despite their early years in obscurity and the dismal pay, long hours, and intense physical demands, drew a core of dedicated caretakers.

However, as contemporary park guardians can attest, it's not about the money; from the time Otto first saw this riot of red rock, he was hooked. In 1907 he wrote, "I came here last year and found these canyons, and they feel like the heart of the world to me." Otto immediately began pushing for protection of the towering rock sculptures and broad, ancient canyons. After five years of passing around petitions and writing letters to editors and politicians, Otto prevailed; in 1911 President William Howard Taft established Colorado National Monument.

Horace Albright saw Otto in action in his rocky realm and recalled that "John Otto was a marvelous guide and knew every inch of his monument, which he tended like a personal kingdom." With pen, pick, and shovel (and, according to those who knew him, an endless cache of energy and patriotism), the Hermit of Monument Canyon, as he was known there, made accessible and enjoyable an area that previously had seemed impenetrable even to locals. A *Grand Junction Daily Sentinel* article in April 1909 said, "[K]eep in mind what this lover of nature, John Otto, is doing. He is asking no credit yet he deserves it all. Singlehanded he has opened this great playground to the world." As a result, the monument was among the most-visited national park units around the time the National Park Service came into being in 1916.

Walter Ruesch, another unsung guardian of cultural and geological history, started out as a hired hand at Mukuntuweap National Monument (now Zion National Park). With integrity and unbridled affection for the place, he rose to custodian of the monument and, ultimately, to superintendent of Zion National Park. His singular devotion to the monument and quiet, dignified nature eclipsed his habit of hurling profanities at whoever was within earshot—he may have suffered from Tourette syndrome long before that disease was defined. When some patronizing higher-ups from the Union Pacific Railroad visited his brilliantly colored temples and towers of sandstone, Ruesch managed to contain himself, but upon their departure, he barked, "Hell, the sons of bitches are gone, but I think the bastards enjoyed themselves!"

As the NPS matured and visitor numbers increased exponentially, rangers were on the scene. They drove skunks from outhouses, bears from campgrounds, and people from harm's way. They protected park resources and visitors during wildfires, earthquakes, blizzards, volcanic eruptions, hurricanes, and inaugurations, as well as many uneventful days. They became well-known among those who traveled to parks and even among those who didn't. Many rangers did indeed devote their lives and, by association, their immediate families' lives to the NPS. Some, like that humble trailblazer Gabriel Sovulewski, were rangers for three decades or more, often moving from park to park wherever they were needed. Many of their names have been lost to time, but their deeds have not; their legacies endure in each park whose resources were secured and in each visitor who made a safe passage.

Mount Rainier rangers outside park headquarters in the early 1930s

Superintendent Horace Albright feeds hotcakes to a trio of bears (mother "Lizzie" and twin cubs "Max" and "Climax") in Yellowstone in 1922.

CHAPTER 12

For the Good of the Game

ABOUT HALFWAY ALONG the 16-mile stretch between the Canyon and Lake areas of Yellowstone National Park, a dozen or so motorists are paused. This is the Hayden Valley, a place where bison and bear "jams" occur with some frequency. At times, some of the park's signature wildlife are actually crossing pavement, though more often they are off-road grazing in the mellow meadow, sagebrush flats, or nearby hillsides.

This 17,000-acre valley at the heart of the Yellowstone Plateau is the bed of an ancient lake, a past

still evident from the forested ridges that mark its former boundaries. For wildlife lovers, it is a place for all seasons—from the raw, windy winter when foxes, wolves, and bison rove the lonely plateau to springtime when glowing green grasses pierce the thawing ground and stretch sunward. Some of the park's hundreds of bird species, including bald eagles and occasional trumpeter swans—North America's largest waterfowl, with a wingspan up to 8 feet—frequent this expanse. The Yellowstone River, clear and conspicuous, takes a sinuous route

An early bear trap built of logs atop a horse-drawn wagon, in front of the store in Yosemite Valley in the early 1900s

cases and there's no need to maneuver for a better vantage point. The perfect spot is the one everyone is already in, straining their ears toward the wild.

A century ago, the relationship park goers had with wildlife was quite different, as was the way the National Park Service managed natural resources. Once feverishly eliminated, predators are now better understood for the critical role they play in the health of ecosystems. Once fished, hunted, and grazed for the benefit of visitors, parklands and waters are now protected from overfishing, domestic animals, and the scourge of invasive or nonnative species. Once fiercely guarded against wildland fires, park acreage devoid of valuable structures now often is allowed, even encouraged, to burn. Contemporary NPS staff work to put to right some of the management mistakes made by their predecessors. And there were many.

The first, and most glaring, error involved the treatment of predators and their prey. The Organic Act has a confusing set of mandates that have been interpreted every which way since its enactment in 1916. While it requires the NPS "to conserve the scenery and the natural and historic objects and the wild life" in parks, it also empowers the Secretary of the Interior to provide "for the destruction of such animals and of such plant life as may be

across the landscape. Though it will drop over dramatic falls after leaving Hayden Valley, it doesn't seem to be in much of a hurry here.

It is twilight on a warm summer evening, and the visitors have stopped to witness one of nature's most hair-raising events. In hushed wonder, they hear the distinctive bay of gray wolves. The atmosphere pulses with the mournful cries of separated pack members. Yellowstone is a park that gets millions of visitors each year, but the many excited people in this spot, on this night, are silent or whispering. Hearing wolves is as good as—and arguably better than—seeing them. A seed of mystery remains in a world that otherwise leaves little work for the mind's eye. How many are there? Where are they headed? Are they coming closer? On this night, cameras stay in their detrimental to the use of any of said parks, monuments, or reservations."

The fledgling NPS had to apply that mandate to the grab bag of parks it had inherited, which had all previously been managed independently of one another. Along with the parks, the Park Service inherited all of the consequences of the beliefs and policies of the army and civilian caretakers who had made and enforced various rules for decades. While all these views were somewhat different, they amounted to the following: fire, predators, and tree-killing insects were *bad*; four-legged megafauna were *good*. In the case of bears, if they weren't strictly good, they at least were fascinating to tourists.

Landscape conservation meant preserving serene places with beautiful views. As so-called aesthetic conservationists, the NPS founders staked their existence on diverging from the US Forest Service model of utilitarian conservation, but as they were also focused on economics, it was critical to park boosters to attract as many tourists as possible. That meant sticking with predator policies that glorified game animals and allayed fears about predators. This approach of entertainment and economics over ecology seems counterintuitive in retrospect, but at the time, knowledge of ecosystem dynamics had only started to bloom.

The movement coincided with the back-to-the-land trend that swept in at the end of the nineteenth century when industrial fatigue had set in. The more time botanists, ornithologists, mammalogists, field biologists, and the like spent observing the natural world, the more startling the revelations about the interactions of species and their connection to their physical environment. Charles Adams of Syracuse University wrote the *Guide to the Study of Animal Ecology* in 1913. Along with

Victor Shelford of the University of Chicago and University of Illinois, Adams developed the idea that there were different classes of land preservation. They surmised that the degree of wilderness existing in a park directly related to the human influences on it. Adams wrote that keeping "reasonable bounds" on disturbances by people had to factor into conservation. The wildest areas would be those where only "nature is allowed to take her course with the minimum of human interference," he said.

Adams and Shelford were early organizers of the Ecological Society of America, founded in 1915 with fellow scientific titans Henry Cowles and Sir Arthur Tansley, who would coin the term "ecosystem" years later. There was also Liberty Bailey, a botanist from Cornell University, whose influential writing sought to reunite humans and nature, two parties whose interactions had been marked mainly by hostility up to that point. In his 1915 book *The Holy Earth*, Bailey seemed to take particular aim at the treatment of predators across the country: "Our minds dwell on the capture and the carnage in nature—the hawk swooping [down] on its prey, the cat stealthily watching for the mouse, wolves hunting in packs, ferocious beasts lying in wait, sharks that follow ships, serpents with venomous fangs," he wrote. "The struggle in nature is not a combat, as we commonly understand the word, and it is not warfare . . . Nature is not in a state of perpetual enmity, one part with another."

However, the NPS was a new organization with a shoestring budget, and such issues were not even on the radar of early park management. The terms that best define the resource management in the early days of the NPS are development, protection of popular features from destruction and exploitation, and wildlife population control. These were Stephen Mather's priorities.

Back in the early nineteenth century, the NPS never even pretended to be a scientific agency. It was Mather's notion that any issue relating to natural resources management (except development) should be farmed out to other federal agencies. If a park had a problem with insects, call the Bureau of Entomology. With anything aquatic, the Bureau of Fisheries, of course. It followed that the Bureau of Biological Survey (the precursor to the US Fish and Wildlife Service) should handle anything related to wildlife, both "good" and "bad." Fire, that "forest fiend," as Mather put it, should be managed with the help of the USFS, which had a well-entrenched suppression policy. So "prevent, detect, and fight" became the fire motto in national parks as well.

Yellowstone Superintendent Horace Albright with an elk calf raised by park rangers at Mammoth Hot Springs and penned there for park visitors to view.

At the National Parks Conference in January 1917, it was clear that there needed to be fewer "scary" animals and more crowd-pleasing ones in the parks. Two years earlier, one of the most effective anti-predator policies in park history had taken effect in Glacier National Park. Congress had allocated $125,000 to the Bureau of Biological Survey to eliminate predators in the Crown of the Continent ecosystem. The hunters and trappers had been highly successful in removing hundreds of thousands of wolves, coyotes, and mountain lions from Montana. At the park conference, attendees extolled the virtues of bison, black-tailed deer, moose, antelope,

elk, and mountain sheep but kept talk of predators to a minimum. Chief Forester Henry Graves did, however, mention the "elk problem" in Yellowstone, insisting that "the whole talent and resources of the Government" should be put into killing predators and, when necessary, feeding game animals. During this time, those animals perceived to be good-natured came to be known generally as wildlife.

After the fact, Horace Albright wrote much about the rationale behind early wildlife policy at the agency: "In those days we really hadn't the time, money, or ability to make close scientific studies of the problem." As for the treatment of predator and prey, Albright explained, "Back in 1916 there were two real, or imagined, threats." The first was how to prevent the extinction of ungulates, a problem they truly feared at the time. The second issue was predators, which already had been under siege for a decade. "This policy had been initiated at the behest of cattlemen and sheep-men during the administration of

Theodore Roosevelt and carried out rather ruthlessly until shortly before we entered the picture," wrote Albright. "It had been a federal policy to placate the ranchers around the outskirts of the park as well as give the soldiers stationed there the opportunity to obtain hunting trophies and furs."

Albright said that as he began to hear scientists such as Henry Fairfield Osborn, president of the American Museum of Natural History and later of the American Association for the Advancement of Science, talk about natural equilibrium, he began to oppose predator extermination. "Mather and I did not see eye to eye on this question," wrote Albright. "He felt the tourists loved to see wild animals, the more the merrier, and he envisaged herds of elk and antelope—the 'gentle ones,' as he called them." Nevertheless, Albright insists he made it clear that killing off predators was "impracticable." The 1917 NPS report he wrote does include the statement that "the killing of wild animals, except predatory when absolutely necessary, is strictly forbidden in Yellowstone Park by law."

It's easy to imagine that, even if Albright disagreed with Mather on the issue, it wouldn't have taken much to silence the second in command. Mather led the NPS as an autocracy with a dash of cult leader personality. Most everyone around Mather, especially Albright, admired him and found it hard to argue with the man. By 1918 Albright's dissent appears to have buckled at the knees. Though the NPS annual report for that year talks about "restoring wild life in America," it reflects little change in thinking: "The National Park Service holds no one of its several public charges in greater reverence than the care, maintenance, and

American Indians and others herd Yellowstone bison in 1925. Superintendent Horace Albright staged these shows to impress visiting dignitaries.

NOBODY BETTER TRY TO CHANGE THIS PLACE

By 1923 cattle prices had dropped, taxes were overdue, and properties were being foreclosed on in Jackson Hole, Wyoming. Ranchers were bailing out in droves. In late July, homesteader Maud Noble held a historic meeting in her three-room cabin, where the striking, pyramidal peaks of the Teton Range were ever-present beyond the cottonwoods and willows, past the Snake River. In attendance were Horace Albright (then superintendent of Yellowstone and still Stephen Mather's right-hand man), Noble, and a handful of other locals hatching a plan to federally protect the area.

The Tetons and Jackson Hole, naturally isolated throughout their history, had recently been discovered by the world, and their limited, if spectacular, resources were stretched thin. Small homesteads were bought and consolidated into large ranch operations; fly-by-night camps and hotels sprouted weedlike to cater to a growing number of tourists. Large-scale development and commercialization were on its doorstep, and at risk was the integrity of the Greater Yellowstone ecosystem, many millions of acres beyond the first national park's boundaries, including the area just east of the Teton Range. If the vast elk ranges, teeming lakes, and wild banks of the Snake were to be protected from exploitation, the NPS had to act decisively.

Albright had been determined to expand the boundaries of Yellowstone to include the Tetons and the Jackson Hole valley since he'd been assistant director of the NPS in 1916, then acting director from 1917 to 1919. The Tetons had everything the first national park didn't: mountain lakes and landscapes that rivaled anything in Switzerland (the scenic benchmark at the time). But the idea was about as popular as saddle sores among most locals, who clung to a picturesque notion of western life that was more romance than reality. When he took the pulse of locals about protecting this area, Albright recalled, "The answer was a menacing consensus—nobody better try to change this place."

Ranchers continued to resist as the economy slumped and presidents from Wilson to Coolidge systematically removed from homestead claims hundreds of thousands of acres of public land in the area, adding most of it to the national forest system. In 1929 Grand Teton became a 96,000-acre national

development of the wild animals which live free and normal lives within its reserves," the report says. "These animals are an exceedingly important part of what is left of that vast heritage of wild life which the march of civilization and the ruthlessness of former generations have elsewhere destroyed."

In the same breath, the emphasis on maintaining game herds at any cost was clear: "In Glacier National Park, increase of predatory animals has made necessary an intensive campaign for their destruction," the report continues. "This is now in progress." In Yellowstone, it explains, "An intensive campaign to destroy predatory animals, such as the wolf, coyote, and mountain lion, has met with gratifying success." Rocky Mountain National Park superintendent Roger Toll (who was later in park that included the extraordinary Teton Range and six glacial lakes at its base. But the NPS wanted more: Jackson Hole valley.

By that point Albright had been working with conservationist-philanthropist John D. Rockefeller to acquire large tracts of land in the lee of the craggy Tetons. At Albright's urging, Rockefeller formed a "shell" business not linked publicly to its famous benefactor (to temper price gouging); the Snake River Land Company advertised itself as a recreation outfit. Rockefeller planned to give that land to the federal government, and the NPS intended to add it to the existing national park. When Rockefeller lifted the veil in 1930, residents were outraged. Wyoming lawmakers demanded a Senate investigation, which happened in 1932. Ultimately, both Rockefeller and the Park Service were absolved of any wrongdoing, but mistrust of the NPS persisted in Jackson Hole for decades.

Throughout the 1930s and '40s, blistering antipark sentiment incinerated several efforts to expand the national park to include the Rockefeller holdings. With no compromise in sight, Rockefeller issued an ultimatum to President Franklin Roosevelt in early 1943: take the land now, or it will be lost to the NPS. Just five weeks later, FDR used his authority under the Antiquities Act of 1906 (thus circumventing any congressional opposition) to establish Jackson Hole National Monument. The new park drew a protective border around 210,000 acres, including Rockefeller's land and a large chunk of the Teton National Forest. Valley tempers flared again over what was seen as another federal sleight-of-hand; armed protests ensued.

Prevailing attitudes in Jackson Hole gradually began to shift after World War II ended. More Americans were visiting national parks, and tourism was renewing local economies. By the spring of 1949, a compromise that required that no president ever again use the Antiquities Act to create a national monument in Wyoming resulted in the 1950 establishment of the 485-square-mile national park now in existence.

Finally, alpine zones and forest joined wetland and sagebrush in one protected tract as habitat for pikas and eagles and everything in between. It took more than three decades for the NPS (with some powerful friends) to pull it off, but now every year millions of people visit Grand Teton National Park, which includes Maud Noble's preserved cabin on the Snake River.

charge at Yellowstone) said his park was greatly threatened by the flesh eaters. "For the good of the game," he said, his park was aggressively tracking predators with dogs and poisoning them.

The migration from that mind-set to the present one—in which apex predators such as wolves, mountain lions, and coyotes are treated as essential to ecosystems—began with a few vocal, passionate scientists who, armed with a growing body of evidence, refused to cow to the old guard at the NPS.

Four thousand feet up on the flanks of 20,320-foot Mount McKinley (a.k.a. Denali) is already far above tree line. That goliath peak, North America's highest, along with other peaks of the Alaska Range, covers much of the southern half of 6-million-acre Denali National Park. Its razor-sharp ridges cast lingering shadows far across a titanic landscape of glaciers, valleys, and braided rivers. Even at lower altitudes, among its lumpy tors it can be cool and windswept in late May, hardly the ideal place to bring offspring into the world.

That is, unless you're a surfbird. Its understated appearance—pale gray mottled with black—belies the fact that it's a phenom in ornithological circles. The surfbird, which dwells from the coast of southeastern Alaska all the way down to Chile's Tierra del Fuego, may have the largest winter range

of any bird in the world. It lives predominantly on craggy coasts, but for reasons only it knows, the stocky shorebird flies 150 miles inland during the breeding season to nest in this stony alpine tundra on Mount McKinley. The bird had been known to ornithologists for a century and a half before its secret nesting spot was finally revealed in 1926.

That long-sought discovery was made by two biologists from the University of California–Berkeley doing fieldwork. It was about four o'clock in the afternoon, still a week short of June, and the pair was only a week into their seventy-two-day expedition when they nearly stumbled into a nest of the elusive bird. First to spot it was George Melendez Wright, a young scientist born in California to an El Salvadoran mother. Even as a teenager, this accomplished outdoorsman was known to grab his backpack, set out solo, and explore undeveloped areas along the coast between San Francisco and the Oregon state line. Joseph Dixon, more of an expedition veteran, had already been on field outings to several existing or would-be national parks, to Alaska a handful of times, and once to the Arctic waters off Siberia.

The surfbird's cozy nest lay on the rocky, shrub-studded mountainside, in a shallow depression along a well-used game trail. Its surface was lined with the finest moss, upon which sat four eggs ("just the loveliest things you have ever imagined," Wright said later), which were tended to by a vigilant male surfbird. Dixon and Wright watched the nest for eighteen hours and, during that time, witnessed several close calls. On one occasion a bighorn sheep came clomping along the game trail. Fearing its nest would get stomped, the surfbird

George Melendez Wright, suited up as a member of the International Park Commission scouting territory in Texas on the US–Mexico border (now Big Bend National Park)

fluttered frantically from the nest and ricocheted off the face of the startled animal, causing it to change course. After averting disaster, the male fluffed out its chest feathers and settled down gently onto the eggs once again. "It seemed almost wrong to look at the nest, thus robbing the bird of a secret it has jealously guarded for so many years," said Wright.

During more than two months in Denali, Wright and Dixon walked roughly 500 miles, jotting down countless, detailed observations and collecting specimens. To those young scientists, the park must have seemed like a candy shop does to a child. Compared to the Lower 48, where even protected parklands had already lost many species (including most predatory ones, from wolves to grizzlies), its diversity must have left them wonder-struck. It was like stepping into a time machine and seeing what Montana or California had looked like before those biologists were born, before human hubris had taken a horrific toll. It was also likely a confirmation that studying natural landscapes, taking the time to wait and to watch, yielded new insights. Humility kept them from assuming they had all the pieces of the nature puzzle. That, along with their patience and tenacity, ultimately would have a lasting impact on the NPS and on national parks nationwide.

The surfbird watchers were mentored by the founding director of Berkeley's Museum of Vertebrate Zoology, Joseph Grinnell (a distant cousin of George Bird Grinnell), who took a frank stance about the purpose of parks that didn't gel with the views of early Park Service leaders. In *Animal Life as an Asset of National Parks*, Grinnell wrote that parks existed mainly for "retaining the original balance in plant and animal life," yet without a focus on science, "no thorough understanding of the conditions or of the practical problems they involve is possible." This was a radical concept to park boosters who believed that Glacier and Acadia and the like were for people alone to admire and enjoy.

With the help of other tireless scientists, Grinnell and Dixon had done exhaustive research in Lassen Volcanic National Park, the southern Sierra Nevada (including Kings Canyon National Park), and Yosemite. The famous Yosemite Transect, as it was called, surveyed mammals, amphibians, birds, and reptiles in a 1500-mile cross section of the state from the San Joaquin Valley east to Mono Lake. It took eight field biologists from 1914 to 1920 to pen more than 2000 pages of field notes, collect nearly 2800 specimens, and take more than 800 photographs. Their results were published in the 1924 book *Animal Life in the Yosemite*, the first major work on life in national parks. In it Grinnell and Tracy Storer talked about "the interrelations of living things." They said, "The longer we study the problem the clearer it becomes that in the natural forests, which, happily, are being preserved to us in our National Parks, a finely adjusted interrelation exists, amounting to a mutual interdependence, by which all the animal and plant species are within them able to pursue their careers down through time successfully."

Grinnell took a no-holds-barred approach to the treatment of predators, explaining that their destruction did not take place in a vacuum; pluck certain species out of the ecological system, and there will be consequences. "The removal of any of these elements would inevitably reduce the native complement of animal life," he wrote in the book. "Nor do we approve, as a rule, of the destruction of carnivorous animals—hawks, owls, foxes, coyotes, fur-bearers in general— within the Park. Each species occupies a niche of

A GRIZZLY AFFAIR

When hotel workers dumped food waste behind hotels in Yellowstone National Park, they inadvertently lured bears. By the 1880s, watching both black and grizzly bears eat garbage had grown into a genuine feature of the national park experience. Into the 1900s, many parks expanded bear shows and even built bleacher-style seating, night lighting, and feeding platforms furnished with fresh meat; one had a large painted wooden sign reading "Lunch counter for bears only." Along park roads and even at picnic areas, visitors wanting a closer look would hand-feed them. Black bears, and even grizzlies, had earned a false reputation as being playful and entertaining. Early NPS leaders commonly presented wildlife as a spectacle and encouraged tourists to associate the wild animals with the children's story "Goldilocks and the Three Bears." Not surprisingly, there were many bear-human conflicts, which often led to the bruins' demise.

The first comprehensive NPS scientific study, published as *Fauna of the National Parks of the United States* (which became known as *Fauna No. 1*) in 1933, argued "that every species shall be left to carry on its struggle for existence unaided, as being to its greatest ultimate good, unless there is real cause to believe that it will perish if unassisted"—including bears. In the spring of 1938, a letter from NPS Director Arno Cammerer arrived at Yellowstone announcing "a system-wide regulation forbidding the public to feed bears in any manner." Anticipating public backlash from what had become a staple of park tourism, he said, "It has been suggested that an appeal to a photographer's sporting instincts would be useful here; that is, point out how much more pride he would have in a photograph attained with difficulty in natural surroundings as against a photograph taken of a bear eating candy which could just as well be duplicated in any city zoo."

its own, where normally it carries on its existence in perfect harmony on the whole with the larger scheme of living nature."

These were barn-burning concepts that the NPS was not ready, or willing, to accept. The push for major development in parks—to make them as comfortable and entertaining as possible for the visiting public—was unyielding. During the years Grinnell and his colleagues were making field observations for their book, the NPS kept a mountain lion in a cage in Yosemite Valley, from the time it was a cub, along with two adult cats from Yellowstone. Its zoo at Wawona included elk

not native to the park. Yellowstone also had zoo-like enclosures at Mammoth Springs that housed bison, bears, badgers, and coyotes.

During this time when the termination of predators was a priority, rangers took on the role private hunters had played, supplementing their incomes with the sale of hides. By the mid-1920s, cougars and wolves had been extirpated from Rocky Mountain, Zion, and Grand Canyon national parks. Bears, however, were crowd-pleasers and were shipped to zoos or killed only if their behavior was deemed problematic. Roadside feeding of bears was not encouraged but was also not prohibited. A 1923 photo shows President Warren G. Harding in Yellowstone feeding Max, a young bear he lured out of a tree with a hunk of gingerbread. In Sequoia, as in most large parks, hundreds of tourists watched feedings each night on Bear Hill; elimination of problem bears became common there. In this period, the NPS also had a category of nuisance animals, such as porcupines, pelicans, and otters, they felt should be reduced in number. They believed that if predators altered "the natural balance of life"—and reduced the likelihood of a good fishing day for tourists—they should be removed.

Professional hunters like Jay Bruce, shown here in Yosemite, were hired to eliminate predators in several high-profile parks.

While development was a matter of common sense to park originators, the emphasis on it, even early on, was alarming to a growing band of wilderness advocates as well as scientists. A young forester, Aldo Leopold, had begun talking about the importance of safeguarding untamed places, and in the early 1920s he first proposed wilderness protection. Leopold had joined the USFS when he was just twenty-two years old, spending more than a decade in the abundant forests of Arizona and New Mexico. It dawned on him that preservation policies in place on land administered by the USFS, which allowed for multiple uses, and the NPS, which focused on development for recreation, were not robust enough.

Leopold was influenced by Arthur Carhart, the first full-time landscape architect of the USFS, who, at the behest of local outdoorsmen (and in

favor of fish and wildlife), rejected development in Colorado's White River National Forest. In 1922 Leopold submitted a proposal to administer the Gila National Forest in New Mexico as a wilderness area where primitive conditions would be maintained—and in 1924 it was done. While it was a decided victory, Leopold was cautious in his optimism that what had happened in the Gila was a concept that would endure. "Let no man think that because a few foresters have tentatively formulated a wilderness policy that the preservation of . . . wilderness is assured," he said.

Designating an area specifically as pure wilderness was a notion that early national park boosters found tough to grasp. To them, the parks *were* wilderness; that's why they'd been set aside from national forests whose "highest use," as famous forester Gifford Pinchot had put it, was human exploitation. In 1925, in an article in *American Forests and Forest Life*, Leopold wisely put his concept in context. He wrote, "Since the pilgrims landed, the supply of wilderness has

Forester William Greeley, was on a quest to find "some way to swing preservationist support to the Forest Service—and away from the increasing movement for national parks," as he put it. His survey of potential wilderness tracts identified more than seventy large areas totaling more than 55 million acres.

Even if wilderness status was a political ploy, purists like Leopold took full advantage of the agencies' tug-of-war to advance their cause. However tenuous, the Gila's new label was like a cairn marking a trail to the future of wilderness preservation. That same year, ecologist Charles Adams wrote in "Ecological Conditions in National Forests and in National Parks" in *Scientific Monthly*: "In recent years there has been an intensive movement to get vast crowds into the national parks, and at such a rate that vast areas of the parks are without question being severely injured."

Criticism of policies in regard to predators and invasive species grew louder by the mid-1920s as well. A group called the Anti-Steel-Trap League joined the influential Boone and Crockett Club, New York Zoological Society, and American Society of Mammalogists to protest trapping and poisoning schemes in parks. Not only did scientists believe the practice was brutish, but they had started to connect the dots between the loss of those species and the effect that had on the landscapes they populated. Alarming trends were already being seen in Yellowstone, where a bison glut was taxing the native flora. By 1925 the NPS was killing or selling off the iconic animals by the hundreds to other public or private interests.

In the 1920s the Ecological Society of America and the American Association for the

always been unlimited. Now, of a sudden, the end is in sight. The really wild places within reach of the centers of population are going or gone. As a nation, however, we are so accustomed to a plentiful supply that we are unconscious of what the disappearance of wild places would mean, just as we are unconscious of what the disappearance of winds or sunsets would mean."

While no doubt due to Leopold's eloquence and influence, the designation of wilderness areas was also a tactic used to keep USFS land away from the NPS, which had begun grabbing it by the fistfuls—from Grand Teton to the Grand Canyon—for national park expansions throughout the 1920s. After the Gila designation, Leopold's boss, Chief

Advancement of Science also officially opposed fish planting, which had been a massive operation in several major parks. They objected to the introduction of any type of nonnative species. As a result, some invasive species, including feral goats in what became Hawai'i Volcanoes National Park and feral burros at the Grand Canyon, began to be eradicated, but fish-stocking policies endured.

With the sense that national parks were cascading toward ruin, Adams, the zoologist from Syracuse, suggested in 1925 that the NPS hire in-house scientists to guide policy. While the old guard may have paid some lip service to the concept, they still traveled well-worn policy paths. Elk-loving Mather was director until 1929, and Albright, who fought heartily for practices—such as bison roundups and bear feedings—that delighted his visitors, was superintendent of Yellowstone until then.

During the latter half of the 1920s, NPS leadership had a lot (perhaps conveniently) distracting them from scientists' alerts. Albright was playing host to a stream of dignitaries, including conservationist-philanthropist John D. Rockefeller Jr., whose support he was trying to garner to add Grand Teton to the national park system (see first sidebar in this chapter). Sequoia nearly doubled in acreage. Three major eastern parks—Shenandoah, Great Smoky Mountains, and Mammoth Cave—came on the scene, as did Bryce Canyon. A historic and bitter fight over territory in the Grand Canyon was flaring up, and forest fires raged out of control in Glacier. If the worrisome wildland fires caused Park Service leadership to pause and think about

fire policy and ecosystem management, they precipitated no evident changes in either arena.

However, whether in response to criticism from the scientific community or to the maneuvering by the USFS, the NPS *did* dip its toes into the wilderness pond in 1927. It designated about 7 square miles north of Yosemite's Tuolumne Meadows as a wilderness reserve for scientific study where no recreation was allowed.

At the same time, there was major pushback against development at Mount Rainier National Park. A trail that circumnavigated the immense, ice-cloaked volcano had been scouted by the influential outdoors group The Mountaineers. When the trail's path became the NPS's preferred auto route and was slated to be graded and tarred, the organization declared war. Such a road would essentially develop all but 25 percent of the park, they argued, giving access to nearly every natural

It's caribou for dinner for this wolf seen along the park road in Denali.

After likely being eliminated from Yellowstone in the early 1900s, mountain lions reestablished themselves and are again a top predator within the ecosystem.

nook. The Park Service's landscape architects took a second look, and ultimately the northern section of the proposed loop road that would have cut through some of the park's most rugged and stunning terrain was deemed "too costly." What is now the 93-mile Wonderland Trail, which passes through old-growth fir and cedar forests and alpine wildflower gardens, might have been a drive-through if not for the growing ire of development critics.

With the road defeated, The Mountaineers pressured the NPS to consider officially declaring Rainier's roadless areas as wilderness. They were not thinking of a scientific reserve like the one in Yosemite but of the Gila, where Leopold had envisioned primitive places that could be navigated only via nonmechanized means. Mount Rainier Superintendent Owen Tomlinson agreed, writing to his higher-ups in DC: "Such action would be in entire accordance with national park policies and ideals, and it would have the effect of assuring those concerned with the preservation of national wilderness areas that the National Park Service is guarding against overdevelopment in national parks."

The NPS, which had no precedent for the change in designation, refused to call resulting roadless areas "wilderness," but it ultimately followed through on The Mountaineers' concept of designating certain areas "to be free from road and commercial development." For the first time it acknowledged that, while the Organic Act of 1916 had been well intentioned, another layer of protection was needed to shield what remained of the wild from the modern world. At Mount Rainier in 1928, the NPS had its first de facto wilderness area set aside for recreational use. Whether it had been designated to appease The Mountaineers or because it was too expensive to pave hardly mattered. It was only the beginning of an imminent chain reaction.

Perhaps encouraged by the success of wilderness advocates, or alarmed that no action had been taken on Adams's push for the hiring of in-house NPS biologists three years earlier, scientists stepped up their ground offensive. Joseph Grinnell echoed Adams in 1928 when speaking to the annual park superintendents' gathering. In fact he repeated what he had said in 1916: scientific research was key to knowing both what was going on in parks and how problems should be addressed. First and foremost, said Grinnell, was the urgent need to leave predators alone. At his behest, the conference adopted a resolution to forbid absolutely the use of steel traps in parks. While the measure didn't impact every park—steel traps were used to capture carnivores at the Grand Canyon until 1930 and in Yellowstone until 1931—the NPS did implement it.

In the waning days of the 1920s, as the stock market fluctuated wildly before eventually bottoming out, the leadership of the fledgling Park Service changed hands. In January 1929, Mather's directorship ended due to a stroke he had suffered late the previous year. Following his resignation and the news that Albright would succeed him, a *New York Times* editorial said, "This means not only that the policies which Mr. Mather developed will be carried on, but that their execution is entrusted to a man who played a large part in framing them." It was the reflection of a nation relieved that the growing park system, which was becoming more well-known and popular, was in good hands.

In one of their last meetings, Albright arranged for his old friend's train to pause in DC en route to the Mather homestead in Connecticut. Albright had finagled a fifteen-minute stop and gathered all the Washington-based members of the Park Service on the platform. Mather had not regained his speech but shook hands with everyone through an open window as they spoke encouragingly to him. He smiled broadly, his aquamarine eyes still flashing brightly, as he waved the walking stick his staff had just given him in thanks. But there would be no more mountain parties on which to bring that cane; Mather died the next year.

Albright, moving in to pick up where Mather had left off, had big shoes to fill, but he had, after all, stepped in for his chief on many past occasions. Lifting Mather's mantle didn't mean that Albright did everything the same; on the contrary, stepping out from behind his beloved mentor's shadow allowed him to consider other prominent viewpoints tapping at the corners of his consciousness. Now that rapping was coming most consistently and loudly from a growing mob of ecologists.

In the decade since Albright had written that the destruction of predators was impracticable, little had changed in NPS policy. But now that he was setting the agenda, Albright put into play some of what he was learning about the way an ecosystem functions. While not willing to go all the way to protecting predators, he agreed that they should be "controlled but not eliminated." It was a small step by the scientists' standards but an airborne leap for the Park Service.

In an even more surprising move, Albright agreed the bureau needed its own scientists and green-lighted the first system-wide scientific research to gather baseline data on all vertebrate fauna. The scientists who would undertake that 11,000-mile odyssey through parks were Wright and Dixon, the two surfbird observers who had endured early, still-bitter spring days in Alaska seeking wildlife and discovery. In the chilly days that lay ahead for science, they perhaps glimpsed something of their own wild destiny, pulling up the collars of their coats and pressing on.

If Albright had expected a bunch of lapdog scientists who would come around to the thinking that parks were for people, he didn't get them. The battle over natural resource policies involving wildlife, wildfires, invasive species, grazing, fish stocking, insects, and overdevelopment would span a century and amount to nothing less than an epic battle for the soul of national parks and their future existence.

At 6643 feet, Clingmans Dome is the highest point in Tennessee, in Great Smoky Mountains National Park, and along the 2180-mile Appalachian Trail. This steep walkway leads to its observation tower.

CHAPTER 13

Livin' in the Garden of Eden

ON THE WEST SIDE of Great Smoky Mountains National Park lies Cades Cove, a spot humming with visitors in summer, when green meadows whisper in reply to warm breezes, and in fall, when luminescent maples make their seasonal curtain call. The cove is a sheltered valley with dark, rich soil that supports abundant shrub and tree species. From above, the valley itself looks like a maple leaf that has floated to the ground: its jagged edges are crowded with hardwood forest, and numerous streams course through its veins. Down in the cove, among the

dogwoods, magnolias, and Carolina silverbells flamboyant with spring blooms, white-tailed deer are abundant, and black bears, coyotes, turkeys, and groundhogs can be seen poking around. In the distance gleams the frosty top of 5527-foot Thunderhead Mountain. To the south lies a ridge that separates this area of Tennessee from North Carolina. Along that border runs the Appalachian Trail, 71 miles of which lie within the national park.

For centuries before it was part of the national park, Cades Cove (once called Kate's Cove after the

VOICES OF THE SMOKIES

At Great Smoky Mountains National Park's Oconaluftee Visitor Center, a fascinating interpretive display includes oral histories of former park residents—such as Jonathan Woody of Cataloochee, who once traded a fish for the extraction of one of his teeth by a local dentist, and Eugene Sutton, who talks about secret signals in the daring days of making moonshine during Prohibition. Life in those hills, says another former resident, Charlie Palmer, "was more like livin' in the Garden of Eden than anything else I can think of." One display concludes simply, "The park would not exist without their sacrifices." More than ninety historic structures, including homes, barns, schools, and churches, are preserved in the park as vivid reminders of those who once lived here. In Cades Cove, you might swear you hear the sounds of mountain children playing Soup Pot or singing "Fiddle-I-Fee," their jubilant voices carried on a dulcet breeze.

wife of a Cherokee chief) was a hunting ground for those American Indians, whose tribe was organized in seven clans: Wolf, Blue, Paint, Bird, Deer, Long Hair, and Wild Potato. They controlled most of the southern Appalachians, settled in the abundant foothills, and worked fertile land along countless waterways. After encountering Cherokees in the area in 1540, a Spanish explorer reflected that tribe members seemed "sedate and thoughtful, dwelling in peace in their native mountains; they cultivated their fields and lived in prosperity and plenty." At its center, Cherokee life was essentially democratic, a system in which women were equal to men in government and at home. After the American Revolution, tribe members clashed with European Americans making inroads, and in 1819 they relinquished most of their territory in the Great Smoky Mountains.

In the days before that decisive treaty was signed, John Oliver and his wife, Lurena, were among the first permanent white settlers of Cades Cove. By 1830 the population was already 271, and by 1850 it swelled to 685. The town that sprang up in the isolated mountain valley included 500-acre

farms, log homes, barns, smokehouses, a grist mill, three churches, and, eventually, a schoolhouse.

Great Smoky Mountains National Park is now a UNESCO World Heritage Site where dozens of those original structures, restored by the National Park Service, can be seen along an 11-mile loop road—on which the Oliver home is the first stop. While you explore the wide, verdant valley, it's easy to imagine the full days of those early settlers: tending abundant cornfields with mules and muscle, smoking hog meat, picking apples, cooling milk in a springhouse, collecting chestnuts, molding iron at the blacksmith's forge, making molasses from sorghum. Aside from the physical labor required just to survive, life in the cove and in other communities sprinkled in the creases of these rolling hills was largely idyllic. Family ties were strong and neighbors pitched in during births, deaths, and most events in between. But the end of their story—the transition of this area from settlement to national park—was not quite so halcyon.

The Great Smoky Mountains, a subrange of the Appalachian Mountains, are an ecological tour de force. The Smokies, formed between 200 million and 300 million years ago, are among the oldest mountains on Earth. Within 800 square miles, more than 17,000 species of flora and fauna have been documented, and scientists figure there could be as many as 80,000 total. The abundant rainfall, northeast-to-southwest orientation, and elevation range from 875 to 6443 feet (the summit of Clingmans Dome) provide the ideal habitat for both northern and southern species. Nearly 95 percent of the park is forested, and roughly a quarter of that is old-growth. In addition to having one of the biggest swaths of temperate deciduous old-growth on the continent, Great Smoky Mountains National Park is the largest protected upland landmass east of the Mississippi River. The Smokies don't have the brash, youthful beauty of the Rocky Mountains; instead, the southern Appalachians' wonder is in their distinguished folds, the wrinkles where time defies human relevance.

On the brink of its tenth anniversary, in 1926 the NPS oversaw a few dozen national park units, most of them in the West. But park advocates,

THAT'S A FACT

The Smoky and Blue Ridge mountains were named for the bluish-purple haze clinging to the hills, which is formed by the release of hydrocarbons from the abundant vegetation. The Cherokee call the area *Sha-co-na-qe*, meaning the "place of blue smoke."

Horace Albright among them, had long felt that, since most of the population of the United States lived east of the Mississippi River, there should be parks closer to those masses. Having national parks within a day's journey of Boston, New York, and Washington, DC, would also bring the national park movement into lawmakers' backyards, possibly increasing understanding and economic support of it. But creating a park in the East to rival Yellowstone or Yosemite raised problems unique to the geography. Western parks had been created on public land, making it relatively easy to draw new boundaries around federally protected areas. That was not the case in the East, where private landowners had long dominated.

Rumblings about creating large national parks in the East had been made for decades, but up to the 1920s, the idea had mostly languished. A dozen or more bills had been introduced in Congress and one national monument had been created in Maine, but little else was accomplished. Even NPS director Stephen Mather initially opposed creating eastern parks. Albright recalled Mather saying, "Nonsense! The wonderlands are in the West. Once people hear about them and more roads are improved, they'll make the trip."

But by 1919 Mather had started pushing for the creation of national parks in the East. Despite the solid foundation the Park Service now enjoyed, there was a gnawing fear in those early days that as long as the bureau was relatively small and limited in its geography, it was vulnerable to the Forest Service and other behemoth federal agencies. Establishing a foothold with even a handful of eastern parks would earn the Park Service a longed-for national identity.

Congress acquiesced that year, and Sieur de Monts in Maine became Lafayette National Park,

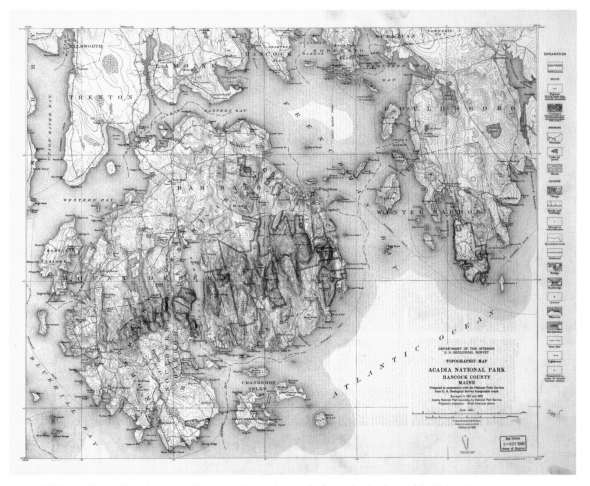

In 1919 Acadia National Park, depicted on this topographic map, became the first national park east of the Mississippi.

named after the French hero of the American Revolutionary War. It was the first national park east of the Mississippi, the first on a coast, and the first to be cobbled together from private land donations. It wasn't until 1929, under Albright's directorship, that the name was changed to Acadia National Park, a moniker that he and park mastermind George Dorr had agreed years earlier had a nice ring to it.

With the precedent set for establishing a national park in the East, and one formed solely from the donation of private land to the federal government, efforts to protect a portion of the southern Appalachians intensified. Two groups—one in Knoxville, Tennessee, one in Asheville, North Carolina—had been competing to have the national park in their backyards but finally combined forces to locate a park equidistant from each location, in the heart of the Smokies. Virginia had homed in on a different 300-square-mile area along its Blue Ridge Mountains, spanning from mountaintops to valley floors with a lavish array of plant and animal life. Georgia, West Virginia,

Kentucky, and even Alabama were also exploring park-eligible sites within their borders.

At the behest of the NPS (and through an act of Congress), the secretary of the interior in 1924 appointed a group of prominent lawmakers to survey the Southeast for potential parklands. In their voluminous report, the group highlighted areas along the Blue Ridge Mountains of Virginia, parts of the Smokies straddling the Tennessee–North Carolina border, and a portion of the Mammoth Cave area of Kentucky. That rough outline was enough to go on, and between 1925 and 1926, Congress authorized three national parks in the Appalachian region: Great Smoky Mountains, Shenandoah, and Mammoth Cave. This was the first of many steps on the way to official park status for all three areas. However, since much of the land that made up these proposed parks was privately held, the land first had

to be purchased—a formidable challenge that created years of chaos in those ancient hollows.

The legislation required that the land be donated to the federal government, so the states went to work acquiring it—no easy task in areas where communities were well established and lumber interests were powerful entities, which essentially meant residents and state lawmakers had to find the funds to pay for it. While people employed by lumber companies were opposed to large parks, many others endorsed them and enthusiastically raised funds. Organizations and individuals pitched in, even schoolchildren. In the late 1920s, the Tennessee and North Carolina legislatures each appropriated $2 million for purchasing 500,000 acres for Great Smoky Mountains National Park. Private citizens in those states emptied their pockets and contributed $1 million to the park cause. It was a phenomenal sum, but by the time the money had been pooled in 1928, land prices had doubled.

Still $5 million short, the states felt their park dreams slipping away. It was a familiar spot for the NPS, which then called on an old friend to help put eastern parks on the map. The NPS persuaded John D. Rockefeller Jr., who had helped Dorr reach his goal of preserving Acadia in Maine, to pitch in once again. Rockefeller's foundation matched the states' funds and contributed $5 million. It also contributed $164,000 for Shenandoah as Virginia struggled to raise enough. Citizens there were encouraged to "buy an acre at $6," and the state managed to cobble together $1.2 million.

With cash in hand, states commenced buying land. Some lumber companies willingly sold acreage at reasonable prices, but others demanded exorbitant fees and conditions—including being able to log the land for fifteen years after the sale. Other companies started madly logging in an attempt to kill the region's national park worthiness. Two potential sales resulted in lawsuits that ended up at the US Supreme Court; in both cases, the loggers were ordered to cease operations and to sell their holdings to North Carolina. As hard as that state's fight was against tree cutters and economics, Tennessee, Virginia, and Kentucky had even bigger battles ahead, with private landowners.

The displacement of people living within what are now Shenandoah, Great Smoky Mountains, and Mammoth Cave national parks has been described as everything from progressive to barbaric. Some 500 to 700 families were displaced from each of those three park areas, all from tight-knit communities like Cades Cove, where people followed the rhythms of the natural world and subsisted on what they grew, collected, hunted, or bartered. They lived more or less on their own terms, engaging with the fast-paced world beyond their borders only when it suited them. From among the ferns, fungi, and mountain laurel, they gathered and sold galax, hemlock, and mistletoe. They cultivated cabbage, field beans, corn, potatoes, and ginseng. They hunted razorback pigs, deer, and pheasants; some raised chickens. While some grazed cattle, most seldom had milk, butter, or beef. They never seemed to have enough salt.

At first, some of these locals were in favor of a park; they had witnessed the destruction wrought by logging and cared about maintaining the integrity of their home places. One such man was Horace Kephart, a transplant to those hills who, over time, was accepted by locals within what would become Great Smoky Mountains National Park. He wrote thoughtfully about what made life and the locals there so unique: "They are creatures of environment, enmeshed in a labyrinth that has deflected and repelled the march of our nation for three hundred years," he wrote. "Time has lingered in Appalachia. The mountain folk still live in the eighteenth century. The progress of mankind from that age to this is no heritage of theirs." By the early 1920s, Kephart said, the lumber industry had turned what was vital to something vile, ruined, and wrecked, and he advocated for a national park in the region to maintain what remained of culture and livelihoods.

In 1930 the NPS took over the protection and administration of the acreage that had been acquired up to that point. Many residents had been told their homes would not be threatened by a park being established around them, but mostly only the sick or elderly were allowed to stay on; the vast majority were forced to leave. Arno Cammerer, who replaced Albright as NPS director in 1933, advised park rangers to act with tact and sensitivity toward the mountain-dwellers. But he was opposed to people living in national parks and had developed a clear bias against them. That same year, a couple of *National Geographic* editors publicly opposed the removal of mountain residents from the Shenandoah area, arguing that visitors were interested in experiencing the unique customs of residents. In response to the *National Geographic* comments, Cammerer said, "There is no person so canny as certain types of mountaineers, and none so disreputable."

When the states approached them about buying their holdings, some residents were desperate to escape a life of isolation, while others fought until their dying days to maintain it, says Katrina Powell, an expert on the removal of families in the Blue Ridge Mountains. "This was a moment in time, of social and educational reform, of paternalistic

Condemnation Act of 1928, which allowed it to condemn properties and seize them by eminent domain. Most residents thus "incentivized" took state buyouts and left, but others stood their ground, many articulately arguing for their constitutional rights. When all else failed, some people had to be dragged from their homes, properties were burned, and countless ties were broken. Lawsuits were filed; John Oliver's descendants were among those who fought bitterly to remain in bucolic Cades Cove.

With the formation of those four eastern parks from Maine to Kentucky, the NPS crossed an invisible barrier from west to east; it was now a true public lands player in the East. While this was a significant change, a chance conversation with the US president a few years later would cause the most monumental shift in the agency's history—and make a man's dream come true in the process.

From the time he first arrived in Washington, DC, from California in 1913, Albright had struck out on weekend excursions to historical sights, dragging along any agreeable body. He trudged around the remnants of Civil War fortifications that surround the capital, visited the storied Chesapeake and Ohio (C&O) Canal, and journeyed to the site of the dramatic battle at Manassas. As he visited these and similar sites, he was thinking they should be national parks with proper protection and interpretation. Mather also had a profound interest in history; he was descended from Cotton Mather, the fervent seventeenth-century

thinking when they figured they knew what was best for mountain folk," Powell said. If people living on desirable plots of land refused to donate or to sell their lands, they were deemed "argumentative" and "uncooperative," she said. Powell grew up near the boundary of Shenandoah National Park hearing stories from removed families still bitter and mourning a lost way of life.

Because Virginia either lacked adequate money to buy the land outright or thought the process intractable, the state passed the Public Park

Home to the John Oliver family cabin, the once bustling community of Cades Cove is now a popular historical area in Great Smoky Mountains National Park.

minister of Boston's Old North Church (was that where Stephen's famous zeal originated?), and his grandfather had fought in the Revolutionary War. When the two were together in Washington, DC, Albright and Mather took lengthy walks to historic spots; they daydreamed about hiking the entire 185 miles of the C&O Canal.

Though they had a lot to worry about in the Park Service's formative years, they never missed an opportunity to advance their cause of bringing historic sites under the NPS umbrella. In 1917, in the first annual NPS report, Albright had argued that his new bureau should have jurisdiction over battlefields and other sites with historical associations, which were then exclusively under the purview of the War Department. As a self-described history buff who spent a lot of time exploring those sites, Albright wondered, "Why should military departments be in charge of places that are attractions for all people?" He had raised the question while drafting the legislation that established the NPS, though pushback from existing agencies caused him and the embryonic NPS to abandon the pursuit.

In early 1929, just after being appointed NPS director, Albright took another swing at it. At a military affairs committee meeting on a frosty January day, he argued that battlefields and the like were unknown or misunderstood without interpretation of the kind the NPS specialized in providing. But the plea fell on deaf ears. One congressman referred to the NPS as the keepers of the nation's playgrounds, and Albright later wrote, "[He] implied that if we had control of the military parks there would be hot dog stands everywhere." Representative Frank James of Michigan commented, "For sentimental reasons we think these parks ought to stay where they are."

By 1930 the NPS oversaw twenty-one national parks and thirty-three national monuments—the vast majority of which were natural and cultural areas in the West—with more than 3 million visitors annually. Over the next few years, the NPS strategically established new historical parks such as Colonial National Historical Park, which includes Yorktown Battlefield in Virginia, in order to set a precedent for its successful management of that type of site. Albright hired both the first chief historian of the NPS and an architectural historian during that time.

Albright had been close to President Herbert Hoover and had hoped to enlist his help in staging a coup to overthrow the War Department's control of monuments, memorials, and battlefields. Hoover was a friend of the parks: Before entering public life, he'd been head of the National Parks Conservation Association, was friends with Stephen Mather, and had spent time in Yellowstone while Albright was superintendent there. As head of the US Food Administration, he had deflected exploitation of park resources during World War I, then as US president from 1929 to 1933 he advocated for the parks. However, Hoover was ultimately unable to fulfill Albright's dream of adding established historical sites to the Park Service. Thanks to a casual conversation Albright had with the next president, however, history would be made.

Soon after taking the oath of office, President Franklin Delano Roosevelt (FDR) took a road trip to Hoover's hideaway on the Rapidan River (now within Shenandoah National Park). It was still April-brisk, but the dogwoods and redbuds were flowering optimistically. Included in FDR's

Secluded among the hillocks and hemlocks of the Blue Ridge Mountains along the Rapidan River, the Hoover camp, or "Summer White House," officially became part of Shenandoah National Park in 1935.

happened upon one of FDR's own pet projects. While he was governor of New York, FDR had tried to make the 1777 Battle of Saratoga site a state park. FDR told Albright, "Suppose you do something tomorrow about this. We'll help you at the White House. And if you get one battlefield, why shouldn't you get the others?"

Albright went to work on Saratoga National Historical Park (which would be established in 1938), and FDR made good on his promise. The Reorganization of 1933, mandated by executive order, handed forty-eight areas over to the NPS, including battlefields, parks, monuments, and military cemeteries. Care of Gettysburg, the Lincoln Memorial, the Statue of Liberty, the White House, and beyond was now up to the NPS, all part of a single system of federal parklands stretching from coast to coast.

entourage was Albright, who was asked to sit behind the president on the way back to Washington, DC. The NPS director knew this was his chance to appeal directly to the president. Albright waited patiently for the right moment to bend FDR's ear. When it arrived, he launched into the importance of making the NPS a truly national bureau with holdings in every part of the country. Besides, he said, it was inefficient to have parks spread out over several agencies. Without realizing it, Albright

In reality, the transfer had given the NPS more than it had bargained for—including Arlington National Cemetery and 700 buildings in the DC area. The NPS also became the tongue-twisting Office of National Parks, Buildings, and Reservations. Less than a year later, it regained its original name—and several years on, Arlington National Cemetery and hundreds of other sites were taken off the NPS's plate. With the 1933 reorganization, Albright had wrested from the Forest Service fifteen national monuments, which the NPS had long sought. Considering the long-standing animosity between the two agencies, those acquisitions must have been especially sweet.

THAT'S A FACT

The tallest tree in the eastern United States is in Great Smoky Mountains National Park. The 191.9-foot-tall tulip tree was measured in 2012 by the Native Tree Society.

The famous fall foliage and misty clouds of Great Smoky Mountains National Park

It had taken Albright sixteen years since the start of the NPS to make the agency a better version of itself, one that both protected the landscapes and purveyed the stories of the nation's most significant natural, cultural, and historical sites. Nearly as significant as rounding out the NPS system, however, was Albright's resignation. Once he had placed that historical piece into the NPS puzzle, Albright left Washington, DC, for good. What he had assumed would be a short-term gig had grown into a two-decades-long mission, one that he was now ready to relinquish.

Albright's contributions, while often overshadowed by Stephen Mather's booming personality, were many and vast. It's fitting that Albright Grove Loop Trail in the northeast corner of Great Smoky Mountains National Park, with its ancient hardwoods and historic cabins, was named for the conservation pioneer. That old-growth cove holding basswood and beech, hemlock, poplar, and magnolia includes some of the Smokies' tallest and oldest trees. It's a steep, winding hike up to the grove along a quiet, fern-lined trail. The murmur of nearby creeks and the whispering of the tree canopy in the wind are about the only sounds you hear. A magnificent tulip tree, 25 feet or more around and nearly 192 feet high, dominates the area. With its steadfast character and sweeping vision of the vast verdure below, it gives you a sense that Albright is still looking out for the well-being of the national parks.

A Civilian Conservation Corps crew in Mount Rainier National Park where they built and repaired structures, roads, campgrounds, and trails

CHAPTER 14

Tree Army

ON MAY 13, 1933, the high peaks of Rocky Mountain National Park were cloaked with steely clouds; 18 inches of snow lay on the ground, and the raw north wind threatened more. At first, just 8 men of the Civilian Conservation Corps (CCC) were dispatched into the park to set up Camp Number One, but within four days there were 150 more. That first camp was at Little Horseshoe Park, one of four CCC camps within Rocky Mountain and the first camp to be occupied in a national park west of the Mississippi. Enrollee Battell Loomis

described those first days this way: "A detail of twenty men shoveled the frozen snow away and leveled the campsite. A field kitchen was erected, four tents were set up, latrines were dug, boulders were blasted away, and 1400 feet of 2-inch galvanized pipe was laid to have water in the kitchen for supper that evening." After darkness also moved in, each man got a cotton-stuffed mattress and six blankets.

By the end of that year, hundreds of young men had been transplanted from teeming urban misery to the vast, tranquil floor of Yosemite Valley. Their

SHE-SHE-SHE CAMPS

The female equivalent of the CCC—though on a much smaller scale—were the "she-she-she" camps started by Eleanor Roosevelt to put to work some of the nation's 200,000 homeless women. The idea was largely scorned, but with the help of Labor Secretary Frances Perkins, the First Lady persevered. In all, 8500 women found work in ninety camps.

U-shaped camp, like scores of others around the country, had barracks large enough to house 225 to 250 men. Like a small town, the camp had a mess hall and kitchen, officers' quarters, a recreation building, a latrine and bathhouse, a hospital, and a "schoolhouse." In the seven years that CCC Company 942 worked among the granite sentinels and ethereal waterfalls of Yosemite, there were ten such camps throughout the park, with a total of nearly 7000 enrollees.

Their tasks ranged from the mundane, including pulling invasive weeds, to the lofty, such as replacing the famous climbing cables and stairway on the slick face of Half Dome. Their ambitious, sometimes dangerous projects included large-scale revegetation, flood mitigation, wildland firefighting, and tree-stump blasting with dynamite. Their work endures in the impressive Wawona Tunnel, the much-photographed Pohono Bridge spanning the Merced River, and many other rustic structures.

Like young men all over the country, those in Rocky Mountain and Yosemite national parks had left behind their families to join the ranks of a growing band of parkland workers. The CCC was just one of newly elected President Franklin Delano Roosevelt's work-relief programs, but it was

among the boldest. FDR had campaigned on the platform of a New Deal for Americans that would get citizens back to work and lift the nation out of the Great Depression. With one-quarter of the population unemployed, families struggled just to survive. In cities, especially in the East, crime, prostitution, and hopelessness were about the only things on the rise.

Following through on an idea he'd floated during his campaign against Herbert Hoover, Roosevelt wanted to tackle multiple national issues at once. Overzealous industrialization had torn the country to shreds, and deforestation, flooding, and Dust Bowl farmlands were its lasting wounds. Hard-won parklands—refuges from such harsh realities—had been coming on line since before the Depression hit. Hoover had appropriated funds for building trails and roads in national parks and monuments, but that money had fallen away as the national economy tanked. Both as governor of New York and then as president, Roosevelt felt it was his generation's responsibility to make up for damage done by their industrialist predecessors. Forests once spanning 800 million acres of the continental United States had been devastated by 1933; roughly 100 million acres remained. "The green slopes of our forested hills lured our first settlers and furnished them the materials of a happy

At Camp Wolverton (as it was later called), one of 11 CCC camps within Sequoia National Park, 1933

to carry it out. "And in creating the Civilian Conservation Corps, we are killing two birds with one stone," he said. "We are clearly enhancing the value of our natural resources, and at the same time we are relieving a[n] appreciable amount of actual distress." Roosevelt proposed the CCC concept to his staff just hours after taking the presidential oath of office. It gelled when his top labor advisor, Frances Perkins (soon to be his secretary of labor) suggested implementing a large-scale, federally financed social welfare program. Although no women were allowed in the CCC, Perkins—the first woman to hold a US cabinet position—was instrumental in shaping the high-profile, prodigious project.

Roosevelt's election heralded a hugely influential period in the history of the National Park Service. The development, organization, and expansion of national and state parks during that time determined their modern shapes. In April 1933, just five days after Roosevelt's Emergency Conservation Work Act was signed, 25,000 men from sixteen cities had signed up for the CCC. The ink was still setting on the legislation when NPS Director Horace Albright swung into action. The bureau was responsible for the herculean task of conceptualizing, planning, and organizing all CCC work in national and state park units. While the NPS no

life," said Roosevelt. "They and their descendants were a little careless with that asset."

As governor, Roosevelt had passed a law to boost statewide reforestation, and as president, he hoped to expand his conservation agenda on the national level and to hire urban young men longer has direct involvement with managing state parks, the Park Service became intimately involved with them during Roosevelt's New Deal years.

By mid-1933 the NPS was ready to take on 12,600 men at sixty-three camps in Sequoia, Yosemite, Hot Springs, Mesa Verde, and Great Smoky Mountains national parks, Colorado National Monument, and the established but undeveloped Acadia and Shenandoah national parks. On May 11, the first three camps officially began operation when young men arrived at Shenandoah and what is now called Colonial National Historical Park.

In the beginning, qualified CCC workers were unemployed males, ages eighteen to twenty-five, most of whom were in families on the relief rolls. Enrollees had to agree to live full-time in camps and to work Monday through Friday. Their pay was $30 per month ($25 of which was sent directly to their families), and they were issued blue denim work suits and sturdy black shoes, as well as a dress uniform of olive-colored woolen trousers, khaki shirts, a black necktie, and a coat. They also had camp lodging and three hearty meals a day at the government's expense. CCC officials actually had to bulk up the traditional army portions because many enrollees arrived malnourished.

It took some time to prepare a ragtag posse of city men for the physical demands that park projects posed. Eligible men were sent to army recruiting stations and given a physical exam. If they passed that, they were enrolled, signed a six-month contract (which could be extended for two years), and were inoculated for typhoid and smallpox. They then underwent two weeks of physical conditioning, including substantial food rations, before being dispatched to parks.

Heavy lifting at glacier's end for CCC men clearing boulders from a trail at Mount Rainier National Park

The bulk of the CCC enrollees came from eastern cities, but the NPS also hired regionally, bringing on board some war veterans and knowledgeable locals, for whom age and camp residence rules were eased. Locals were essential for their understanding of the terrain, materials, and climate in their areas. In order to uphold NPS landscape and building standards under the guidance of architects, engineers, and foresters, the agency could also hire a select group of skilled workers, such as blacksmiths and machine operators.

To meet the president's goal of 250,000 workers by July 1, 1933, the Park Service and the Forest Service also enrolled American Indians, who, unlike other enrollees, were not required to overnight in camps. African Americans worked in separate "colored" camps; some camps were initially mixed race, but complaints from locals near those camps ended that practice. The Emergency Conservation Work Act prohibited racial discrimination, but segregation was not considered discriminatory at that time.

While NPS superintendents developed and oversaw the work programs, the army kept peace at the camps. The bugle sounded at 6:00 a.m., and after fifteen minutes of calisthenics and a large breakfast of pancakes, cereal, or ham and eggs, the crews would head to their work sites. During an eight-hour shift, they took an hour lunch break, and when they returned to camp, they could choose from many leisure activities. In every camp, lights were out by 10:00 p.m., followed by a bed check.

Camp buildings fronted a cleared space that was used for assemblies and sports activities including baseball, basketball, and boxing. Sometimes camps held events to raise funds for equipment; for instance, enrollees in Rocky Mountain National Park once put on a minstrel show in the town of Estes Park, Colorado. Occasionally dances with local girls were arranged. Enrollees were encouraged to bring guitars, ukuleles, mandolins, or harmonicas to pass time in camp and create unity; spelling bees and singing contests were popular. Every camp had a library with about fifty books and various magazines.

In addition to a busy cook, the camps generally had a chaplain, a dentist, a doctor, and an educational advisor. Evening classes were held at every camp, and more than 90 percent of enrollees participated in them; 57,000 men were taught to read and write while in the CCC. As the program matured, vocational training was emphasized to prepare workers for jobs after they left the corps. The NPS was responsible for this job-related training, as well as for designing lectures to help enrollees understand the particular region to which they were assigned. In natural areas, forestry work was discussed; in historical parks, various periods in American history were illuminated. The NPS also championed professionally guided field excursions during which the young men could study the relevant geological, biological, cultural, or historical significance of their parks.

New York Times headlines trumpeted the growing popularity of the CCC. On June 22, 1933, the *Times* said, "237,984 Enrolled at Forest Camps; Officials Expect 70,000 More in Civilian Corps Before the Month Ends." On June 3, the *Times* announced the CCC's push into western parks: "6,940 Going to Forests: Civilian Workers Depart Today for Idaho and Montana." It was no doubt a thrilling, if intimidating, move for boys more accustomed to population density and pavement than to glaciers and grizzlies. Of the corps

The CCC worked to develop and protect Rocky Mountain National Park, allowing visitors to soak in such magnificent views as this one of Longs Peak, the park's tallest mountain.

men who worked in Montana, for example, doing extensive work in Glacier National Park, thousands were in-state recruits but others came from as far as New York. One enrollee from Brooklyn told the *Daily Missoulian* of his time in a Montana camp: "It took a little time to become accustomed to trees instead of people. The sighing of the wind in the great trees was a sound of mystery and at first terrifying after the roar of the densely populated cities we came from . . . Coming out here was a great break for me."

Of course, not all enrollees from New Jersey or Chicago who were plunked down in the Wild West were so inspired. Whether the enrollees were homesick or displeased with the labor or rules—some mistakenly thought it would be a "walk in the park"—the CCC had a fair number of desertions, 8 percent on average. It also had firings and at least one mutiny plot staged by New Yorkers in Yellowstone, which was foiled. Others in the CCC were proud of their low desertion rate, and those encamped at Mount Olympus National Monument (now Olympic National Park) hung a sign over their camp entrance announcing "We Can Take It."

By October 1934, there were 102 camps in national parks and monuments, and 263 camps in state parks, in most of the Lower 48, as well as in Alaska and Puerto Rico. Earlier that year, the NPS had also enrolled men to work in what is now Hawai'i Volcanoes National Park. In 1935 the CCC again extended its reach, to the US Virgin Islands.

In places where tourists were likely to cross paths with CCC members, camp officials took weekend shifts to address questions from the public. NPS higher-ups also tasked field officers with contacting local newspapers to soothe anxiety about influxes of young men into their communities and to rally support nationwide. Ultimately, the CCC was Roosevelt's most popular Depression relief program. A nationwide opinion poll taken in 1936 showed more than 80 percent of Americans were in favor of extending the program, with the strongest support in the Rocky Mountain and Pacific coast states.

Having millions of men devoted to parks was a boon for the NPS, which had a major backlog of projects due to staffing and budget shortfalls. During the nine years the CCC was in place, it built more infrastructure in national parks east and west than in the history of the system up to that period. Hundreds of miles of trails and roads were constructed as well as thousands of buildings including lodges, visitor centers, museums, employee housing, and restrooms. The CCC also worked on firebreak construction, erosion mitigation, and insect and tree disease control. Of course, the workers also planted trees: more than 2 billion of them.

Few national parks in the East were untouched by the wilderness corps. The infrastructure of the relatively new Great Smoky Mountains National Park was built largely by twenty-three CCC camps. Thousands of men pushed hundreds of miles of roads through tough terrain and built bridges, campgrounds, and fire towers. From

CCC men chop wood for use in their rustic but picturesque camp. As it did in many national parks, the CCC worked tirelessly to prepare Rocky Mountain National Park for increased tourism.

PARKITECTURE IN THE CCC YEARS

During the height of the CCC in the late 1930s, the rustic, "all-American" parkitecture style began to decline. Architects' changing philosophies rejected the pricey, labor-intensive nature of parkitecture in favor of simplicity and new construction materials as the international style took hold. Structures were designed with symmetry and a lack of ornamentation. They were often low-profile buildings in textured and stained concrete but were still built to meld into the background. Writing in the NPS's *1940 Yearbook: Park and Recreation Progress*, landscape architect George Nason summarized the shift away from the carefully cultivated rustic tradition; structures intentionally made to look unrefined were a protest to progress, he said. "The glorified pioneer structures of today are a species of tawdry circus showmanship," wrote Nason, "not examples of simple honesty. They are designed to awe rather than usefully charm." By the time the United States entered World War II at the end of 1941, national park rustic style was all but abandoned.

1933 to 1942 in Shenandoah, an estimated 10,000 young men planted hundreds of thousands of trees, shrubs, and native plants, many of which were grown in three CCC plant nurseries from seeds collected within the park. One of their largest eastern projects was the Blue Ridge Parkway. The great scenic byway, which spans 469 miles from Shenandoah to the Great Smoky Mountains, was largely built by four CCC camps whose workers labored from 1935 until the end of the program in 1942; construction flagged post-CCC, and the road was not officially completed until 1984. The CCC helped finish the Appalachian Trail, working on stretches in Shenandoah and the Great Smoky Mountains, as well as in Maine near the trail's northern terminus. It's a testament to the quality of their work that—unlike in many other areas— none of the Appalachian Trail spans the CCC built have needed rerouting for sustainability.

In the West, the scale of the work was also immense. At the Grand Canyon, where they labored for eight years, the CCC completed hundreds of projects on the North and South rims and at the bottom of the canyon. They improved the steep Bright Angel Trail from the South Rim to the canyon floor and completed the Colorado River Trail. They ran telephone and electric lines, some across the gaping mouth of the canyon. At Rocky Mountain National Park, they built miles of new trails and roads, campgrounds, amphitheaters, sewer systems, fire towers, and guardrails on the new Trail Ridge Road across the Continental Divide. In the Sierra, CCC men helped finish the Pacific Crest Trail and the John Muir Trail. Dozens of camps completed projects too numerous to catalog.

The NPS estimated that work in national parks and monuments amounted to more than $9 million in permanent improvements, and in state parks, the value was $27 million for the first two years alone. The Park Service gauged that the CCC did in two years what would have taken the NPS alone twenty years to complete. In *National Parks and Emergency Conservation Work*, NPS public relations chief Isabelle Story estimated that each

CCC BY THE NUMBERS

Years in operation: 9

Men employed: more than 2 million

American Indian enrollees: 80,000

Monthly salary: $30

Number of national parks and monuments worked in: 94

State parks constructed: 711

Trees planted: 2 billion–3 billion

Trails and roads built: 138,000 miles

Lodges and museums built: 205

Drinking fountains installed: 1865

CCC camp pumped $5000 per month into local economies and millions of dollars into the national economy as supply orders for clothing and equipment were filled. Families received cash infusions from their young men, and the enrollees grew strong with steady meals and physical labor—a boon for natural resources and for human ones, as the president had hoped.

The scale and speed at which park projects were completed was lauded by most people, from the president to the general public, but not everyone was on board; conservationists expressed alarm at the scale of construction. There were too many roads and trails making pristine wilderness accessible, they argued, and too many new structures spoiling once-modest landscapes. Taking notice that none of the money was being spent on scientific objectives, biologist George Wright cried foul. In response, the NPS hired a slew of biologists, which then numbered twenty-seven in total—the most up to that time. It was a paradoxical time in which scientists were gaining influence amid a flurry of ecological disruption wrought by CCC activities.

Whatever its perceived drawbacks, the CCC employed 5 percent of the total male population and lifted countless families from poverty. In addition to the CCC's financial and ecological effects, Roosevelt and other supporters cited its rescue of young men from the idle life that threatened the fabric of the nation. The president felt that bringing young men out into healthful surroundings had far-reaching effects, and he summed up the success of the CCC in this way: "More important, however, than the material gains will be the moral and spiritual value of such work . . . We can eliminate to some extent at least the threat that enforced idleness brings to spiritual and moral stability."

The impacts of the CCC were lasting. Those rustic rock-and-timber buildings and bridges that characterize the national park style are still enjoyed by visitors; many are now on the National Register of Historic Places. But the conservation corps did much more than that, as Roosevelt had intended. Up to that point, the idea that wild areas were worth saving and worth seeing had existed mainly among the wealthy and educated. Under the CCC, national parks and conservation went more mainstream. The CCC workers themselves brought the concepts of conservation and preservation back with them to city-dwellers, and the CCC's work gave them a tangible sense of the need for it. The CCC's so-called beautification projects also made parklands more accessible to average Americans who built relationships with landscapes they might never have seen otherwise.

In various accounts given at that time, and in oral histories recorded since, few men expressed regret about enlisting in Roosevelt's Tree Army. Darrel Stover of Yosemite's Company 942, Camp Cascades No. 6, was asked if he would repeat his experiences. He replied, "Yes, I would do it all over again. It was a new life for a nineteen-year-old kid. I, like so many of the others, enlisted as a teenager and came out a man. And it happened in the most beautiful place in the world, Yosemite."

One Rocky Mountain enrollee, who referred to those in his ranks as the "Green Guard of the Roosevelt Revolution," described the positive impact the detail had on him. He wrote, "A few months ago I was broke. At this writing I am sitting on top of the world. Almost literally so, because National Park No. 1 CCC Camp near Estes Park . . . is 9000 feet up. Instead of holding down a park bench or pounding the pavements looking for work, today I have work, plenty of good food, and a view of the sort that people pay money to see . . . We are going to have a hamburg steak tonight. And I am on the payroll."

One of the original 14 designs of national park posters done for the NPS by Works Progress Administration artists, intended to lure a poverty-weary public to parks.

Tireless field biologist Joseph Dixon weighs and measures a newborn fawn in California in 1928.

CHAPTER 15

The Realization Is Coming

THE GIANT FOREST in Sequoia National Park is a place that defies time. Days begin and end, generations come and go, civilizations rise and fall, and still the trees reach up and out toward a future beyond each day's admirers. This 1800-acre grove boasts a mind-blowing 8400 sequoias, including several of the largest trees in the world. On a plateau where the General Sherman Tree stands, visitors mill around beyond protective fencing, posing for pictures with Earth's largest living tree—and largest living organism, by volume. The behemoth is 103 feet around at its base, and it reaches 275 feet up into the air. At 2200 years, it is older than the Great Wall of China.

Sequoias grow naturally only on the western slope of California's Sierra Nevada, generally at 5000 to 7000 feet in elevation. This species, *Sequoiadendron giganteum*, can reach more than 300 feet and live more than 3000 years. Near the General Sherman Tree is the President Tree—named for Warren G. Harding—which is 3240 years old and has upwards of 2 billion leaves.

Photographs taken today or tomorrow may serve as reminders of the moment when your neck was cricked awkwardly as you scanned for treetops and the giants were put in proper perspective. But the substance of the place is captured only when you are there in flesh and bone, beneath their shade, inhaling the loamy scent of water, soil, and time.

The Giant Forest scratches the surface of the embarrassment of riches that are Sequoia and neighboring Kings Canyon national parks. Besides the megatrees there are extreme peaks, gaping canyons, and riotous rivers. And from the foothill chaparral to Mount Whitney, the highest peak in the Lower 48, there's a lot of backcountry to explore. The High Sierra Trail heads east across the park from the Giant Forest for roughly 50 miles and ducks between the glaciated peaks of the Great Western Divide at 10,700-foot Kaweah Gap. Then it descends into Kern Canyon before intersecting the epic John Muir and Pacific Crest trails. From there it's a day's trek to the 14,494-foot summit of Mount Whitney. Along the way, hikers cross steep gorges, gushing creeks, windswept valleys, and alpine meadows filled with glacial ponds, hot springs, waterfalls, and plenty of granite.

In Kings Canyon park, bordering Sequoia to the north, one small spur road runs along the magnificent namesake canyon, glacier-carved to a depth of more than 8000 feet—one of the deepest in the United States—but the pavement soon stops. From road's end at Zumwalt Meadows, surrounded by rock domes and sentinels and wild waterfalls, you get a taste of—and, perhaps, a thirst for—the fertile backcountry. Whether for a day or a month, you can venture into hundreds of thousands of wilderness acres, never once having to retrace your steps.

Except for the trees, the Giant Forest looks quite different from how it did in the 1930s. By then early park developers had done a whole lot that harmed the very places they were sworn to protect. In Sequoia, there had been no stopping the onslaught. Visitation soared after a road finished in 1903 linked the Sierra foothills to the grove. A veritable town sprouted in the grove, including several campgrounds, hundreds of cabins and platform tents, a gas station, restaurants, latrines, shops, a hospital, and parking lots.

John Muir had said of Sequoia, "Most of the Sierra trees die of disease, fungi, etc., but nothing hurts the Big Tree. Barring accidents, it seems to be immortal." But he hadn't lived to see the impact of so many tree huggers. True, bugs and blight don't care for the taste of the tannic acid in the cinnamon-hued bark and branches of the sequoia. And its thick bark makes it virtually impervious to fire from above or below. Though many sequoias are struck by lightning, few of the mature trees are killed by these strikes. Some wear black scars, evidence of injuries from which they have healed. But sequoia root systems are shallow, making them vulnerable to toppling in high winds, particularly when that base has been compromised by

Wildlife policies that favored game animals over predators, the introduction of foreign species that crowded out local flora and fauna, fire suppression, and widespread development that facilitated the entry of millions of people all were practices with dire results—and all were present in Sequoia and the other "natural" parks. Much of the criticism of those actions came to a head in the 1930s, a decade in which the emerging voice of scientists at the NPS seemed poised to change everything.

For a decade, Colonel John White had noticed stress on the Giant Forest and other groves and had been agitating for change. The superintendent had arrived in Sequoia in 1920, still relatively fresh from military service in Europe during World War I, knowing little about the unique environment. But he set out to learn as much as possible, and over his twenty-seven years of service in Sequoia, White developed a conservation philosophy based on his own observations of strain on the environment and on an acceptance of the new science that explained what he was seeing. This was, of course, often at odds with prevailing NPS ideology and policy. White's responsibility as caretaker of the world's largest living things seemed as big as *they* were, but White wasn't one to back down from a tussle, of which there were many.

By the time White had settled into Sequoia with his wife, Fay, and their daughter, Phyllis, it was clear no new sequoias were taking root. The giants had failed to regenerate, but no one knew why. Cutting-edge ecologist Charles Adams had written much about the trouble in Sequoia in a *Scientific Monthly* article in 1925. He concluded that overdevelopment was killing the Giant Forest.

soil erosion. Being stripped of their protective root cover by trampling feet or hooves, car tires, construction, or floods is enough to bring down the immense evergreens.

The National Park Service believed it was acting in the best interest of the resources, but sometimes, even armed with substantive research, it chose to ignore facts in favor of the agency's agenda.

Plant pathologist Emilio Meinecke, who had been hired by the NPS to study the issue, also deduced that people were the problem; they were compacting the soil over shallow roots or wearing it away during construction and touring.

These two scientists might have saved themselves a lot of trouble by trusting the superintendent's observations, which culminated in 1927 when White vented about the huge leap in tourism over the time he'd been head of the park: nearly 90,000 visitors in that year, compared to about 28,000 in 1920. "We have been somewhat in the position of an engineer who might be required to build a dam across a rushing stream without an opportunity to divert the water," he said. White built fences, relocated parking lots, and replaced soil in an effort to slow wear and tear on the trees from careless motorists, who sometimes ran into the trees, and from thieves who pried off pieces of bark to keep or sell as souvenirs.

White said the Park Service's biggest problem was how to develop parks "without devitalizing them; to make them accessible and popular, but not vulgar; to bring in the crowds and yet to maintain an appearance of not being crowded." He went head-to-head on many occasions with the park's main concessionaire, and when the company wanted to add additional cabins in 1931, White balked. The NPS director ultimately allowed the increase in structures, but White, who had also fought to cap guest capacity, won a significant victory at the same time; the concessionaire could build its new cabins, but it had to limit strictly the number of people who could stay in each. It was the first time the Park Service had put a limit on tourism development of any kind. At that time White also broached the topic of entirely removing the structures in the Giant Forest. The idea, which no doubt seemed radical, was rejected by the NPS, but the superintendent persisted.

In the meantime, White seeded sequoias in the park's own nursery and replanted them in the forest, never realizing the missing link to sequoia regeneration: fire. Seeds are released from cones when they are subjected to extreme heat, the kind that accompanies a blaze. While this was not known at the time, White disagreed with the NPS policy of fire suppression because it allowed the buildup of other vegetation—so-called fuel—at the base of the big trees.

But the NPS followed the lead of the US Forest Service, which prevented fires and fought them at

Sequoia National Park experimented early on with prescribed burns to reduce forest undergrowth, but soon after, fire suppression became policy for the early NPS. Decades passed before fire reclaimed its rightful place in the natural process.

reporters on not sensationalizing recent wildfires in the area: "I am indeed glad to see that the *Los Angeles Times* is treating these fires as of so habitual occurrence as scarcely to be news," White said. He saw fires as part of the life cycle of forests—a system that, with human interference, had gone haywire. White called people who feared fire raging in the Giant Forest "scareheads." The Big Trees had been in the path of wildfires for eons, he wrote, "yet they still raise their spears or crowns of blue-green foliage to the azure of our Sierra skies."

Still, letting nature-caused wildfires burn and intentionally setting them (a practice now known as prescribed burning), both of which thin out forests and prevent a catastrophic buildup of fuels, was highly controversial. Forests had become so dense from decades of fire suppression that any fire could quickly burn out of control. Even scientists like Adams who believed fire suppression was necessary recommended against it; it was now just too risky.

New scientists within the bureau began to bring to light these many human impacts—from fire suppression to overuse—on national parks. The first parks-wide biological survey, green-lighted by Horace Albright, was the brainchild of George Wright, who joined the NPS as a naturalist in Yosemite in 1927. Wright had seen things that disturbed him: overabundant deer, few predators,

all costs. The USFS policy made sense, to a degree, because that agency had to protect resources that could be logged and sold—resources that were, of course, worthless if burned. For the NPS, parks were a product of another kind; scenery was their commodity. The NPS believed that fires must also be fought in national parks in order to retain their appeal and, therefore, their economic value. Wildfires had been terrifying and costly events, in general, for westerners. What the NPS ignored, to its peril, even in the face of emerging science, was that fire was essential to the health of landscapes and, ultimately, entire ecosystems.

Eventually White came to understand the role of fire in the Sequoia park ecosystem, at least in part. He did not see it as the evil many others did. In 1928 he wrote a letter to a newspaper, complimenting and bears habituated to humans—it seemed to him the natural world was way off balance. The NPS top brass may have agreed to the biological survey because Wright, who had great personal wealth, funded it himself. Regardless, the survey was launched in the summer of 1929 and Wright, Joseph Dixon, and Ben Thompson went to work documenting wildlife conditions and drawing conclusions about how to mitigate the impacts of human activity in parks.

The NPS Wildlife Division was formed by Albright in 1933, composed of those three scientists plus a secretary. While they were dubbed the *Wildlife* Division, their observations and suggestions extended to many areas of park life. That same year, the release of their paper *Fauna of the National Parks of the United States* (*Fauna No. 1*, of three), which laid out those years of field research, raised the first real red flags.

The report did not mince words: "When a roster of typical wildlife problems from the whole national park system was assembled, a very wide range of maladjustments was revealed," wrote the authors. They covered a staggering array of topics and prescribed a number of treatments, including restoring depleted habitat, dealing with species' overabundance (caused by humans' reduction of predators), reestablishing extirpated species, eliminating exotic species, and reducing disturbances to breeding grounds. They established some hard truths, including that "a park is an artificial unit, not an independent biological unit with natural boundaries (unless it happens to be an island). The boundaries, as drawn, frequently fail to include terrain which is vital to the park animals during some part of their annual cycles." The authors lamented the conservation of mere scenery and suggested that future parks, or the expansion of current ones,

should contain "year-round habitats of all species." The report represented the first time dissent over the treatment of natural resources in parks was coming from *within* the NPS.

While Wright was admired and respected, the policies he and his colleagues suggested met with resistance; sometimes the Park Service simply ignored the prescriptions, and sometimes it was a bit more complicated. Take, for example, the issue of carnivores. *Fauna No. 1* suggests that "the rare predators shall be considered special charges of the national parks in proportion that they are persecuted everywhere else." At least in theory, the NPS agreed; since 1931 it had recognized that wolves and mountain lions and the like were an important part of the ecological picture. Killing them wasn't totally banned, but it had been significantly curtailed.

But also in 1931 Congress passed the Animal Damage Control Act, which required the government to destroy or control predators that threatened domestic livestock. The directive to control predators made it convenient for the Park Service to bend to the will of vocal agriculture interests and to do what it ultimately wanted to do anyway: make parks attractive and acceptable to the traveling public. Often it was only when the NPS was called out in the media that policy shifted, as was the case with pelicans in Yellowstone, which were being killed for preying on fish. A vocal conservationist, Rosalie Edge, raised the ire of bird lovers over what she called the "senseless slaughter" and embarrassed the NPS into changing its tune.

The year 1933 was a big one in the annals of natural resource management at the NPS. That February, Albright contributed an article to *Scientific Monthly* called "Research in National Parks," which made clear the inherent conflict between his early NPS guard and the ecological imperative of its newcomers. While he wrote that "science is fundamental" to parks, Albright also said, "Being equipped by nature with the most complete and magnificent laboratories imaginable, it was inevitable that scientific research should become an important and popular activity of the National Park Service. Nevertheless, it is one of the newest developments in national park work, which is primarily of a human welfare nature."

Again, science took a backseat to people. It's possible Albright felt threatened by the implication that early policy had been ruining parks; scientific research at that point was jeopardizing

the founders' legacy. Scientific studies had upset the romantic idea that there were pristine parks, true wild areas, remaining. It must have been a tough pill to swallow for people who had, until so recently, been the clear front-runners in achieving immortality through their national park conservation efforts.

In 1934 the NPS Wildlife Division was uprooted from the University of California–Berkeley campus and replanted in Washington, DC. The move put the division's work under the noses of policy makers, and in some ways it was the three scientists' most influential moment. That same year the new NPS director, Arno Cammerer, made *Fauna No. 1* the official policy of the NPS, at least in theory. While the scientifically supported recommendations regarding fire, pests, and diseases were clear—let them run their course—field managers were torn between *Fauna No. 1* and certain superintendents who resented Wright and others for telling them how to run *their* parks. For example, NPS biologist E. Lowell Sumner pleaded for scrapping a plan to improve the road through Titus Canyon in Death Valley National Park; in his view, it would be better to remove the road entirely and let the rare plants and animals there recover from a disturbed state. He was disregarded.

But it was also a time of crisis with ungulates in large parks, which may have made NPS leadership more inclined to listen to ecologists who had predicted such distress. An overabundance of elk was decimating

Before scientists understood the importance of fires to ecosystems, preventing and extinguishing them was seen as essential to preserving nature and protecting visitors.

ground cover in Yellowstone, and the NPS feared deer would be the end of wildflowers in Yosemite. Wright's colleague Thompson was direct with Cammerer: no pristine or even close-to-pristine "first- or second-class nature sanctuaries are to be found in any of our national parks under their present condition," he said.

Fauna No. 2, written by Wright and Thompson, was released soon after the Wildlife Division made its cross-country move, and like the first report, it was equal parts illuminating, instructive, and philosophical. Progress had been made since the Wildlife Division had been founded, they reported; natural resources were sounder than at any time since the establishment of the NPS. But there was still a long way to go.

Some of the most intriguing aspects of *Fauna No. 2* are its philosophical underpinnings of ecology, which would dominate conservation rhetoric in years to come. The authors talk about the "psychological and zoological" imperatives of wildness. They ask, "How can the secret beauty of wilderness be opened to the people and remain unspoiled? This is the greatest question we have to meet if we are to save this and every other national park as truly primitive areas." They called on Aldo Leopold, who was both a visionary wilderness advocate *and* a practical forester and wildlife manager, to explain. "The salient geographic character of outdoor recreation, to any mind, is that recreational use is self-destructive," Leopold had written in his essay "Conservation Economics." "The more people are concentrated on a given area, the less is the chance of their finding what they seek." At a conference that year, Wright leveled with the assembled national park superintendents, in his diplomatic way: "We know that it is impossible to keep any area in the United States in an absolutely

primeval condition," he said, "but there are reasonable aspects to it and reasonable objectives that we can strive for."

Wilderness preservation ideals were also gaining traction elsewhere. Newly ordained Secretary of the Interior Harold Ickes had developed strong opinions about conservation while knowing Stephen Mather and Horace Albright. From day one, Ickes was at near-constant odds with Arno Cammerer, who was at that point plotting development in the big new eastern parks. Just two months after entering office, Ickes said, "If I had my way about national parks, I would create one without a road in it. I would have it impenetrable forever to automobiles, a place where man would not try to improve upon God."

Into the 1930s, the NPS continued to set aside small, somewhat random park areas as research reserves similar to the one in Yosemite, without consulting scientists. There were twenty-eight such areas in ten parks, including some in Yellowstone, Grand Canyon, Rocky Mountain, and Zion. But without a congressional mandate, even those areas preserved specifically to study their primeval characteristics were as vulnerable as any other part of the parks.

Around that time Bob Marshall, then chief forester at the Office of Indian Affairs, wrote Ickes about establishing a national wilderness policy: "In order to escape the whims of politics . . . [wilderness areas] should be set aside by an act of Congress . . . This would give them as close an approximation to permanence as could be realized in a world of shifting desires," he said. A consummate mountaineer and extreme outdoorsman once tracked by a grizzly (he survived by playing dead), Marshall

This path heads into Santa Elena Canyon in Big Bend National Park, the largest expanse of roadless public lands in Texas.

voiced disgust with the NPS, which he felt had wrecked its reserves by catering to tourist hordes.

In a tone channeled later by environmental writer Edward Abbey, Marshall wrote forcefully about the dire need for untrammeled spaces: "As society becomes more and more mechanized, it will be more and more difficult for many people to stand the nervous strain, the high pressure, and the drabness of their lives," he wrote. "To escape these abominations, constantly growing numbers will seek the primitive for the finest features of life." The hope for wilderness lay in national forests, Marshall contended, and he pursued wilderness earmarking within the USFS. Marshall's campaign for a national system ultimately resulted in roughly 14 million acres of wilderness within national forests.

In 1934 the term "wilderness parks" joined the NPS vernacular with the establishment of Everglades and Big Bend national parks. When Congress authorized the Everglades as a national park, it required that it be permanently preserved as wilderness and insisted that no development "interfere with the preservation intact of the unique flora and fauna and the essentially primitive conditions now prevailing." Unlike earlier parks created to safeguard scenery, Everglades was the first park established to protect vast ecosystems as wildlife habitat. Scientists had been studying the area since the late nineteenth century, broadcasting its biodiversity and voicing concern over the intense development that was already engulfing much of southern Florida.

Another issue was the persistent plume hunters who were slaughtering flocks of birds with alarming efficiency, leading the Audubon Society to join the fight. May Mann Jennings, head of the Preservation Committee at the Florida Federation of Women's Clubs, led the charge. The effort resulted in public and private land donations that grew from 960 acres in 1916 to 4000 acres in 1921. That area, Royal Palm State Park, became the centerpiece of the national park when parkland acquisitions were finally complete years later, in 1947. At the dedication ceremony, President Harry Truman said, "Here is land, tranquil in its quiet beauty, serving not as the source of water, but as the last receiver of it. To its natural abundance we owe the spectacular plant and animal life that distinguishes this place from all others in our country."

Also in 1934, a major moose die-off occurred in Isle Royale National Park, in Lake Superior off the coast of Michigan. A few years earlier, an up-and-coming wildlife biologist had studied the animals there and had predicted such an event. Adolph Murie had observed that, without any predation, the moose population had boomed beyond the carrying capacity of the 45-mile-long island, and the entire ecosystem was suffering as a result. Murie recommended culling the moose population by relocation, hunting, or introduction of wolves to the island. His proposal languished, as did life on Isle Royale, until the 1934 die-off and a wildfire two years later that torched the island.

Soon after that, Murie joined the NPS as a staunch advocate of wilderness values in national parks. In that same year, construction began on the Blue Ridge Parkway—a conspicuous example of park development that revealed the gulf between the priorities of Murie and fellow NPS biologists and that of their bosses. The biologists were advocating natural conditions that, for the most part, disallowed human manipulation. To them, an ideal wilderness state didn't prioritize one indigenous species over another and didn't allow humans easy access into every recess of a park. Wilderness advocates agreed.

Just after the new year ticked to 1935, forward thinkers and policy shapers met in the nation's capital for the first meeting of the Wilderness Society, of which Bob Marshall was one of the founding members. Among them were former journalist and Mather man Robert Sterling Yard, attorney Harvey Broome, accountant Harold Anderson, explorer Ernest Oberholtzer, soil conservation and

water management expert Bernard Frank, forest examiner Benton MacKaye, and ecologist Aldo Leopold. Each had deep roots in the outdoors, covering nearly every nook of the country, and they used their passions and diverse expertise to drive the movement forward.

In the fall of that year, in a piece called "Why the Wilderness Society?" Leopold wrote that the "hammer of development" had such momentum that he feared wild places would be pounded to road dust before their worth was recognized. "The Wilderness Society is, philosophically, a disclaimer of the biotic arrogance of *Homo americanus*," he said. "It is one of the focal points of a new attitude—an intelligent humility toward man's place in nature."

Pioneering NPS wildlife biologist Adolph Murie, shown here at Igloo Canyon in Denali, was the first scientist to study wolves in their natural environment.

But almost as soon as those enthusiastic ecologists and advocates reached for the stars, those aspirations began to slip through their grasp. Before long, the same old fears seemed to creep back into NPS land management. Murie experienced this firsthand on several occasions. Predator control was again plaguing Yellowstone, where managers wanted to protect game animals from coyotes. Murie was sent to study the problem, and his highly unpopular conclusion was that the NPS policy protecting predators (a recent rule still on shaky ground) should be upheld. Murie was a straight shooter, and more than one person demanded he be fired.

Undaunted, Murie went on to study wolves in what's now Denali National Park, where the canids were being blamed for the drop in bighorn sheep numbers. "It looked as though certain influential sportsmen would get Congress to pass a bill requiring wolf control in the park, thereby threatening the Service's basic management policies," NPS ecologist Sumner wrote years later. But Murie had "presented the biological facts so effectively that pressure for wolf control subsided," Sumner said.

Rather than focusing on a single organism, Murie looked at whole ecosystems, concluding that "life is richest where greatest diversity exists in the natural order." In 1935 Murie protested the clearing of a large, partially burned area on the western slope of Glacier National Park. To log that area would be "sacrilegious," he said, because its decay and regrowth would provide a different—though necessary—type of habitat for park wildlife. The NPS felt the burn area would be an ugly scar if left as is, and Murie lost the fight.

Camping along the High Sierra Trail at Kaweah Gap, a pass through the Great Western Divide, in Sequoia National Park

Murie's loss represented two things that were going on in the United States at the time. First was the construction of the Hoover Dam, started in 1931 and completed in 1936, a glaring example of how to bend nature to the will of humanity. The second was the push to respond to the recreational desires of Americans. As the nation languished beneath the weight of economic depression, accounts of unrestrained places where some serenity might be found were popular in the mainstream media. The glaciers and gorges and deep, quiet forests; the alpine wildflowers; and the great elk herd of the Olympics were things of mystery and hope. The Recreational Area Study Act passed in 1936 sought to identify those outdoor needs.

Biologist Wright had done some preliminary work for the study to identify places where parks mainly for play—not ecological conservation—could be situated. It seemed odd, even to him, that he should be tagged to give such input, but he concluded that establishing more parks for the specific purpose of recreation would ease the stress on sensitive, overrun parks like Yosemite. That work in part led to the first national recreation area (Lake Mead in 1936) and the first national seashore (Cape Hatteras in 1937).

But Wright would not live to see that happen. While on duty for the NPS, he was killed in a car accident when returning from Big Bend National Park, at age thirty-one. Roger Toll, the superintendent of Yellowstone, was also killed in that crash. Of his longtime friend and colleague, with whom he had explored Alaska, Thompson said, "George was an unusually effective champion of his cause— idealistic, hard working, highly sociable, keenly perceptive of other people, always generous, and unconcerned about personal status."

Ultimately, Wright's work endured—although not right away—both within the Park Service and in the larger field of conservation biology. He and other pioneering scientists, led by Joseph Grinnell, had looked at the natural world in such a way that they could see the interplay species had with their environments, including the role habitat plays in the health of species; the symbiosis of plants and animals in ecosystems; the purpose of predators; and food chain dynamics. Their contributions are still evident in the management and preservation of countless parks. In *Fauna No. 1* Wright had written, "[O]ur national heritage is richer than just scenic features; the realization is coming that perhaps our greatest national heritage is nature itself, with all its complexity and its abundance of life, which, when combined with great scenic beauty as it is in the national parks, becomes of unlimited value."

Wright and the other early NPS ecologists also were champions of the remarkable experiences possible in parks, if they were managed to prioritize nature. In his own way, so was Sequoia Superintendent John White. By the time he spoke at the superintendents' conference in 1936, he had been at Sequoia for nearly two decades, and his voice resonated. During a speech entitled "Atmosphere in the National Parks," he said, "We should boldly ask ourselves whether we want the national parks to duplicate the features and entertainments of other resorts, or whether we want them to stand for something distinct, and we hope better, in our national life."

White had been pushing back hard on the proposed Sierra Way, a road that would have cut clear through Sequoia's backcountry. A highway scheme popular with local businesspeople, it would have rivaled Glacier's Going-to-the-Sun Road or

IF YOU LIKE ANSEL ADAMS, YOU'LL LOVE GEORGE GRANT

As the first chief photographer of the NPS, from 1929 to 1954, George Grant traveled more than 500,000 miles and captured upwards of 40,000 images in at least 140 parks. His photographs formed a documentary reservoir used in all manner of NPS publications and projects. (In this book, his photos appear on pages 103, 122, 125, and 156.) Grant's eye was unique and his work iconic, though few know his name. The credit line on many of his images reads only "National Park Service." Grant shares the title Eminent Photographer with several others who have contributed a large body of work to the bureau, including its third director, Arno Cammerer.

Shenandoah's Skyline Drive. Both White and the NPS had initially supported at least parts of the project, but that soured as the opposition from scientists and private groups like the Sierra Club intensified. The acting NPS director at the time, Arthur Demaray, told Interior Secretary Ickes what he thought of the Sierra Way: It was an "unjustifiable and destructive invasion of a great national resource, the primitive and unspoiled grandeur of the Sierra," he said. As evidenced by the huge roadless area encompassing the Middle Fork of the Kaweah River, the project was defeated.

A second generation of leadership began to rise within the NPS, one that invested more moral responsibility in preserving roadless terrain. It would take decades before legislative protection for wilderness came on the scene. A necessary first step in that direction was a critical shift in mindset such as was seen in 1938, when a national park was formed encompassing Mount Olympus National Monument and large swaths of Olympic National Forest.

Just a few months later, at a Northwest Conservation League meeting in Seattle, speaking with the zealousness with which he fought for the park, Ickes declared that the NPS would do differently by Olympic. He said, "When a national park is established, the insistent demand is to build roads everywhere, to build broad easy trails, to build air fields, to make it possible for everybody to go everywhere—without effort . . . But let us preserve a still larger representative area in its primitive condition for all time by excluding roads. Limit the roads. Make the trails safe but not too easy, and you will preserve the beauty of the parks for untold generations. Yield to the thoughtless demand for easy travel, and in time the few wilderness areas that are left to us will be nothing but the backyards of filling stations." Ickes commented also about the drawbacks of fame for national parks and the need to protect them from abundant admirers. How best to shield Olympic? "Keep it wilderness," he said.

With a victory of a kind for the lonely Olympic Peninsula, wilderness backers ramped up their campaign for California's popular Kings Canyon —once a favorite refuge of Mather and Muir before him. Muir had compared it to Yosemite, calling Kings a "grander valley of the same kind." In the wake of ranchers and timber companies, of irrigators and hydroelectric entrepreneurs—who sometimes fought among themselves, to the benefit of park advocates—local residents had been striving for some level of preservation since the 1870s. The Sierra Club had joined the fight in 1892 and never let up, but at least a dozen legislative attempts at protection between 1911 and 1926 had sunk. However, pressure from the Sierra Club and, later, the Wilderness Society was key to the Forest Service's inclusion of a primitive area in its rival Sequoia National Forest plan. The USFS courted wilderness purists while fueling local sentiment that the so-called land-hungry NPS was apathetic to their economic needs.

In the mid-1930s, Ickes and the NPS fought back with both fists, launching a media blitz that would have made Mather proud. Ickes even employed Ansel Adams to photograph Kings Canyon and then circulated those images. In the relentless campaign to win over Californians, the NPS made a lot of promises and compromises, not all of which it kept. As the push toward a park edged ever closer to success, the battle between the two agencies got downright dirty. Accusations flew back and forth over wiretapping, bullying, burglary, and even bribery. On the heels of a political scandal that discredited the main local congressional opponent of the bill and swayed other members of Congress to support the park, Kings Canyon became a national park in 1940, joining only a handful of wilderness parks under the NPS umbrella.

It was a complicated time for the Park Service; it had embraced the Everglades as its first wilderness park, as well as Isle Royale, Olympic,

Big Bend, Joshua Tree, and the Channel Islands in the 1930s with Kings Canyon following in 1940. From 1933 to 1941, NPS lands expanded from 8.2 million acres to more than 20 million acres. The national park system was maturing, was well-known and well loved. But any commitment to science that had grown during that decade seemed to falter.

Years later, Sumner reflected on the 1936 passing of his pioneering colleague, which he felt had precipitated the subsequent demoting of science at the Park Service: "During the first few years after George Wright's death, the continuing momentum of projects already underway largely overshadowed a vague, disquieting impression that the needs of the biological program were not receiving the same understanding and support at the highest level that they once had," he said. Not long after that, Sumner wrote a paper entitled "Losing the Wilderness Which We Set Out to Preserve," again emphasizing the importance of carefully managing primitive areas to retain their wilderness characteristics.

The 1930s closed with a final blow: the death of Joseph Grinnell, the University of California–Berkeley professor who had been a consummate mentor and adviser to a generation of NPS scientists. His influence and ideas would live on, though the onset of World War II and the role parks were thrust into during it would shelve concepts of ecological connectivity indefinitely. That same year, the number of biologists at the NPS shrank to just nine, a third of what it had been just a few years earlier on George Wright's careful watch.

PART III
1940–1979

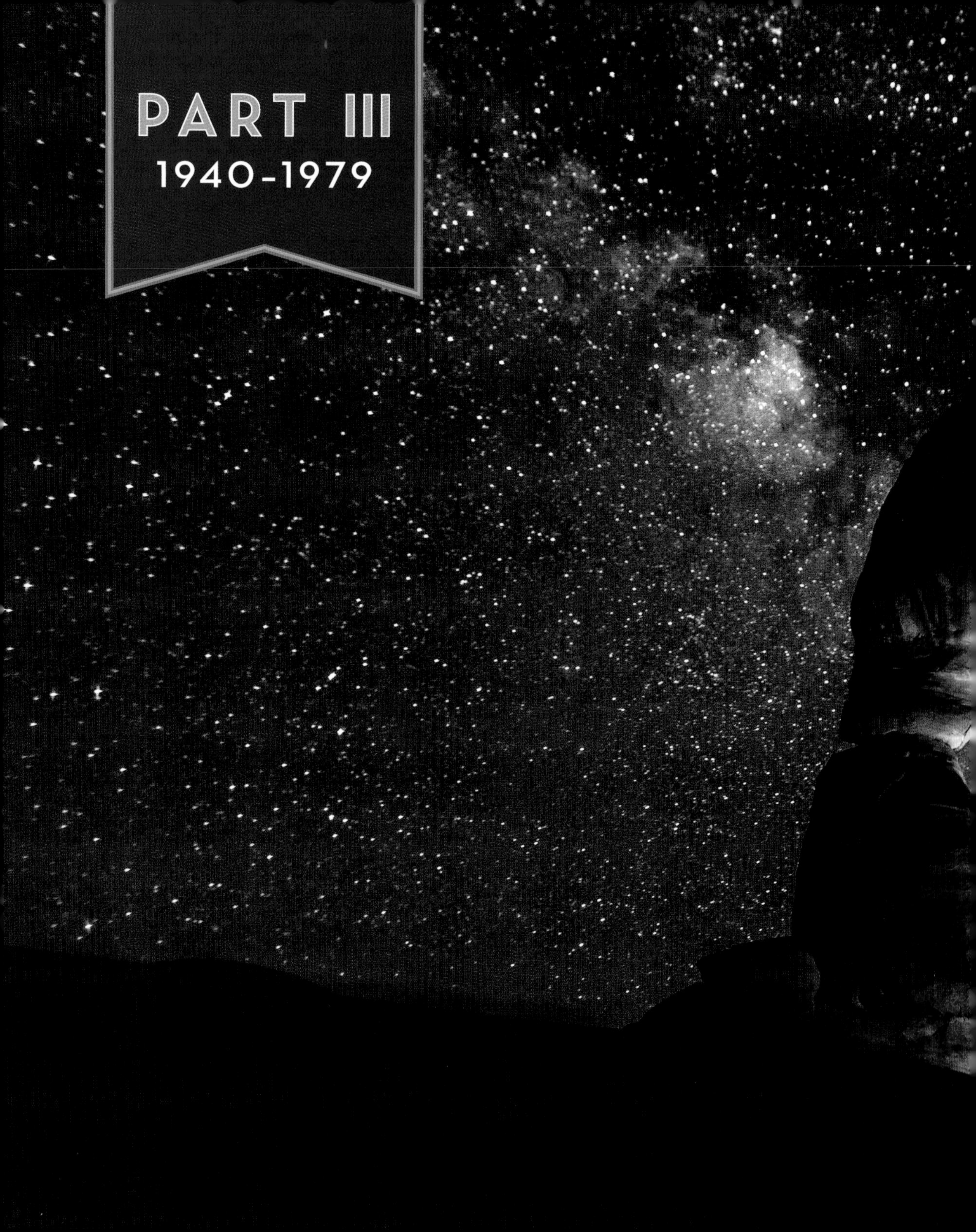

CHAPTER 16

Parks During World War II: A Nation Worth Fighting For

ON THE MORNING of December 7, 1941, US Navy officer Alfred Kame'eiamoku Rodrigues was on duty at the Bishop's Point base at the entrance to Pearl Harbor on Oahu, Hawaii. When an alarm sounded at the approach of enemy aircraft, twenty-one-year-old Rodrigues raced to the armory. From there he could see red Rising Suns on the wings of incoming Japanese planes. Rodrigues began firing his .30-caliber revolver at the aircraft overhead, which, he recalled, were flying so low he could see the faces of the pilots.

The horror that unfolded that day left 2341 Navy, Marine Corps, Army, and Army Air Force and 49 civilian personnel dead. The majority of those killed were on the USS *Arizona*, which sank after its forward ammunition exploded and burned for two days. Most of the 1777 sailors killed on the ship remain entombed there, and above them there is now a powerful memorial. The site is part of the World War II Valor in the Pacific National Monument, made up of nine areas in Hawaii, Alaska, and California—five of which are in Pearl Harbor. The offshore memorial, a long white cylinder whose ends flare upward, stretches across the waist of the sunken ship, appearing to float on the surface of the harbor. Its architect, Alfred Preis, described the design as having a low center, which expresses initial defeat, but with ends that are raised to convey strength and stability. "The overall effect is one of serenity," he said.

The USS *Arizona* (BB-39) burns after the Japanese attack on Pearl Harbor on December 7, 1941.

The United States was shaken to its core by the bombing of Pearl Harbor, which drew the nation into World War II. Within a matter of weeks, prosperity turned to austerity. The Civilian Conservation Corps was dissolved, the National Park Service budget was slashed, staff dropped away in large numbers (many swapped ranger uniforms for military ones), and park development and expansion was shut down. Although national parks remained open, gas was being rationed, rubber was in short supply, and sightseeing by bus or automobile was frowned upon. Visitation dropped 55 percent from 1941 to 1942.

At the dawn of the new decade, the NPS Wildlife Division had been absorbed into the US Fish and Wildlife Service and became the Office of National Park Wildlife. The move was a startling

indication of the Park Service's desire to get out of the science business while the thinking of foresters continued to dominate policies affecting national parks. At the time, those joining the ranger ranks were primarily trained in forestry, and most perpetuated the politics and practice of fire, insect, and predator suppression in their individual parks. After the United States entered WWII, research, publications, and monitoring programs were all tossed aside. Wilderness was relegated to the background as well—any activists remaining on the home front had their hands full deflecting poachers groping for park resources.

The 1918 director's report had concluded that "any argument that the use of the national parks will noticeably increase the production of wool or meat is ridiculous beyond expression." But at the onset of World War II the NPS had the same arguments, as if scripted, with a similar cast of characters. Parks were again beset by claims that their resources were needed to win the war; just as in the first world war, if it could be eaten

THAT'S A FACT

The National Park Service headquarters moved to Chicago during World War II so its Washington, DC, headquarters could be used for wartime activities.

or used to manufacture something, someone demanded to exploit it. This time around, the loggers, hunters, and ranchers locked horns with two tough conservationists: NPS Director Newton Drury and Secretary of the Interior Harold Ickes. Drury, who had come to the NPS from heading the Save-the-Redwoods League, took a proactive approach to managing parks during wartime. He and Ickes focused on how parks could contribute to the war effort without suffering irreparable harm.

During the nearly four years the United States was embroiled in the war, stands of virgin hemlock and red spruce were targeted in Great Smoky Mountains National Park; Yosemite's meadows were again favored for grazing; mineral deposits in Death Valley and Organ Pipe Cactus national monuments were sought; and, once more, the Olympic Peninsula's Sitka spruce were on the chopping block, as were those in Glacier Bay National Monument. Ickes and Drury agreed that park resources should be used solely as a last resort. They felt any concession, big or small, threatened the mandate outlined in the Organic Act of 1916. They fought to prevent, in Drury's words, a "breakdown of the national park concept."

Still, the NPS faced daily harrying, often in the public forum. A former head of the USFS, William Greeley, was editorialized in the *Seattle Post-Intelligencer* in 1943. He believed that Olympic "should do its part towards victory by giving up certain of its fine grade, old growth timber to the war effort. The principle of the draft should extend from our boys to our resources. Nothing is too sacred to do its share."

Infantry soldiers haul a 37-millimeter gun up a mountain pass in Alaska during training.

Most extractive advances were rebuffed—but not all: tungsten was mined near the northwest boundary of Yosemite, salt was harvested in Death Valley, and spruce was culled from the temperate rain forest of the Olympic Peninsula in an area in the process of being added to the national park. To deflect grazing demands, the Park Service calculated that its employees, and others within the Interior Department, could cut their beef consumption by one-third to offset the request—which they offered to do. Nevertheless, some grazing permits were granted during the war; cattle grazing in parks increased by about 14 percent and sheep grazing by roughly 5 percent—a remarkably low amount considering the intensity of the advances.

Kalaloch Lodge in Olympic National Park served as a US Coast Guard outpost. A radar station was built in Redwood National Park (disguised as a barn and farmhouse) and monitored by a thirty-five-member Army Air Corps crew working twenty-four-hour shifts. Other defense installations appeared in Acadia, Hawai'i Volcanoes, Glacier Bay, and Olympic parks. There were military maneuvers in Hawai'i Volcanoes and Mount McKinley (now Denali) national parks. Extended training for troops took place in Yellowstone, Yosemite, Isle Royale, Shenandoah, and Death Valley. Cabrillo and Fort Pulaski national monuments were used for coastal defense and closed to the public. Part of Badlands National Monument was used as an Air Force gunnery, and Joshua Tree National Park supplied the proper conditions for desert warfare training.

Other parks served as training grounds for winter warfare for ski troops, paratroopers, and saboteurs who would work behind enemy lines. The Paradise and Tatoosh lodges in Mount Rainier served as base camp for the US Army Eighty-Seventh Mountain Infantry Battalion (later combined with the Tenth Mountain Division). During these mountain maneuvers—in heavy snow, at high elevation, in subzero temperatures—soldiers experimented with food rations and tested clothing and equipment such as ski wax, sunscreen, and stoves. And, of course, they trained on snowshoes and skis. One expedition in May 1942 summited the 14,411-foot mountain and was documented in a ski-training film.

Members of the civilian National Ski Patrol acted as guides and shared winter survival tips, including avalanche awareness. Those volunteers bested troops (who'd routinely returned to camp hypothermic) in clothing from L. L. Bean and Bass, schooling soldiers about the best gear available to endure winter conditions. The Tenth Mountain Division went on to fight in the roughest terrain of the Italian Alps, seeing combat on 114 days. They

suffered significant casualties—992 were killed in action and another 4154 were injured. "There is hardly an area in the National Park System that has not made some direct contribution to aid in winning the war," Drury said.

Scientists were largely reactive during that time, and a handful were dispatched only when an issue had gotten too big to ignore. At times when they asserted science-based policies in regard to hot-button issues such as downsizing bison herds or ending bear shows in Yellowstone, they met a staunch opponent in former NPS Director Horace Albright. While Albright was in the private sector by that time, he often weighed in, particularly when it came to Yellowstone, where he had been superintendent for a decade.

As Albright had told biologist Joseph Dixon in the 1930s: "Yellowstone has always been the 'bear park.' I would rather see bears not appear at all in other parts of the system than see any material change in the bear shows at Yellowstone." The statement was classic first-guard NPS: parks are for people, and the animals there must be managed to delight them. Albright also argued with Drury about efforts to end bear and bison feeding and the orchestrated bison stampedes, saying that national parks were not "biologic units." But Drury stood

US military planes fly over mountains in Alaska in February 1942.

or unconsciously there is built up within all who have had such experiences an increased faith in our country. Can these experiences fail to strengthen the conviction that this is a nation worth fighting for?"

The NPS director, who had served in the army in WWI and perhaps knew from experience, also insisted that parklands promoted healing. He made sure soldiers had full access to parks before, in between, and following deployments. Military rest and recreation camps were set up in Carlsbad Caverns, Grand Canyon, Mount McKinley (now Denali), and Sequoia national parks. Out of 6.8 million visitors to national parks in 1943, 1.6 million were soldiers.

In his magazine article, Drury recounted: "A new form of use has arisen. Since Pearl Harbor, approximately two million members of the armed forces have visited the areas administered by the National Park Service. There is significant meaning and definite justification of the national park concept in the fact that increasing thousands of members of the armed forces are being given opportunities they never had before and may never have again to see the inspiring beauty of this land of ours. A typical letter from the commanding officer of one battalion states: 'Officers and enlisted men of this battalion join with me in expressing our appreciation to you and the members of your staff for the enjoyable time spent at Grand Canyon. I am sure the pleasant memories of this battalion's visit to Grand Canyon will long be remembered as a most worthwhile and educational trip.'"

by the *Fauna No. 1* policies outlined by Wright and his colleagues. "[O]ur aim . . . should be to place each wild species . . . on its own, without dependence on man, and occupying its natural niche in the biota of the park," said Drury.

Drury used the press to wage his own public relations battle against extractive interests; he took to the radio, gave speeches, and wrote magazine articles about NPS war efforts and the importance of parks. Parks inspired patriotism, gave inspiration, and renewed courage, he said; Americans were fighting in Europe to protect the values that homeland parks embodied. From coast to coast, national parks were icons to be preserved and not profited from. "Pride in America swells in the hearts of all who look upon the mile-deep chasm of Grand Canyon, the geysers and hot springs of Yellowstone, the thundering waterfalls of Yosemite, the towering Sequoias, and the sweep of mighty forests on the Olympic Peninsula," Drury wrote in *American Forests* magazine. "Consciously

Drury also opened many park facilities, including Lava Beds National Monument, as recuperation areas for the military. "In war, no less than in peace, the national park areas serve as havens of refuge for those fortunate enough to be able to visit them," he wrote. "Affording an environment that gives relief from the tension of a warring world, the parks are, even now, being looked upon as a factor in the physical and mental rehabilitation that will be increasingly desirable as the war progresses."

From 1943 through 1945, Yosemite's posh Ahwahnee Hotel was transformed into a navy hospital. Injured sailors and marines convalesced amid rivers, rock walls, and waterfalls with temporary recreational additions that included a pool hall, pub, movie hall, dance band, bowling alley, and

US troops and NPS rangers offload supplies on Denali's Kahiltna Glacier during an attempt to summit the peak in 2013.

Pearl Harbor survivors salute during the seventy-first anniversary ceremonies at the World War II Valor in the Pacific National Monument.

library. Their time there helped to reintegrate them slowly into mainstream society.

The same was true of many survivors of Pearl Harbor who, after retiring from military service, volunteered at the national monument to interpret that day and to share their memories with a new generation. Some of those witnesses to infamy were drawn back to fully process the shock of those events. Some came to visit with the spirits of friends they never saw again after that day, who remain forever in the depths of Pearl Harbor and, as one volunteer described it, eternally in their hearts.

Master Sergeant Richard Fiske, US Air Force (retired), volunteered for many years. One of his special duties was to place two roses every month at the USS *Arizona* memorial at the request and expense of Zenji Abe, a Japanese pilot who had been part of the attack that day. After laying down the flowers, Fiske played taps on his bugle. He told countless visitors he understood that Abe was just obeying orders that December day, and he no longer harbored any ill will toward him or others. In time that particular tune, of hatred and hostility, had changed.

Motorists stop for a photo-op in Great Smoky Mountains National Park circa 1950. Annual park visitation grew steadily following World War II, topping 33 million in 1950, and then skyrocketed to nearly 80 million in 1960.

CHAPTER 17

An Investment in Good Citizenship

TRAVELING NORTHWEST out of Moab, Utah, in just a few miles the road meets the strapping Colorado River, which forms 11 winding miles of the southern boundary of Arches National Park. A couple of miles farther west is the main entrance to the park, where the road switchbacks as it climbs the side of a canyon, gaining some 1200 feet in elevation. Along this roughly 20-mile-long main artery running nearly the length of the park lies one of the West's most alluring landscapes. Arches is a grab bag of geological masterpieces molded by time, temperature, and water. Sprawled out in every direction are mythical-looking spires, ruddy sandstone fins, soaring monoliths, and mysterious hoodoos with names including the Three Gossips, the Tower of Babel, and the Parade of Elephants.

The park also contains the densest concentration of natural stone arches in the world—more than 2000 have been discovered thus far. They include spans beneath which you could only crawl and others that would curve over city office buildings with room to spare. The Statue of Liberty could recline comfortably—twice!—along the length of Landscape Arch. The rock formations are geological oddities owing to the kind of rock here and a precise amount of precipitation (roughly 8 to 10 inches each year) that slowly erodes it. The products of those forces are sandstone sculptures, hardened chunks of buff- and salmon-colored clay molded as if by an unseen artist.

Arches gives the initial impression of being harsh, even barren, but it is a changeable land. Since 1970, forty-three arches have collapsed. The fragile, high-desert ecosystem brimming with cyanobacteria, algae, fungi, and lichen supports an astonishing array of desert plants, but it can be irrevocably damaged by mere footsteps. There's something peculiar about the light here; it seems more a living thing with breath than a mere by-product of Earth's angle toward the sun. When sunlight floods this desert expanse, a jumble of red-rock spans, sky-piercing pinnacles, and gravity-defying balanced rocks materialize.

On a sunrise hike to Delicate Arch, the whole place appears lit from within, pulsating with a reddish-orange warmth. The walk to the arch that was also called the Chaps and Old Maid's Bloomers in times past skirts the remains of the John Wesley Wolfe Ranch, a reminder of the uneasy existence eked out by homesteaders in this area of Utah in the late nineteenth century. Cross over the Salt Wash, and a short spur leads you to a striking panel of centuries-old Ute petroglyphs depicting a bighorn sheep hunt. Climb up over a cairn-studded slickrock face, follow the trail through a sandstone saddle filled with the scent of nearby pinyon and juniper, and edge along a cliff blasted from rock to reach the iconic freestanding arch. You can debate whether it is delicate, or perhaps defiant, as you repose within a sandstone amphitheater facing the arch upon its open-air stage.

Of Delicate Arch, a more than 50-foot-high beauty with a backdrop of the snow-dusted La Sal Mountains, writer and agitator Edward Abbey said, "For a few moments we discover that nothing can be taken for granted, for if this ring of stone is marvelous then all which shaped it is marvelous, and our journey here on earth, able to see and touch and hear in the midst of tangible and mysterious things-in-themselves, is the most strange and daring of all adventures."

Abbey worked as a seasonal ranger in Arches in the summers of 1956 and 1957, greeting tourists, teaching them things about the place, and occasionally disciplining them and/or saving their hides. He lived on the Willow Flats, near the improbably Balanced Rock—a chunk of stone the size of three tractor-trailers atop a pinched neck. That was at the end of what was then the main passage into the park: a rutted, occasionally flooded mess of a road.

Abbey's memoir about his time in the park, *Desert Solitaire*, is both a love letter to the landscape and a bitter rebuke of the forces that had begun to change Arches and other national park units by the mid-1950s. "Progress has come at last to the Arches, after a million years of neglect. Industrial Tourism has arrived," he scoffed. In Abbey's second season there, the Delicate Arch Trail was completed and just over 25,000 people visited the park. That same year saw the completion of a new entrance road that set the park on a path to unfettered popularity. Visitation increased by 106 percent the next year, topped 100,000 in 1962, and doubled again by the

Passing between the sheer sandstone walls of a narrow slot canyon in Arches National Park

HIKING

simply that the parks are being loved to death," said Wirth. "They are neither equipped nor staffed to protect their irreplaceable resources, nor to take care of their increasing millions of visitors." He told the administration that national parks had been beset by 50 million visitors in the past year and predicted that, by the NPS's fiftieth birthday, in 1966, there would be 80 million. In his impassioned appeal, Wirth went on to sell a package of park improvements that would be rolled out over the next decade. The program was called Mission 66. A major overhaul of park infrastructure and management, it shaped the parks into what we know today.

In peacetime following World War II, tourism rebounded spectacularly to prewar levels but investment in parks did not. The NPS director at the time, Newton Drury, made no effort to obscure the conditions in some parks, made deplorable by wartime neglect, scant agency budgets, and a crush of visitors. To solve what he called the "dilemma of our parks"—to protect and develop them—required a major and consistent influx of cash. But during the postwar period economic stimulus via public works flowed more readily into roads, housing, and dams. Parks slipped further into disrepair, and their owners—the American public—would have to rage against the decline before turning Congress's head.

As the 1950s dawned, Drury resigned, Arthur Demaray served briefly as NPS director, then Conrad Wirth was installed, serving from 1951 to 1964, under four presidents—the longest of any director to date. The US economy was bulking up, as were

time Arches National Monument was redesignated as a national park in 1971. It now exceeds 1 million visitors per year, a 3700 percent increase from Abbey's day.

Whether or not Abbey knew it, just two months before the twenty-nine-year-old ranger took up residence in what he described as his "little tin government housetrailer," the gauntlet for major change in parks had already been thrown down. In January 1956, National Park Service director Conrad Wirth briefed President Dwight Eisenhower and his cabinet on the state of the national park system. "The problem of today is household incomes, but funding for parks was still low. As more Americans steered their shiny Fords, Chevys, and Chryslers out of suburbs blooming with tract housing and onto smooth new interstate highways to visit national parks, the parks' disrepair became impossible to ignore. Americans were becoming accustomed to a certain level of comfort, predictability, and consumption. The lack of working toilets in Shenandoah or the trash piling up in Yosemite Valley would not do. Many people also had more leisure time and wanted to spend it playing; in 1955 they spent $14 billion on recreation, a huge leap since before World War II.

The backlash against park deterioration and ruined vacations was tantamount to an angry mob congregating on the NPS's doorstep. Media coverage of the situation was widespread and relentless. In his 1953 *Harper's* magazine column, "Let's Close the National Parks," popular historian Bernard DeVoto decried damage done by vandals and slumlike conditions in campgrounds. While championing devoted, hardworking NPS staff, he chronicled the downhill slide of parks in the shadow of miserly congressional appropriations. DeVoto wrote that the NPS was being required "to operate a big plant on a hot-dog-stand budget."

He figured the amount needed to clear maintenance backlogs and to position parks better for the onslaught of tourists would not be forthcoming, so he suggested the park system be reduced to a size for which Congress was willing to pay: "The Service is like a favorite figure of American legendry," he wrote, "the widow who scrapes and patches and ekes out, who by desperate expedients succeeds in bringing up her children to be a credit to our culture . . . But it stops there, short of the necessary miracle . . . So much of the priceless heritage which the Service must safeguard for the United States is

beginning to go to hell." The whole situation was, he argued, a national disgrace. For years, many other national magazines and newspapers railed against the declining state of parks, often quoting Wirth, who spoke candidly about the dire nature of the problem.

A landscape architect by training, Wirth had been chief land planner for the NPS and had been intimately involved in the New Deal development of parks prior to becoming director. Wirth framed the Mission 66 scheme patriotically and fiscally—just as FDR had the Civilian Conservation Corps—as a way to strengthen both moral fiber and bank accounts. Wirth told Eisenhower, "To put the national parks in shape is an investment in the physical, mental and spiritual well-being of Americans as individuals. It is a gainful investment contributing substantially to the national economy, as I have mentioned. It is an investment in good citizenship." Swept by Wirth and the tide of public opinion, the president and Congress eagerly endorsed the Mission 66 program—to the tune of $1 billion over ten years.

Wirth announced the program at a banquet sponsored by the NPS, the Department of the Interior, and, tellingly, the American Automobile Association. Once again, as it had when the NPS came into being, the automobile would precipitate another wave of park development. Some 60 million cars were registered in 1955, double the number a decade earlier. Better highways and cheaper cars made parks from California to Maine closer than ever to booming population bases. The millions of visitors that Frederick Law Olmsted Sr. had imagined in 1865 had finally materialized. Less than a century later, in 1955, Yosemite, Yellowstone, Rocky Mountain, Shenandoah, and Great Smoky Mountains national parks annually

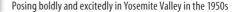

of postwar America. Single-family homes, personal vehicles, and new shopping centers, where people could get everything they needed in one spot, drove the demand for what people expected to find on vacation in their parks. This desire and the need to manage crowds made planning, technology, and architecture hallmarks of Mission 66. Wirth told park superintendents to make bold changes and be imaginative about taking their parks above and beyond the so-called stagecoach economy on which many were originally based.

The result was new and updated roads, entrance stations, trails, ranger stations, observation towers, campgrounds, picnic areas, parking, wayside exhibits, amphitheaters, staff housing, water, sewer and power lines, and, of course, visitor centers. Quaint log museums gave way to more than a hundred bunker-style visitor centers—from Antietam to Zion—that functioned as one-stop shops for Main Street America. Here, crowds could meet a ranger, hear an interpretative talk, watch a film, embark on a short nature walk, admire museum displays, use restrooms, and even buy their postcards to send back home. Park Service modern displaced Park Service rustic as the new parkitecture.

The relative enormity and concrete flatness of the new visitor centers was criticized as having an urbanizing effect on parks. But Wirth and his hundreds-strong staff of landscape architects, engineers, and structural architects believed the functional style—which lacked the eye-catching grandeur of the rustic structures—ultimately distracted less from the surrounding landscape. The mod structures also cost less to build and to maintain than their more romantic predecessors. The

saw between 1 and 2 million visitors *each*—and nearly all arrived by car.

For those who may have needed some convincing to visit the parks, given the bad press they'd been getting, Sinclair Oil Corporation ran a series of full-page advertisements. They highlighted the Everglades, Mesa Verde, and other parks and made specific mention of Wirth and his new initiative: "From coast to coast, *Mission 66* means better vacations for you" one ad said, explaining that improved roads, sanitation, overnight facilities, and interpretive activities were part of the bargain. Standard Oil Company sponsored a radio program on parks; Phillips Petroleum distributed a guide to Mission 66 improvements.

Far from being the sole vision of an NPS director, Mission 66 was a response to the demands cookie-cutter approach to park facilities made them immediately recognizable to people who may have been to Yellowstone but not yet to Grand Teton.

Mission 66 also catered to the popular passion for recreational tourism by adding facilities specifically for play, including ski lifts, marinas, skating rinks, aerial tramways, and stables. And while accommodations had been improved for those wanting to greet a new day inside a park, improved roads and centralized activity gave rise to the day-use model that endures today.

Whether people came to the national parks because they were enticed by the upgrades or were driven by postwar affluence, visitation system-wide more than doubled from 1956 to 1966; Wirth had predicted 80 million, but the total by then was, in fact, 133 million. For Wirth, the NPS, and the visiting public, Mission 66 made good on its promise. It also perpetuated the NPS founders' vision of parks as places for people to enjoy. It confirmed that national parks and monuments, and everything in between, were close to the hearts of average Americans. As Wirth had said at Eisenhower's cabinet meeting, "The national parks have become a real part of the American way of life." To this day, Mission 66 is seen as a kind of golden age of the NPS, when citizens and members of Congress alike supported large-scale investment in parks.

But not everybody was happy about it. To its critics, Mission 66's devotion to development spelled disaster for parks. Their dissent, which grew louder and more influential during the decade-long program, ultimately helped precipitate the modern environmental movement. Conservation groups such as the National Parks Conservation

Association, Sierra Club, and Wilderness Society mostly had shared a long, mutually beneficial partnership with the NPS up until this point. Now, at the root of the disagreement between them was the meaning and purpose of "wilderness."

To Wirth and his old-school NPS contingency, one of Mission 66's main goals was the preservation of national park wilderness areas per the 1916 Organic Act mandate: to protect parks for use and enjoyment into the future. Their rationale was that, since an influx of park goers was inevitable, the best response was to contain public use with development. The documents upon which the Mission 66 program was based reveal that Wirth was focused on moving development out of sensitive areas and putting it in attractive and accessible areas that did not encroach on major park features. He wanted to know from superintendents what problems they had been encountering in protecting natural conditions, including "animal populations, plant associations, forestry management." Wirth also wanted more and better roads, it seems, to get people in and out of parks as quickly as possible. His number-one policy recommendation for Mission 66 was that visitation to national parks "should not be actively encouraged." The fact that fifty parks were added to the system during the mission's decade was also a sore spot for the director, who felt that system growth only diverted limited funds.

But these intentions, strategies, and opinions were not disclosed beyond the NPS ranks. The landmark Mission 66 plans were made and rolled out in grand fashion, without the consultation of historic NPS friends and confidants. These stakeholders, seeing only public relations blitzes announcing massive development in parks and fearing for the quintessence of wild places, felt

RECREATION ON A PLATTER

Bear shows finally ended in Yellowstone National Park in 1942, as park management reduced the amount of trash at the "public" dumps. This was done partially because of the growing understanding of the ecological importance of managing wildlife under natural conditions and partially due to the drop in visitors and their refuse when the United States entered World War II. But garbage disposal at parks didn't change; dumps remained open, and bears with a taste for people's scraps kept coming back. Roadside feedings by visitors also continued with scant recourse from park officials. As post-WWII visitor numbers increased at all parks, so did incidences of human injury and property damage.

Bears in parks were little understood until Olaus Murie (brother of Adolph) studied their movements and feeding habits in Yellowstone in the early 1940s. A biologist for the US Fish and Wildlife Service, he strongly opposed allowing bears access to any unnatural food sources. Not one to mince words, Murie responded bluntly to inquiries about the rights of tourists to see bears while visiting a park: "It is a question of whether we are justified in sacrificing some of the main purposes of a park, and endangering lives and property, in order to maintain a special display, furnish cute bear antics, however stimulating this may be to the public," he said. "I think the quality of a national park experience can be improved if we do not try to hand the visitor his recreation on a platter, but let him make at least a little exertion to find it." That mind-set, while familiar to present park goers, represented a major shift in thinking that prioritized the good of wildlife over the desires of humans.

Later came the famous Craighead study—named for the twin brothers who spent twelve years studying Yellowstone grizzlies—that tracked bear movements, habits, and numbers starting in 1959. The Craigheads were in favor of depriving bears of humans' snacks, but they endorsed a gradual weaning. This would acclimate bears to a post-trash existence in which they'd have to work harder to find food as well as minimize the human-bear clashes that would likely result from bears looking to supplement their diets from backpacks, cars, and campsites. If the dumps must be closed, said the Craigheads, ungulate carcasses should be made available to the bears until the situation stabilized. But the story didn't end there (see chapter 19).

alienated—and came into the ring swinging. Ed Abbey, that lover of sand verbena and solitude, took to calling the NPS the "National Parking Service" with a "Development Fever Faction." Ansel Adams, the famous photographer of parks, commented that with Mission 66, "the illusion of service-through-development has triumphed over the reality of protection-through-humility."

(He later backpedaled, however, saying that the program was undoubtedly well intended and an "excellent program of providing 'necessities' in terms of expected travel increases.")

Outside the parks, and across the country, open space was being gobbled up to satisfy a staggering appetite for subdivisions, making land that enjoyed federal protection that much more unique and valuable. Inside the parks, ecology was being over-shadowed by the Mission 66 build-a-thon. In 1950 the Park Service employed 150 landscape architects but only 8 scientists. NPS ecologist E. Lowell Sumner reflected on why programs dedicated to archaeology and history soon recovered to prewar levels but biology programs did not. "Interest in man's own activities of conquest and struggle has preceded by centuries an interest in understanding and protecting the natural environment on which he depends for his future survival," he said. The period he called the "eclipse for biology which lasted from 1942 to 1963" was marked with what he termed roadblocks and frustrations.

As the concept of wilderness continued to take shape, the Park Service was pressed to justify many of its own policies and actions. Such was the case in the Everglades when a row arose over building in what was then designated a wilderness park. The development prospectus, managed by the park's first superintendent, Daniel Beard (who had been a field biologist since the 1930s), had an ecological emphasis. But the hands-off approach, which banned hotel construction, didn't sit well with the locals. The state had donated a million acres toward the park with the understanding that it would be developed as a tourist attraction, they argued. Ultimately Wirth, champion of Mission 66, caved to the demand, and a hotel, cabins, and a swimming pool were built at Flamingo in 1959.

Whether conservationists were concerned with the Everglades, the Great Smoky Mountains, or Grand Teton, a paradox was becoming clear to many: the NPS was developing parks for a growing number of visitors but doing little to protect the resources those people were leaving home to experience.

Some progress was being made against artificial management of natural resources, particularly in terms of ending bear feeding and reducing predator kills. However, rangers continued to stock fish, fight forest fires, spray pesticides, poison "pests," feed bison in winter, and thin herds of bison, deer, and elk that (without being kept in check by predators) were decimating grasses, shrubs, wildflowers, and saplings.

NPS biologists kept pushing for policies that would restore some balance to the natural world, and they were backed up by outside groups. In the illuminating book *Preserving Nature in the National Parks*, Richard West Sellars shares a 1958 letter from Olaus Murie (who was the head of the Wilderness Society at the time) to Sumner in which Murie said that Mission 66 had caused "a confused outlook, in which the biological program suffers." While the Park Service might have splendid people, Murie said, its leadership was out of touch with what was taking place in regard to scientific understanding.

Nevertheless, the biologists pressed on, educating park goers about the breadth of natural resources while stealthily advancing their beliefs about wildlife management. NPS scientists were housed in the NPS Division of Interpretation after WWII, when they returned to the NPS from the US Fish and Wildlife Service. Under that division and without a strict scientific mandate, publications produced by the biologists in the 1950s were geared toward tourists. One glowing example of this is the 1953 *Birds and Mammals of the Sierra Nevada* written by Sumner and Joseph Dixon, which included their extensive field studies in Sequoia–Kings Canyon parks. This fascinating volume mixes scientific observations with messages intended to get readers thinking about the true benefit of park resources: "What is a giant sequoia worth, in dollars, as it stands deep in a forest where hermit thrushes sing?" they wrote. "What is the value of a sunset? Of a national park? Of freedom? We commonly say that their value is intangible, not properly expressible in dollars and cents. But that does not make them less precious."

They also defended some still-derided predators: coyotes. "Like people, coyotes vary," they wrote; "not all people rob banks, not all coyotes eat livestock . . . Traps and poison have silenced the coyote's howl over vast areas where once its nightly serenade seemed as much a part of the West as the smell of sagebrush and the limitless unfenced vistas. Can anyone, however devoted to hastening the 'economic maturity' of the West, watch this scene without some regret?" Photos illustrating the volume show a group of coyote pups emerging from their den and a mother bear standing guard while her cubs rest in the tree branches above.

But NPS leadership maintained the standoff until an eminent ecologist publicly shamed the bureau by shining a light on the lack of basic ecological research in parks. In a speech he gave at the Sierra Club's Sixth Biennial Wilderness Conference in 1959 entitled "Ecological Islands as Natural Laboratories," University of Michigan ecologist Stanley Cain warned that the NPS was missing a bet by not prioritizing science: "The first difficulty, as I see it, is that the research activities of the Service are directed toward immediate pressing problems," he said. "It is largely a matter of trouble-shooting." To Cain and others, the NPS's habit of only stepping in at the eleventh hour was counterintuitive. Instead the agency had to understand *why* an ecological shift was taking place. To know that, it had to have a clear handle on what resources each park had and how those ecosystems functioned. Cain concluded

the Park Service needed "a formal, continuing, and sufficiently massive program of ecological and systematic research."

Following the rebuke, Park Service biologists were thrown a bone: a $28,000 research budget for the entire park system. It was a paltry amount compared to the hundreds of millions being spent on physical development—and sadly similar to the annual allocations of the early 1930s. But Sumner recalled that it had a remarkable psychological effect and it encouraged research institutions to collaborate with the NPS.

The result was a somewhat revolutionary ream of in-house reports highlighting critical ecological conditions in many parks. Two came in 1960. The first was the far-reaching "Back Country Management Plan for Sequoia–Kings Canyon National Parks." It began with a detailed definition of "wilderness," which had been and would continue to be a touchy issue for the Park Service: "A wilderness is a large, undeveloped, wild area extending beyond roads and developments for permanent occupancy, in which one can experience solitude, quiet, beauty, a sense of adventure, and feelings of remoteness from modern civilization, including mechanized transportation—and in which the drama of natural forces is permitted to unfold without interference except for such management practices as may be required to counteract major destructive influences." The second report came from a committee chaired by the Everglades' superintendent, Dan Beard. The internal report, which Sellars cites in his book, said that park resources were "actually endangered by ignorance" because of the cold shoulder given to scientific research and management.

But identifying the problem and doing something about it were still oceans apart at the NPS.

Sumner himself described that era in this way: "Meanwhile, in the parklands themselves, biological time-bombs had gone on ticking through all the years of inattention. Now giant sequoias were leaning and falling with attention-getting frequency and people were asking why, fears were being expressed that DDT was becoming an ever greater biological hazard, that the saguaros of Saguaro National Monument were vanishing, that Yosemite Valley was becoming choked beyond recognition by an unnatural and hazardous invasion of trees, that feral goats threatened the survival of unique vegetation in the national parks of Hawaii, and that Everglades National Park was dying of thirst."

As always, there were people within the NPS who shared the belief that research was critical to protection of resources. And there were some, albeit on the fringes, who shared a philosophy of wilderness with outside conservationists—some had even made progress at the NPS policy level, such as in the "Back Country Management Plan for Sequoia–Kings Canyon" report. But these advances came fitfully, like stumbling over scree, on a park-by-park basis. There was no Park Service–wide recognition, a situation that caused a gap between NPS leadership and their former conservation champions on the outside. In that gap lay the essence of wilderness character: What was it? How should it be defended?

The visitor center overlooking Antietam National Battlefield is typical Mission 66—a modern approach intended to blend into its surrounding. The light gray masonry and the way the building's tiers follow the slope evoke the region's tradition of fieldstone wall and bridge building.

The answer to those questions had been rooted decades before Mission 66 was conceived, when the first influx of cars swarmed the parks. Public relations guru Robert Sterling Yard, who'd been hired by Stephen Mather, had split from the Park Service largely over the issue of how easy the NPS was making it to get to and move within parks. Despite having worked tirelessly writing copy that successfully lured Americans to parks, Yard had a change of heart when he felt parks were becoming *too* popular. In 1923 he expressed growing alarm that no laws existed to "specify in set terms that the conservation of these parks shall be complete conservation."

The upswing in building during the CCC years only heightened that anxiety. In Yard's first article for the Wilderness Society's publication, *Living Wilderness*, he wrote, "The fashion is to barber and manicure wild America as smartly as the modern girl. Our duty is clear." He continued,

KEEP IT DOWN!

The National Park Service's Natural Sounds and Night Skies Division works to protect and restore darkness and quiet to parks. Seeing and hearing landscapes as they were millennia ago is a growing rarity and a vital component of maintaining wilderness character. In "dark sky" national parks, visitors can enter a celestial world that is lost to artificial light pollution in most other places. The International Dark-Sky Association has recognized several US national parks, including Big Bend, Death Valley, Natural Bridges, Hovenweep, and Chaco Culture National Historical Park, as some of the darkest skies in the world that can be accessed by the general public.

Noise pollution is just as big a problem as light interference—for resident wildlife and visiting humans—so the NPS and partners are studying soundscape maintenance and experimenting with quiet zones in parks, as well as working (with much difficulty) to reduce aircraft overhead. Which are considered some of the quietest national parks? Great Basin, Isle Royale, and North Cascades top the list.

"Furthermore, we believe that the great majority of careless and casual enjoyers of the out-of-doors (and what American does not enjoy his out-of-doors?) would join heartily in preservation if only he realized the exquisiteness of primeval nature, the majesty of much of it, and that once destroyed, it can never be returned to its thrilling sequence from the infinite."

Yard had a kindred spirit in Aldo Leopold, the eloquent scientist and naturalist (and longtime US Forest Service employee). In his 1938 essay "Conservation Esthetic" in *Bird-Lore* (later *Audubon*)—which became part of his renowned volume *A Sand County Almanac*—Leopold encapsulated the conflict between recreationists and wilderness purists: "Like ions shot from the sun, the weekenders radiate from every town, generating heat and friction as they go. A tourist industry purveys bed and board to bait more ions, faster, further . . . Bureaus build roads into new hinterlands, then buy more hinterlands to absorb the exodus accelerated by the roads . . . But to him who seeks something more, recreation has become a self-destructive process of seeking but never quite finding, a major frustration of mechanized society."

Recreation was becoming as big a threat to public lands as logging or mining ever could be, Leopold believed. It seemed history was repeating itself; the same issue of use versus preservation that had given rise to the national park movement itself and led to the founding of the Park Service came roaring back. The *use* in this case was millions of visitors coming to parks to play, and the *preservation* was an attempt to safeguard certain areas from those masses. For Leopold, wilderness had to be preserved in a natural state, had to have lines drawn around it that permanently differentiated it from easily accessed and influenced nature.

The NPS had its own definition and understanding of the concept of wilderness. In essence, the bureau reasoned that without a "front country," where people oohed and aahed at viewpoints and roasted marshmallows at campgrounds, there would be no backcountry. If most people limited themselves to features readily accessible by car, the rest would remain, essentially, wild. And if there was no backcountry, no scenic vistas to admire or great expanses to contemplate from afar, there would be essentially no purpose for parks. One could not exist without the other.

This had been the logic used by Stephen Mather and Horace Albright, and it was more or less the rationale under which Wirth was operating in the Mission 66 decade. Among the so-called propaganda distributed during Mission 66 was an NPS publication called "The National Park Wilderness," which was a response to the growing criticism of development. Right up front it posed the question: What is a wilderness area? "Ten people will give you 10 different answers to the question," it said. "Does wilderness preservation mean discarding the tradition of National Park hospitality and require rationing of visitors, elimination of lodges and campgrounds, or other radical changes? . . . The National Park Service seeks a sane and practical middle ground, with no compromise whatsoever with the basic and traditional purpose of the National Parks."

The publication went on to allow that wilderness could have a trail, a campsite, a fence, or even a fire lookout. But its basic quality had to be defined in terms of "personal experience, feelings, or benefits." It concluded, "Wilderness is a physical condition. Wilderness is also a state of mind." In this regard, the NPS and its critics seemed in alliance, but they ultimately parted ways over whether or not there should be areas within national parks that were permanently protected from human influence. The rift grew, and "wilderness" soon became a political concept, one that would contribute to landmark environmental legislation passed throughout the 1960s and 1970s.

In the thick of it all was Ed Abbey, who ventured onward from the stone sentinels and desert profusion of Arches, first as a seasonal ranger in Organ Pipe Cactus National Monument, then at Everglades National Park and Lassen Volcanic National Park, where he was a fire lookout. As much as he raged against the onslaught of industrial tourism and against the NPS for facilitating it, he also wrote, "As government agencies go, the Park Service is a good one, far superior to most." He could unleash a ream of expletives on bureaucrats but called NPS rangers in the field capable, honest, and dedicated.

Despite the changes at Arches, Abbey did return to it for one last season, in 1965, drawn back to what he called its spiritual appeal. The simplicity of the desert and the clarity of its light were a kind of remedy for him—as they still are for many—to a modern society of endless concrete, two-car garages, and societal expectations. At night, when the steel-and-glass army of cars has marched off, an utter darkness seeps over the landscape, a celestial dome forming overhead. National parks, and Arches in particular, are among the few places left where you can see night skies more or less as they were millennia ago. Using Delicate Arch as a portal, you can look up into the Milky Way and down the very gullet of Earth's galaxy, existing at that moment in communion with wild wonder.

Neve Glacier and Snowfield Peak in the rugged North Cascades, where glaciated peaks jut from thickly timbered valleys

CHAPTER 18

Those Wild Sixties

THE TRAIL UP to Cascade Pass zigs and zags gradually, first lined with ferns and moss-draped conifers; then, as it emerges from the forest, it opens up to a surreal panorama of the lower half of North Cascades National Park. Snow and ice can persist here right up to Independence Day, but when it dissolves into mountain streams, countless waterfalls roar to life and ice drops from hanging glaciers with a thunderous clamor. This meadow is then brilliant with red columbine, pink-studded heather, and glacier lilies in shades of yellow that mimic summer sun.

At the pass, marmots warm themselves and pikas scamper among rocky outcroppings. Deer or bears may be seen foraging in the flowers. Views to the northwest of Johannesburg Mountain, Forbidden Peak, and 8672-foot Eldorado Peak beyond hint at the ruggedness of this park's terrain. Deep, narrow valleys rise to mountain horns and spires, swathed with more than 300 glaciers that feed more than 125 alpine lakes and countless waterfalls. There are few roads here but 400 miles of trails, including the Pacific Crest National Scenic

In 1956, beatnik Jack Kerouac, author of *On the Road*, worked as a fire-spotter based in a one-room fire lookout on Desolation Peak in what is now North Cascades National Park. His novel *Desolation Angels* is based in part on his sixty-three days there. In his nonfiction essay "Alone on a Mountaintop" in *Lonesome Traveler*, he comments on his motivation for wilderness immersion: "I came to a point where I needed solitude and just to stop the machine of 'thinking' and 'enjoying' what they call 'living,' I just wanted to lie in the grass and look at the clouds."

Trail, which cuts across the southern edge of the park. In the north, peaks with names such as Challenger, Fury, Terror, and Despair convey how both climate and topography have made this place as extreme as it is stunning.

This seldom-visited national park had fewer than 24,000 visitors in 2014; it is made up of 93 percent designated wilderness, remaining as untamed as it was when established in 1968. It lies at the center of more than 2 million acres of federally designated wilderness, the largest area of that kind in the Lower 48. It is one of the most diverse ecosystems in the world.

For nearly sixty years, Pauline "Polly" Dyer and others from the North Cascades Conservation Council (NCCC) have been instrumental in keeping northern Washington wild. The day Dyer, now in her nineties, became an environmentalist might be pinned to the one on which she met her future husband, John. The woman with the megawatt smile was hoofing it up a trail on Deer Mountain near Ketchikan, Alaska, when she struck up a conversation with a rock-climbing Californian wearing a red cap with a Sierra Club pin on it. Not long after that, the two were married and moved to Washington State, where they

stepped out at every opportunity to explore the Olympic Peninsula and the Cascade Range. They became active in The Mountaineers, established the Pacific Northwest chapter of the Sierra Club (the first branch outside California), and were founding members of the NCCC.

But Dyer's feelings about the wild world ran deep from an early age. "I remember climbing up all kinds of hills in Alaska, and always, standing at the top, I just wanted to wrap my arms around the whole spectacle and protect it," she says. In 1953 the Dyers cut their conservation chops on a campaign to keep loggers out of Olympic National Park and then, along with The Mountaineers, turned their attention to preventing a project that would prove pivotal in the wilderness movement.

In the northwest corner of Colorado, straddling the Utah border, is a complex landscape of mountains, plateaus, canyons, and rivers. Here, on the southeast flank of the Uinta Mountains in Dinosaur National Monument, despite extreme aridity, more than 1000 plant and animal species subsist. It's a land where two desert rivers—the Green and the Yampa—combine spectacularly at Steamboat

Now in her mid-nineties, conservation icon Polly Dyer continues to work for wilderness protection.

Rock in Echo Park. Layers of rock, some more than a billion years old, in shades of cayenne and ecru and exposed by millions of years of river cutting, are dappled with vegetation.

The explorer Major John Wesley Powell was intrigued by the area and challenged by its rapids on his passage down the Green and Colorado rivers in 1869. In 1915 just 80 acres of this area were set aside for public enjoyment; in that region is the richest deposit of Jurassic fossils ever discovered. The fossil remains paint a picture of this speck of Earth as it was 149 million years ago when stegosauruses and other dinosaurs cut across a savannah of conifers and ferns. It wasn't until 1938 that Dinosaur was enlarged to 210,000 acres to encompass its spectacular river corridors.

The enlarged park enjoyed relative obscurity for a decade or so until it landed in the crosshairs of the Colorado River Storage Project. By the late 1940s, major dams had been built throughout the West, including the gargantuan Hoover Dam on the Colorado and the Grand Coulee Dam on the Columbia. Engineering was lauded as bringing

security and comfort to a blossoming population base amid dry lands. Upper and Lower Colorado Basin states wanting a more secure water supply from the Colorado and its tributaries were anxious to get their dams. Whatever would lie beneath the reservoirs, however scenic or soothing, took a backseat to consumer and commercial water consumption.

Echo Park, right smack in the middle of Dinosaur National Monument, where those two potent rivers meet, had a bull's-eye on it by 1950. National Park Service Director Newton Drury had initially fought the dam but ultimately let the rivers slip away. The plan to build the Echo Park and Split Mountain dams pitted federal agencies against each other and put members of the NPS family at odds. What was the point of federal protection if it couldn't prevent something like this? The loss of Yosemite's Hetch Hetchy not that many years before still stung conservationists, and when a January headline in the *Salt Lake Tribune* that year declared "Echo Park Dam Gets Approval," history seemed to be repeating itself. NPS maps showed the areas to be flooded and projected ahead to tourist facilities that would be built to cater to those recreating at the reservoir.

It seemed a done deal—until a veritable who's who of wilderness boosters, including Polly Dyer, stepped up their game. The potential loss of Echo Park was laid out before *Saturday Evening Post* readers in a 1950 article by a Utah native and popular voice of the day, Bernard DeVoto. In "Shall We Let Them Ruin Our National Parks?" he wrote, "No one has asked the American people whether or not they want their sovereign rights, and those of their

The wild Yampa River and Steamboat Rock from Harpers Corner Trail in Dinosaur National Monument

Fossilized camarasaurus skull and vertebrae in the Quarry Exhibit Hall at Dinosaur National Monument

descendants, in their own publicly reserved beauty spots wiped out." DeVoto speculated that visitation to all national parks would continue as long as they contained something worth seeing. But "a good many of them will not be worth visiting if engineers are let loose on them," he said. Luminary landscape architect Frederick Law Olmsted Jr. appealed to the Department of the Interior to change its plans and put the dam somewhere else. The loss would be catastrophically great, he said, if the project proceeded.

Arthur Carhart was a landscape architect with the US Forest Service who decades earlier had thwarted a summer-home development in a national forest in Colorado in favor of wilderness; it was, in fact, the first time the wilderness preservation concept had been applied to federal land. He had long ago left the Forest Service but continued to promote conservation causes as a popular writer, and he was a leading voice opposing the damming at Dinosaur. Carhart's engaging style drew others

to the battle, and during that time he strategized with Howard Zahniser of the Wilderness Society (and future author of the Wilderness Act of 1964) and Mardy and Olaus Murie. Like Polly and John Dyer, the Muries were a conservation power couple, lovers of wooly places and creatures, and potent advocates for their protection. In the 1920s they had moved meaningfully through little-known outback Alaska tracking caribou and then on to Jackson Hole, where Olaus exhaustively studied elk for the Bureau of Biological Survey. Together the Muries defended and encouraged national parks such as Olympic and Grand Teton as well as those vast roadless tracts in Alaska. While directing the activities of the Wilderness Society from 1945 to 1961, Olaus had been an NPS ally and during that time helped the agency deflect a dam scheme in Glacier National Park.

But the fight for Echo Park was a defining one that drove an ideological wedge between wilderness advocates and the NPS. Defense against dams in Dinosaur was a test of the Park Service's instinct and ability to protect parks—and, in the eyes of the Muries, Zahniser, and others, the NPS was failing.

Sierra Club head David Brower also barreled to the frontlines during the Echo Park dam fray. The club's book, *This Is Dinosaur*, edited by western icon Wallace Stegner, gave would-be activists a clear look at what would be lost to the dam. "How much wilderness do the wilderness-lovers want? ask those who would mine and dig and cut and

IF YOU LIKE ALDO LEOPOLD, YOU'LL LOVE SIGURD OLSON

Visionary ecologist Sigurd Olson not only helped draft the Wilderness Act of 1964, he was also influential in the protection of Voyageurs National Park and Point Reyes National Seashore. In between stints as the head of the National Parks Conservation Association and the Wilderness Society, Olson was on the NPS Advisory Board, consulting Secretary of the Interior Stewart Udall on national park and wilderness issues. During one of Olson's many moving speeches, he talked about the intangible values of wild places, saying, "It is hard to place a price tag on these things, on the sounds and smells and memories of the out of doors, on the countless things we have seen and loved. They are the dividends of the good life."

Photographed the year the Wilderness Act passed (1964), Sigurd Olson called wilderness a "spiritual necessity."

dam in such sanctuary spots as these," wrote Stegner. "The answer is easy: Enough so that there will be in the years ahead a little relief, a little quiet, a little relaxation, for any of our increasing millions who need and want it." Murie gave a snapshot of the area's wildlife and a perspective on the ecological importance of wilderness. In a move pioneered by Robert Sterling Yard with his national parks book forty years earlier, every member of Congress got a copy of *This Is Dinosaur*.

The smaller wilderness groups at the time—the Sierra Club, the Wilderness Society, and the National Parks Conservation Association (NPCA)—combined forces with the big guns of the day, including the National Wildlife Federation, Audubon Society, Izaak Walton League, and Garden Club of America. They coordinated to lobby Congress, rally members, and broadcast their beliefs.

Sigurd Olson, president of the NPCA, spoke at a meeting of twenty-eight conservation groups in 1954, telling them that wilderness "serves as balance wheels to the speed and pressures of a high-powered civilization." Speaking about the Organic Act, the Park Service's mandate, he said, "It is good for moderns to experience the wilderness. It is part of the cultural background of America . . . Any development in any national park or monument which destroys [it], is breaking faith with the original intent of Congress to pass these areas on unimpaired." Olson felt, as many of those in the battle against the Dinosaur dam did, that if the Park Service was defeated in Echo Park, then the future was dim for a national wilderness preservation system.

The gathering was covered by media near and far, and the bout between the development-hungry and those who stood in front of that rolling ball, hoping to slow its momentum, was soon

A Girl Scout fishes for trash on April 22, 1970, the first annual Earth Day.

DC, office. They gave him a confidential copy of the legislation that was taking shape and tried to explain how it differed from NPS policy of the day. Zahniser described a wilderness-forever future in which places would be described not in terms of *use* but *character*. Brower said of the fledgling wilderness bill, "The concept has great promise for the days coming soon, when the zoning we have always understood to exist in the parks will need this careful spelling out to counteract pressures such as we hardly used to dream of."

Despite the brevity of the meeting, clearly it had an impact on Wirth, who dispatched a three-page written response. In it he said, "It is our belief that such primeval areas of national parks and monuments are, in fact, already wilderness areas with adequate protection against future nonconforming use . . . In these circumstances, it is our view that nothing would be gained from placing such areas in the National Wilderness Preservation System as provided in the bill . . . Therefore, I hope you will appreciate the fact that we view with some apprehension any proposed law which will deal with our fundamental objectives and policy. What we have now can hardly be improved upon."

This was a peculiar moment of feast and famine for the NPS. While it had the financial and ideological backing of the nation with Mission 66, the agency was deflecting blows aimed at its core. Feeling its identity—and perhaps its very existence—threatened, the NPS at first actively opposed any federal legislation to protect wilderness, claiming it was gratuitous and intrusive.

over. Congress approved the Colorado River Storage Project in 1956 but left Echo Park out of it. Dinosaur's rivers would not be dammed for power, irrigation, or drinking water. And the Yampa would remain as it is today: the only free-flowing tributary in the Colorado River system.

With that victory in the bank, wilderness champions were emboldened to stand up to other proposed national park development. The obvious choice was Mission 66. The increase in infrastructure promised was immense, from roads and visitor centers to comfort stations and campgrounds—and the Wilderness Society and Sierra Club made no secret of their opposition. The bad blood between the Park Service and wilderness backers endured.

In February 1956, the same month in which Zahniser wrote the first draft of what would become the Wilderness Act, he and Brower met briefly with NPS Director Conrad Wirth in his Washington,

A STEADYING PRESENCE

In a July 1963 article in *American Forests* magazine, Senator Clinton P. Anderson wrote, "Wilderness is an anchor to windward. Knowing it is there, we can also know that we are still a rich nation, tending our resources as we should—not a people in despair searching every last nook and cranny of our land for a board of lumber, a barrel of oil, a blade of grass, or a tank of water." The Wilderness Act celebrated its fiftieth anniversary in 2014.

But eventually the Park Service got on board, though reluctantly, after President John F. Kennedy's administration endorsed the bill in the early 1960s.

A major influencer of the NPS's eventual support was, no doubt, Stegner's now-famous "Wilderness Letter" sent to a member of the Interior Department's Outdoor Recreation Resources Review Commission, which was studying the values of wilderness at the time. Stegner wrote: "Something will have gone out of us as a people if we ever let the remaining wilderness be destroyed; if we permit the last virgin forests to be turned into comic books and plastic cigarette cases; if we drive the few remaining members of the wild species into zoos or to extinction; if we pollute the last clear air and dirty the last clean streams and push our paved roads through the last of the silence, so that never again will Americans be free in their own country from the noise, the exhausts, the stinks of human and automotive waste. And so that never again can we have the chance to see ourselves single, separate, vertical, and individual in the world, part of the environment of trees and rocks and soil, brother to the other animals, part of the natural world and competent to belong in it."

More than a wilderness manifesto, Stegner had written a love letter to the wild world: "Even when I can't get to the backcountry, the thought of the colored deserts of southern Utah or the reassurance that there are still stretches of prairies where the world can be instantaneously perceived as disk and bowl and where the little but intensely important human being is exposed to the five directions of the thirty-six winds, is a positive consolation. The idea alone can sustain me," he said.

Stegner personally handed Secretary of the Interior Stewart Udall a copy of the "Wilderness Letter" after meeting him in Washington, DC. Stegner's intensely personal reflections and plea struck a chord with the secretary, and when Udall was asked to speak at the Sierra Club's Seventh Biennial Wilderness Conference in April 1961, he read the "Wilderness Letter." That crowd included Supreme Court Justice William O. Douglas (a vocal fan of untamed places, says friend Polly Dyer), Brower, Olson, icon Ansel Adams, and other influential folks.

From there, Stegner's defense of what he called a "geography of hope" went viral, so to speak, and was referenced as far away as sub-Saharan Africa. The "Wilderness Letter" appeared in full in the *Washington Post*, where it got the attention of Capitol Hill.

Zahniser also spoke at the Sierra Club conference, about wilderness forever, not mentioning the Park Service or Forest Service by name but alluding to their historic fiats, which seemed to be fading into the past as more Americans came to understand that wilderness was not a luxury but a necessity, as legitimate as any use those agencies sanctioned. "We saw that safeguarding wilderness involves the wildness of ourselves and of other visitors to the wilderness," he said, "for we all have an inborn tendency to make over wilderness rather than to adapt ourselves to it."

With public and political sentiment warming to their philosophy, the wilderness crusaders redoubled their efforts to create a system of primitive landscapes with an extreme level of protection. From the time of that frosty 1956 meeting with Wirth, Zahniser pumped out sixty-five more versions of the proposed wilderness legislation and defended it at eighteen congressional hearings, amounting to 6000 pages' worth of testimony. "Let us be done with a wilderness preservation program made up of a sequence of overlapping emergencies, threats, and defense campaigns," he wrote.

Polly Dyer worked closely with Zahniser during this time, as did Olson and Olaus Murie. Did they sense then that history would hold fast to them as the creators of America's *next* best idea? No, says Dyer modestly, "We didn't think about our role in it at all; we just focused on the end result." But getting there wasn't as easy as explaining to lawmakers that in wilderness were critical reserves for human health, happiness, and humility. Even with the backing of the Oval Office and the Senate, the bill died in committee in 1962 in the heat of intense opposition from loggers, ranchers, and miners. Another attempt stalled in the House the next year because of similar opposition.

But Zahniser was a listener and peacemaker who, without ever letting go of his overall goal, compromised to arrive at a bill that would please wilderness backers *and* pass the Eighty-Eighth

Congress. Compromises that included grazing and prospecting in some areas were written into the bill (actions that would later be banned), and when the House vote was tallied in July 1964, only one member had dissented. Zahniser had condensed the act's purpose into its first line: "In order to assure that an increasing population, accompanied by expanding settlement and growing mechanization, does not occupy and modify all areas within the United States and its possessions, leaving no lands designated for preservation and protection in their natural condition." The legislation created the National Wilderness Preservation System and immediately added to it 9.1 million acres of wild America, giving them a higher level of protection than ever before.

Zahniser died just a few months before the bill's signing, but his toiled-over words live on in ways he could have scarcely imagined. "It is a bold thing for a human being who lives on the earth but a few score years at the most to presume upon the Eternal," he had said. "Yet we who concern ourselves with wilderness preservation are compelled to assume this boldness." When President Lyndon Johnson signed the bill in the White House Rose Garden on September 3, he remarked that the legislation's bipartisan support reflected a strong national consensus for the importance of planning ahead. Another historic era in preservation had begun, Johnson said: "I believe the significance of this occasion goes far beyond these bills alone. In this century Americans have wisely and have courageously kept a faithful trust to the conservation of our natural resources and beauty."

Today the National Wilderness Preservation System (NWPS) protects as designated wilderness

Numerous creeks thunder downhill from the glaciated peaks of the North Cascades.

more than 109 million acres in more than 750 areas, in all but six states. By some estimates, an additional 200 million acres of land in the public domain have wilderness characteristics deserving of that protection. More than half of the current national park system is federally designated wilderness, and another 135,000 acres within parks are currently proposed. Despite its once-fervent snubbing of the wilderness concept, the NPS now manages 40 percent of the NWPS (nearly 44 million acres), the largest chunk of wilderness of any federal agency.

But now is no time to rest on laurels of victories past, says current NCCC president Karl Forsgaard, because the twenty-first century has been a mixed bag for wilderness. "There are still roadless areas [eligible for wilderness protection] that haven't been protected for one political issue or another," he says. "Others have been trashed. What is left now is even more precious." Echoing a speech Zahniser gave in Seattle just two weeks before his death, about the importance of local activism near wild spaces, Forsgaard says, "The lands that have been protected are under constant pressure. If nobody is paying attention, if nobody cares about what could go wrong, wilderness will be lost. It requires enormous vigilance."

With jagged peaks jabbing at the sky, virgin forests, and a moody climate, the North Cascades still appear as a work in progress, like a place nature isn't quite done with yet. To Polly Dyer's joy and astonishment, gray wolves returned there on their own several years ago, a sign that the system is righting itself from human impacts suffered long ago. Only time will tell if the North Cascades will get wilder still, but due to the boldness of past and present wilderness apostles, it will be left to its own devices.

A nanny mountain goat with her kid on Yellowstone's Sepulcher Mountain near the Wyoming–Montana border

CHAPTER 19

The Mood of Wild America

IN THE WANING DAYS of July, on the west end of the valley cut by Swiftcurrent Creek in Glacier National Park, campers are pitching tents and dishing up dinners. The last of the day's light adorns the surrounding high peaks of the Lewis Range, including Mount Grinnell (8851 feet), Mount Wilbur (9321 feet), and Mount Gould (9553 feet). From this area, named Many Glacier, patches of ice can be seen clutching mountain flanks along the Continental Divide. More than 700 miles of trails run through the park, and some of the most beguiling hikes begin here.

Ecosystems from every compass direction converge in Glacier, and the result is a landscape that is as diverse—from old-growth forests to sapphire-tinted alpine lakes—as it is dramatic. It is a hub from which life radiates outward. Rain or snow falling on Triple Divide Peak might flow into the river systems of the Columbia (to the Pacific), Mississippi (to the Gulf of Mexico), or Saskatchewan (to Hudson Bay). Glacier is what

John Muir called "the best care-killing scenery on the continent."

Near the campers, rangers have set up spotting scopes and trained them on a distant cliffside. From afar the object of curiosity looks like a shrinking snowfield among ancient gray jags far above the valley floor. Upon closer inspection, the white blob is a breathing thing, a long-haired, shaggy beast perched at a pulse-pounding height on a rock ledge hardly wider than its body. Its soft cloven hooves grip the outcrop like rubber climbing shoes, and it can cross nearly 12 feet in a single bound. Any tightrope walker would envy its poise, as any long jumper would its athleticism.

Seemingly immune to precariousness, the burly mountain goat munches away on whatever green bits it can find. With its distinctive looks—pointed horns, long face, trademark beard—the mountain goat is the park's icon. Though they are called billies and nannies, they are more closely related to the antelope or musk ox than a wild goat. Picking such remote dining spots is a strategy for staying off the menu of predators such as mountain lions, coyotes, wolves, and the occasional grizzly bear— though bald eagles might knock a goat kid off a cliff and scavenge its remains. This "escape terrain" is the preferred haunt of mountain goats, the steeper the better.

Hours pass, the sun drops away, and still the intrepid creature can be seen inching along the ledge, grazing its way into tomorrow. The next day, it is nowhere in sight. Did it pass the night, beneath a star-thick sky, on that sliver of stone? Or did it climb to a steadier piece of ground and succumb to one of those keen predators?

Glacier is the core of the Crown of the Continent ecosystem, which remains one of the most ecologically intact areas of the temperate regions of the world. The park has nearly all of its original plant and animal species, including all of its native carnivores—even the rare wolverine and Canada lynx. Made up of several ecosystems, from breezy prairie to wind-scoured tundra, resulting in a rare, rich bank of biodiversity, it is one of the environments envisioned by ecologists fifty years ago when they fought to manage national parks in a way that would protect, restore, and maintain them for future generations.

That fight began in earnest in the early 1960s when ecologists, both within and outside the National Park Service, gained a prominently placed ally, Stewart Udall, who was appointed Secretary of the Interior in 1961. Udall, a former congressman from Arizona, started heeding warnings about the

A stunning profile of peaks emerges along Glacier's Going-to-the-Sun Road.

lack of science in NPS management almost immediately. A fan of nineteenth-century naturalist George Marsh, Udall dragged Marsh's *Man and Nature* out of relative obscurity, calling it "the beginning of land wisdom in this country." Udall expressed the desire for the NPS to represent the purest conservation arm of an Interior Department devoted to that cause. He sided with criticism that the Mission 66 project was running off the rails and shifted its gears from development to research and resource protection. Nature must take precedence over human needs, said Udall.

He had read the internal report "Get the Facts and Put Them to Use" written by NPS naturalist (and later assistant director of Resource Studies) Howard Stagner, which was highly critical of the bureau's overall natural resources management. The Stagner Report, as it was known, reiterated many of the basic objectives outlined in George Wright's *Fauna No. 1* nearly three decades earlier, while incorporating some newer science. "The animals indigenous to the parks shall be protected, restored, if practicable, and their welfare in the natural wild state perpetuated," the Stagner Report said. "Their management shall consist only of measures conforming with the basic laws and which are essential to the maintenance of populations and their natural environments in a healthy condition."

At the time, Yellowstone had reached a crisis point with its overabundance of elk. The NPS was getting an earful from the public about downsizing the northern range herd by thousands of animals. Some people didn't want them culled at all; others wanted to be able to come into the park and hunt

Secretary of the Interior Stewart Udall and First Lady "Lady Bird" Johnson soak up Grand Teton National Park from a raft on the Snake River in 1964.

them—a position NPS Director Conrad Wirth supported early on, while his underlings did not. Conservationists and academics were asking what the scientific basis was for any of the policies followed in parks.

The answer was that no overarching ecological road map was being followed. Criticism of that fact led Udall to appoint an outside wildlife advisory board. He also commissioned two reports—from outside groups, which was entirely novel at the

LETTING BEARS BE BEARS

A rise in general environmental awareness in the 1960s and specific concern about the hazards of open-pit garbage dumps led to an Executive Order in 1970 that banned dumps on federal lands. After the closure of huge trash heaps in Yellowstone and Yosemite, visitors were advised not to feed bears and to store food securely. (Mostly) bear-proof garbage cans were installed throughout parks.

As the Craighead brothers, who had spent a dozen years studying them, had predicted, the bears still sought food from humans, leading to the killing of nearly 100 "problem" grizzlies in Yellowstone in the early 1970s. In a population that the two researchers had estimated at fewer than 200 bears, it was a major blow. Because of fear of their extinction, grizzlies were listed as threatened under the federal Endangered Species Act (ESA) in 1975.

That protection, along with the emergence of a new generation of bears that were not hungry for human food, resulted in the rebounding of populations in the 1980s. Parks hazed bears investigating nonwild food, installed storage lockers at campsites, and required backcountry hikers to secure food in (truly) bear-proof canisters.

A recent University of California–Santa Cruz study concluded that Yosemite's bears subsist on diets similar to those of their forebearers a century ago. In Yellowstone, grizzlies bounced back spectacularly, and bears now number several hundred in the greater ecosystem. This has prompted the federal government to consider removing that population from the ESA list. But conservation groups vow to fight that move, arguing that delisting would be premature. Now climate change threatens the food security of bears.

time—to look at the elk issue, in particular, and at what mechanisms the NPS was using to make such decisions.

The first report was led by a University of California–Berkeley ecologist, A. Starker Leopold (son of famous wildlife biologist and wilderness advocate Aldo Leopold). His 1963 report *Wildlife Management in the National Parks*, known as the Leopold Report, confirmed the NPS decision to cull the herd as an "integral part of park management," reinforcing that it should be done only by the Park Service. The report extinguished the firestorm over the elk issue—at least temporarily.

It also presented a philosophy by which parks should be managed and envisioned an endgame the NPS should work toward, both of which were a profound shift in how the agency interpreted its mandate. Up to that point, the Park Service had believed national parks existed to provide enjoyment for people and focused its energies and resources largely on that aspect of its founding legislation. But the Leopold Report pointed out that "in the Congressional Act of 1916 which created the National Park Service, preservation of native animal life was clearly specified as one of the purposes of the parks."

To that end, the Leopold Report recommended that "native species of wild animals should be present in maximum variety and reasonable abundance." Mere *protection* of natural resources,

SMOKEY BEAR HAS FLIPPED

Safety, science, and stewardship are the primary concerns of the National Park Service Wildfire Management Program. Fire is one of the biggest forces for change in parks, with the potential to alter landscapes more often than earthquakes, volcanic eruptions, or major floods.

Yosemite, a crown-jewel park, has the "largest and most complex fire program in the NPS," says its chief of fire and aviation management, Kelly Martin. It is a tough and often thorny place to manage for fire because of its international stardom, millions of visitors, number of historic structures, borders with public lands managed by other federal agencies, compliance with state and federal air pollution regulations, proximity to inhabited areas, and expansive wilderness areas.

Martin cites the 1963 Leopold Report as putting the importance of fire in ecosystems on the front lines of resource management. The report says nature-caused fires are part of ecological maintenance and that controlled burns could be beneficial. Fire is dynamic, an essential-to-ecosystems process for the procreation of big trees, including sequoias and lodgepole pines, whose closed cones open in a fire's heat. Fire makes soil nutrients out of organic matter and makes the ground fertile for seeds. Fire creates a new, or improved, diversity of habitats. It clears canopies to allow light to reach new seedlings. Aspen, willow, birch, and an abundance of flowers and grasses emerge from nitrogen-rich soil.

Though the Park Service embraced US Forest Service–preferred policies of fire suppression before the Leopold Report, "The NPS broke ranks with other government agencies when it picked up on the fire piece from Leopold," says Martin. Leopold had mourned, in particular, the state of the big trees in Sequoia NP. With dense undergrowth rendering the star attractions unrecognizable, the grove no longer resembled the place once worthy of inclusion in the national park system, the report said. Fire proponents soon got what they wanted when

which had been the main priority of the NPS for some time, could no longer be the primary goal; resources had to be actively maintained and, in some cases, restored. "Americans have shown a great capacity for degrading and fragmenting native biotas," wrote Leopold. "So far we have not exercised much imagination or ingenuity in rebuilding damaged biotas. It will not be done by passive protection alone."

The major management shift the report suggested was that the Park Service "recognize the enormous complexity of ecologic communities and the diversity of management procedures required to preserve them." No magic bullet would allow all parks to be kept "as nearly as possible in the condition that prevailed when the area was first visited by the white man." But the report's authors were confident that "a reasonable illusion of primitive America could be recreated, using the utmost in skill, judgment, and ecologic sensitivity." This ideal "vignette," as they referred to it, "should be the objective of every national park and monument."

experimental burning was started in 1964. Soon Sequoia NP had a whole new way of managing fire. This was a historic departure for Sequoia, whose eventual superintendent, Walter Fry, had "subdued" seventy-two fires in Sequoia and General Grant (later incorporated into Kings Canyon) national parks from 1905 to 1915.

An article in *Westways* magazine expressed the magnitude of the departure. "Smokey Bear has flipped. When last seen, the furry fire fighter had chucked his hat, shovel and badge and was running stark naked through the forest babbling something about rangers setting fires . . ." But it was an idea whose time had come, and the new policies soon spread to Kings Canyon and, ultimately, to Yosemite.

Since the 1970s NPS resource managers have been using naturally ignited fires, and setting their own, to restore ecosystems and to reduce the likelihood of megafire events where fire has been historically suppressed. Now what's known as prescribed burning restores health to the big trees. And fires at higher elevations are allowed to burn themselves out. But as humans have crowded parks and their borders, it has gotten increasingly difficult to manage for natural conditions. Exacerbating factors, climate change foremost among them, make wildland fire management an unpredictable priority. "No fire season is the same," says Martin, when severe drought conditions like those experienced in California intersect with declining budgets. "The public thinks we can put every fire out, but we can't," she says; sometimes they are too costly or too dangerous to fight.

The 2013 Rim Fire, fought by hundreds of firefighters from several federal agencies, burned 400 square miles, including a large chunk of the northwest flank of Yosemite NP. During the fire, NPS Director Jonathan Jarvis commented on the uphill battle federal land managers are fighting to get fuel reduction funds. Without money to do forest thinning and planned burns, he said, "You get an incredible fire year." A map on the wall in Martin's firehouse office shows the Rim Fire burned out where there had been old fires and controlled burns. Without mitigation, says Martin, the west side of the park—including the Mariposa Grove of Giant Sequoias—is at high risk for a major event. "It's just waiting for a catastrophic fire," she says.

Most biologists agreed with the basic conclusions of the Leopold Report, but others criticized the mythical goal of recreating the moment in which Europeans first laid eyes upon future parklands—never mind that American Indians had seen and used many of those areas for millennia. NPS biologist Adolph Murie cautioned against the overengineering of landscapes. "We should be guardians not gardeners," he wrote in his critique. But Murie understood that the authors of the Leopold Report did not mean that parks should be *literally* recreated to imitate primeval conditions. Like other ecologists' use of the term "balance of nature," the phrase "vignette of primitive America" wasn't meant to indicate a desire for a static environment. Ecologists, and Leopold in particular, knew better than anyone that natural conditions fluctuate, sometimes widely, as part of healthy ecosystems. Leopold acknowledged there were limitations that made the vignette impossible. "Yet, if the goal cannot be fully achieved it can be approached," he said.

In many cases "management" meant leaving natural processes to play out on their own. "Wildlife should not be displayed in fenced enclosures; this is the function of a zoo, not a national park," said the report. "In the same category is artificial feeding of wildlife. Fed bears become bums, and dangerous." In every case, Leopold recommended that the best agency to study and solve NPS problems was the Park Service itself. And research it must. "Management without knowledge would be a dangerous policy indeed," said the report. "The goal, we repeat, is to maintain or create the mood of wild America," said Leopold. "Above all other policies, the maintenance of naturalness should prevail."

The second report authorized by Udall came from the National Academy of Sciences. The conclusions of what was referred to as the Robbins Report (for chair William Robbins) were aligned with Leopold and Stagner—and E. Lowell Sumner and George Wright before them all. Robbins perhaps expressed more outrage over the shirking of science that had become the norm at the NPS: "It is inconceivable . . . that property so unique and valuable as the national parks . . . should not be provided with sufficient competent research scientists in natural history as elementary insurance for the preservation and best use of parks," the report remarked.

Robbins spent a lot of time defining the reason certain national parks were established and acknowledged the contradictions in the NPS mandate: "There are differences of public opinion on the major purposes of the national parks. One extreme wishes the national parks to be developed as neon-lighted vacation resorts; another wishes them left as nearly primeval as possible," the report said. It acknowledged Leopold's "vignette of primitive America" by saying that "the ideal, though admirable, may not be fully attainable; yet it is desirable to move in that direction."

The Robbins Report acknowledged the tenuous interplay among what was, what is, and what should be. "The Committee recognizes that national parks are not pictures on the wall," the authors wrote; "they are not museum exhibits in glass cases; they are dynamic biological complexes with self-generating changes. To attempt to maintain them in any fixed condition, past, present, or future, would not only be futile but contrary to nature." In every case, said the report, "Naturalness, the avoidance of artificiality, should be the rule."

Park management had been criticized by outside entities before, but the systematic approach taken by Udall in eliciting two very public, very scathing reports put NPS leadership on a ledge with

Environmentalism went mainstream in 1970 with "Save Our" stamps issued by the US Postal Service.

a spotting scope trained on them. But in many ways, those reports backed up what the Park Service's in-house scientists had been saying for decades: We need comprehensive research in parks to know what's there and how it's changing. We need backup to implement policies that may be unpopular but necessary, such as selective culling, prescribed burns, removal of some built structures, etc. And we need a serious budget and staff to accomplish all this.

The reports were not so much a wake-up call to NPS scientists as to their bosses. And that's exactly what they got. In the same year Leopold and Robbins were unleashed, Udall dispatched a memo to outgoing NPS Director Conrad Wirth—soon to be replaced by George Hartzog—advising him to "take such steps as appropriate to incorporate the [reports'] philosophy and the basic findings into the administration of the National Park System."

Why had the conclusions of Wright and other NPS scientists, spanning decades, largely been swept under the rug, whereas Leopold's became public policy? It was in part the influence of an ecologically minded secretary of the interior. But in the 1960s the general public also was gaining an awareness that only scientists, or particularly well-informed citizens, had in the 1930s. The modern environmental movement was taking root in the wake of highly publicized biodisasters, including oil spills off the California coast, pollution in Lake Erie, and massive bald eagle die-offs from insecticides. The movement became part of American culture when Dr. Seuss's *Lorax* spoke for the trees and popular musicians sang about the destruction that humans had visited upon Earth, such as Joni Mitchell's lament in "Big Yellow Taxi" that "they paved paradise and put up a parking lot."

The road to rewilding parks in the way envisioned by the Leopold Report was, as its authors had anticipated, an enormous and complex one. It required a reshaping of the organization—scientists should be elevated to sit alongside other decision makers, the report said—and a sort of lobotomy that removed the emphasis on tourism from Park Service minds and replaced it with ecology. But it required even more than that—it meant admitting that the way things had been done traditionally within the Park Service was wrong-headed, even destructive.

To some old-timers, who may have started with the NPS when distant parks were semiprivate fiefdoms, the changes in decision-making and management meant the wrenching away of influence and power. The changes also meant tempering the sentimental spirit of the Park Service, whose romantic creation story and idyllic past protectors lingered in its consciousness. What resulted, in part, was righteousness and stubbornness on the part of the established gatekeepers. (They may not have given much credence to science, but they knew a cornered animal fought its way out.)

Territorial disputes cropped up almost immediately between new "research scientists" in parks and established "wildlife rangers" who, with park superintendents generally on their side, believed nobody knew their parks better than they did. An edict dispatched to park superintendents from the Washington office, such as "make sure anything you build doesn't affect the ecology of that spot," was more often than not just ignored. The science-minded might put up a fuss, but much like in the pre–National Park Protection Act days in late nineteenth-century Yellowstone, there simply was no enforcement mechanism in place to do anything about it.

A 1963 speech given by Assistant Secretary of the Interior John Carver Jr. is a good example of how high emotions were running at the time. At the NPS Conference of Challenges in Yosemite, he railed against what he called the near-occult practices the NPS deployed to deflect outside influences. Carver read a job description for a position in the bureau that said the candidate should be "imbued with strong convictions as to the 'rightness' of National Park Service philosophy, policy, and purpose." He continued: "This has the mystic, quasi-religious sound of a manual for the Hitler Youth Movement. Such nonsense is simply intolerable. The National Park Service is a bureau of the Department of the Interior, which is a department of the United States government's executive branch—it isn't a religion, and it should not be thought of as such."

Secretary Udall's 1964 *Letter on National Park Management*, which laid out the principles that would direct NPS management plans, seemed to rise above the heated rhetoric in search of middle ground. It referenced what was known colloquially as the Magna Carta of the National Parks—a letter Secretary of the Interior Franklin Lane had written to first NPS Director Stephen Mather in 1918—and reaffirmed that document's core principles. "The accomplishments of the past are not only a source of pride—they are also a source of guidance for the future," Udall wrote. In regard to natural areas, the primary objective of the NPS was to "provide for all appropriate use and enjoyment by the people that can be accommodated without impairment of the natural values. Park management shall recognize and respect wilderness as a whole environment of living things whose use and enjoyment depend on their continuing interrelationship free of man's spoliation."

Udall's short manifesto belied the mind-boggling complexity of putting new scientific priorities into play. One complication included the obvious lack of funds

The front page of the April 23, 1970, issue of the *New York Times* reports on Earth Day events. The caption reads: "Throngs jamming Fifth Avenue yesterday in response to a call for the regeneration of a polluted environment."

This photo was taken during the translunar phase of the *Apollo 11* Mission in 1969. For many people, images like these highlighted the finite and fragile nature of the Big Blue Marble.

budgeted by Congress to do scientific research in parks. NPS funding for research projects was a paltry $105,500 in 1965, in part because some in Congress didn't think the Park Service should be conducting scientific research. One member of the House appropriations subcommittee commented, says Richard West Sellars in his book *Preserving Nature in the National Parks*, that "research was not any business of the Service." At a conference of national park scientists in the late 1960s, E. Lowell Sumner said NPS research budgets were still "*peanuts* in comparison to those of larger and more powerful branches and divisions of the Service." This left the NPS leadership groping for resources to carry out the mission thrust upon it.

Muddling the process was pressure from the executive branch on down for the Park Service to respond to an agitated nation's recreational needs. This task was undertaken by an innovative new NPS director who would usher in another era of transition and expansion of the national park system.

Though the mountain goats of Glacier may prefer life on the edge, many species do not—yet that is where they found themselves in the late 1960s. Continuous waves of human intrusion on nature's processes left many wild things teetering. By that time only 500 bald eagles remained in the Lower 48. Grizzly bear populations were hovering in the danger zone. Peregrine falcon numbers were dismal, and Florida panthers were few and far between. While the fight for their survival was reaching its pinnacle, a reprieve was not yet at hand.

The diamondback terrapin prefers to live in brackish marshes like those found in Gateway NRA's Jamaica Bay Wildlife Refuge.

CHAPTER 20

Parkscape USA

LOOK OUT UPON the surging tide from Breezy Point in Gateway National Recreation Area, and all urban chaos lies behind you. With bay and ocean segments in New York and New Jersey, the park lets visitors break away from the crush of city life and maybe see a resourceful red fox in woodlands, a delicate piping plover among sand dunes, or a sturdy blue heron riding salt-kissed breezes—all remarkably close to the Big Apple.

In 1972, on the same day Golden Gate National Recreation Area was formed on the Pacific coast,

26,000-acre Gateway was established as a portal for millions of people to get to know the national park system on the East Coast. It's made up of disparate areas, including ocean beaches, maritime forests, freshwater ponds, salt marshes, and a wildlife refuge. These diverse ecosystems support an impressive array of species; one such creature is the diamondback terrapin, the only turtle in North America specifically adapted to brackish water. Its home is Jamaica Bay, where in early summer visitors might catch sight of female turtles laying pinkish eggs in shallow sandpits. The volume of bird species (more than 300) and butterfly varieties (more than 70) using Gateway as a home base or as a migratory stopover is rivaled only by the number of *people* who gravitate to it: more than 6 million in 2014.

The existence of these first two nature-based urban national parks is owed, in large part, to George Hartzog Jr., who was appointed the seventh head of the National Park Service at just forty-three, in January 1964. Born and raised in poverty in a small South Carolina town, he was a Methodist preacher by age seventeen, a lawyer soon thereafter, and an army captain along the way. Hartzog joined the NPS when he was twenty-six, first as an attorney, then as superintendent of Rocky Mountain and Great Smoky Mountains national parks. As superintendent at the Jefferson Expansion National Memorial in downtown St. Louis, he oversaw the construction of the famous Gateway Arch.

During Hartzog's run as director, the nation was undergoing seismic shifts. The costly Vietnam War was peaking, as were equal rights movements for women and minorities. While generations were divided and social tensions mounted, outdoor recreation seized the nation, and environmental awareness also became a front-page item. Land use was rapidly transitioning from open green space to private enclaves, causing citizens and public officials to fret about many Americans' lack of recreational opportunities, which were viewed as a possible antidote to national anxiety.

Elected officials were troubled that, while middle-class suburbanites certainly were traveling

As ecological awareness grew, wildlife managers emphasized observation (over interaction) with park fauna such as in Yellowstone, where this placard was displayed in 1961.

to parks, people in cities—and that was most of the population—were losing touch with a proud outdoor tradition. They believed this meant most Americans were also losing out on the benefits to spirit, body, and mind that contributed to the overall health of the nation. The NPS had been dabbling in reservoir-, river-, and beach-related park designations (Congress authorized several such parks, though none were officially established until 1964), and there was tremendous pressure to add more. But the task of recreational planning had been stripped from the NPS by the creation in 1963 of a new agency within the Department of the Interior: the Bureau of Outdoor Recreation.

In 1958 Congress had created the Outdoor Recreation Resources Review Commission (ORRRC) to respond to the pressing desire for more public park spaces. The group, chaired by financier and philanthropist Laurance Rockefeller, had to identify

HI KIDS!
Don't feed the bears.
Be sure Dad keeps the
car windows rolled up.
Over 40 people have been
hurt by bears this year.

what was needed and where and how that need might be satisfied. In studying the recreation issue, the Census Bureau carried out a National Recreation Survey that polled 16,000 people about their lives and relationships to open spaces. It was meant to be a detailed investigation of what the public was doing in the out-of-doors, and it didn't disappoint.

In 1962 the ORRRC released its report, *Outdoor Recreation in America*, based on that and other studies. The results showed that roughly 90 percent of Americans participated in at least one form of outdoor recreation in the summer of 1960, which amounted to a total of 4.4 billion separate outings during that time. As demand grew for park experiences, available land supply was dwindling; the report said, "The resources for outdoor recreation—shoreline, green acres, open space, and unpolluted waters—diminished in the face of demands for more of everything else." The committee projected that by the year 2000, the number of outings per year would triple. (Their prediction was high but remarkably close; by 2012 Americans were taking 12.4 billion outdoor excursions annually.) The report specifically looked ahead to the needs of those at the start of the twenty-first century, "so that the outdoors may be available to the Americans of the future."

A primary focus of the report was city dwellers' growing estrangement from the natural world, despite the uptick in outdoor activities by a certain population segment. The wild "no longer lies at the back door or at the end of Main Street," the report said. "More and more, most Americans must traverse miles of crowded highways to know the outdoors. The prospect for the future is that this quest will be even more difficult." Rockefeller and the other report writers were troubled that "few places are near enough to metropolitan centers for a Sunday outing." Outdoor opportunities were most urgently needed near urban areas, which had the fewest facilities per capita and the most intense competition for land use. The report's authors said, "Immediate action should be taken by federal, state, and local governments to reserve or acquire additional water, beach, and shoreline areas, particularly near centers of population."

Rockefeller's committee recommended forming the Bureau of Outdoor Recreation (BOR) to help bring structure to outdoor recreation planning, and with the passage of the National Outdoor Recreation Act in 1963, it became the Department of the Interior's newest federal agency. The BOR's task was to guide the creation of *recreational* park units alongside the NPS. Now middle-aged, the Park Service had never before had a partnership with another federal agency to supposedly "help" do its job identifying potential parklands and lobbying Congress for their creation. It was an unnerving time for NPS leadership.

Influential NPS directors George Hartzog Jr. (left) and Horace Albright (right) both guided the agency and parks through pivotal moments. Here in Harpers Ferry, West Virginia, they are celebrating the agency's fiftieth anniversary in 1966.

East Pond at Gateway NRA's 9000-acre Jamaica Bay Wildlife Refuge is a great place to view migrating birds; 332 species have been spotted there.

The ORRRC also recommended forming a heavy-hitting Recreation Advisory Council, consisting of the secretaries of the Departments of the Interior, Agriculture, and Defense; this council issued its recommendations in 1963. A major objective of the council was the establishment of national recreation areas (NRAs), specifically in areas where the population within a 250-mile radius exceeded 30 million. Those NRAs should, they said, "be areas which have natural endowments that are well above the ordinary in quality and recreation appeal, being of lesser significance than the unique scenic and historic elements of the national park system, but affording a quality of recreation experience which transcends that normally associated with areas provided by state and local governments." Basically, these new urban parks didn't have to be as beautiful as Yosemite, but they had to be better than city dwellers' current park prospects.

At that moment of disquiet and desire, Hartzog inherited the unenviable job of proving the continued relevancy of the Park Service to Capitol Hill. Not long ago, it was a bureau with carte blanche over its territory. Now it was experiencing a major shift in the treatment of much of its backcountry due to the 1964 Wilderness Act, and the Leopold Report and others were cranking the gears of ecological management. Now the NPS was being told that its power to earmark additional playgrounds for people would be shared. Was there really still a place for an agency with seemingly over-the-hill ideas?

The NPS was competing with as many as twenty other federal agencies to oversee urban recreation areas. While cooperating with the recreation bureau, the NPS director was no doubt looking for ways to keep the Park Service in the mix, to be a solution to the problems of development and disconnection facing the nation. In response, Hartzog launched a new agenda: Parkscape USA, a framework in which to grow the national park system in size and scope. His agenda would lead to an era of great expansion, but it also became the next installment in the ongoing tension between the "use" and "protection" directives inherent in the NPS's founding mandate. Hartzog found himself time and again having to defend and champion the seemingly opposing imperatives of preservation and public recreation.

Hartzog knew that cities lacked sufficient outdoor outlets for the recreation-minded and that, with more free time, hordes of people were hitting the roads en route to wilderness parks. But many others—lacking lengthy vacations, the resources to travel, or the interest in vast wilderness areas—languished amid pavement, glass, and steel. Making national parks more pertinent to that population became his mission. Areas like the National Capital Parks–East and Rock Creek Park in Washington, DC, represented the connection Hartzog wanted to encourage between city dwellers and open space, history, and culture.

The NPS director believed bringing the masses, many of whom were minorities, into the fold would do much to strengthen the base on which the NPS stood. He knew saving wildlands in Alaska required the support not just of people who might hike there but of people in New York City and Chicago who might never see or even hear of Denali. Reflecting on that time many years later, Hartzog said, "That was an important part of the expansion: to make the park system relevant to an evolving urban society, because I still contend that wilderness will never be preserved by the people who manage it. Wilderness will be preserved by the people who elect representatives to the Congress."

Hartzog was also an eager supporter of President Lyndon Johnson's "Great Society" vision for the nation, which called for urban renewal, beautification, conservation, and the prevention of crime and delinquency. The theory went that the country could not be great unless its cities were. Urbanites' lack of communion with nature was troubling for Johnson, who said, "The loss of these values breeds loneliness and boredom and indifference." Unrest dominated some cities, including Los Angeles, which erupted in violent riots in the Watts area in 1965. Over the next few summers, 167 other cities similarly rebelled, largely along racial lines, resulting in hundreds of deaths, thousands of injuries, and billions of dollars in damage. Johnson believed changing the conditions that led to despair was the only way to prevent urban strife. Hartzog felt that encouraging people to get off city blocks and get into parklands could go a long way to curing those ills.

Among the top grievances listed in a poll of urban minorities was a lack of decent recreational opportunities. Hartzog spoke of this before a House committee meeting on the establishment of Golden Gate NRA. He said, "Millions of young people are being reared in asphalt and concrete jungles completely isolated from their natural and cultural inheritance, and they are growing up with no appreciation of the important values that undergird our Republic."

Parkscape USA initiated programs designed to get city dwellers, especially young people and

Blue Hen Falls in Cuyahoga National Park, where bald eagles nest in secluded woodlands, is a natural oasis close to the urban centers of Cleveland and Akron, Ohio.

minorities, into the parks; offerings included Summer in the Parks, Parks for All Seasons, and Living History programs. They not only got people into green spaces but facilitated activities and implemented an education program to, as Hartzog said, "foster environmental perception." The director found a strong ally in the First Lady, who was on the front lines of beautification in the capital park areas. The planting of nearly 1 million new bulbs, plants, and trees (including the now-famous cherry trees, a gift from the Japanese government) and other improvements did much to brighten Washington's gloomy face. "Lady Bird" Johnson, the "First Lady of the National Parks," traveled to other units around the country to witness wonder and woe firsthand, and she had a way of coaxing members of Congress into giving Hartzog what he wanted.

But the urban park emphasis had naysayers, many within the NPS. Among them were park purists who believed the Park Service should focus on large-scale "nature" and on conservation rather than *use*. Detractors didn't count the protection of those urban enclaves as contributing to the preservation of nationally significant resources. Besides, after the Leopold and Robbins reports prescribed a focus on ecology, wasn't there already plenty for the NPS to work on? A Park Service preoccupied with urban park units as well as big reservoirs and national recreation areas created by mammoth dams grew ever distant from those ecological priorities.

In 1967 principal NPS research biologist E. Lowell Sumner (by then a thirty-plus-year veteran of Park Service bureaucracy) remarked, "So far the stage for actual recovery has only been set. An enormous amount of work, extending over many years, must be done to accomplish the goals of restoration and maintenance that have been established. But it is clear that the tools and the know-how are at hand, or can be obtained. It is also clear that another recession like the last would bring irreversible ecological destruction to many of the national parks. To save these world-famous treasures we must learn this lesson from history."

In 1968 the NPS issued its *Administrative Policies for the Natural Areas* (known as the Green Book), which emphasized the active management outlined in the Leopold and Robbins reports. It also tethered past to present by retelling the story of the birth of the national park idea with science at its core. The Green Book quoted Lieutenant Gustavus C. Doane, the astonished young soldier who escorted the famous 1870 Washburn Expedition through Yellowstone, which was an influential step in the founding of the first national park. Doane later said of Yellowstone, "As a field for scientific research, it promises great results; in the branches of geology, mineralogy, botany, zoology, and ornithology it is probably the greatest laboratory that nature furnishes on the surface of the globe." But the Green Book was but a small notch on a set of giant, slow-turning gears.

In the meantime, Hartzog had to contend with critics who felt that urban parks, which began as far-from-pristine wild enclaves, would erode the quality of the NPS brand. The idea of urban parks flew in the face of their romantic notions of what constituted national parks and the experiences they believed people should have in them. While they didn't deny that urbanites needed parks, they felt the NPS wasn't the right master. NPS Chief Historian Robert Utley wrote during that era, "The National Park Service rank and file for the most part opposed the idea of urban parks and still do. They were a big departure from the traditional . . . They thought Hartzog should put his energies into caring for traditional parks and getting more [of them]."

But Hartzog believed the NPS had a responsibility to respond to the needs of the nation. So he pushed on, envisioning Gateway and Golden Gate NRAs as prototypes to be replicated in urban areas nationwide—though he kept that to himself since it was not a popular idea with President Richard Nixon, who took office in 1969. It became a reality to some extent: Santa Monica Mountains NRA was established near Los Angeles, Cuyahoga Valley (now a national park) near Cleveland, and Chattahoochee River NRA outside Atlanta. For many people, those parks were the first, and in

A ranger engages schoolchildren at a beach in Golden Gate NRA.

some cases the only, interface they ever had with the natural world.

Director Hartzog also believed the NPS should support the ongoing equality and environmental movements. The year before he accepted the directorship, Hartzog had stood on the National Mall elbow to elbow with 250,000 others while Dr. Martin Luther King Jr. delivered his rousing "I Have a Dream" speech. As King called out the shameful condition that forced African Americans into exile in their own country, devoid of the inalienable rights promised to all people by the Declaration of Independence, Hartzog was listening. Two national park rangers—one black and one white—flanked King on the steps of the Lincoln Memorial, a place that held special meaning for Hartzog. The sixteenth president was his father's idol, and the elder Hartzog often evoked Lincoln, imploring (as Lincoln's mother had of her son) that George "be somebody."

As director, Hartzog appointed the first African American, the first woman, and the first American Indian to high-profile positions within the Park Service. In an interview in 2005, Hartzog reflected on his role in expanding the NPS ranks. Agency gatherings had generally been a sea of white male faces into the 1960s, when Hartzog began to actively recruit women and people of color. Of the importance of park units that told the stories of women and minorities, he said, "[O]ur diversity is a reality and to me it's a source of pride. We're the only nation on the face of the earth that is created like this nation."

For fifty years, the NPS had been an evolving entity reflecting the shifting interests and needs of the nation; under Hartzog, it continued to be. He was instrumental in the passage of the National Historic Preservation Act of 1966, the most far-reaching preservation legislation ever enacted, and numerous historical parks were inaugurated during his reign. Hartzog also pushed for the first (and only) cultural park, Wolf Trap National Park for the Performing Arts in Virginia, established in 1966. And, despite what his detractors perceived, he also supported the budding environmental movement in his own way.

Hartzog took office just months before the passage of the Wilderness Act of 1964, which had a lasting impact on the NPS. Though he testified on behalf of the legislation, he couldn't have been called a true supporter of it. The concept clashed with the more democratic view he had of parks; Hartzog felt that wilderness, as the bill's proponents saw it, excluded large numbers of people. It made more sense to him to keep options open for possible future development. That is why he tried to market the concept of a "man's influence on the wilderness"—a kind of buffer zone where some modest development was possible between heavily developed park areas and restricted wilderness areas. The wilderness backers weren't buying it.

Hartzog did strive for balance among the many vocal factions at the time. He recalled, "I tried to work with them. I tried to hear their concerns. And I tried to take them into account. I figured when I was catchin' hell from both [the development-minded and the environmentalists], I was somewhere in the right spectrum."

Hartzog was also a believer in the need for a science-minded service. And instead of simply paying lip service to the new ecological framework the way his predecessors had, he called on the framer himself. Hartzog had long admired A. Starker Leopold, and after Hartzog had made several attempts to hire him, Leopold finally accepted the director's offer to be the NPS's first chief scientist. No doubt the two had moments of friction, since Hartzog had a dualistic view of the purpose of parks. "I still believe parks are for people," he said. "If people aren't in parks, then it's not a park . . . But that doesn't mean it's for all people for all things at all times. There's got to be limitations on it."

Leopold stayed in that role, as well as being chair of the Department of the Interior Advisory Board on Wildlife Management, fixing on goals and policies, and methods for enacting them, from 1968 to 1972. During that time, Hartzog was instrumental in the passage of the Wild and Scenic Rivers Act of 1968, after the designation of Ozark National Scenic Riverways in 1964 had made preserving untamed stretches of water a reality. And he played a key part in passing the National Trail Systems Act of 1968, legislation that ultimately added new categories to Park Service holdings.

But there were contradictions. "The spirit of Parkscape USA," Hartzog said in a 1966 *National*

A hiker looks southeast toward San Francisco and the Golden Gate Bridge from the Marin Headlands in Golden Gate NRA.

Geographic article, was embodied in Glen Canyon NRA. The construction of a dam there had created an enormous reservoir, Lake Powell, where stunning red-rock canyons had once been visible. Eight of the NRAs added to the system during Hartzog's time were reservoirs, a creature roundly despised by conservationists. While a huge number of nonprofit conservation organizations were hatched during that time, and many of them told the NPS what it should do to prioritize nature, the NPS generally listened only when the suggestions aligned with its own immediate agenda. Some nonprofits called for an end to crowd-pleasing, century-long traditions such as the Yosemite "Firefall," a bonfire pushed over the edge of Glacier Point and carried by water 3200 feet down into Yosemite Valley. Other organizations called for the elimination of all car-camping areas and even razing the classic Old Faithful Inn.

The Conservation Fund (which would merge with the World Wildlife Fund, now known by the acronym WWF, in 1990) released a powerful manifesto on park values in 1972 that included eight targeted recommendations. A couple of them eventually became NPS policy, while other suggestions called attention to issues that would become more acute in time, persisting up to the present day. The group, which included ecologist Stanley Cain and river-runner and wilderness historian Roderick Nash (author of the immensely popular book *Wilderness and the American Mind*), talked about determining the human carrying capacity of each park and setting quotas based on that. "The choice is ours," they said, "whether the parks shall remain the 'crown jewels' of our outdoor heritage to be cherished, protected, preserved, and worthy of our rigorous self-imposed restraints, or permitted to degenerate into the commonplace."

The general public besieged the NPS with its own growing sense of responsibility toward parklands too. Environmentalism had gone mainstream with the publication of Rachel Carson's *Silent Spring*, the introduction of Earth Day, and the ascendance of the Sierra Club. David Brower, that group's former executive director (with more than seventy first ascents and the facilitation of ten new national parks and seashores to his credit), said in 1971, "Wilderness is the bank for genetic variability of the earth."

That same year, Barry Commoner's book, *The Closing Circle: Nature, Man, and Technology*, was published. The self-described intransigent biologist got straight to the point: "This is the

THE BILLION-DOLLAR PARK

As early as the 1890s, admirers of California's colossal redwood trees began to fret about the trees' rapid demise beneath the saw-toothed blades of eager loggers. It wasn't until 1920 that Congress told the Interior Department to look for an area that might make a suitable national park with the gentle giants at its core.

The National Park Service and the Save-the-Redwoods League surveyed the coast and dispatched advice, but decades more passed as the species' numbers dwindled. By the 1960s, at least 90 percent of the original 2 million acres of coast redwoods—some of which had been living since the height of the Roman empire some 2000 years before—had been felled. The league spent decades cobbling together funds to acquire potential parklands from logging companies, which it then donated to the state for protection.

It took until 1968, with less than 5 percent of the redwoods remaining, for Congress to act, and the new federal preserve placed 58,000 acres under the care of the NPS, President Jimmy Carter followed up on former President Johnson's action by adding another 48,000 acres to Redwood National Park in 1978, where many previously logged acres continue to undergo restoration.

Today the national park, and the state parks that flank it, are comanaged by the state of California and the NPS as a World Heritage Site and an International Biosphere Reserve. Within the national park's temperate rain forest, where countless creeks course along valley gullies, lies the world's tallest known living tree. Named Hyperion, after the father of Helios, the Greek sun god, it is more than 379 feet high. "When all the bills are paid, it is estimated that the cost of the expanded park may be as much as one billion dollars—and worth every cent of it!" Hartzog wrote in his memoir, *Battling for the National Parks*. Laying down footsteps among those titans, careful listeners may catch a whisper from centuries or millennia past or recognize the gritty squawk of a golden eagle, at home in its sky-high canopy.

ecosphere, the home that life has built for itself on the planet's outer surface," he wrote. "Any living thing that hopes to live on the earth must fit into the ecosphere or perish. The environmental crisis is a sign that the finely sculptured fit between life and its surroundings has begun to corrode." The book brought the term "sustainability" into vogue and introduced Commoner's four laws of ecology: "Everything is connected to everything else . . . Everything must go somewhere . . . Nature knows best . . . There is no such thing as a free lunch." A general societal viewpoint began to emerge that the

planet had been abused—air, water, and soil had been polluted and resources had been ravaged—and that humans were responsible.

Significantly, the Nixon administration answered that public outcry with a rapid-fire and stunning spate of federal legislation: the Clean Air Act (1970), the Endangered Species Act (1973), the Clean Water Act (1972), and the law that created the Environmental Protection Agency (1970). While all these laws greatly affected management of national parks, the one that most altered the ground rules for the NPS from the 1970s onward was the

LWCF: FIFTY AND FABULOUS

The Land and Water Conservation Fund (LWCF), which recently turned fifty, has been a critical tool in preserving roughly 5 million acres; the National Park Service has used it to secure land in Grand Canyon National Park and others. When it was devised five decades ago, the concept seemed straightforward enough: devote up to $900 million every year from offshore oil and gas drilling royalties to create and protect valuable parcels of federal land.

But year after year, Congress has been diverting those funds (totaling roughly $30 billion so far) that should have been used to make strategic preservation investments. If the LWCF is reauthorized and fully funded into the future, it will renew a pledge made to the American people a half century ago, and it could be a powerful tool to help secure a future for vulnerable ecosystems throughout the national park system.

National Environmental Policy Act (NEPA) of 1969, which requires all federal agencies to consider the environmental impacts of proposed actions. NEPA also permits public input into the process, which allows all citizens—including conservation advocacy groups—to comment on how, in the case of the NPS, national parks should be run. Coming into compliance with all of those new legislative pieces meant that the Park Service would need more scientific knowledge about park resources at all levels than it currently had.

Into the 1970s, the Park Service made fitful progress establishing several scientific research centers, which would coordinate with research offices in individual parks. The number of in-house scientists increased, and so did their budget (somewhat). But despite having the Leopold Report author at the helm of its scientists, the NPS was still not able to create a thorough, collaborative program to manage science. After the departure of Leopold as chief scientist, as rapidly as ecological thinking had risen in the consciousness of policy makers, it fell again. Although "wilderness" parks

such as Guadalupe Mountains (1966) and North Cascades (1968) were added to the national park system and portions of existing parks were federally protected under the 1964 Wilderness Act during this time, the NPS regressed to old habits. The scientific voice was muffled by reshuffling to lower tiers those scientists who had been elevated to report to the director. The meager funds earmarked for research were often pilfered for other work within parks.

Ultimately, Hartzog's leadership brought about the addition of more than seventy park units, including large natural units such as Canyonlands and Redwood national parks and wilderness-grade parks such as Voyageurs. A handful of national seashores were also established during his run, including Fire Island, Cape Lookout, Assateague Island, Cumberland Island, and Gulf Islands, as well as national lakeshores such as Sleeping Bear Dunes, Apostle Islands, Indiana Dunes, and Pictured Rocks. Nearly 3 million acres (an increase of

Extremes characterize Guadalupe Mountains National Park where teeming habitats range from gypsum sand dunes, succulents, and shrub desert to semiarid grasslands and coniferous forests filled with firs and pines.

about 10 percent) were added to the park system during Hartzog's term, and his efforts eventually led to the preservation of more than 47 million additional acres, including massive additions in Alaska amid tremendous controversy.

But he wouldn't be around to celebrate that victory firsthand. In 1972 Hartzog became the first NPS director to be forced to resign. Despite being a consummate negotiator and roundly admired, he ruffled President Nixon's feathers when the Park Service revoked a special permit that had allowed one of the commander-in-chief's friends to dock a houseboat in Florida's Biscayne National Monument.

Hartzog, the Outdoor Recreation Resources Review Committee, and the Bureau of Recreation are long gone (the recreation bureau was abolished in 1981, when the NPS resumed many functions once taken from it), but some of their greatest achievements endure. For example, one of the ORRRC's recommendations led to the creation of the Land and Water Conservation Fund (LWCF) in 1965, which requires that some of the annual profits from offshore oil and gas leases be spent on conservation on local, state, and federal levels. Hartzog acquired new NPS lands largely with that tool. The LWCF was a kind of promise—a gift from policy makers a half century ago to future leaders—to keep conservation at the core of American values.

"The need for people to get outdoors and have an association with the land is inherent in us

as human beings," Hartzog said. His two mold-breaking parks, Gateway and Golden Gate, were added to the park system mere months before the director's departure. Now more than 20 million visitors per year shake off their city shackles there—more than twice the numbers at Yosemite, Grand Canyon, and Yellowstone combined. Visitors to those urban parks swim, hike, camp, paddle, hang-glide, bird-watch, horseback ride, bike, or simply wait, watch, and listen. At Gateway, they might glimpse a seal basking in the sun at Sandy Hook or an eastern gray tree frog that, within a few eyeblinks, camouflages itself from brilliant green to brownish gray while its lively warbling vibrates summer air.

Picketers in Fairbanks, Alaska, in December 1978 protest the Antiquities Act with signs reading "Save our land from what?" and "What about state's rights?"

CHAPTER 21

"Park Barrel" Politics

AS YOU BUZZ OVER Wrangell–St. Elias National Park in a single-engine Cessna, the immensity of the place comes into focus. Black peaks prod fleecy clouds, glaciers loll like massive tongues, and braided rivers carve slews of channels through the Alaskan backcountry. Wrangell–St. Elias is roughly bisected by the Chitina River, which flows from the enormous Logan Glacier on the eastern edge of the park. The noble, colossal Wrangell Mountains make up the northern half of the park, and the younger, steeper Chugach

Mountains populate the south. The 127-mile-long, 6-mile-wide, 3000-foot-thick Bagley Icefield spills from the stony peaks of the Chugach onto valley floors via dozens of named glaciers.

The runoff from this largest subpolar icefield in North America and its valley glaciers sustain a multitude of life-forms such as spawning salmon, hungry grizzlies, grazing moose, and crag-hopping Dall sheep, as well as mighty stretches of boreal forest filled with breezy stands of spruce, poplar, willow, blueberry, aspen, and more. The park's name refers to both 14,163-foot Mount Wrangell, one of the largest active volcanoes in North America, and Mount St. Elias, which, at more than 18,000 feet, is the second-highest peak in the United States. Spanning more than 13 million acres, it is the largest US national park—and yet it is seldom visited.

This rugged land—with the largest proportion of designated wilderness in the national park system, at 10 million acres—is not an empty landscape, as many believed fifty years ago. But back then, what it had to offer depended upon who you asked.

In the early 1960s, the US Army Corps of Engineers was moving ahead on a scheme to dam the Yukon River at Rampart Gorge for hydroelectric power. Nine Alaska Native villages would have been drowned by a reservoir the size of Lake Erie.

The Alaska Conservation Society—started in 1960 by local bush pilot Ginny Wood and her husband, Morton, a ranger at then–Mount McKinley (now Denali) National Park—rose up against the dam. They passed petitions, contacted Congress, and publicized prolifically. In 1965 Ginny wrote in "Ramparts We Watch," published in the *Sierra Club Bulletin*, "Perhaps we may find that Alaska's most valuable resource, even in terms of the market place, is not water power and an industrial potential, but space—spectacularly beautiful space that is not all filled up with people and industry as is so much of the rest of the world."

The Woods, and their close friend and fellow activist Celia Hunter, represented a faction of local Alaskans who experienced the backcountry as something more than shopping malls for extractive industries. Ginny and Celia had been flying

tourists around the state already and had pooled their money in 1952 to build Camp Denali (still in operation), nearly 100 miles into Denali National Park. They also started Tundra Treks in the late 1950s, leading backpacking trips into the wilderness, the first tourist business of its kind in Alaska. Ginny wrote about the "qualities of the spirit that diminish as the wide open spaces recede," which she understood could easily happen in Alaska if they let down their guard.

The massive dam proposal was splashed across national media, and when Secretary of the Interior Stewart Udall did all he could to defeat the stoppering of the wild Yukon, the plan fell apart. Rampart Gorge, the salmon that run the Yukon, and the vast wetlands that serve as critical breeding grounds for millions of waterfowl were ultimately protected in 1980 when Yukon Flats National Wildlife Refuge was established.

But another challenge quickly rose. In 1969, just a decade after Alaska had become a state, a consortium of oil companies announced a plan to build an 800-mile-long pipeline to deliver oil from Prudhoe Bay in the north to Valdez in the south, leaving a visible scar on Alaska's wild face. A National Park Service committee in the midsixties had proposed thirty-nine sites (with Wrangell–St. Elias at the top of the list) where it suggested the NPS urgently step up its acquisitions. However, politicians hungry to develop resources—from oil reserves and timber to fishing camps and vacation homes—on those hundreds of millions of acres of federal land refused even to meet with NPS representatives. Now alarm bells rang in the environmental community; oil spills from wells and tankers had already made national headlines as the cash-strapped state clung to that resource as its ace in the hole. They could do little to slow the momentum of the Trans-Alaska

Pipeline, which crosses three mountain ranges and 800 rivers and streams, but they vowed to fight for what remained of untamed Alaska.

Before any interests could lay claim to portions of Alaska's 375 million acres of "public" land, however, its rightful tribal owners would have to be compensated. By the late '60s, Native groups had filed suit over aboriginal land claims, prompting Secretary Udall to freeze any action— from drilling to camping—on public lands until the issue was resolved. Overnight it seemed everyone, from oil giants to state politicians and national environmental groups, was cozying up to Alaska Natives—the Aleuts, Athabascans, Eskimos (including Inuit and Yupik), Haidas, and Tlingits—wanting Native claims withdrawn from the areas they considered valuable.

The Native population, much of which had suffered terribly both economically and socially by that time, was eager to secure access to lands they considered ancestral while being paid for the rest. What resulted was the Alaska Native Claims Settlement Act (ANCSA), passed at the end of 1971, which allowed indigenous people to choose 44 million acres for their own use. In return for releasing other aboriginal land claims in the state, Native groups were paid nearly $1 billion.

The rest of the landmass was then ostensibly up for grabs, with one key exception. A powerful amendment to the act, engineered by NPS Director George Hartzog, ignited one of the most acerbic conservation controversies in history. That provision allowed the secretary of the interior to withdraw millions of acres of existing public land

"The Mountain" looms large for this backpacker in Denali National Park.

for consideration as national parks, wildlife refuges, forests, and wild and scenic rivers. By 1972 the NPS was administering 7.5 million acres in four parks in Alaska but had sent recommendations (derived from the work of its field-based Alaska Task Force) to add twenty-plus areas spanning more than 40 million acres to the national park system.

Current NPS historian Chris Allan, based in Fairbanks, is an expert on that time period. He says many outsiders saw Alaska as the country's last chance to safeguard true wilderness areas (later called national interest lands), but Alaskans of all backgrounds and motivations protested what they called the "locking up" of *their* land. They figured they could use, manage, and develop state resources better, and they wanted Alaska to be as free of federal interference as possible. They prided themselves on their self-sufficiency in the far north and felt huge parks threatened that spirit.

In the midst of that storm, says Allan, the NPS became a "lightning rod for anxieties," an entity toward which a century's worth of enmity and mistrust of the federal government was channeled. The NPS was also suffering an image problem locally, due to Alaskans' perception that the feds were indifferent in their management of existing national parks in the state. Up until the time of Alaska's statehood, due to a lack of resources the Park Service had only a handful of employees on the ground to manage the seldom-visited Mount McKinley (now Denali) and Glacier Bay national parks. Paradoxically, though they opposed federal takes, locals were irked that the NPS acted as an absentee landlord of the public land that did exist in Alaska.

Hartzog's Alaska Task Force said as much in its report, "Operation Great Land," which suggested the NPS get its act together before seeking public support for additional parks in the state. The Park Service had neglected to establish a public presence and had done nothing, it said, "except give lip service to the broad concept" of the potential for and purpose of parklands in Alaska. It would need to take a much more active role on the ground, the task force said: "the time has come for action, not words."

Into the 1970s the Park Service scrimped in the management of parks in the Lower 48 in order to bolster its in-Alaska staff and improve access for visitors. At the same time, negotiations had begun to sort out how to apply one controversial section of ANCSA, 17 (d) (2), which allowed the secretary of the interior to withdraw up to 80 million acres of land from development for conservation purposes. Those "d-2" lands, as they became known, had to be withdrawn by the secretary within nine months of ANCSA's passage, and with input from all parties they were, at least preliminarily, set aside in March 1972.

Federal officials, supported by environmentalists focused on preserving whole ecosystems, and would-be resource extractors, backed by state leadership and many locals, became enmeshed in round-the-clock meetings, scouting trips, heated and lengthy debates, and not a little barb throwing. During those talks, millions of acres were lost and gained like chess game pawns; some areas swelled to a size that made conservationists giddy. Others were not so gleeful. Congressman Nick Begich, once a key player in the passage of ANCSA, called the conservation proposals (and preservation proposals, for many included cultural resources) a massive land grab. Alaska Attorney General John Havelock threatened lawsuits over what he dubbed a sellout of Alaskans.

Opponents decried the conservation proposals as "park barrel politics" designed to benefit everyone except the state.

Between the time of the initial d-2 withdrawals and the final ones several months later, the NPS raced to essentially double-check that it had suggested the best possible additions to the national park system. In his administrative history of the Park Service during that time, NPS historian Frank Williss wrote that the Alaska Task Force worked tirelessly in the field before making its final determination: "After weeks of virtually around the clock effort the Service recommended that Secretary [of the Interior Rogers] Morton withdraw for study for potential additions to the National Park System eleven areas totaling 48,945,800 acres." The biggest chunks of that were 13.4 million-acre Wrangell–St. Elias and the 11 million-acre Gates of the Arctic.

The secretary's final d-2 withdrawals included twenty-two areas spanning nearly 80 million acres for possible addition to the national park system. They included most of the land suggested by the Alaska Task Force (41.7 million acres' worth), though several areas were scaled back by hundreds of thousands or even millions of acres. Despite the land lost, the members of the task force seemed pleased with the result. Williss wrote that the planners commented, "We got all the rock and ice we asked for" at Mount McKinley (now Denali) and suggested that Wrangell–St. Elias be called Great Glacier National Park.

Bill Brown, a member of the Alaska Task Force who went on to live and work in the far north for many more years, summarized that historic period this way in his foreword to Williss's book: "There was drama here, every bit as moving as that passed down from the legendary campfire

at Yellowstone. But all this was only prelude. The work now being done and yet to do gives us the chance to recapitulate the early days of Park Service history. Here is a place where new legends wait to be born, where new heroes can prove their mettle." What Brown meant was that the protection of these massive open spaces was exciting, and revolutionary to a certain extent, but their value had to be proven to the rest of the nation and, not incidentally, to Congress.

The historic ANCSA legislation required that Congress implement the interior secretary's selection of d-2 lands by December 18, 1978; otherwise, the lands would be fair game for developers. For years, efforts to solidify the national interest lands in flux were dead ends, until Jimmy Carter was elected president in 1976. During his campaign, he had vowed to act on ANCSA, and as that deadline approached, lawmakers took action. On Congress's first day of work in 1977, Arizona Congressman Morris "Mo" Udall (brother of former Secretary of the Interior Stewart Udall) introduced House Resolution 39, the precursor to the Alaska National Interest Lands Conservation Act (ANILCA) of 1980.

Opponents immediately jockeyed for revisions. As written, the bill was a conservationist's dream, but it met opposition from all the usual suspects, and then some, including a portion of Alaska Natives who felt that "wilderness" threatened their subsistence rights. Central to the debate were the issues of use and access on d-2 lands: Would Alaskans be able to hunt and fish as they normally had? Could they fly in or take snowmobiles? Would there be areas where logging, drilling, or mineral exploration would be allowed? How much would

THE PRESIDENT'S MAGIC WAND

Unlike national parks, which require an act of Congress, national monuments can be created from existing federal land by the president without congressional input, through the power of the 1906 Antiquities Act. This brief piece of legislation's influence has reached far and wide. The original purpose was to safeguard archaeological sites; some of the best examples now protected are Bandelier, Montezuma Castle, Gila Cliff Dwellings, Hovenweep, and Canyons of the Ancients.

But the Antiquities Act's open-ended wording has led to the protection of heritage and the environment as well. The legislation reads, in part: "The President of the United States is hereby authorized, in his discretion, to declare by public proclamation historic landmarks, historic and prehistoric structures, and other objects of historic or scientific interest that are situated upon the lands owned or controlled by the Government of the United States to be national monuments."

The catchall phrase "scientific interest" has been used to justify the inclusion of some of the largest and most controversial national monuments. From the beginning, environmental resources were given as much weight as cultural ones, an interpretation that has had a lasting impact both on states with monuments and on the responsibilities of the National Park Service. "It was a very forward-thinking law," says Stanley Bond, current chief archaeologist of the Park Service. "And it's still a very important mechanism for preserving cultural and natural sites in the United States."

Presidents have defended their use of the Antiquities Act as a way to protect places from immediate threats and—as Carter did in Alaska—to end bureaucratic deadlock. While the far-reaching authority has been wielded by fourteen presidents since Teddy Roosevelt, with some expected push and pull, some lawmakers have argued adamantly that the Antiquities Act flouts the democratic process by circumventing Congress. Opponents have argued it denies access to resources where mining, grazing, logging, or hunting might have taken place. Conservationists counter that parklands contribute significantly and consistently to local and national economies in a more sustainable way than resource extraction.

About one-third of national *parks* began their conservation lives as national *monuments* (Congress can change their designation), and there are now nearly eighty NPS-managed national monuments in all. Some were created by acts of Congress, but most were not.

become "instant wilderness," as conservationists referred to it, which would restrict all those activities? During the days of input and debate over the bill, Alaska Governor Jay Hammond, a former bush pilot, made a statement that would prove prophetic in the rough air that lay ahead for ANILCA: "It is not easy to be both the oil barrel to the nation and national park to the world."

The final bill showed some major concessions on both sides, ensuring that no one was 100 percent satisfied. The NPS lost national "park" acreage in nearly every proposed unit to the newer category of "preserve," which allowed for fishing, hunting, and fuel and mineral extraction—if it didn't harm the overall health of the natural resources. Still, before the bill came up for a vote, Mo Udall called it "surely the greatest conservation opportunity ever to be placed before the House of Representatives." HR 39 passed 279–31 in May 1978, but whatever contention had been experienced up to that point was a relative speed bump compared to the wall the bill would hit in the Senate.

The Senate version of the bill was virtually unrecognizable, and largely unacceptable, to conservationists, despite some effort being made at compromise. The bill and a provision to extend the d-2 deadline for a year were both killed by Alaska Senator Mike Gravel. NPS historian Williss writes that Gravel saw the bill as a slippery slope toward a total federal takeover. "They don't want just this, they want all of Alaska," Gravel said. Instead of letting the deadline pass, President Carter made a bold move, as the NPS had recommended numerous times and Secretary of the Interior Cecil Andrus had warned Carter would. With the stroke of a pen—a move that would dog him, and Gravel for that matter, for decades—the president used the Antiquities Act of 1906 to set aside seventeen national monuments totaling 56 million acres. It was the broadest application of the legislation in history. The secretary withdrew another 40 million acres for conservation consideration.

The withdrawals were intended to prevent Alaska from becoming, as Andrus said, "a private preserve for a handful of rape, ruin and

run developers." Carter saw the monument designations as a stop-gap measure intended as a placeholder, a starting point from which Congress could debate access and refine uses as it moved toward passage of ANILCA. The proclamations succeeded in achieving a level of protection for those national lands until final determinations could be made—but the nuance of Carter's actions was lost on many Alaskans.

By and large they did not take the news well. The *Anchorage Times* called the move a dirty deed, and the state filed a suit challenging the federal withdrawals. There was talk of state secession. An overalls-clad, straw-stuffed effigy of Carter with a noose around its neck was burned at a rally in

Protest signs opposed to the "tyranny" and "dictatorship" of the NPS in conserving public lands were posted in Eagle, Alaska, the epicenter of Antiquities Act dissent in the late 1970s and early 1980s.

Fairbanks. During Carter's visit to the Alaska State Fair in 1979, his Secret Service detail read the ire of the crowd and suggested he stay in the vehicle. He didn't but did have in tow double the agents normally on deck. Years later, Carter remembered seeing a baseball-tossing booth there where players took aim at his likeness; the image of Ayatollah Khomeini, leader of the Iranian regime that held Americans hostage at the time, was another target but was not nearly as popular.

In Eagle and Glenallen, two towns in the shadow of new monuments, the locals were furious. A resolution adopted in both towns promised that "we do not intend to obey the directives and regulations of the National Park Service." The new director of the NPS Alaska Area Office was greeted with signs reading "NATIONAL PARK SERVICE EMPLOYEES and anyone else advocating a dictatorship (including those locally who support National Park Service activities under the Antiquities Act) ARE NOT WELCOME HERE!" Placards stuck to car bumpers read "Take this monument and shove it!"

Jack Boone, a longtime Eagle resident and city council member, described the mood in a town where people hunted, fished, and trapped on nearby public lands in order to feed their families: "They lived a subsistence lifestyle. They strongly opposed this action . . . I felt at the time . . . that sending the Park Service as the agency to manage an area this lightly used was like using a cannon to kill a mosquito—totally inappropriate," he said. Many of his neighbors had left the Lower 48 to escape what they felt was too much government interference, only to find themselves smack in the middle of it in rural Alaska.

Bob Howe, who did some of the early field studies of what became Yukon-Charley Rivers National

Preserve and wrapped up his longtime NPS career as superintendent at Glacier Bay, described the feeling this way: "People were happy with the way life was, and they wanted to keep it that way. Federal government would be restrictive and they didn't want anything to do with it. One of the reasons they had come to that part of Alaska was to escape that bureaucracy that would change their way of life. That was the basis of all the problems." And the locals, particularly in Eagle, certainly devised colorful ways to make their opinions known. "There were a couple of graves by the main intersection with the toes of boots sticking up out of the headstones [which] indicated that these were Park Service people," said Boone.

The NPS historian at the time, Bill Brown, said that Carter's monuments designation was seen by many Alaskans as unconstitutional, and he said it "just blew the lid off" the fragile détente that had existed between locals and the NPS up to that point. All of the work he and other members of the Alaska Task Force had done over the previous several years, to reassure residents that traditional land uses would be maintained, "was wiped out. All of their fears were realized," he said.

"Except for the conservation community who welcomed this 'into the breach' way of holding on to these areas and preserving the work done over the many years, basically Alaska went into open revolt." Tempers were so high that it did little good to try to explain that traditional subsistence uses, as well as firearms and the use of aircraft, would be allowed in the monuments.

Eagle councilmember Boone says locals definitely wanted to make the Park Service nervous and uncomfortable but would never have taken it further than that. "To the best of my knowledge there was never any actual seriously contemplated violence against any Park Service person, from Eagle," he said. "I've heard there was in other parts of the state but . . . never any here."

While a frosty demeanor and idle threats dominated the reaction to federal presence in Alaska, there were also some hairy moments. Members of the 1979 Ranger Task Force received many personal death threats. Shots were fired through office windows at night. At Wrangell–St. Elias, an NPS plane was torched and another had its cables cut. Rangers there had to leave their homes when they received a bomb threat.

Much as Jackson Hole locals had done after the designation of Jackson Hole National Monument in Wyoming decades earlier (see Nobody sidebar, chapter 12), Alaskans staged an act of civil disobedience. Hundreds converged on the town of Cantwell in January 1979 for the Great Denali–McKinley Trespass. During the course

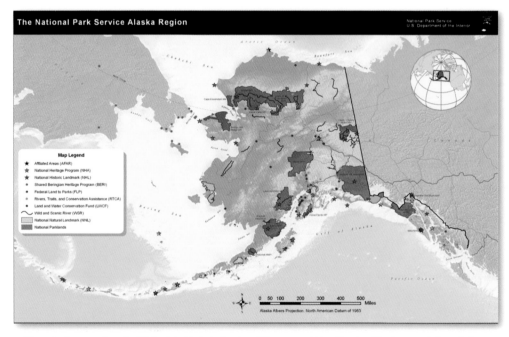

The scale of conservation of public lands in Alaska is clear from this map on which national parklands appear in large dark green swaths, most of which were set aside through political maneuvering in the late 1970s and early 1980s.

of a two-day protest, an estimated 1500 residents crossed into the newly designated Denali National Monument (which would become part of the national park a year later) and engaged in as many illegal activities as possible. They lit bonfires, set traps, shot some birds, ran dog teams, drove their snow machines around, and even skydived.

Meanwhile, ten NPS rangers, who had arrived from the Pacific Northwest to back up the small cadre of law enforcement already at McKinley, more or less stood by and watched. The resistance was relatively peaceful, but it didn't escape the notice of the Park Service that many of the protesters were heavily armed. A *Spokesman-Review* (Spokane, Washington) article from the time says that, while rangers made no arrests at the protest, they warned that "federal regulations governing national monuments in Alaska would be strictly enforced in the future." As the Park Service began to establish a presence in the new monuments, despite scant resources they made good on that promise; they patrolled enormous areas, making contact with as many people as possible to talk about the new rules, and wrote tickets for violations.

However unpopular, the monument designations had lit a fire beneath Congress to determine, through legislation, the final status of those many millions of acres that had already been withdrawn by Carter and Secretary Andrus. What level of conservation protection would each parcel ultimately have? What uses would be allowed? For the better part of the next two years, the push to pass ANILCA was mired by outside lobbyists, inside politicking (including much take-it-or-leave-it bluster from Alaska lawmakers), and a shift of power in the House from conservation to conservative.

As the nation's capital started heating up in the summer of 1980, so did the debate over various amendments to the bill. It seemed lawmakers were getting nowhere, but the presidential election that November unseated Carter in favor of Ronald Reagan, who promised to undo as much protection of public lands in Alaska as possible. After that, both sides were motivated to pass a version of ANILCA that safeguarded some of Alaska's resources and allowed for economic development of others. The compromises included Andrus permanently removing from protection 40 million acres he had reserved in 1978, which consisted mainly of potential wildlife refuges.

But many more potential parklands remained in the bill—certainly not all that conservationists wanted, but definitely more than Alaska's elected officials did. The bill also ensured that presidential authority could never again be used to proclaim a national monument in Alaska. The concessions were tough for Mo Udall, who, shortly before the House voted on a version of the bill that had already passed the Senate, said, "Neither I nor those who support me consider this legislation to be a great victory for the cause." Despite the lackluster endorsement—following nearly a decade of political machinations—the House passed ANILCA, and Carter signed it on December 2, 1980, in the waning days of his presidency.

While conservationists back then were disappointed, the bill is now thought of as one of the most significant moments in conservation history. The act redesignated many of Carter's national *monuments* as national *parks* and ultimately preserved 104 million acres as ten national parks and preserves, two national monuments, two national conservation areas, twenty-five wild and scenic rivers, and nine wildlife refuges. It tripled the amount of public land in the country that could not be developed and more than doubled the acreage in the national park system.

One of those significant additions was Wrangell–St. Elias, which alone protects nine of the highest sixteen peaks in the United States. Borders were also drawn around places where marine ecosystems, prehistoric artifacts, critical habitat, and migration corridors are now protected. On the day he signed ANILCA, Carter addressed criticism that the legislation would cripple the state's economy: "The price of not protecting the environment would be far greater and far more lasting," he said. "Much of the damage cannot possibly be repaired at any price. We protect it today or we lose it for all time."

In the decades following the passage of those extraordinary land acts, legislators once vilified returned to Alaska, including President Carter and Congressman Mo Udall. On those occasions, they were largely greeted by cheers instead of jeers. Udall commented that people were still waving their hands at him, but this time were using all five fingers. Most Alaskans came to accept the millions of visitors their parks draw annually, the tens of thousands of jobs the parks support, and the $1 billion-plus they pump into local and state economies each year. As President Carter said in 1980, "We were determined to preserve portions of Alaska. . . . We dared to act with foresight instead of hindsight." In attempting to consider the equal demands of industry and ecology, he said, "We struck a balance."

In late 2013, in an NPS-sponsored teleconference with some 90,000 students—including many in the shadow of Wrangell–St. Elias National Park—the former president talked with schoolchildren about his bold, once-unpopular moves that were driven in part by the consideration of generations to come. Addressing a high-school student's question about the role of today's youth in protecting the environment, Carter said, "You should be constantly alert throughout your life . . . . and protect [the earth] with all of your resources and all your intelligence and all your strength."

It's hard to know what Alaska would look like now had that sweeping legislation not been enacted. Would more oil pipelines slice through solitude? Would healthy populations of wolves and bears exist? Would there be a backcountry like that in Wrangell–St. Elias, where, if you had a lifetime of exploration, you still would not know it all? Would places where the sight of a gyrfalcon climbing effortlessly over treetops, a river otter propelling gracefully through a cold mountain stream, or a wolverine lumbering powerfully through deep, soft snow be the exception, not the norm? All those who fought to keep Alaska wild no doubt hope each generation to come will be as unacquainted as the last with that possibility.

"Helen of Many Glacier Hotel," an American Indian, operates the hotel's switchboard in 1925; she is one of many tribal people who had a complex relationship with conservation and the NPS.

CHAPTER 22

Civilized Off the Face of the Earth

ON A HOT AFTERNOON in late June, Joshua Little Owl stands beneath the visitor center canopy at the Little Bighorn Battlefield National Monument in southeast Montana. It's the only shady spot as far as the eye can see. The sky is relentlessly blue, with a small handful of clouds that quickly retreat into vastness. To the north is the Yellowstone River; to the south the Little Bighorn River flows in the shadow of the Wolf Mountains.

This is Little Owl's second year as a National Park Service interpretive ranger, and he's addressing

visitors who sit facing Last Stand Hill, now a quiet, breezy hillside where a simple, gleaming memorial marks the 1876 fall of US Army Seventh Cavalry troops. It was on a day like this, hovering around 100 degrees, when Lieutenant Colonel George Custer and more than 260 troops in his immediate command were killed by Northern Plains Indians.

Little Owl, a lanky, twenty-two-year-old member of the Crow tribe, asks the gathered group, "How many want to hear the battle talk where Custer wins? Anyone want to hear that

NPS Director Stephen Mather and Blackfeet Indian Chief Curly Bear meet again at Glacier National Park. Several years earlier Curly Bear had visited Mather in Washington, DC, as part of a delegation protesting the use of non-Indian names in the park.

talk?" Muffled laughter is the reply in this place, sacrosanct due to lost lives, including as many as 100 Lakota Sioux, Cheyenne, and Arapaho warriors.

But it is also a site of intersecting emotions where histories collide and demand reflection. Were Custer and his men bravely following orders to drive tribes back to reservations? Or were they invaders trying to overtake indigenous people on land that legally belonged to them? The tension broken by the quiet chuckles, Little Owl welcomes the visitors to the monument and to the Crow Reservation that surrounds it, "swirling like water around a stone," as Northern Cheyenne Chief Two Moon described Indian bands circling Custer during his final moments.

Little Bighorn, which became part of the national park system in 1940, is one of dozens of sites focused on American Indian events, including such stirring places as Arizona's Tonto National Monument, Ocmulgee National Monument in Georgia, Iowa's Effigy Mounds National Monument, and the Trail of Tears National Historic Trail. But scratch the surface of the history of European Americans in what is now the United States, and encounters with indigenous people pervade nearly every aspect. The histories of Acadia and the Everglades, of Denali, Yellowstone, and Yosemite—and dozens of lesser-known places in between—are woefully incomplete without the Indian perspective. The Park Service has estimated that Native Americans have cultural and historical ties, some stretching back thousands of years, to more than 40 percent of NPS units. But up until

the 1980s, Native Americans were mentioned only a handful of times in agency documents spanning nearly a century.

George Catlin, penning the first notion of a "nation's park" in the 1830s, felt the existence of American Indians was imperiled by Euro-Americans pushing across the finite frontier and hoped all life there might be safeguarded from western expansion. Following in the boot steps of the Lewis and Clark Expedition, the painter bobbed along the wide, silted Missouri River into the Dakota Territory in 1832 in search of Indian subjects for his paintings. Observing the seemingly endless prairie (once nearly 340 million acres constituted the river's basin), Catlin was overcome by the "thousand hills, and bluffs, and dales, and ravines" and the herds of antelope, bison, and elk congregating there. The artist spent the better part of a decade documenting Native Americans, painting portraits and scenes that remain invaluable for their chronicling of everyday Indian life and culture. Catlin recorded some of the final moments that many tribes spent in their homelands.

The Indian Removal Act, signed by President Andrew Jackson in 1830, eventually strong-armed most Native people from the East onto reservations west of the Mississippi River. Out of fear, ignorance, greed, or a combination of the three, Euro-Americans saw Indians as competitors for resources, as a problem to be solved, as a wildfire to be extinguished. Speaking to Congress soon after signing the displacement bill, Jackson said, "It gives me pleasure to announce to Congress that the benevolent policy of the Government, steadily pursued for nearly thirty years, in relation to the removal of the Indians beyond the white settlements is approaching to a happy consummation."

American Indians were not quite so pleased or optimistic, and a council of the Cherokee Nation commented, "We wish to remain on the land of our fathers. We have a perfect and original right to remain without interruption or molestation. The treaties with us, and laws of the United States made in pursuance of treaties, guaranty our residence, and our privileges and secure us against intruders. Our only request is, that these treaties may be fulfilled, and these laws executed . . . But if we are compelled to leave our country, we see nothing but ruin before

us." Several years on, those treaties were trampled and the tribe lost a Supreme Court battle, losing their ancestral homeland in western Georgia, where gold had recently been discovered. Roughly 4000 Cherokees died while being forcibly marched along the Trail of Tears to a reservation in Oklahoma.

Catlin had focused on depicting American Indians because he felt they "had been invaded, their morals corrupted, their lands wrested from them, their customs changed, and therefore lost to the world." While his national preserve idea

George Catlin's *See-non-ty-a, an Iowa Medicine Man 1844/45* was one of many of the artist's American Indian–themed works meant to highlight the plight of Native people.

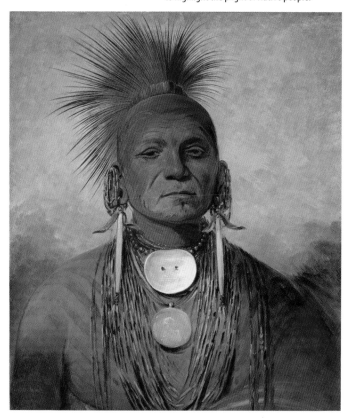

The Navajo, like many tribes, lived in conflict and compromise in relation to US conservation lands. Ansel Adams documented this Navajo woman and child in Arizona's Canyon de Chelly.

In that same decade, and with his own sentimental flair, conservation icon Henry David Thoreau wrote extensively about his encounters with Indian culture, primarily the Penobscot. In his *Indian Notebooks*, he admired the Native ability to "see the great spirit in everything." In *The Maine Woods*, based on his travels in the 1850s, Thoreau reiterated Catlin's hope for an Indian Territory where Native people would live traditional lives: "Why should not we, who have renounced the king's authority, have our national preserves, where no villages need be destroyed, in which the bear and panther, and some even of the hunter race, may still exist, and not be 'civilized off the face of the earth'?"

Thoreau's interactions with American Indians informed much of the writer's later work and beliefs and that of his admirer John Muir. Muir closely patterned his *Travels in Alaska* on Thoreau's *Maine Woods*, and the evolution in his thinking about Native people followed a similar arc. Both men initially held fast to predominant racist beliefs about American Indians, but those beliefs became muddled by their appreciation for Natives' understanding and interpretation of the environment and their adaptability and relative harmony with the wild. Ultimately, on opposite coasts, Muir's and Thoreau's attitudes about American Indians shifted dramatically over time.

Prior to spending significant time with the Penobscot, Thoreau had described them as "greasy-looking," "dull," "shabby," and "sinister."

was of course pursued zealously, its architects did not embrace Catlin's belief that indigenous people should remain in those special places. Ultimately, all but a minuscule number of American Indians were evicted from eventual parklands, and the artist's wish for cultural longevity and harmony among species and between men would be only that. In 1851 the western migration of white pioneers and the advance of the railroads precipitated the Indian Appropriations Act, which "consolidated" western tribes onto reservations. But even then, treaties were broken time and again, and reservation land was chipped away at by Euro-Americans hunting natural resources. It was one such event that ultimately led to the Battle of Little Bighorn.

Similarly, until Muir forged friendships with members of the Tlingit nation in coastal Alaska, he had described the Indians he encountered in California as "lazy," "dirty," and "superstitious." In his book *My First Summer in the Sierra*, Muir wrote, "Perhaps if I knew them better I should like them better." In time Muir did come to respect Native beliefs and customs, and both he and Thoreau came to see (at least some) American Indians as key to human understanding of the environment. Native Americans saw themselves as part of a sacred circle in which all life was connected, a concept both Thoreau and Muir embraced and advanced. Muir's later writing includes descriptions of Indians as "wise," "stoic," and "dignified." Thoreau adopted terms including "steady and reliable" and "beautiful simplicity."

❖   ❖   ❖   ❖

Whatever effect those two behemoth interpreters of the natural world had on the conservationists who followed them, their attitudes about American Indians were not retained. Many early conservationists acted as if potential parklands were empty spaces waiting to fulfill their destiny of delighting and enlightening Euro-Americans. But, in reality, many would-be parklands were places where American Indians lived year-round or seasonally. Here, they rocked babies to sleep, tended critical crops, drummed and danced, hunted for food and hides, made art, held reunions, shared stories from time's beginning, built shelters,

and retreated to for spiritual guidance and fulfillment. A dozen or more tribes had frequented Yellowstone—one of them lived there permanently. A mixed band of Ahwahnechee, Paiute, and Miwok used Yosemite. The Blackfeet, Salish, Kootenai, and at least four other tribes crossed Glacier's mountain passes, paddled cool lakes, and strode across verdant meadows. Their vision-quest cribs—low rock walls arranged for protection from the elements—still rest on the flanks of more than thirty mountain peaks in that area. At least eight tribes had a relationship with the Grand Canyon.

Paradoxically, well into the midnineteenth century the West was known as the "Indian wilderness," a term that inextricably linked aboriginal people to

An American Indian, possibly a member of the Havasupai, contemplates the Grand Canyon.

A MONUMENTAL LEGACY

In the Antiquities Act's 110-year-history, the moniker "national monument" has been given to sites for a multiplicity of reasons—from preserving 5000 years of Inupiat Eskimo culture in the Arctic to safeguarding a Caribbean island and coral ecosystem. Twenty percent of national park system units are monuments, including the ruins of prehistoric Indian civilizations, desert ecosystems, an African burial ground in Lower Manhattan, lava beds, historic forts and battlefields, dune fields, the cool recesses of Muir Woods, and even the indelible beacon of the Statue of Liberty.

Despite the controversy that has checkered the legislative life of the 1906 Antiquities Act and the reputation of national monuments as lesser parks, the legislation has ensured protection of some of the nation's most unique resources, says NPS Chief Historian Bob Sutton: "A lot of people look at NPS units that are designated as national *parks* like they are far more important than others," he says. "But within the Park Service we don't see them any differently."

What would have become of these places without the antiquities legislation? NPS chief archaeologist Stanley Bond answers, "We just have to look at the scale of development today to know that many of those places would have been lost to it."

areas still considered feral and inhospitable. No one knows precisely when the term "wilderness" came to mean a place rich in natural resources and romantic solitude and lacking people, but that interpretation relied on separating "Indian" land from potential "pleasuring grounds" (as the law establishing Yellowstone National Park states).

That shift allowed conservationists to deny the relationship living bands of Indians had with their millions of acres of homeland. National park proponents' mythology perpetuated the ideas that aboriginal people either saw so-called wilderness areas as scary and uninhabitable or that they were careless with those resources. What was at best an oversight and at worst violent dispossession allowed conservationists to ignore the long histories and vast knowledge base that American Indians maintained as sustainable users of their resources. Had Native Americans been treated as possible allies instead of speed bumps, and had their ecological awareness been respected and tapped, natural resource managers might have avoided missteps based on prevailing assumptions that ultimately endangered treasured ecosystems.

Instead, with surprising efficiency and within just several generations of the nation's founding, Euro-Americans had taken control of nearly every square mile of land that had been occupied for thousands of years by other people. It was perhaps because of that startling efficiency, cruelly administered, that the majority of tribes that encountered conservation schemes saw them as just another phase of conquest by an advancing colonizer. They were treated, in turn, as outlaws opposed to the

One of the oldest continuously occupied sites in North America, Canyon de Chelly has more than 2500 archaeological sites dating as far back as 1500 B.C.

conservation ideal and, for the most part, removed from desired parklands.

By the time the NPS was established, the goals of Indian removal had largely been fulfilled, and it was convenient to think about much of the land it wanted to "protect" as vacant and unaffiliated. This situation often resulted in a strange paradox, particularly in the case of national monuments, many of which are protected by the Antiquities Act of 1906 *because* of their Native-based histories and artifacts. For decades after its founding, the NPS was guarding and interpreting archaeological Indian resources of past tribes while keeping present tribes, who often had ancestral ties to those areas, behind federal fences.

In the case of Mukuntuweap National Monument, established in 1909, the Park Service succeeded in renaming it Zion in 1918, a name that later stuck as it became a national park. The group known as the Basketmakers once hunted, gathered, and grew crops in that hypnotic desert oasis. Their descendants, the Paiute, spent time at what they called *mukuntuweap*, or "straight arrow," and still live in southern Utah. The changing of the name rejected the cultural ties one living band of people had with the place in favor of another: the white Mormon pioneers who called it Zion. Even Mesa Verde, which preserves the astonishing cliff dwellings of the Ancestral Puebloans—from which at least twenty-four tribes trace their roots—has a name given to it by Spanish explorers.

Native populations did endure in some parks, whether living within parks (Yosemite and Grand Canyon), living in reservations bordering parks (also true of Grand Canyon), and/or using parks seasonally or for traditional purposes (Glacier). In every instance, records indicate that these "relationships" were considered little more than the source of many Park Service headaches.

In some cases the NPS worked uneasily with American Indians by directly employing tribe members on any one of many tourism development projects. At the Grand Canyon in 1919, infrastructure construction was stalled for lack of workers. Dozens of Havasupai, some of whom had washed dishes and done housekeeping and other odd jobs for the main park concessionaire, were hired by the NPS to do manual labor. They built walkways, dug ditches for a sewage treatment plant, and built a bridge spanning the Colorado River. While most were intentionally kept out of the viewfinders of visitors, some of those families lived at an old village site within the park—until the Park Service decided it was unsightly. The

Navajo riders circa 1904 in Canyon de Chelly, which became a national monument in 1931

Havasupai were then moved to a new village where they paid rent to the federal government. That setup ended in the mid-1950s, when all tribe members were exiled to a 518-acre chunk of their original homeland—roughly 30 roadless miles from the park. Congress returned 185,000 acres to the tribe in 1975—with the help of Arizona Congressman Mo Udall—and restored traditional use rights to nearly 100,000 more acres of parkland. But the damage had been done: wage

labor and reservation life had forever changed the way tribe members used their canyon.

Sometimes what seemed mutually beneficial was generally exploitative, such as the pseudocultural exchanges in Yosemite. Annually from 1916 until 1929, Yosemite held Indian Field Days, the purpose of which was "to revive and maintain interest of Indians in their own games and industries, particularly basketry and bead work." The encouraged activities were those that neatly fit into white preconceptions of Native life. Cash-prize contests were held for authenticity of dress and crafts, and photos were snapped of tourists alongside participants in feathered headdresses and in front of tepees. When the field days were past their prime, the Park Service began a quiet, careful plan to systematically drive tribe members from the park. In 1935 park leadership forced the remaining American Indians living in Yosemite Valley into cabins built by the government. Each structure was roughly 430 square feet—for six to eight family members. Future units alleviated crowding, but never again did the original residents of that area live as they chose to. The last of the Indian Village in Yosemite Valley was razed in the 1960s.

At Glacier National Park, the Great Northern Railway drummed up business for decades by promoting the park as an Indian destination. At the behest of the railroad, a group of Blackfeet—the "Glacier Park Indians," as they were advertised—toured the East performing war dances for massive crowds. If tourists were then enticed to travel to Montana, they were met at the railroad station by Blackfeet and toured tepees in the park. The arrangement was no longer advantageous to the profiteers when the car usurped the railroad as the preferred mode of park transport. After that, the NPS was less inclined to tolerate the tribe's traditional uses of parklands—hunting, fishing, and gathering timber—despite the fact that the Blackfeet had treaty rights to do so. While whites who'd homesteaded in the area were allowed to carry on with their subsistence activities (and concessionaires with their profit making), American Indians were tossed out and sometimes jailed. Blackfeet have fought that policy to the present day, because their oral history contradicts the details of an 1895 treaty that supposedly ceded the eastern half of the

park to the US government. Some tribe members maintain that the "agreement" was only a lease that expired seventy-five years ago.

Similarly, at Mesa Verde, Navajo day laborers performed for tourists a ceremony that had some Pueblo influence but was otherwise completely unrelated to the people, the place, or its history. In *Indian Country, God's Country*, Philip Burnham said the practice "was like dancing fandango at a Celtic ruin." Of course, to the tourists who threw coins, it mattered little; the performers were Indians who fit tidily into a narrow racist profile.

Other early Park Service leaders recognized the deep connections Native people had with would-be parklands and sympathized with their plight; some were even made honorary members of tribes with whom they interacted. Sometimes that led to a compromise with tribes, often because they would not bend completely to park powers.

In 1915 Blackfeet tribe members Bird Rattler, Curly Bear, and Wolf Plume traveled to Washington, DC, to confront Stephen Mather and Horace Albright. Standing around Mather's small, crowded desk in traditional garb, including tall feathered headdresses, they formed a striking juxtaposition. The Blackfeet were there to demand that Native names given to natural features in the Glacier area be respected and maintained by the federal government. Robert Marshall, chief geographer of the US Geological Survey, was also there, and he told the delegation that white people would not be able to say or spell the Indian names, so the best the feds could do was to try to translate them. But even that posed problems, said Marshall, because the translations were often names the Park Service didn't like, such as "Jealous Woman's Lake" at Glacier. The Blackfeet said they wouldn't tolerate the present name, Lake McDermott, so the group eventually settled on Swiftcurrent Lake, the name it retains.

For his part, Mather promised that any names assigned henceforth would be Blackfeet ones, but the horse was long out of that barn; out of 663 geological features in the Glacier–Waterton region, many already had monikers given by whites. Some of those are Native-sounding words, but many were either misinterpretations of the original Native name or total fabrications. Even the famous Going-to-the-Sun Road that bisects the park, thought to have come from a Native legend, was likely conjured up by Euro-Americans. Thoreau had written in his journals that "the Indian language reveals another wholly new life to us." But at many locations within the national park system, Indian place names were lost, as was knowledge of migration routes, hunting techniques, harvesting practices, prayers and songs, creation stories, botanical properties, climate observations, fire behavior, ecosystem balance, and sacred inspiration.

Policy shifted somewhat in the 1930s when the Indian Reorganization Act, or "Indian New Deal,"

halted tribes' loss of land, relaxed restrictions, and restored some traditional uses. It also reserved some rights and privileges for tribes during the creation or expansion of parks, which became significant in Alaska in the 1970s and '80s. During those New Deal years, the Park Service seemed to soften on tribal relations. For instance, in 1931 Canyon de Chelly became a national monument whose 84,000 acres lie completely within the boundaries of the Navajo Nation. It is still the only national park unit that is completely owned by a tribe and comanaged by the tribe and the NPS. Visitors can travel into its three major mystical canyons—de Chelly, Monument, and del Muerto—only with a Navajo or Park Service guide.

Also indicative of that era of softening is the creation of Death Valley National Monument, by President Hoover in 1933. Inside the roughly 2 million-acre park lived members of the Timbisha Shoshone tribe, who have stayed on there since its occupation by the Park Service, though tension has been their constant companion. For example, the NPS insisted that tribal families leave their chosen homesteads and live in a village at Furnace Creek, in adobe houses built by the Civilian Conservation Corps.

The US government, perhaps threatened by the renewed self-determination and revival of tribalism encouraged by the Indian New Deal, passed a series of laws and policies in the 1950s and '60s. That so-called Indian Termination Policy stripped more than a hundred tribes of federal recognition and nearly 2.5 million acres of "trust land"; a few tribes eventually regained both, but most did not. It was a twisted assimilation scheme but appears to have amounted to a land grab by the federal government, which then sold a lot of that land to private entities. Tribes including the Timbisha

Shoshone suffered, as a result, from an anti-Native backlash. Those adobe homes—which they never wanted to live in to begin with—were washed away by fire hoses in an attempt to drive the Indians from the park; it did not. Death Valley became a national park in 1994, and soon after that, the Timbisha Shoshone Homeland Act of 2000 was passed, providing trust land on which the tribe could permanently live within the park. In the preface to that legislation, tribe member Pauline Esteves wrote, "Our people have always lived here . . . Then others came and occupied our land . . . We never gave up. The Timbisha people have lived in our Homeland forever and we will live here forever. We were taught that we don't end."

Not until 1987 (the year prior to the end of the Indian Termination Policy) did the NPS seriously attempt to invite Native people back into the discussion and management of their historic resources and to broaden park stories beyond those of white settlers. With the release of the *Native American Relationships Management Policy*, the NPS finally began the process of recognizing and consulting American Indians connected with parklands system-wide. Instead of contrived dances or attempts to hide the links between American Indians and national parks, they are now mostly celebrated.

The National Tribal Preservation Program, established in 1992 as an amendment to the 1966 National Historic Preservation Act, requires the NPS to work cooperatively with Indian tribes, Alaska Natives, and Native Hawaiians to protect resources and traditions. The landmark Native American Graves Protection and Repatriation Act, which went into effect in 1996, affirms the rights

Blackfeet Indians in Glacier National Park, an area that they called the "backbone of the world"

of those three groups to custody of human remains and other objects of significance.

In its 2001 report, *Rethinking the National Parks for the 21st Century*, the National Park System Advisory Board said, "We are coming to understand that parks become richer when we see them through the cultures of people whose ancestors once lived there." NPS interpretation at sites such as Mesa Verde, Olympic, and Glacier national parks is now generally focused on the rich, often sophisticated relationships aboriginal people had with those places.

The next step, which is ongoing, is to add multidimensional storytelling that allows the

Located within Havasu Canyon, a southwestern branch of the Grand Canyon, and still accessible only by foot, Supai is the capital of the Havasupai Indian Reservation. It lay within the national park boundaries until the land was returned to the tribe in 1975.

includes the use of the word "massacre"—the first time the actions of federal troops against Native Americans has been described as such at a national park.

At Sand Creek and beyond, the narrative of westward expansion may ultimately be reframed from a clash of cultures to a conquest of one culture by another. The challenge is to avoid diminishing the loss of life on either side and to prevent casting the American Indian in roles popularized by later sympathizers as either simply "victim" or "environmentalist" or the white settler as merely "villain." History and those who made it are much more complex.

Little Bighorn—where the Battle of the Greasy Grass, as it's known to American Indians—took place, is also now working to get it right. While sharing some of his encyclopedic knowledge of the fighting, Josh Little Owl encourages visitors to consider the 250 books in the monument's bookstore—each of which, he jokes, gives a different version of the event.

Because of the scale of loss during Custer's Last Stand, the battle movements have been largely guessed at, despite the fact that dozens of Indian accounts emerged in subsequent years. Those perspectives of the intense fighting with the Seventh Cavalry are now becoming part of the park's narrative. More than a century after the army placed 249 markers to denote where Custer's men died,

descendants of those former park inhabitants to share the stories of their ancestors themselves. That's an effort worth making, says Mark Dowie, a journalist who has written widely about "conservation refugees" around the world. "It's a healing process for Native American people to tell their stories, and it's a side of the story that has to be considered," he says.

At Colorado's Sand Creek Massacre National Historic Site, established in 2007, the Arapaho and Cheyenne fought the Park Service for the right to lead the interpretation of what happened there in 1864. Their ancestors believed they were under the protection of the US government, when instead a village of women, children, and the elderly was attacked by US soldiers, leaving 150 dead. The brutal events were once a disjointed footnote of the Civil War but are being retold with the addition of once-disenfranchised voices. This telling now

Red granite markers identify fallen American Indians on the killing fields at Little Bighorn Battlefield National Monument where the landscape has changed little since 1876.

the NPS installed a handful of markers showing where Indian warriors fell.

By then the name of the park had been changed by Congress from Custer Battlefield National Monument to the one it has now. That same act authorized an Indian memorial to be erected at the site: "The public interest will best be served by establishing a memorial . . . to honor and recognize the Indians who fought to preserve their land and culture," said the legislation.

The "Peace through Unity" theme was adopted with the guidance of Oglala Lakota and Cheyenne elders; the memorial was dedicated in 2003 and completed in 2013. The circular structure is made of massive granite panels and wrought-iron sculptures through which the hills and sky are visible. Visitors enter through a spirit gate, which welcomes the souls of the Seventh Cavalry troops, whose memorial can be seen from the gate's opening. The names of fallen Indian warriors are inscribed on the walls, and also honored are the Crow and Arikara scouts who joined Custer in an attempt to defeat enemy tribes. On the Cheyenne panel, tribe member Wooden Leg sums up one of the most analyzed battles in US history this way: "We had killed soldiers who came to kill us."

Civilized Off the Face of the Earth   **251**

Previous: From a Russian word meaning "treeless heights," but far from barren, tundra comprises much of Alaska, including Denali (seen here). *Below:* The NPS's Murie Science and Learning Center partners with the Denali Education Center to give kids of all ages hands-on experiences; they hike, sleep outside, and explore at Denali Discovery Camp.

CHAPTER 23

Wildernesses at Your Feet

SOMEHOW A STEADY RAIN seems fitting weather in which to troll beneath a canopy of redwoods, looking for life. Drops brush past branches far overhead and slap into puddles with a hypnotic tempo. Glenn Plumb, chief wildlife biologist for the National Park Service, leads a sodden but lively group of schoolchildren in a rainbow of ponchos through Muir Woods. It's late March and the explorers are searching for bats hanging out in fire-hollowed trunks of the tremendous trees. Plumb has brought a camera that, when mounted

on a telescoping pole, can peek 30 feet up. "Nobody has ever looked *inside* these trees before with a camera," Plumb tells the kids. "Let's see what we can find." It seems to add to the thrill this day, the idea that there are frontiers still to reach, discoveries yet to be made.

Muir Woods National Monument is the San Francisco Bay Area's only old-growth coastal redwood forest—and one of the last in the world. Trees average 600 to 800 years of age, but some have passed 1200 years' worth of days here. They are the main lure for visitors worldwide, but there are also owls and voles, ferns and slugs, salmon and skunks, as well as ten bat species, to be noted. For these young naturalists with awakened senses, it is a brimming trove. "The kids absolutely loved it," says Plumb. "We are driven to discover. It's a human condition."

Muir Woods is part of Golden Gate National Recreation Area, which includes various sites along the north California coast covering more than 80,000 acres and 90-plus miles of shoreline. Plumb, the students, and volunteers were taking part in a park-wide BioBlitz there in 2014. Each year the BioBlitz—a collaboration between the NPS and the National Geographic Society—moves to a different national park unit where citizen scientists work with career scientists to find and document every type of plant, animal, and insect (and more) they encounter. What the volunteers gather in a twenty-four-hour period is a snapshot of all life in that park, often a staggering array of species in the backyard of millions of people.

Since the program started in 2007, BioBlitzes have involved tens of thousands of scientists-for-a-day who have documented thousands of species. The collaborations are so popular that many other parks and communities have held their own versions. Several have been done in the Boston Harbor Islands NRA—thirty-four biodiverse islands spread out over 50 square miles, a short ferry ride from downtown. Harvard entomologist and visionary naturalist E. O. Wilson joined in the 2008 BioBlitz there. Of the islands, Wilson has said, "There are wildernesses at your feet."

During the Golden Gate NRA BioBlitz, volunteers combed several sites such as Crissy Field's waterfront for rare birds and native plants; they searched the coastal scrub and chaparral of Rancho Corral de Tierra for the California red-legged frog and San Bruno Elfin butterfly. In all, 300 leading scientists and naturalists from the area joined forces with roughly 6000 volunteers to record more than 2300 species, from microorganism-rich biofilm to towering trees. They examined leaves and tracks, picked up bugs, and netted fish. Their high-tech field notebook was a smartphone app they used to upload photos, location information, and notes, all of which were fed into Park Service databases. BioBlitzes are helping to build an inventory of all natural resources in parks that can be monitored into the future. Over time, what's in parks and what's gone missing are key indicators of ecological health.

This type of crowd-sourced inventory and monitoring had not likely been envisioned by critics of Park Service science in the 1980s and 1990s. While the sheer amount of land conserved by the NPS in the 1970s was encouraging, ecology was more of a concern than ever. When in the late 1970s outside park watchers again sounded the alarm, the NPS acted by permanently placing a scientist at the level of associate director, just in time to respond to a congressional request for a checkup on parks.

The first service-wide survey, the *State of the Parks* report, was "designed to identify and characterize threats that endanger the natural and the cultural resources of the parks." Released in 1980, the report was dismal. It concluded that "park units representing all size and use categories, and all types of ecosystems, reported a wide range of threats affecting their resources. These threats, which emanate from both internal and external sources, are causing severe degradation of park resources." Parks were too crowded and too built up and didn't have nearly enough staff. The size of buffer zones outside

Female grizzlies can have from one to three cubs, which stay with her for up to three and a half years.

The report concluded, "The results of this study indicate that no parks of the System are immune to external and internal threats, and that these threats are causing significant and demonstrable damage. There is no question but that these threats will continue to degrade and destroy irreplaceable park resources until such time as mitigation measures are implemented. In many cases, this degradation or loss of resources is irreversible. It represents a sacrifice by a public that, for the most part, is unaware that such a price is being paid." The NPS's response to Congress, which came the same month President Ronald Reagan occupied the Oval Office, promised that each park would develop a resource management plan (RMP) including comprehensive resource inventories, prioritized problems, and necessary staff and funding. Park superintendents, in response, began to take a sincere ecological approach to park management for the first time—albeit briefly.

Before they could sink their teeth in, as if on cue an economic recession struck the nation. Attentions were diverted, and at that moment, the mortality of grizzly bears in Yellowstone could not have been less on the minds of lawmakers. The austerity-focused executive branch trickled down to the NPS as Secretary of the Interior James Watt instructed park leadership to focus less on ecology and wilderness and, once again, make visitor services its primary management goal. By 1982 the NPS had basically thrown its hands up and abandoned the objectives outlined in the *State of the Parks* report.

parks had also shrunk significantly, threatening migratory species and introducing air and water pollutants. The Park Service blamed a paltry budget and lack of scientists—who made up, the NPS estimated, just over 1 percent of its staff—and asked for congressional support.

The unsettling report—which cited roughly 4300 dangers to national parks—once again thrust service-wide crises into the limelight. While individual superintendents had a line on how conditions were degrading in their parks, those problems had not been well documented and had never been coalesced into one troubling picture until the *State of the Parks* report. (The National Parks Conservation Association's *Adjacent Land Survey* from 1979 had prompted the NPS to take its own look.) Therefore the magnitude of the problems system-wide came as something of a surprise to park leadership—and why shouldn't it have, considering the NPS still lacked an adequate research body that might connect the dots on various threats?

Whether due to the tight purse strings in Washington, or because the expansion of the national park system in the 1960s and '70s had been so great and so controversial, the '80s were a period of relative quiet during which the dust of decades past was settling. Among the few additions to the system during that time were Timucuan Ecological and Historic Preserve in northern Florida, the first and only unit of its kind with salt marshes and wildlife, a nineteenth-century plantation, and American Indian roots. Nevada's stunning Great Basin National Park also came on the scene, along with the distant but deserving National Park of American Samoa. The biggest headline from that era is the staggering rise in visitation, despite the lack of disposable income among average Americans. Roughly 220 million people visited parks in 1980, and that rose to an all-time high of more than 287 million in 1987.

When the economy rebounded, the NPS was infused with cash but still failed to complete RMPs for each park. It had abandoned a planned expansion of its scientific research program, though it did put in place national monitoring programs for air quality and mining threats. But that did not placate the General Accounting Office (GAO), whose 1987 report was headlined "Limited progress made in documenting and mitigating threats to parks."

The GAO gave many examples of that limited progress, including this: "The Park Service's budget for resource management increased considerably between 1980 and 1984, from $44 million to $93 million. Within the twelve national parks GAO visited, additional funds were used to resolve some significant problems, such as the removal of plants and animals harmful to park resources and the repair of deteriorating historic structures. Nevertheless, officials of these twelve parks judged that 255, or 80 percent, of the total 318 threats reported in 1980 were still unresolved as of December 1985." One of the GAO's many recommendations was that a system-wide approach to researching and monitoring park resources and conditions be implemented. Where had that been heard before? It was as if the specter of George Wright had returned to haunt the NPS.

Morale within the NPS continued to wither in the heat of renewed scrutiny. Some limited progress was made, particularly in training park superintendents and others within the Park Service on environmental laws and ecological management principles. But a whirlwind of directors, division chiefs, expectations, directives, and admonishments left the NPS ranks to a certain extent suspended or paralyzed. Looking forward to the 1990s, and to the close of the twentieth century, the Park Service knew daunting days lay ahead. But much like that remarkable subalpine wildflower, the glacier lily, which busts through snow on a still-blanketed white meadow—promising the return of spring—the Park Service would emerge eventually from its own winter.

One sign of that came when, in 1985, a massive eco-error was made right. About fifty years after the last gray wolf was seen in Glacier National Park, a dozen wolves walked from Canada into the northwest corner of the park to hunt. That next spring, one of the females made her den inside the park; it was the first time that had happened in the Lower 48 in a half century. Breeding packs eventually followed, and within a decade, upwards of sixty wolves lived in northwestern Montana—by then they were protected by the Endangered Species Act and accepted as critical ecosystem members. While it may not have been good news to mountain goats grazing above Many Glacier, ecological balance was being restored.

RETURN OF THE WOLVES

In Yellowstone from 1914 to 1926, at least 136 gray wolves were killed. While the occasional wolf might have been seen after that, into the 1940s there was no evidence of packs in the park. An antipredator campaign had exacted immense losses for that ecosystem, one of the largest intact temperate-zone ecosystems on Earth, which has Yellowstone and Grand Teton national parks at its center. By the middle of the twentieth century, nearly every wolf in the Lower 48 had been eradicated. By 1978 the few that remained were protected under the Endangered Species Act. And then the comebacks began.

In Yellowstone in the late 1990s, more than thirty wolves captured in Canada were released in the park. By 2007 an estimated 1500 wolves roamed Montana, Wyoming, and Idaho, including 171 in Yellowstone. That number has declined substantially since then due to disease and a decline in elk—wolves' preferred meal. Despite the population drop, by 2012 endangered species protection was stripped from gray wolves in all three states. Wolves in the Lower 48 now occupy less than 5 percent of their historic range, but they can still be found in seven national parks. Ten parks in Alaska maintain wolf populations as well.

Unlike a century ago, we now understand gray wolves to be smart and social, with deep family ties and observable empathy toward pack mates. Recent studies have also shown that the presence of such apex predators is critical to the overall health of entire ecosystems. The comeback of that keystone species seems to have boosted biodiversity throughout the Greater Yellowstone Ecosystem. Elk kills feed grizzly bears and other scavengers during low food years. Fewer elk also means more berries for bears—a critical late summer food supply. As elk numbers drop, wolves are also increasingly preying on the park's overabundance of bison. The wolves' displacement of coyotes has been a boon to small mammals and birds of prey as well.

In Glacier National Park and the larger Crown of the Continent ecosystem, the wolves' return has improved conditions for aspens, willows, songbirds, beavers, and trout. It's too early to say whether the return of gray wolves to these two areas will lead to ecosystem recovery on a large scale. Those ecosystems are complex puzzles that are simply missing certain pieces after centuries of manipulation.

A Yellowstone Delta Pack wolf in 2013 when 95 wolves in 10 packs were counted in the park

NPS rangers introduce young visitors to the wild wonders of the Boston Harbor Islands.

Yet in 1991, at seventy-five years of age, the NPS had reached a crossroads. It held a symposium in October of that year in high-country Colorado to take a hard look at issues and solutions. Its findings, widely known as the *Vail Agenda*, were published the next year, including this warning: "The Park Service is in danger of becoming merely a provider of 'drive through' tourism or, perhaps, merely a traffic cop stationed at scenic, interesting or old places." Challenges lay ahead, the report said: natural resources managers still did not have a clear idea of the biodiversity in parklands, and no good mechanism was in place to take on the herculean task. But there were also opportunities; the authors believed what was learned about the ecology of parks could be used to understand the rest of the biosphere (the sum of ecosystems worldwide) and to educate the public about environmental issues.

Both of those possibilities, in fact, developed into critical functions of today's Park Service. The bottom line for the *Vail Agenda* authors was that there were still amazing ecological aspects to parks, and it wasn't too late to dive in, document them, and report back to the world. It was perhaps the most optimistic natural resources assessment up to then—the Park Service envisioned a future in which it was both ambassador to the world and environmental leader, putting 110 percent into both of its dual Organic Act mandates.

It would require a major commitment at all levels of the NPS and a major turnaround in priorities, and those who were skeptical could not have been faulted for their cynicism. NPS Director James Ridenour voiced what most people no doubt were thinking, given the spotty history the Park Service had in following through on such battle cries. He said, "It is clear to me that we will

Glacier lilies, which bloom near receding snow, are a hallmark of warm days in the Montana high country, including Glacier National Park.

need an ongoing commitment and process to keep our collective feet to the fire to make sure that our efforts do not just generate another report to gather dust on a shelf." NPS historian Bill Brown, who knew a thing or two about mobilization for a conservation cause from his work in forming Alaskan parks, also responded to the *Vail Agenda*. He said the NPS needed to highlight "what the parks must be in our society, how they must be nurtured with people and resources to accomplish the social purposes that we as a nation have agreed upon for them."

Between the *State of the Parks* reports in 1980 and 1993, the agency's natural resource budget increased fourfold, from roughly $23 million to about $95 million, and this included research money. But, surprisingly, in 1993 there were just 100 researchers out of more than 1100 natural resources management staff—the same number there had been in 1980. These figures were documented in NPS historian Richard West Sellars's book *Preserving Nature in the National Parks: A History*, which

came out in 1997. Its irrefutable and comprehensive picture of institutional neglect of the environment, drawn by an insider, made the Park Service sit up and take notice. Along with the input of groundbreaking, impasse-busting new director Robert Stanton, it did what every other analysis over the past sixty years had failed to do: trigger change within the NPS in regard to ecological management.

Perhaps the biggest change in the history of science at the NPS dawned with the new millennium when Stanton announced his Natural Resource Challenge in 1999. He'd barely taken office when Sellars's critical review of the lack of attention to scientific research and understanding within the NPS hit the newsstands. Years later Stanton reflected on that time: "One of two things could've happened," he said. "I could have gone into denial saying, 'Well, we're doing the best we can' and then just happily float down the river, or I could say that Dr. Sellars had identified areas for which we need to be giving more attention." In late 2014 Stanton talked again about his response to what he called Sellars's "in-depth, no holds-barred" analysis. He said, simply, "We took it to heart."

Stanton's matter-of-fact approach displaced the NPS's hallmark defensiveness in favor of an instinct for proactivity that quickly rallied support around the big idea. At last a system-wide *action* plan was coming from the top; at last the national crusade that Bill Brown had called for was taking shape. Stanton announced the Natural Resource Challenge at Mount Rainier, at a ceremony celebrating the park's one hundredth anniversary: "This action plan represents our strong commitment to

FIGHTING OVER FIRE

The biggest fire in National Park Service history tore through nearly 800,000 acres—36 percent—of Yellowstone in 1988. That fire season had begun much like any other, with twenty mostly lightning-caused fires, eleven of which burned out by themselves. The other fires were being watched, until severe drought conditions and the adverse effects on tourists (not to mention the attention of nightly news anchors) led to the NPS's decision on July 21 to suppress all fires.

But it was too late. The fires were expanding and combining, and within a week nearly 100,000 acres had been torched. Despite the efforts of 25,000 firefighters, including two marine battalions and hundreds of aircraft, by the end of August the fire was gulping down thousands of acres per day. When the weather turned cool the fire abated, though it was not officially extinguished until November. In all, the fire cost two lives (outside the park), $120 million, and nearly 10 million gallons of water.

During and after the fire, accusations indicted the Park Service's "let it burn" policy. The NPS had been lackadaisical in its response, critics said—but the facts dispute that charge. The NPS relied on detailed prediction models to know when to step in and when to let fires play out. From 1972 to 1987, 235 relatively small fires were allowed to burn nearly 34,000 acres before being naturally extinguished. In 1988 nearly 250 fires were ignited in the Greater Yellowstone Ecosystem. Seven of those were to blame for 95 percent of the torched acreage in the big blaze. Of those fires, five had begun outside the park, and three of those were human-caused blazes that firefighters attempted to put out immediately.

The combination of forces that came together that summer in Yellowstone—seemingly "routine" fires combined with relentless drought and ferocious wind—were, in retrospect, largely unimaginable. Today, fire policies system-wide are somewhat stricter but virtually unchanged. Despite the national outrage at the event, ecologically speaking, there was little to fear. New forests of lodgepole pine have risen amid the wreckage, and what was once mourned by many as dead and gone again bristles with life.

The 4238-acre Alder Fire in Yellowstone in August 2013

From seasonal ranger to fifteenth director of the NPS, here Robert Stanton (second from left) is seen during the filming of *Spencer's Mountain* in Grand Teton with Warner Bros. staff and stars and seasonal park ranger William Kinardy (second from right).

programs, shared more knowledge with colleges and universities, and strengthened its ties to the scientific community. A variety of vital signs also began to be monitored at many parks: weather and climate are recorded at nearly 250 park units, the type and number of birds in nearly 200, fire regimes and fuel dynamics in more than 100, coastal and oceanographic features and processes in about 30, and much more.

preserving our country's precious natural heritage for this and future generations," he said. "Preserving our natural resources far into the future now requires active and informed management based on sound science." Fifteen years later, Stanton still speaks proudly about the critical role conservation nonprofits played in rallying public support around the need. He also credits the "strong, *strong* bipartisan support" he says Congress showed, and an obvious trust in and support for the National Park Service to rise to the challenge. And that it did.

A multimillion-dollar budget infusion—estimates range from $75 million to $100 million—and a revision of culture put science at the fore of decision making. This influx of funds paid for comprehensive inventory and monitoring programs that would have made George Wright grin. The NPS began to know in depth, for the first time, what it was protecting. It expanded natural resource

Stanton then went a step further when he asked the National Park System Advisory Board to make recommendations essentially about how the Park Service should be interpreting its mandate in the next century. *Rethinking the National Parks for the 21st Century*, published in 2001, challenged the tenet that had been the focus of the Park Service since its very beginning. It urged the NPS "to re-examine the 'enjoyment equals support' equation" and warned that parks could no longer be managed "as islands with little or no connection, cultural or ecological, to their surroundings." This warning would have made any number of past NPS ecologists cheer. Stanton remarked recently that he's pleased each director who has succeeded him has picked up the mantle of his Natural Resource Challenge. He says, "All have embraced the letter and the spirit."

Wildlife biologist Glenn Plumb, who spent a dozen years at Yellowstone where he oversaw the reintroduction of gray wolves, sees the evolution of science in the Park Service in three phases. In the first phase, it was largely the recipient of research and ideas about ecology and park resources. In the second phase, in the 1960s, efforts were made

HIGHER GROUND

The National Park Service is already experiencing and anticipating some major changes in parks due to climate change. Adaptation planning extends beyond natural resources to protection of parks' vast cultural, historical, and recreational resources. Rising sea levels and storm surges have already impacted many units, including damaging dozens of structures at Gateway National Recreation Area during Hurricane Sandy. Now the Park Service is getting ahead of the curve in low-lying coastal parks and beyond. It's moving sensitive objects and equipment to higher ground and installing mobile displays, accommodations, and dining facilities that can all be moved out of harm's way.

to balance out the historic lack of scientific management of natural resources. The third phase is now providing leadership in dealing with some of the biggest ecological challenges to date. "There's more recognition that some of the best and most highly productive scientists in the country are here at the Park Service," Plumb says. Add a now-robust research permitting system, and the result is thousands of projects being done by outside institutions and a growing body of collaborative work taking place in parks each year. That work has never been more important, as external threats identified as far back as the *State of Parks* report in 1980 continue to intensify.

From American Samoa to the San Juan and Channel Islands, from Boston Harbor Islands to the Virgin Islands and all coastal and land-locked national parks in between, the key to

understanding conditions in, and threats to, parks is mastering science. Likewise, emphasizing science in national parks will put them at the core of US conservation.

And that begins, in part, in Muir Woods with those budding explorers who walked, waded, and crawled around, passing the day in revelation among millipedes and salamanders and swallowtail butterflies. Among them might just be the next crop of NPS scientists who take to heart safeguarding those sanctuaries, a new and diverse cohort who communicate the relevancy and necessity of parklands to their generation. Plumb smiled when remembering one middle schooler who, when invited to help scope out bats, walked boldly and fearlessly into the hollow of a redwood. "Yup, that's it, get right in there," Plumb said. "See? Everybody can do science."

Monocacy National Battlefield shares the story of a skirmish that, while technically a victory for the Confederates, was broadly a defeat because it gave the Union critical time to reinforce Washington, DC.

CHAPTER 24

Keeper of National Memory

IN THE NORTHWEST CORNER of Colorado flows a wild and free river, the last such tributary in the Colorado River system. The Yampa swells to brimming with snowmelt in the spring and early summer, spurring class II to class IV rapids that are renowned for whitewater rafting. After surging from the Rocky Mountains, the Yampa and Green rivers part ways in Dinosaur National Monument to cut countless curves through remote canyons and silver-leafed sagebrush plains.

It's a special place, a life-affirming one, for veteran Garett Reppenhagen. After nearly four consecutive years of active duty overseas, as a US Army sniper in Iraq, Reppenhagen returned home. The time he spent in Dinosaur, in the company of other vets, helped him begin to heal from the traumas of war. "It was the highlight of my whole year," he says. For a handful of years, a group of veterans gathered in the park, often using their sole vacation time and paying their own way there, to spend nearly a week rafting the Yampa while doing backbreaking work for the National Park Service removing invasive tamarisk. There was something curative about the combination of hard labor, wild river, and camaraderie. "Out there it's harder to disguise yourself and what you're made of," Reppenhagen says. "You're stripped down to who you are. You admit that there's wear and tear, that humans are fragile. For some reason it becomes more acceptable to expose your feelings and fears. That's when the recovery begins."

Getting outdoors had become a habit for Reppenhagen, the Rocky Mountain regional coordinator for the Vet Voice Foundation, a role he assumed soon after returning from war. "When I got home from Iraq, I grabbed my tent and water purifier and I headed out," he says. Reppenhagen, who suffers from post-traumatic stress disorder, hadn't thought much about it at the time, but he sensed he needed to be away from civilian life, which was filled with too many now-foreign elements. "It was instinctual to hit the trail," he says. "I was going stir crazy. When I came down [from the mountains], I felt a lot better." Reppenhagen (whose father served in Vietnam and grandfathers served in World War II) says being in the woods or on the river helps dissolve feelings of powerlessness, of loss of purpose and lack of mission that beset so many vets. "You're motivated to go over the hill, around the next bend, scale the mountain you didn't think you could," he says. The power of getting back to basics, of relying on your will and wits, infuses you with strength and accomplishment.

National parklands have long been places for healing, for recovering from wartime—for veterans and civilians alike—whether in the backcountry of Rocky Mountain National Park or at Perry's Victory and International Peace Memorial, commemorating a pivotal naval battle in the War of 1812. Many national parks, such as the latter, also preserve wartime tales. How does a nation acknowledge the sacrifices of war? How does it mend and move forward? Often it does so by establishing some common ground whose surface is paved with stories.

On a fall morning, the rolling hills of Chickamauga in northern Georgia are laden with low-slung clouds. In the woods and fields where Union and Confederate forces clashed 150 years ago, it's not hard to imagine how an enemy, whether in blue or gray, could appear as if from nowhere and threaten one's existence. Ambrose Bierce, one of the nineteenth century's most prominent writers, was a first lieutenant in the Union Army at Chickamauga, and while he was no stranger to battle at that point, he was disturbed by the intensity of that conflict. "There was sharp fighting all along and all day, for the forest was so dense that the hostile lines came almost into contact before fighting was possible," he wrote. In a state of heightened awareness, their wool collars must have felt scratchy in the Southern swelter, and their adrenaline must have surged at the snap of twigs beneath approaching feet.

For nearly three days soldiers fought desperately for control of nearby Chattanooga, Tennessee, the "Gateway to the Deep South." The Union ultimately lost the Battle of Chickamauga but won the decisive Battles for Chattanooga, paving the way for the Union's lethal thrust into the South. In the weeks following the Battle of Chickamauga, Union General Ulysses S. Grant and Confederate President Jefferson Davis took in the scene where 34,000 casualties (including President Abraham Lincoln's own brother-in-law) had been suffered. Citizens also were drawn to the battlefield, some in search of

Civil War soldiers in their Northern Union blue, in an unidentified camp

Williams Rosecrans, who had been removed from duty after the Chickamauga loss, stirred the crowd with an emotional address: "The survivors of that battle, both Blue and Gray . . . are assembled together to consider how they shall make it a national memorial ground, which people of all time shall come and visit with the interest due to the greatness of the events which occurred on that battleground. It took great men to win that battle, but it takes greater men still, I will say morally greater, to wipe away all the ill feeling which naturally grows out of such a contest." While national cemeteries had been designated and some monuments to the fallen had been erected, this effort to preserve an entire battlefield was a wholly new way to reflect on those events.

loved ones, others for a sense of the second-bloodiest Civil War battle, where, as Bierce later put it, "skill, valor, accident, and fate played each its important parts." The gunsmoke had cleared, but no doubt the acrid smell and bitter taste of loss both lingered regardless of which side they were on.

Twenty-five years after the war ended, in 1890, Chickamauga and Chattanooga National Military Park became the nation's first such reservation. As the legislation creating it says, the park preserves the landscape where the battle took place and marks the forests, fields, and hills where some of the "most remarkable maneuvers and brilliant fighting" of the war occurred. The park was the brainchild of two Union brigade generals who invited Confederate veterans of the battle to aid in its protection, which they did, wholeheartedly.

In 1889 thousands of soldiers from both sides gathered for a barbecue near where they had fought for their lives and beliefs. Former Union General

That same year, equal numbers of veterans from both sides got to work clearing decades of overgrowth and marking battle lines. The military park among those quiet farms and forests of Georgia put on the map—and into the hearts of a generation with still-smarting war scars—the importance of protecting battlefields in their original condition. A national effort to bring together North and South, literally and figuratively, and to heal war wounds grew from there. Veterans led the way; huge joint reunions of former enemies were held at Gettysburg in 1888 and a year later at Chickamauga. Within a decade of Chickamauga's designation, the battlefields at Shiloh, Gettysburg, and Vicksburg also became national military parks; Antietam, the location of the bloodiest one-day battle in American history, was established as a national battlefield in 1890.

From the very start of battlefield preservation, the designated purpose was to analyze what transpired at each place. The sites were intended to honor soldiers but also to be places to study military strategies and maneuvers. For many years, they were used to conduct military training exercises, now a bygone practice. While the mandate to focus on the tactics and results of battles endures, over time the NPS has expanded its answer to that initial question of "what happened here?" The thing about stories is that they have, at a bare minimum, two sides. In the case of the Civil War, the NPS has spent decades trying to balance perspectives and prejudices that, in some cases, had solidified into tradition and belief.

At the Confederate Cemetery of Appomattox Court House National Historical Park lie the remains of 18 Southern troops and one Federal soldier. General Robert E. Lee surrendered to Ulysses S. Grant at nearby McLean House, ending the Civil War.

Getting at the subtleties of such a well-known conflict is a challenge, says ranger Rick Hatcher at Fort Sumter National Monument. "It's an immense responsibility," he says. "And an aspect that's continuously evolving." Should the war contribute to national identity? And, if so, in what ways?

Interpretations of individual events and, indeed, of the purpose of the war itself continue to evolve. At Fort Sumter, where the first shots of the war were fired, exhibits have shifted from a focus on military movements to interpretation of the causes and consequences of the conflict.

NPS Chief Historian Bob Sutton says his agency continues to wrestle with the question of why each side entered the conflict. "Obviously, there were many causes: political, economic, and social, which are all correct," he says. "But why was the political cause such that it would lead to a civil war?" Getting to that is like peeling away layers of an onion, he says. The NPS does that at more than seventy-five national park units related to Civil War events with engaging exhibits and live discussions of states' rights, human rights, and constitutional rights—and at the center is the institution of slavery.

From that stepping-off point, at Shiloh, Gettysburg, and more, the NPS broadens the discussion of the war to the practice of slavery,

concepts of freedom and citizenship, and the antebellum economy of the South. Statistics the Park Service uses in displays are powerful: the economic "value" of slaves in the United States in 1860 was $3 billion, more than the combined worth of all railroads, factories, and banks nationwide. But it is the human objects that are often the most stirring, the tangible links from past to present. Monocacy National Battlefield, roughly 40 miles northwest of Washington, DC, still looks much like it did in the summer of 1864 when its farms became killing fields in one of the decisive yet less-celebrated events of the lengthy war. There the artifacts of soldiers and civilians—a tattered boot, a bullet-pierced canteen, a jagged amputation saw, haunting photographs, and some heartbreaking letters—are all powerful tale-telling tools.

While the Civil War rightfully looms large among conflicts fought on American soil, there are others. As the keeper of national memory, the National Park Service manages dozens of sites focused on marking and interpreting pre-Colonial battles, the Spanish American War, the French and Indian (Seven Years') War, the Revolutionary War, the War of 1812, the "Indian Wars," the Mexican American War, and World War II. Only a handful of states do not have an NPS site devoted to a battle fought on home turf.

Some units, like the impressive, angular ramparts of Castillo de San Marcos National Monument in northern Florida, bear witness to centuries of conflicts. The Park Service takes visitors first over a huge drawbridge and into the narrow Sally Port, the only way in or out of the fortress. There visitors get a sense of the strength of the fort and why it's still around. Outer walls

The Stone House, here with soldiers and a carriage outside in 1862, served as a field hospital for two major Civil War battles at Manassas; still visible in one of the rooms are the names carved by two soldiers being treated there, only one of whom survived.

guardrooms there is still-visible Colonial-era graffiti scrawled by bored soldiers who practiced the alphabet or etched images of sailboats on high seas. Spanish soldiers—or, rather, historical reenactors—still troll the fortress in long royal-blue coats and colorful three-point hats.

The NPS is also tasked with commemorating the American involvements in conflicts overseas. From the west end of the Reflecting Pool in West Potomac Park—a.k.a. the National Mall—in Washington, DC, the Lincoln Memorial faces the World War II Memorial. The Lincoln Memorial is flanked by the Korean War Veterans Memorial, the Vietnam Veterans Memorial, and the District of Columbia War Memorial, which honors residents of DC who fought in World War I. There is, at present, no monument to all 4.7 million veterans who served in the Great War. Legislation signed in the waning days of 2014 allowed for adding a structure honoring WWI veterans to the NPS's Pershing Park, an area on Pennsylvania Avenue adjacent to the White House.

are as thick as 19 feet at the base, constructed with *coquina*, a native but uncommon limestone that, unlike its wooden predecessors, was able to withstand the impact of cannon fire. The Spanish built the castillo between 1672 and 1695, and it is the only military construction remaining in the United States from the seventeenth century.

The NPS has preserved some fascinating aspects of the garrison, making walking around like getting postcards from the past. Within the fort's rooms and ramparts, the Park Service protects and maintains the experience of having been there as a soldier, a refugee, a prisoner, or a worshiper. The intimate chapel with the gently curved ceiling still has elaborately carved porticoes that once held treasured religious objects. In the

Walking among the columns, flags, fountains, and inscriptions can be a hair-rising, wedge-in-the-throat-producing experience. Omnipresent on signs and statues are words such as "courage," "bravery," "heroism," and "sacrifice," used to describe troops who served their country in places they initially may have been unable to pinpoint on a map. Many, of course, did not return. But still, their pulse is felt among the haunting, 7-foot-tall steel statues of soldiers caught in suspended animation, in hard

After his friend was killed in action, a grief-stricken American infantryman is comforted by another soldier, in the Haktong-ni area of Korea in August 1950.

a partner, or children. Though they might lack a future, lost soldiers had pasts that mattered. They also left people behind whose grief could not be contained but whose burden might be lightened, ever so slightly, by laying something down at the wall. Those items also give insight into a complex moment in history in which Americans, embroiled in an unpopular conflict, made the ultimate sacrifice. As time passed and the offerings became more frequent, the general public became de facto curators of an expanding museum collection telling countless stories that, woven together, begin to form a narrative of the impact of war on society.

Those offerings are collected by NPS rangers and, once vetted, are inventoried and securely stored outside the city at the Museum Resource Center (whose acronym, MRCE, is pronounced "mercy"). The number of items in storage now exceeds the number of names on the panels by nearly ten times, and the backlog is enormous, says Janet Donlin, who has been at the MRCE for several years. "It's a really dynamic collection, and there's always a lot to do," she says. Fundraising is ongoing for the Education Center at the Wall, which eventually will be built adjacent to the memorial and will honor not only Vietnam veterans but also the nearly 7000 troops killed in

hats and ponchos, at the Korean War Memorial. Their heartbeats reverberate off the polished black granite panels of the Vietnam Veterans Memorial. Visitors may leave these memorials, but those monuments do not leave them.

Nowhere among the memorials are there political statements—that is all beside the point now, says NPS Museum Resource Center director Bob Sonderman. These are all, in a way, sacred spaces for recognition, reflection, and healing. This is especially true for the memorial to Vietnam vets. Since construction started more than three decades ago, the monument has grown into something organic owing to the items intentionally left there by visitors: first a Purple Heart, then dog tags, birthday cards, teddy bears, American flags, photographs.

Though not mandated to keep the offerings, the NPS grasped their importance early on. They weren't merely things; they represented a life, a person who had parents, perhaps siblings, post-9/11 conflicts. When it's complete, some of the remembrances will be displayed in permanent and rotating exhibits.

While the MRCE staff declines to ascribe meaning to bags of M&Ms, baby pacifiers, and the like left at the wall (99 percent of which is left without attribution), certain items stand out, says Sonderman. Take the custom-built motorcycle left by a group of veterans with instructions that it not be ridden until every prisoner of war or soldier missing in action from Vietnam has been accounted for. Then there's the empty champagne bottle and two accompanying wine flutes that had obviously been used, says museum technician Joanne Westbrook. "There's something so human but also timeless about pouring a libation," she says. "And something so powerful about the role of these items in coming to terms with loss."

❖   ❖   ❖   ❖

Though the NPS is charged with preserving histories of conflicts—in stories, exhibits, structures, and relics—the fate of these places full of national memory is not set in stone. In keeping priceless historical and cultural sites from crumbling around the visitor, the NPS has a colossal task. There are the ordinary but

damaging elements of time and weather and, as the climate changes, the extraordinary ones, such as floods and fire. Parks include more than 27,000 properties that are on the National Register of Historic Places. Sites are as diverse as the Best Farm at Monocacy National Battlefield, from whose barn Confederate sharpshooters fired at the enemy, and the Gettysburg Lincoln Train Station, where the president alighted to give his now-famous address nearby.

We have come to understand that we congregate on those battlefields, at those forts, cemeteries, and memorials, for reasons as numerous as the tens of millions of people who go there each year. We try to calculate the costs of war from Bunker Hill to Baghdad, to tally the toll of human misery and loss, to get a sense of the days when, as President Lincoln described it, "the heavens are hung in black." Without these places, we drift untethered from the events that have molded us, those that form our national recollection.

NPS rangers from Antietam National Battlefield carry the remains of an unknown Civil War soldier recently discovered at the park.

RESTORING TARNISHED TREASURES

Throughout more than 400 national park units, there are, by some accounts, tens of thousands of historic structures—including centuries-old spots such as Spanish forts and Native pueblos—in need of maintenance and restoration. Many are original parkitecture structures that, while well built, have been heavily used for a century.

To address a growing demand for specialists within the NPS who could preserve these invaluable cultural resources, the Historic Preservation Training Center (HPTC) was founded in 1977. Since then the center has trained and dispatched dozens of preservation specialists to do historic architecture, carpentry, masonry, and woodcrafting at sites from Hawaii to Puerto Rico. National parks and monuments, battlefields and cemeteries, all need repair; roofs, bridges, statues, and windows require maintenance. "Some of the most iconic buildings in the park system," and much more, have work waiting to be done, says HPTC director Chris Anderson.

Budgets are now threadbare, and this important work has slowed considerably, says Anderson, but "the importance of timelessness, quality, sensitivity, and ability" have not diminished. Included in that enormous maintenance backlog are structures built during the era of the Public Works Administration, 1933–39, and Civilian Conservation Corps, 1933–42. Now, many structures built during the Mission 66 era, characterized by intense construction and arguably less quality control, are also weakening in middle age.

The NPS reports that only 57 percent of its historic structures, 53 percent of its cultural landscapes, and 52 percent of its recorded archaeological sites are in good condition. The rest are less so. At parks nationwide, these resources are at continued risk from storms, rising sea level, vandalism, fire, and budget cuts. One prominent example of this is Ellis Island, which had to pack up into off-site storage nearly 22,000 priceless objects and a million archive pieces after Hurricane Sandy in 2012. They were not expected to return to that museum until sometime in 2016. Waterfront parks such as Castillo de San Marcos National Monument have been scrambling in recent years to either fortify against coming storms or to clean up after them.

Having a fortress in St. Augustine was so important to Spain that they spent more than a quarter million pesos—upwards of $35 million today—to build Castillo de San Marcos (now a national monument).

Among the tributes to soldiers' sacrifices on the National Mall, the Korean War Veterans Memorial is one of the most haunting.

Beyond those places of congregation, Iraq vet Garett Reppenhagen and his crew seek another tether, a refuge in the wild. As John Burroughs wrote, "I go to nature to be soothed and healed, and to have my senses put in order." For days on end, Reppenhagen and his buddies conquered the Yampa's whitewater and breathed in the cool backcountry air encircling stands of willow and box elder. They worked strenuously, both physically and mentally, and they rested on cottonwood-shaded banks, listened to chirping colonies of prairie dogs, and watched golden eagles and peregrine falcons ride thermals above canyon cliffs. They were in the company of one another, and of ancient rivers, dinosaur bones, and American Indian petroglyphs; of wildflowers and mountain lions. A direction had been chosen; their course was clear. The Yampa offered that much to them, and they took it, gladly.

CHAPTER 25

We Differ as the Waves

IN ANACOSTIA, a neighborhood in southeast Washington, DC, the view has changed some since Frederick Douglass lived his final years, from 1878 to 1895, up on a rise called Cedar Hill. The rolling farmlands eventually sprouted many homes, but the Anacostia River continues to flow in the forefront, and Douglass's multiacre estate remains very much the same. Climb atop the grassy hummock shaded by oak, hickory, and southern magnolia, and you'll pass through the stately columns and enter through the double wooden doors into a place that appears as if the famous abolitionist stepped away only moments ago. There are his glasses, his violin atop the piano, even his barbells—Douglass was something of a fitness nut, walking 5 miles to and from his office most days. There's his chair at the head of the dining room table, set on wheels so that his 6-foot, 200-pound frame could be mobile while he told animated stories to gathered political or literary luminaries. Underground Railroad conductor Harriet Tubman was a guest here, as was women's suffrage leader Susan B. Anthony. In the pantry, a bottle of Chateau Margaux from the 1890s awaits uncorking.

The Frederick Douglass National Historic Site preserves an astonishing 70 to 80 percent of the home's original furnishings—artwork, rugs, lamps, tables—which is likely the highest rate of authenticity of any unit in the entire national park system.

The room that may best capture the Lion or Sage of Anacostia, as Douglass was known, is his library. With a fire glowing in the wood-burning stove behind him, the self-educated former slave would sit for hours in a bulky leather chair at his rolltop wooden desk, polishing speeches and writing prolifically. His beloved mastiff was likely curled up at his feet. No doubt Douglass often stood in front of the packed bookshelves, running his fingers along the spines of his 1000-volume collection. On his desk still sits a copy of Solomon Northrup's *Twelve Years a Slave*, the autobiography of a free man kidnapped in the North and forced into slavery in Louisiana. President Abraham Lincoln's cane is also here at the historical site, a gift to Douglass from the First Lady following the assassination.

Douglass advised Lincoln on the treatment of African Americans during the Civil War. He felt that when a black man became a soldier, his citizenship was irrefutable; the Fourteenth Amendment granting that right was ratified in 1868. The two had a lot in common and became friends; Lincoln had only about a year of formal schooling but was an insatiable reader and self-taught scholar. Like Douglass, he was a tall man with a commanding presence. They were both captivating orators and spoke eloquently about social injustices they had witnessed and sought to eradicate. Next to Lincoln's cane is Douglass's death mask, which preserves the fleeting moments of his mortal

journey. Look closely at the mask, National Park Service ranger Braden Paynter advises excitedly, to see some of Douglass's still-visible beard hairs.

All of the invaluable items in the house, and their power to evoke the presence of an intriguing, acclaimed historical giant and the time in which he lived, might have been scattered to the wind if not for the efforts of Douglass's second wife, Helen Pitts, says Paynter. The two met while Pitts was working as a clerk for Douglass, and they married shortly after his first wife died. Pitts attended Mount Holyoke, an elite women's college, and was active in the abolitionist and suffragist movements. Pitts was from a wealthy, progressive white family, but blacks and whites alike were critical of the interracial union. Douglass responded with his guiding principle that color did not set apart members of the human family. Besides, he posited, "What business has the world with the color of my wife?" Pitts formed a nonprofit organization that ultimately secured this physical piece of Douglass's legacy. The Park Service took over the estate in 1962 and opened it to the public a decade later.

Cedar Hill is, no doubt, a historical landmark, but it is hardly a static place. Douglass, and others in his orbit, set a standard with their lives and work that many still strive to emulate. Douglass's descendants, for example, still actively work on ending modern-day human trafficking. The site is a place in which to reflect but also to examine the now, says Paynter. He lifts a portable video camera and proudly shows a visitor clips from the latest annual oratorical contest held at the park, for which schoolchildren memorized and recited portions of Douglass's speeches. As each grade-schooler took the stage, their surprisingly sturdy voices filled the room with Douglass's sagacity, challenging the present to confront lingering injustices.

EXPLORING UNDERGROUND

The first person to explore many underground miles at what is now Mammoth Cave National Park was a teenage slave named Stephen Bishop. At age seventeen, in 1838 the self-educated young man began guiding visitors among the subterranean marvels and became legendary for his fearless exploration and discoveries. Fellow slaves Mat and Nick Bransford (also owned, as Bishop was, by the cave's owner) and their descendants guided at Mammoth Cave for more than a century.

Materson "Mat" Bransford was the son of the affluent Tennessean Thomas Bransford and a slave woman. He began guiding at Mammoth Cave in 1838 and, even after slavery was abolished, Mat remained there for the rest of his life.

From Cedar Hill, visitors can look northwest to the Washington Monument, part of the NPS's National Mall and Memorial parks. Opposite that gleaming obelisk, at the end of the 2000-foot-long Reflecting Pool, is the Lincoln Memorial. Nearly seventy years after Douglass's death, hundreds of thousands of people filled that space during the civil rights–inspired March on Washington. It was a muggy day in late August when Dr. Martin Luther King Jr. walked up to the podium to deliver his moving "I Have a Dream" speech.

Gilbert Lyons, now an NPS ranger at the Lincoln Memorial, was there at the rally. As the crowd swelled and surged forward, he held his ground right up front where he could see King. "As he spoke, the words flowed out of his mouth just like honey," Lyons recalls. A high price was paid by many in the civil rights movement, but Lyons knows it ultimately amounted to something great. "They tried to silence Lincoln by assassinating him. It didn't work. King went out there and he spoke and they tried to silence him. And what happened? The word got louder and louder and you can see now the country is pulling itself together," says Lyons. It's the whole span of that long, complex history that unfolds on the goose-bump-raising steps of the memorial, when you look up into the gargantuan, smooth marble likeness of the sixteenth president.

There are now more than three dozen NPS units that specifically highlight black history—from the African Burial Ground National Monument in downtown Manhattan and the Brown v. Board of Education National Historical Site in Kansas to the New Orleans Jazz National Historical Park in Louisiana and the Tuskegee Airmen National Historic Site in Alabama. Dozens more NPS units tell the stories of other historically marginalized groups: Hispanics, Latino Americans, Asian Americans, Pacific Islanders—and women.

From New York Harbor to San Francisco Bay, and in Alaska, Hawaii, Puerto Rico, and beyond, national parks tell stories of strife, courage, conflict, and triumph. At these sites, NPS interpretation transcends whichever race, ethnicity, or gender the park is associated with and celebrates the character of a person, or group of people, who distinguished themselves from others of their time. Yes, Harriet Tubman was African American; yes, she was a woman. But as a conductor on the Underground Railroad, leading hundreds of slaves to freedom—and as a spymaster for Union forces during the Civil War—she was above all ingenious, brave, and tireless, sometimes incomprehensibly so. Ditto for Rosa Parks, Booker T. Washington, and George Washington Carver, all African Americans who have NPS units celebrating their grace and grit.

The Golden Spike National Historic Site in Utah recognizes the invaluable contribution of 11,000 Chinese workers in completing the first transcontinental railroad. Central Pacific Railroad Company president and California Governor Leland Stanford said in 1869 that, without their tenacity, "it would have been impossible to complete the western portion of this great national highway." The Manzanar, Minidoka, and Tule Lake internment camps, called "segregation centers" during World War II, soberly capture the history of more than 120,000 Japanese Americans and those of Japanese descent living in the West who were removed from their homes and imprisoned by the federal government.

While parks tell the stories of all Americans, minority visitation to national parks is minimal. The most recent NPS poll on the topic of race revealed that, in 2008 and 2009, 78 percent of park visitors were non-Hispanic whites. Latinos accounted for 9 percent and African Americans for 7 percent of visitors. Asian Americans made up roughly 3 percent. Visitation did not correlate with the racial and ethnic makeup of the country at the time, which was 64 percent white, 16 percent Latino, 13 percent African American, and 5 percent Asian. The roughly 1 percent each of American Indians, Alaska Natives, and Pacific Islanders was the exception.

Adding to the urgency of effectively linking these groups with their national park system is the fact that the demographics of the nation are shifting dramatically. The non-Hispanic white population is predicted to peak in 2024 and then begin a decline.

Soldiers help an elderly evacuee of Japanese descent exit a railroad car in Lone Pine, California, while en route to the Manzanar War Relocation Center in 1942.

Between 1892 and 1924, a panoply of languages would have combined in a cacophony in the Great Hall of what is now the Ellis Island Immigration Museum; in this spot, more than 12 million immigrants were processed as they entered the United States.

By 2050 Hispanics are projected to be roughly 30 percent of the US population; African Americans, 15 percent; and Asian Americans, 9 percent.

Joseph Sánchez, head of the Park Service's Latino History Research and Training Center, says that at a moment when the NPS is strategizing to be more relevant to minorities, and Latinos in particular, "It matters a great deal whether or not Latinos believe in the national park idea because it is a national institution that preserves and protects heritage and patrimony that represent the face of America." He believes everyone must be educated about their history and culture, and some of the best places to do that are in national parks. "The National Park Service is, after all, a national cultural center where Americans come to learn about themselves and their history . . . Latinos share in the heritage and legacy [of] what has become the United States," says Sánchez.

Hispanic Americans can find their history in many park units—a history that, says Sánchez, stretches back to the days immediately following Christopher Columbus's landing in the New World. At the Presidio of San Francisco, the story of doña Juana Briones de Miranda comes to life. At the beginning of the nineteenth century, she was a Mexican American pioneer, entrepreneur, landowner, and traditional healer—while raising eleven children. Her father was a soldier, and the Briones family lived near the site of El Polin Spring in the modern-day Presidio. While she lived there, Juana sheltered and tended to sick and abused soldiers.

Farther south, the César E. Chávez National Monument in Southern California explores the riveting life of the Latino labor leader and charismatic activist who established the first headquarters of the United Farm Workers, whose motto is "¡Sí, Se Puede!" (Yes, we can!). But those national parks should not just be for Latinos, says Sánchez. "All Americans need to learn that the history of the United States is not about English traditions but also about Hispanic traditions as well as those of Native Americans, Asian Americans, and African Americans," he says.

All told, though many lesser-known parks dedicated to minority and female pathfinders see a fraction of the visitors of crowd-pleasers like the Lincoln Memorial and the Statue of Liberty, they are no less deserving. To the contrary, they offer a peek into times and places we *think* we know well.

Take the Charles Young Buffalo Soldiers National Monument in Ohio, where visitors learn about a man who barreled through barriers of inequality by rising to the rank of colonel in the US Army and led a regiment of Buffalo Soldiers guarding Sequoia National Park. Young and his regiment may have been the first nonwhites to protect both the concept and terrain of national parks, but they certainly weren't the last. Both women and minorities make countless contributions to the core of the NPS.

Betty Soskin is the NPS's oldest full-time ranger; in late 2015 she was in her mid-nineties. She's based at the Rosie the Riveter–World War II Home Front National Historical Park in Richmond, California, which has the country's highest concentration of intact WWII structures in the country. Soskin talks frankly to visitors about working as an African American woman in a segregated union hall in Richmond during the war. It was a complicated time when women were being urged to fill jobs building airplanes, ships, and other war tools—even while women couldn't serve in combat. African American men served in segregated units, risking their lives to fight for the freedom of a nation in which they suffered painful, shameful racism. Soskin, recognizing the paradox, says, "I've outlived my rage without outgrowing my passion."

That fervor includes helping shape the narratives that are told at her fledgling park unit. "Who gets remembered depends on who's in the room remembering," she says. And when she recounts details of her near century to her tour takers, she says, "No matter who they are, they can find themselves in that history, and they're wiping their eyes." Her message is for everyone, but it has special meaning for some. "I want to tell every young African American woman that she is part of this

HOME OF THE BRAVE

When African American classical singer Marian Anderson was denied the stage at a private venue, First Lady Eleanor Roosevelt invited her to perform at the Lincoln Memorial on Easter Sunday 1939, with the help of the National Park Service. When Secretary of the Interior Harold Ickes introduced Anderson to a crowd of 75,000—and to many more listening to the broadcast at home—he began, "In this great auditorium under the sky, all of us are free." Evoking the life and sacrifice of the president at whose feet he stood, Ickes said, "Genius draws no color lines."

story," she says. Soskin didn't visit a national park until midlife (Yosemite was her first); family vacations to enjoy nature were largely for the white middle-class "RV crowd" back then, she says. But now she understands the importance of people from every walk of life going to national parks. "I quickly began to get a sense that they are our greatest gifts," Soskin says. "They are resources that I now feel are *mine*."

That's the message the NPS wants all underrepresented populations to get: this land is your land, too. "Traditionally, we have told the white male history stories, but that's changed. We are committed now to telling all Americans' stories," says Julia Washburn, the NPS's associate director for interpretation and education. There are so many layers of human experience represented in parks that everyone can see themselves and their legacies, she says. That's particularly clear at the Statue of Liberty National Monument, where a legacy of adaptability and overcoming adversity is palpable. There, in New York Harbor, where the East and Hudson rivers flow into one, it seems that looking back reveals a way forward.

Long before it was named Liberty Island, this had been a popular place for Algonquian tribes (descendants of the first humans to colonize North America 12,000 to 13,000 years ago) who harvested rich oyster beds there for several hundred years. By the mid-1600s, the tribes had been driven north and west by European colonizers. As new settlements grew in and around Manhattan amid booming trade and commerce, citizens of other countries were enticed by the prospects of better lives there. Whether they came across the Atlantic or Pacific or over southern or northern borders, from the last ice age to the twenty-first century, willingly or unwillingly (in the case of slaves), immigrants have long made up the United States.

More than 40 percent of Americans alive today can trace their origins to the period from 1892 to 1954 when 12 million people first planted wobbly legs on American soil at Ellis Island. From 1855 to 1890, nearly 8 million others entered via nearby Castle Garden, which is now Castle Clinton National Monument, as riveting a place as Ellis Island. They'd spent weeks aboard crowded, filthy ships, but they knew they'd survived the journey when, beginning in 1886, they glimpsed Liberty's torch, hoisted high above the harbor.

This granite likeness of Dr. Martin Luther King Jr. is as enduring as his heroic legacy and messages of tolerance and peace.

Whether immigrants throughout history have landed in the United States seeking opportunity or fleeing famine, war, religious persecution, or drought is of little consequence. Despite disparate origins and the struggles that many immigrants still undergo, the United States' populace now has staggering, enviable diversity. While recent immigrants didn't sail into New York Harbor, those newer arrivals' stories will soon be told there as well. At Ellis Island, the NPS is still expanding immigration narratives at the Peopling of America Center, whose second phase should open in the near future (if enough funds are raised). That piece will focus on the immigration experience from the closing of Ellis Island to the present day. Whether immigrants arrived in the 1890s or in 2015, all have stories of what has been and hopes of what will be as they contribute to the fabric of communities and the foundation of a nation.

Robert Stanton, the fifteenth NPS director and the first African American to hold that position, likes to remind people that he and Frederick Douglass joined the Park Service the same year. "I donned the green and gray in Grand Teton in June of 1962, and on September 5, 1962, President Kennedy signed the legislation, passed by Congress, designating the Douglass home as a national historic site," he remarked in October 2014. Similar to Douglass, Stanton was part reformer, part diplomat while director from 1997 to 2001, during which time he led the Park Service into a new era of scientific awareness.

Stanton knows that one of the biggest challenges facing the NPS is engagement of all citizens. They will be the savior of parks, he says, when all people, regardless of race, culture, or gender recognize themselves in the shared resources guarded by the Park Service and become necessary stewards of them. Stanton also loves to quote Douglass and feels the international icon of human rights, with his messages of interdependence, speaks directly to today's national conversation about diversity. Douglass said, "It must in truth be said . . . that no possible native force of character, and no depth or wealth of originality, can lift a man into absolute independence of his fellow men, and no generation of men can be independent of the preceding generation . . . The highest order of genius is as dependent as is the lowest. It, like the loftiest waves of the sea, derives its power and greatness from the grandeur and vastness of the ocean of which it forms part. We differ as the waves, but are one as the sea."

Kids on a snowshoeing field trip make discoveries in the slowed, hushed backcountry of Glacier National Park in winter.

CHAPTER 26

The Adventure of Seeing

ON A BROILING JULY DAY in Yosemite Valley, in a swath of shade cast by a Douglas fir, a dozen school-age children cluster around Erik Westerlund, a National Park Service interpretive ranger. In the midst of introducing himself he's interrupted by a loud, throaty call from a huge black bird on a nearby tree branch. Westerlund swivels around quickly, nearly losing his stiff-brimmed straw hat, and gestures for the group to follow him. While jogging over to see the bird, he points up to it and asks, "Who's ever heard of a raven before?" A few hands shoot up and some kids call out, "I have!" Westerlund, who's led thousands of programs at Yosemite, excitedly lists some of the ravens' qualities: they are among the smartest birds in the world; they mate for life; they are nature's cleanup and recycling crew.

On this day Westerlund is leading some of his favorite park visitors, junior rangers, who earn badges, patches, and certificates for completing activities and talking with rangers. "I love being out in the field and turning people on to natural history," he says. Every year roughly 800,000 kids become junior rangers at hundreds of national park units—their motto is, "Explore, Learn, and Protect!" Millions more visitors (including grown-ups) take nature and history walks, sit by campfires, or gaze at galaxies with interpretive rangers. Across the NPS, rangers boast an astonishing array of expertise—from Civil War strategies and tactics at Antietam National Battlefield to the speleogenesis of the marble underground at Oregon Caves National Monument.

Westerlund and thousands of other interpretive rangers throughout the park system uphold a proud tradition that is as old, and in some ways older, than the NPS itself. In the days between the establishment of the first national park in 1872 and the founding of the NPS in 1916, learning emerged as a principle purpose of parks. The great champion of Yosemite, John Muir, jotted in his notebook in 1896: "I'll interpret the rocks, learn the language of flood, storm and the avalanche. I'll acquaint myself with the glaciers and wild gardens, and get as near the heart of the world as I can." Muir knew, as do others who walk in the shadow of Half Dome, that a place cannot truly be known through superficial sightseeing. As early as the turn of the twentieth century, interpreters were leading students of every level into living park laboratories and tapping into the essence of those places.

Muir's belief was embodied by Rocky Mountain National Park booster Enos Mills. As a mountain climber, peak guide, and entrepreneur, Mills introduced guests to his own backyard, which joined the park system in 1915 largely due to his efforts. As a young man walking on a beach near San Francisco, Mills had met an elderly man.

Unfamiliar with the area, Mills asked the white-bearded gentleman about the beach kelp. The older man's thoughtful response began a lifelong friendship between the two. That man, who happened to be John Muir, inspired Mills to devote his life to conservation. In his 1920 edition of *The Adventures of a Nature Guide*, Mills wrote about describing things in a way that gives them breadth for visitors. "The nature guide (interpreter) is at his best when he discusses facts so that they appeal to the imagination and to the reason, gives flesh and blood to cold hard facts, makes life stories of inanimate objects," he said.

Walking near Yosemite's nature center at Happy Isles, Westerlund explains to his charges that they will walk in complete silence and use all their senses—look, listen, touch, smell, and taste. "If we're lucky we'll make some astonishing discoveries," he says. The nearby Merced River coursing steadily by their side, they follow excitedly, pausing to spy on a cluster of iridescent green bottle flies, sample some elderberries, examine bear scratches on an alder tree, and study the structure of a Douglas fir cone. Stopping to smell the leaves of a California laurel, an evergreen with smooth, shiny leaves, Westerlund explains to his wide-eyed protégés that various tribes who once frequented the area used the aromatic plant as a mosquito repellent and to relieve congestion. Passing around and sniffing the pungent leaf of the bay tree, the kids agree that it would certainly clear a stuffy nose.

This afternoon walk evokes one taken by Rocky Mountain's Enos Mills and the children of his nature school more than a century earlier. "Stepping softly and without saying a word, we slipped through the woods and peeped from behind the last trees into a grassy opening by the beaver pond, hoping for a glimpse of a coyote or a deer," he wrote in *The Adventures of a Nature Guide*. "On the way home we turned aside from the trail to investigate a delightful bit of forested wilderness between two brooks. We were explorers in a new country."

The philosophy of nature interpretation was transformed after acclaimed journalist and fiction writer Freeman Tilden had a chance meeting with NPS Director Newton Drury in the 1940s. Their conversation led Tilden to devote his writing life to national parks. His 1951 book *The National Parks: What They Mean to You and Me* was called by publishing titan Alfred Knopf the best book ever written on the parks. Tilden's penetrating observations and general philosophy evoked Muir and Mills while revealing a weakness in park interpretation of his day. The NPS had numerous interpreters and an impressive array of university connections, but Tilden felt there was something missing. "The early Greek philosophers looked at the world about them and decided that there were four elements: fire, air, water, and earth," he wrote. "But as they grew a little wiser, they perceived that there must be something else. These tangible elements did not comprise a principle; they merely revealed that somewhere else, if they could not find it, there was a soul of things—a Fifth Essence, pure, eternal, and inclusive."

Tilden insisted that park interpretation should strive to illuminate that intangible element in order to better connect people to those places, their history and substance. He called it the adventure of seeing—a technique for bringing to life dinosaur bones, rocks, cliff dwellings, missions, and more. But how do you turn people on to mountains and trees and open their hearts to the struggles and triumphs and daily minutiae of people long dead?

As a guide, Tilden wrote several principles of interpretation: objects need to relate to the personality and experience of visitors; interpretation is information plus revelation; it should provoke, not instruct; it should aim to represent the whole instead of one part; it should approach kids differently than adults. In the tradition of Mills and Muir, Tilden felt that thoughtful interpretation would lead to understanding, appreciation, and ultimately protection of park resources. As the father of modern park interpretation, his philosophy still shapes the experiences of hundreds of millions of park visitors.

Tilden's techniques are alive and kicking at Independence National Historical Park in Philadelphia, which encompasses Independence Hall (where the Declaration of Independence and US Constitution were signed) and the pavilion where the Liberty Bell is housed. The interpretation by NPS ranger Ed Welch breathes life into these events long past; his take on the Fifth Essence lends meaning to the place where a nation was born and its government created. How does he resurrect men gone to dust centuries ago and conjure the intangible notions of freedom and self-governance?

With a booming voice, Welch demands that visitors summon those original statesmen at their various posts in the Assembly Room, which looks very much as it did in the eighteenth century. It is July 1776, and in the crowded room, the gathering is preparing to vote on whether or not to adopt the Declaration of Independence. Welch moves briskly around the room pointing to various spots: here is Thomas Jefferson, architect of the document, at center stage, and over there are John Hancock, Benjamin Franklin, John Adams, and Samuel

of defiance, the prospect of a government by the people. "This *right here* was the beginning of our republic," says Welch.

With hundreds of millions of visitors to national parks each year, it would be impossible for interpretative rangers to make contact with each one. Countless interpretive installations in visitor centers and numerous wayside exhibits fill the gaps, as do short films and those omnipresent Park Service brochures crafted specifically for each place. Among the most compelling items are original artifacts that act as powerful threads connecting then to now. In some parks the object is *the* symbol materialized, such as the Liberty Bell and the Statue of Liberty; other items are subtler though they have a no less powerful effect. At San Antonio Missions National Historical Park, those three-centuries-old places of refuge are brought to life by an enormous brass key on display, once lifted by a living, breathing person, allowing entry to one of those fortified communities. At Dinosaur National Monument, the actual teeth and bones, once covered with skin and dirt and saliva, of oversized behemoths are present. The preserved, cramped slave quarters at the Kingsley Plantation within Timucuan Ecological and Historic Preserve give shape to the cruel institution of slavery and put a lump in the throat of those who enter them.

Adams, all engaged in heated conversations or contemplations of their rebellious maneuvering. They dip quills into silver inkstands and light taper candles as the day wanes. All don the powdered wigs popular at the time and are clad in fine suits, stockings, and buckled shoes. It is a sober, not celebratory, event; by declaring their independence from England and its king, these men are committing high treason and could be hanged. The visitor is invited to pull up a seat—dragging heavy chair legs across the wood floor—beside these giants of history and conjure the din of debate, the mood

SUNNY SIDE UP

Eleven years after the signing of the Declaration of Independence, the Constitutional Convention met in the Assembly Room in 1787. In the days before the US Constitution was created and signed, the gathering debated about issues affecting their burgeoning nation. Ranger Ed Welch points out the Rising Sun Chair—the original seat occupied by George Washington, who presided over the meetings. Carved into its crest rail are a sun, a liberty cap, and a liberty pole. "[Benjamin] Franklin made a strange comment about the chair," says Welch. "He'd been sitting there looking at the sun—was it rising or sinking?"

On the day the Constitution was signed, Franklin was gratified to see that the sun was rising. Reflecting on the progress of those historic days and years, Washington wrote, "We are not to expect perfection in this world; but mankind, in modern times, have apparently made some progress in the science of government."

As technology takes over, the NPS is expanding its interpretive offerings while straddling a digital divide. Most parks have their own web pages with varying degrees of electronic resources; some parks offer coded signs smartphone users can scan to access park information, texts with weather and traffic information, Facebook and Flickr pages, podcasts, and apps.

But there is societal debate about how wired parks should be. For example, should mobile phone and Wi-Fi access be ubiquitous to encourage the digitally dependent to feel welcome in parks? During a recent pilot project, the Park Service has been looking into offering Wi-Fi at several parks but emphasizes that coverage would be confined to developed areas—the NPS insists it will not be wiring the backcountry. It could be helpful, the Park Service says, in offering visitors real-time information on construction, traffic delays, weather, and the like. The NPS has also reminded detractors that it

would be done only in a way that keeps telecommunication infrastructure hidden and minimizes environmental impact. Making parks digitally accessible is an issue that arouses both outrage and excitement; while it may appeal to highly connected millennials, critics fret over lost solitude. Can you get back to nature while the person standing next to you is streaming videos of puppies on YouTube?

It is not a new issue, really, since the NPS has adapted previously to changing societal norms. These arguments sounds a lot like the ones, way back when, over whether or not to allow cars in parks, or electric lights, or swimming pools—all of which were ultimately approved. In his 1936 manifesto *Atmosphere in the National Parks*, superintendent of Sequoia National Park John White pushed back against what he saw as the dumbing down of the visitor experience. "The interest of the people is perhaps the most difficult of all to define in these perplexing days of social and economical changes," he wrote. "Visitors demand opportunity for physical and aesthetic enjoyment of park scenery, but also for amusement, entertainment, and instruction. There

Interpretive ranger Erik Westerlund administers the junior ranger pledge after a nature walk in Yosemite.

is a natural and steady pressure to place amusement and entertainment above other requirements." The debate over technology also evokes Ed Abbey's rant against industrial tourism. Abbey and many others like him have experienced parks in a deliberately unwired way, and they resist intrusion.

Meanwhile the Park Service, concerned as it was a century ago about staying relevant to the general public, has embraced digital tools as a way to reach and retain young visitors. To many in that demographic, standing around waiting for Old Faithful to erupt once an hour is for chumps; instead, you can get alerts about predicted blows by following the Twitter handle @GeyserNPS. In its forward-looking document *A Call to Action:* *Preparing for a Second Century of Stewardship and Engagement*, leading up to the NPS centennial, the Park Service has "go digital" as one of its main objectives under the heading "Advancing the NPS Education Mission." A digital platform doesn't have to change the way nature is traditionally experienced, it says, and it might even entice more people to experience it.

Julia Washburn, associate director for interpretation and education of the NPS, says changes in society and the ways people learn must be embraced. "We take our role very seriously as a trusted source of scientific and historic information," she says. "That makes it all the more important that we be working hard on reaching a

Bar None

It's a design recognized by billions of people: the slim brochure with the black bar running down the length of its cover, announcing the name of the national park in contrasting white block letters. The famous unigrid design was created by Massimo Vignelli in the mid-1970s, and though it has evolved, it's still the template on which the brochures for more than 400 parks are based. When it adopted the unigrid system, the National Park Service had been looking for a way to reduce costs by streamlining literature production. What it got was a consistent, legible, and recognizable design that would be simple enough to encompass hundreds of diverse parks.

The bar design has a layout that unites parks while also distinguishing them, and it has become a universal symbol that reliable information lies within. Since Vignelli's day, the design and editorial staff at the Harpers Ferry Center—in a breezy building on a wooded perch near the confluence of the Potomac and Shenandoah rivers—has worked with park interpreters to create original content that fits within that modular grid layout. Text and graphics including maps and other images orient visitors to the park and help connect them to the natural, political, or social history of that place. The unigrid brochure—part teacher, part memento—plays an increasingly important role in connecting hundreds of millions of people to the essence of each park.

On a May morning, visitors to the South Rim of the Grand Canyon descend 1120 feet to Cedar Ridge on a ranger-guided hike along the South Kaibab Trail.

Remnants of the original slaves' cabins on the 19th-century Kingsley Plantation, part of Florida's Timucuan Ecological and Historic Preserve

changing audience and engaging those minds. Technology in parks is controversial; some people believe they should be a last bastion, but the reality is that, if we want people to explore and learn, these devices can be a catalyst to an authentic experience."

Whether adding technology means compromising Tilden's interpretation standards is difficult to say. Purists believe Muir would not have yapped on his iPhone while roaming in his Range of Light—he said, "Only by going alone in silence, without baggage, can one truly get into the heart of the wilderness. All other travel is mere dust and hotels and baggage and chatter." But, inspired by the choicest treasures of nature before his eyes, might he have tweeted pithy observations? We'll never know. No doubt, however, he would have

been in favor of the NPS reminding the gadget reliant to look up and to power down. One sign near Old Faithful reads, "Enjoy Yellowstone's natural sounds, please turn off your cell phone."

Our best places, preserved as parks, remain unparalleled platforms from which to launch a lifetime of learning about the nation's natural, cultural, and historical resources. The NPS and its interpretive staff are the caretakers, curators, and ambassadors of those countless pasts, and to a visitor with a kernel of curiosity, their work can prompt life-altering experiences at breathtaking locations.

Take a walk at Lily Lake, at nearly 9000 feet, on a cool June afternoon with Rocky Mountain National Park seasonal ranger Leslie Brodhead, and she will change the way you look at those small wonders: wildflowers. She will get down on her hands and knees, magnifying glass in hand, and introduce you to that secretive, shade-loving beauty, the spotted coral root orchid. If its delicate-looking white and pink petals catch a ray of sun, they shimmer like a thousand disco balls. Troll the wilds of Yosemite with Erik Westerlund and his junior rangers, and you will discover treasures. These rangers will make you wonder if you've spent the afternoon alongside Enos Mills or maybe John Muir himself.

At the end of their time together, Westerlund asks if his group is ready to take their pledge: will they continue to study nature, help care for parks and the planet, and commit to performing three random acts of kindness? After hearing "yes" all around, the ranger hands each child a wooden badge with a carving of Half Dome. Toting their new treasures—which some handle as carefully as a Fabergé egg—the kids rejoin their adults and fan out in different directions across the valley, with a growing understanding of the complexity of the natural world and of that elusive soul of things.

The church facade at Mission San José, one of four walled communities protected and interpreted at San Antonio Missions National Historical Park

CHAPTER 27

Paid in Sunrises and Sunsets

THE SUN HAS JUST begun to speckle yellow upon the Yosemite Valley floor, but already the place is abuzz. Slack-jawed sightseers click cameras; rock climbers inspect gear and eyeball routes; hikers consult maps to confirm trails in one of America's most beloved parks. At the start of the Mist Trail, along the surging Merced River, National Park Service ranger Chris Leonardi swings a loaded backpack onto his brawny frame. It'll be another hot July day, and on this trail, one of the park's most visited, he'll have his work cut out for him. "Waterfall hikes are

always popular, and people hear the word 'mist' and it makes this trail even more attractive," he says. The trail leads to the tops of 317-foot-high Vernal Fall and 594-foot Nevada Fall beyond, two giant cataracts that take awe-inspiring plunges over huge granite boulders. It also provides hiker access to the well-loved Half Dome Trail and is a feeder for the 211-mile-long John Muir Trail, which winds its way through the strapping High Sierra.

On a busy summer weekend, as many as 5200 people might hoof it along the Mist Trail's steep terrain, and Leonardi will make contact with as many as possible. His beat is called "preventive search and rescue," and as its name suggests, it's about alerting visitors to hazards in order to pre-empt incidents.

The day promises many certainties, plus an equal number of uncertainties. For sure, Leonardi will answer a stream of questions: Where's the bathroom? Where can I refill my water bottle? How far is it to the falls? He will also ask many: Where are you headed today? Are you bringing lots of water with you? He will offer endless heads-ups: Past the bridge, the trail gets very steep and rocky. The more than 600 sand-slick, polished granite steps down from the falls are very slippery. Don't go in even calm-looking water, because it can easily knock you off your feet.

If something goes wrong for one or more hikers, Leonardi will rush to their aid and, in some cases, try to save their lives. Heart conditions, dehydration, scraped and blown knees, and turned ankles are all common on this stretch. Hikers throughout the park ask for help when they're injured, tired, cold, wet, hungry, thirsty, or lost. Like many rangers in Yosemite, Leonardi has specialized skills including emergency medical training (with a wilderness upgrade) and Yosemite-specific expertise such as swift-water rescue and technical ropes training.

Pausing at the Vernal Fall footbridge, Leonardi reflects on summers past when too many rescues and a heartbreaking number of body recoveries have taken place along the Mist Trail—30 percent of search-and-rescue incidents in the park happen there. One particular accident that looms heavily in recent memory involved two young brothers who bystanders said were "just" wading in the river and moments later were swept to their deaths. At times Leonardi has to rein in visitors who ignore fences, railings, and warning signs, putting themselves, and their would-be rescuers, in peril. "Sometimes I have to be the 'fun-killer,'" he says. But if that prevents a trip to the Yosemite Medical Clinic, or worse, so be it. If Leonardi were to offer every visitor some simple advice, it would be "Plan, prepare, and be aware of your surroundings. Stay on the trail." According to Yosemite's deputy chief of emergency services, David Pope, "Nearly all of our fatal accidents occur when visitors leave the trail."

THAT'S A FACT

Fewer than 20 percent of the roughly 22,000 National Park Service employees are rangers. The dozens of other critical roles include building and maintenance jobs like electrician, mechanic, carpenter, and plumber as well as landscape architect, historical architect, museum specialist, historian, and visual information specialist. Of course there are also biologists, hydrologists, botanists, geologists, and ecologists, as well as accountants, budget analysts, supply clerks (toilet paper, anyone?)—and the busiest of all—custodians.

Despite warnings to stay on the trail at Lower Yosemite Fall, many visitors scramble over slick granite boulders to get a closer look.

Ubiquitous in their sedate olive uniforms and stiff-brimmed hats, NPS rangers are a species recognized, and roundly admired, nationwide. While they have always been seen as the go-to park employees, their role has shifted in recent decades. In a 1972 follow-up edition of *Oh, Ranger!* the NPS's seventh director, George Hartzog, hinted at a changing time in society and in parks. "The park ranger has had to become a specialist in handling people, and people's problems, as well as protecting forests, historic buildings, and wildlife," he wrote. During the pivotal time he penned that, national parks established in metropolitan areas including New York and San Francisco introduced a host of law enforcement issues more typical to the Bronx than to Bryce Canyon. With increasing numbers of people, even remote parks started seeing more accidents and crimes. An Interior Department report in 1970 compared Yellowstone, Grand Canyon, and Yosemite to small cities with tens of thousands of people on-site daily. The number of serious incidents in parks leapt from 2300 or so offenses in 1966 to roughly 5900 in 1980.

Part of the jump in crime involved the antiestablishment youth movement popular at the time, in which young people actively rejected the values of their parents and other authority figures. Large groups congregated in Yosemite, in particular, where they sometimes shouted disrespectful epithets at rangers, calling them "pine pigs" and "tree fuzz." Tensions came to a head in Stoneman Meadow on July 4, 1970. Rangers' attempts to quiet raucous, drug-fueled partiers escalated into a riot during which rangers were yanked from horses and visitors were beaten. At the end of the day, 30 people had been hospitalized and 135 had been arrested—and the incident had gotten national press.

The NPS could no longer deny that it was on the front lines of societal upheaval and that it needed backup. Soon thereafter, Yosemite built its jail facilities, which are still in use today. With resounding congressional support, in March 1971 the NPS established a law enforcement wing, the entity out of which the "gun" ranger eventually emerged. Balance was not immediately achieved, however, as illustrated by the death of the first NPS ranger to be killed in the line of duty. Kenneth Patrick, forty, was shot to death while pursuing poachers in Point Reyes National Seashore in August 1973. And in the next year, a *US News and World Report* story about a disturbing incident at Wind Cave National Park, in which wildlife was slaughtered, suggests the public's nagging sense of lawlessness in parks: "[T]he sheer ferocity of vandals, mostly youngsters, but often adults too, knows few bounds," it said.

Despite the clear need to rein in disorder, the Park Service had an identity crisis as it struggled with the necessity of its new role. A 1975 NPS memo stated that "the ranger who wants to wear a sidearm to fulfill an image of himself as a 'law officer' is not measuring up to the ranger image." But the very next year, the NPS was given the power under the General Authorities Act to carry firearms, make arrests, and serve warrants. Rangers resisted the directive, but in 1980 the NPS mandated extensive training for law enforcement rangers and required them to carry guns. As the ranks of armed rangers grew and the counterculture movement fizzled, some stability was achieved, but it took both sides letting go of some deeply rooted prejudices. A 1977 NPS report entitled *Youth's Perceptions of National Park Rangers* (which concluded that impressions were generally favorable) called on both parties to keep an open mind. "Stereotyping

WOMEN'S WORK

Women constitute just under 40 percent of National Park Service employees, including many who perform the same duties as male law enforcement rangers, some excelling in areas still seen as male bastions. Lisa Kahn has been patrolling Yosemite's backcountry for a decade. The rugged, remote terrain she covers on foot is marked by few trails but is cut by abrupt canyons, surging streams, and alpine heights. Kahn makes contact with various people she comes across, checking wilderness permits and campers' bear-proofing of food. She packs a firearm and is prepared to use it. Kahn picks up copious amounts of human waste and (used) toilet paper and admits the bugs can be brutal.

"Keeping perspective and not getting tripped up by the little stuff is the hardest part of my job," she says. Being immersed in wildness is a major perk. "You are in love. You are so excited to be alive out here," she says. "I never feel afraid. This is where I feel at home."

Lisa Kahn is one of eight backcountry rangers who patrol assigned areas of Yosemite's wilderness for nine-day solo stretches.

a ranger as just having an enforcer role, or youth as just being a hippy deviant, does not fully reflect the roles of either in a park setting," it cautioned.

Up until the early 1970s, law enforcement ranger work was viewed as too grueling or dangerous for women. Even in parks where male rangers were allowed to carry firearms before the 1980 requirement, women were not. Not until 1971 were women sanctioned to carry a gun and go through law enforcement training. In 1978 women were given official permission to dress in the "men's" uniform (rather than in short skirts, pillbox hats, and cheap replicas of a badge that some visitors mistook for a children's souvenir).

Now more than 3800 rangers all dress the same but have highly varied responsibilities. Law enforcement ("gun") rangers, as opposed to interpretive ("fun") ones, deal specifically with upholding the rule of law in parks and responding to emergencies. They are federal law enforcement agents, and national parks are their exclusive jurisdiction. If you're in a national park unit and call 9-1-1, that's who will respond. Law enforcement rangers carry firearms and make arrests for anything from scrawling graffiti to committing murder. The US Park Police, made up of nearly 600 federal officers, is a somewhat different entity that has authority in mainly urban parks in New York City, Washington, DC, and San Francisco.

In terms of crime, statistics show that parks are safe places. In 2012 national park units had nearly 283 million total visitors—plus tens of thousands of NPS and concessionaire employees living on-site or nearby—and saw 109,000 total reported incidents. In comparison, the US population that same year was roughly 313 million and experienced 10.1 million crimes.

All "gun" and "fun" rangers are sworn to uphold the mandate outlined in the Organic Act of 1916; they all must protect park resources while enabling the enjoyment—and, now, safety—of visitors. But not just interpretive rangers get asked where the bathroom is, or where to see the bears or the best sunsets, or what kind of tree that is. Law enforcement rangers, from Harry Yount—Yellowstone's first game warden and de facto ranger, hired in 1880—to the present have been renaissance women and men. In Yosemite some rangers could just as soon discuss the hydrology of the park's rivers as rescue someone from them. They are individuals who are so good at what they do, they are often poached by other federal agencies or private entities, which pay temptingly more.

And yet many remain in parks, fielding surprising inquiries, such as "What time do you turn off the geysers?" in Yellowstone (oh yes, they've heard it all), and answer with a good-natured smile that the geysers are on nature's schedule. They dispatch endless words of advice, such as that flip-flops are not the best choice of footwear to climb 14,259-foot Longs Peak in Rocky Mountain National Park (oh yes, they've seen it all). And they keep their composure even if Joe Visitor reminds them in a less-than-amiable tone that he "pays the ranger's salary" and he will walk in whatever he damn well pleases.

In addition to the mental and emotional demands, the physical challenges law enforcement rangers face are many. They work in temperatures ranging from subzero to more than 110 degrees Fahrenheit, in places from glaciers to deserts, from oceans to rivers and reservoirs—never mind the grizzly bears, killer bees, venomous snakes, scorpions, and poisonous flora that populate their beats.

A look at the NPS's online Morning Report, which tracks incidents in all parks by date, gives a glimpse of the breadth of challenges rangers nationwide respond to on a typical summer day: "Visitor Seriously Injured When Thrown by Mule"; "Lightning Strike Injures Park Visitor"; "Missing 13-Year-Old Hiker Found by Rescuers"; "Rangers Rescue Kayaker." These rangers may be on foot, horseback, skis, all-terrain vehicle, boat, truck, roped belay, aircraft, or even dogsled. In addition to their search-and-rescue activities, rangers face other dangers. On any given day, in Yosemite and beyond, they may pull people from mangled vehicles, intercept a drug smuggler, confront a wanted fugitive, or break up a brawl. In 2012, 137 rangers were assaulted—one of whom was killed by gunfire.

Many law enforcement rangers learn critical skills during their roughly twenty-four weeks of intensive study at the Federal Law Enforcement Training Centers, where employees of ninety other federal agencies also train. Many have additional schooling, including emergency responder, first responder or wilderness first responder, and emergency medical technician training. In some parks, including Denali and Mount Rainier, an elite legion of climbing or mountaineering rangers specialize in resource protection and rescue in places few people dare to go. At Denali, during a typical thirty-day patrol in the Alaska Range,

Since the 1920s, Denali rangers have patrolled with dog teams; on "good" days, they may cover more than 30 miles.

A Yellowstone ranger manages a grizzly bear jam along Chittenden Road where visitors use binoculars and zoom lenses for a better look.

mountaineering rangers will spend most of their time above 14,200 feet. Search-and-rescue and mountain rangers in some parks rely heavily on highly skilled volunteers.

In a park like Yosemite, where millions of people crowd the valley in the warmer months, rangers might use all that training in a single day. For supervisory park ranger Chris Bellino, a day can go from mind-numbing paperwork to life-saving adrenaline rush in a flash. Bellino has led many high-wall rescues on the park's centerpiece sentinel, El Capitan. Rising more than 3000 feet from the valley floor, it is the world's largest granite monolith. Bellino recalls recent injuries on the wall that, due to their severity, have required helicopter assists. Unpredictable wind and weather conditions make any rescue on the sheer rock extremely dangerous. Add a helicopter, whose rotors may come within five feet of the rock face—with a pilot whose nerves apparently are also made of steel—and the rescues can be pretty dramatic. Such high-risk patrols take a toll, mentally and physically, says Bellino. "Trying to live up to the expectation of jack-of-all-trades saps a lot of your personal time and energy," he says. "You work yourself into the ground here."

While these types of rescues, whether in Grand Teton or the Grand Canyon, generally come at no cost to the injured (unless blatant recklessness is involved), the NPS spends plenty. The 2348 search-and-rescues conducted throughout the park system in 2013 cost the NPS nearly $4 million. The year prior saw 2876 search-and-rescues costing $5.2 million.

The vast majority of visitors to national parks are interested in law-abiding activities, and they look to rangers of every kind to help facilitate that. Yosemite has 120 law enforcement rangers, divided into three districts, though most are concentrated in the valley where the majority of visitors are. That may sound like a lot of personnel, but budget shortfalls over the past several years have left noticeable gaps in what was once a twenty-four-hour patrolled park. In order to keep the peace within the crowded seven square miles of the valley, law enforcement rangers like Cullen Tucker are ever watchful. Every day, the park offers a unique policing challenge, he says, in a geographically isolated place. "When people come here, they bring their problems with them," he says. "It would be very eye-opening for the public to know how much stuff actually happens here."

Tucker has seen many incidents around alcohol and drugs, rowdy parties, speeding, traffic accidents, and stabbings. By midsummer 2014, he had already stopped three fistfights between visitors. When deciding whether to write a citation or to arrest someone, often he asks himself, "Is this person a danger to himself or others? Are they a threat

At 8000 feet up the western face of Mount Rainier, during a joint training exercise, an NPS climbing ranger awaits the arrival of an army unit that aids in high-altitude rescues.

to park resources? Are they ruining someone else's vacation?" Yosemite is in this third-generation ranger's blood—his grandfather, mother, and father were rangers before him. To him the park is home, and he defends it with a sense of ownership. But that doesn't mean budget shortfalls don't take a toll, as does the constant pressure on law enforcement rangers to wear many hats—and wear them well. "We're stretched thin," he says. "It's exhausting work."

"You get paid in sunrises and sunsets" is the saying about how NPS rangers are compensated for their work. One of the perks of the job is that rangers' offices are often amid some of America's most treasured landscapes. Whether that fact makes up for the long hours, low pay, constant hazards, and unrealistic expectations of the role—sometimes amid soul-crushing bureaucracy—may depend on the day. Despite the many changes to ranger responsibilities over the past century, they remain among the most highly respected professionals in the nation, as iconic as the places they work in.

In his 1919 annual report to Stephen Mather, Yosemite Superintendent W. B. Lewis wrote: "The successful ranger must be honest, courteous, and patient and at the same time firm, equal to

emergencies, and of good judgment . . . To find men in whom all of these qualifications are happily combined is not easy, but when once found they should be encouraged in every possible way."

If Lewis were to walk into his park today, that is what he would find. In Yosemite rangers may be patrolling the valley or the wilderness, sharing a joke with visitors or issuing a ticket, preempting a tragedy or responding to one. Or, like their boss Deputy Chief Ranger Michael Stansberry, they might leap up from their lunch, reposition their trademark hat, and rush over to help an elderly woman on a scooter stuck in the sand. Those "greenies," as they are known, will show goodwill, intelligence, and remarkable technical skill. They will beam their "all-in-a-day's-work" smile when they have risen to a challenge. And like Stansberry, Tucker, Bellino, Leonardi, and so many others, they will appreciate it when a visitor turns back to add one more thing to their encounter: "Thank you."

Yellow pond lilies, here in a Yellowstone lake, provide food and shelter for many fish and underwater insects.

CHAPTER 28

The Everglades Is a Test

THE BEST TIME TO WALK the Anhinga Trail in Everglades National Park is in the dry season from December through April. The path winds through saw-grass prairie and across one of the two major sloughs, or freshwater channels, that slowly surge southward through the park. These are the glades, or open expanses, that gave the park its name. This is one of the premier wetland trails in the park system, offering excellent wildlife viewing year-round, says ranger Jennifer Wilcox. The dry season offers

a bonus, she says: "The alligators and anhingas are breeding, and the shrinking Taylor Slough concentrates the wildlife."

To the anhinga, a long-necked, graceful-looking waterbird, this is paradise: abundant, shallow freshwater means good fishing grounds; the cypress trees are perfect for nesting; potential mates are plentiful. In addition to the spear-billed anhinga, herons and egrets are common, and there are alligators—lots of them. Those steel-jawed, iron-sided reptiles act as an architect of the Everglades, a keystone species that bulldozes homey holes in the marshy ground, creating habitat for fish and turtles, which also feed birds, otters, and the occasional bobcat.

Here at Royal Palms—a popular area on the east side of the park that was once a state park—lies the Gumbo Limbo Trail, named for the sturdy, red-tinted tree that thrives within this subtropical hardwood hammock. On natural "hills" that are only inches above sea level, the hammocks boast dense copses of broad-leafed trees; it is a habitat type unique to south Florida. The Everglades is where southern tropical Caribbean conditions meet a northern temperate environment, creating a subtropical ecosystem where hammocks like this one combine oak and maple with mahogany, royal palms, and gumbo-limbo. In their shade grow fluorescent-green ferns and logic-defying air plants that subsist on water and nutrients absorbed without the aid of roots or soil.

The Everglades has nine distinct habitats in all, supporting a deceiving array of biodiversity, including species found nowhere else on Earth. It spans 1.5 million acres, from the Ten Thousand Islands area on the Gulf of Mexico down through the southern tip of the state and out into Florida Bay, encompassing dozens of keys and coral reefs. The freshwater and saltwater areas, pinelands, prairies, marshes, and mangrove forests constitute the largest remaining subtropical wilderness in the Lower 48. Among thousands of species of flora and fauna, the many rare and endangered ones include the American crocodile, Florida panther, and manatee. The park is a World Heritage Site, an International Biosphere Reserve, and a designated wetland of international importance.

Despite strong jaws, sharp teeth, and a veritable suit of armor, American alligators were nearly extinct in the 1960s; the population has rebounded and they are now found in six national parks, including the Everglades.

During the popular A Kite's-Eye View program at Gateway NRA, kids fly a camera-enabled kite. When it lands, students see the images instantly on a laptop and can compare them to nearly century-old images to assess how the landscape has changed.

While the Everglades may seem an ideal world to the anhinga, since it was established as a national park in 1947 it has been in peril, inched back from the brink time and again, only to face new threats. Tally up the current issues it faces, and the sum may equal its most challenging time on record.

Lured by rich soil and sunny skies, northern folk migrated south, where roughly 3 million acres of prairies, sloughs, grasses, and plains stretched from central Florida down to the Florida Keys. By the late nineteenth century, those settlers were clearing land for agriculture in central Florida; many saw the Everglades as a swamp that needed to be drained for farms and homes and cleared of hostile bugs, plants, and animals. More people required more land, and more draining, and so it went.

While the Everglades didn't suit the settlers' purposes in its original form, it wasn't worthless land at all. When Lake Okeechobee overflowed its banks, as it did naturally and regularly, 450 billion gallons of water fanned out into the Everglades and nurtured an assemblage of plants and animals found nowhere else on Earth. But, ironically, artificial draining of that land made farmers struggle to satiate their crops in years of drought. And when it did rain or storm with hurricane force, the settlers often got flooded out.

Whether residents of central Florida needed more water or less, in the same year the Everglades became a park—securing protection for less than half its historic footprint—they looked to the US Army Corps of Engineers to solve their problems. The epic system of canals, levees, and reservoirs the Corps built in response would have been a triumph if it hadn't been such a success—meaning that it impounded and diverted a massive amount of water away from Everglades, 1.7 billion gallons per day, which left the ecosystem thirsting for the old days. By the 1950s it was clear the ecosystem was suffering: the number of breeding wading birds dropped by 90 percent; sixty-eight plant and animal species were quickly headed the way of the dodo; and Florida Bay sea grass was dying, along with the marine life it sheltered.

Finally, in 1999, at the behest of an alarmed public, the Corps of Engineers came up with a plan to restore the natural ecosystem of south Florida. Since hydrology is the key to its health, efforts have been focused on getting the water right, on restoring the best possible quality and quantity of water to the ecosystem. That $10.5 billion Comprehensive Everglades Restoration Plan, approved by Congress, was launched in 2000. Ecologists cheered—that is, until the bureaucratic heel-dragging began. According to a 2014 report by the National Research Council, restoration progress, which has been mostly focused along the edges of the ecosystem, has been modest. The council points to weaknesses in planning, implementation, and follow-through funding. The report also expresses concern that some early effects of climate change are already being seen in the Everglades: sea-level rise is currently causing saltwater intrusion into freshwater habitats, and changes in temperature and precipitation patterns threaten to deny the Everglades even more water.

What's happening in the Everglades is one of the best examples of how the natural resources of a national park can be greatly impacted by outside forces. Since the 1980 *State of the Parks* report, when external threats to parks were first carefully documented, there have been few solutions and many more problems. The Everglades, for example, are cut off from their lifeblood freshwater and threatened by increased population and development (with their demands for limited freshwater) on the park's perimeter, phosphorus runoff from bordering farms, invasive species, and climate change.

Many more external forces threaten the rare biodiversity banks of many national parks. Unlike a century ago, parks that were once remote (some requiring days to reach) are now surrounded by development: housing and retail space, farms and ranches, mining and logging, highways and parking lots. This has several adverse effects on wildlife. First, it fills in former open space that acted as de facto parklands. Buffer zones that wildlife once relied on as additional habitat in which to breed and feed are now vanishing. Since elk and bears don't read maps, on the occasions they cross beyond park boundaries they're often the subject of human-wildlife conflicts—such as the backlash against wolves, grizzlies, and bison that leave Yellowstone.

Those open spaces were also in many cases used as migration corridors for species moving between seasonal ranges or by members of a population looking farther afield for a mate with genetics different from theirs. Restoring connectivity is an effort that current NPS Director Jonathan Jarvis has said recently is of paramount importance in managing not just parks but entire ecosystems. In a place like Yellowstone, that means managing species not only within its 2.2 million acres but also in the 18 million acres around it—a formidable challenge requiring the cooperation of other public and private entities. Precedent has been set with efforts such as the Path of the Pronghorn, the first federally designated migration route in the country. The 93-mile corridor connects the pronghorns' summer stomping grounds in Grand Teton National Park with their wintering grounds in the Upper Green River Basin. The project is a collaboration among the Park Service, the US Forest Service, and the Wildlife Conservation Society. Without more efforts like these, many species face tough times ahead.

Another major challenge for the Park Service is what comes *into* parks. One obvious blight is pollution—of both air and water. The quality of valuable "airsheds" is being compromised by industrial, vehicle, and power-plant emissions—in Great Smoky Mountains, Joshua Tree, Kings Canyon–Sequoia, Rocky Mountain, Acadia, Grand Canyon, and Big Bend national parks, and others. Air pollution levels now regularly exceed national ambient air quality standards (as defined in the 1970 Clean Air Act) in 128 parks. Those particulates also poison plants and animals; some bat species in Mammoth Cave National Park have high mercury levels, and mercury may be causing reproduction problems for peregrine falcons in Big Bend National Park. Ozone is damaging pine trees in Kings Canyon–Sequoia.

Air pollution fouls water quality too—high mercury levels in fish in the Everglades and Acadia have been documented. A recent study focused on western parks showed that the average concentration of mercury in some fish species at parks in Alaska, California, Colorado, Washington, and Wyoming exceeded the Environmental Protection Agency's human health criterion. That poses a threat to people and also wildlife, including birds and mammals, when foraging and reproduction success are compromised. Colleen Flanagan, an NPS ecologist and coauthor of the resulting paper, *Mercury in Fishes from 21 National Parks in the Western US*, said the report is a wake-up call. Some progress is being made in improving air quality as an increasing number of coal-fired power plants go off-line, but only time will tell if that is enough. The issue of water quality is particularly relevant to the sixty or so national parks with coastal jurisdiction that are working to protect and to restore damaged coastal ecosystems and marine life.

NPS superintendents have been challenged to become more engaged in what goes on outside of their parks' boundaries, to defend vigorously their resources when activities that threaten them crop up. It would be a departure for the Park Service, which tends to shy away from such conflicts, but it is not without precedent.

Until her retirement in October 2014, Theodore Roosevelt National Park Superintendent Valerie Naylor and her staff kept a close eye on the energy boom at their door. Near that park, the former Badlands ranch where the conservation-minded president developed some of his environmental ethics, regional oil and gas wells have multiplied in recent years. They are suspected to have caused a recent major uptick in health- and visibility-damaging pollution. The development is also disrupting quiet and daytime views, as well as nighttime dark skies. Naylor and her staff have been fighting development plans (new ones come almost weekly) that encroach upon the 70,000-acre park by making lots of calls, writing tons of letters, and providing testimony. Their negotiations haven't managed yet to stop any industry development—which is marked by noise, flaring, and odor—but they've had some success in pushing it back from the park borders to try to maintain visitors' appreciation of its sandstone pillars, river-swept valley, and teeming grasslands.

Similar drilling has threatened Glacier's eastern border. Other dangers loom large: Uranium prospectors have been sniffing around the Grand Canyon for years. In Alaska, an open-pit copper and gold mine is being mulled near Lake Clark National Park, and another copper mine is being vetted near Gates of the Arctic and Kobuk Valley national parks. A hydroelectric plant planned for the edge of Joshua Tree would siphon groundwater from that desert area. Thousands of active

The shallow, slow-moving waters of the Everglades are ideal habitat for the long-necked, graceful anhinga.

mining claims, many of which have been staked in the past few years, are located close to national parks.

Invasive species are also crossing park borders and contributing more to ecosystem change and instability than would have been imagined a century ago. They include all types of organisms, from the microscopic to the cloven-hoofed; 20-foot-long, 200-pound Burmese pythons in the Everglades are a particularly alarming example. More than 6500 nonnative species have been logged in parks; 70 percent of those are plants. Roughly 5 percent of parklands have been overtaken by invasive species, and at least 650 species have invaded marine parks.

Invasive species will hitch a ride on pretty much anything—clothes, cars, tents, firewood, boats, boots—and are generally brawny colonizers displacing native species with brutal efficiency. They don't change just the look of a place, but can dramatically alter wildlife habits and food sources and fire regimes. Just one example is white-nose syndrome, a fungus suspected of being carried from one cave to another by humans, which is killing millions of bats. It now affects populations in Mammoth Cave, Cumberland Gap National Historical Park, Great Smoky Mountains, and Acadia.

With roughly 35 percent of total visitors to the national park system concentrated in the top ten most-seen national park units, *people* coming into parks can also be a problem. At Muir Woods, traffic and parking woes have caused increased vehicle emissions and other damage to park resources—for example, when exasperated visitors pick any old spot in which to leave their car. At Yosemite, where the population of the valley on any given summer day rivals a small city, the integrity of both the national park concept and wilderness characteristics are of increasing concern. Both conditions would likely have sent John Muir running for the hills, and some modern-day conservationists are calling for caps on visitor numbers.

Some parks have imposed trail and traffic limits, such as the 400-per-day maximum on the number of people permitted to climb Yosemite's Half Dome, which lies within the park's federally designated wilderness area. There's also a trailhead quota to regulate the number of backpackers in wilderness areas in Sequoia–Kings Canyon. Under a plan passed in 2014, Yosemite will limit the number of day visitors in cars in the valley to 20,100, just under the number it currently receives on a typical summer day; others will have to ride the shuttle. Parks such as Sequoia, Zion, and Denali (beyond mile 15 on the park road) have sought to ease traffic by requiring shuttle use to access popular areas. Many others, including Acadia, Grand Canyon, Mount Rainier, Colonial National Historical Park, Bryce Canyon, Rocky Mountain, and Glacier, strongly encourage visitors to ride their shuttles.

Simply put, visitors are also expensive. The Park Service spends half its annual budget on visitor services and facility operations and maintenance. Another 20 percent is spent on managing and planning around the NPS's core mission. The remaining 30 percent is spent on stewardship of the natural, cultural, and historical resources in its care. Despite where most of the dollars go, the Park Service continues to limp along with a maintenance backlog of nearly $11.5 billion. Parks are showing signs of strain as some pipes, roads, boat ramps, trails, and campgrounds crumble. In the Everglades, the Flamingo Visitor Center needs a new roof, and the park's boat docks and campgrounds need rehabilitation. In Death Valley, park roads are crumbling. A recent NPS transportation assessment revealed that 90 percent of nearly 10,000 miles of park roads are in poor to fair condition. Roughly 36 percent of trails (6700 miles out of 18,600 total) are in poor or seriously deficient condition.

Maintenance doesn't constitute the only cutbacks; some major parks have had to reduce law enforcement shifts, and some smaller parks are understaffed to the point of paralysis, with roads, visitor centers, and campgrounds closed. Currently the NPS budget is one-fourteenth of 1 percent of the national budget—a modest investment in a bureau whose work generates billions of dollars for local economies and supports hundreds of thousands of jobs. Accounting for inflation, the Park Service budget declined 15 percent from 2003 to 2013 despite polls showing that nearly all Americans—regardless of political affiliation—want to see parks fully funded and up and running year-round. This was never more apparent than during the federal government shutdown in late 2013, which hit the Park Service and surrounding communities with major revenue losses and reminded a bewildered public of the tremendous daily value of those many resources.

Perhaps the biggest challenge of all is climate change. The longtime poster children for this unrelenting pressure include Glacier National Park's glaciers, which will likely be gone by 2030, as well as those at Olympic and Mount Rainier national parks. But the problem is much bigger than retreating freshwater reserves; the severity of flooding and mud slides at Mount Rainier in 2006—which caused millions of dollars in damage—is attributed by scientists to glacial recession, shifting precipitation patterns, and warmer temperatures. Other effects of climate change—rising temperatures and historic droughts, coastal erosion from rising sea levels and more intense storms, and bigger and hotter wildfires—all threaten park resources, be they ecological, historical, cultural, or practical (think restrooms, trails, and roads).

Going, going . . . a century of climate change has reduced the Boulder Glacier in Glacier National Park to slivers of ice.

The Park Service can do certain things to mitigate the effects of this global environmental shift: reduce its own carbon footprint, restore ecosystems, build coalitions that value biodiversity. But however unfortunate it sounds, it's unrealistic to imagine the Park Service can stop or in any way reverse the advance of climate change in parks on its own.

One of the NPS's main functions now is educating park visitors about what humans do to contribute to climate change and what that means for park resources and the planet on the whole. In

A CCC FOR TOMORROW?

The Civilian Conservation Corps (CCC) represents the past and present of the National Park Service, and some believe it could be in its future. The NPS now has a Youth Conservation Corps for fifteen- to eighteen-year-olds who work in dozens of parks doing construction, restoration, preservation, and research. The Park Service also has robust volunteer programs for youth and adults, but no CCC-like project to alleviate unemployment while benefiting parks. Citing the success of President Franklin D. Roosevelt's popular 1930s program, as well as the need to clear a multibillion-dollar maintenance backlog in parks, some organizations are pushing for a new National Parks Service Corps.

The National Parks Conservation Association (NPCA), for one, has called for at least 10,000 jobs to be created to do CCC-type work and more, including mitigating modern issues such as climate change. Secretary of the Interior Sally Jewell testified before Congress in 2009 (she was then a trustee of the NPCA) about the willingness of millions of Americans to roll up their sleeves and get to work in parklands. She made reference to the tough economic times in which the CCC mobilized so many citizens to conserve and protect its most vital resources while benefiting society at large. A new corps, she said, "can help our nation capitalize on the potential for our national parks to produce significant civic benefits, stimulate local economies, educate Americans about our shared heritage, and protect our national treasures for the use and enjoyment of our children and grandchildren." Surely FDR would approve.

the summer of 2014, the NPS Climate Change Response Program hosted its first Climate Change Academy in collaboration with the nonprofit No Barriers Youth. Ten high school students from Ohio spent twelve days in Alaska's Kenai Fjords and Denali national parks seeing firsthand the harmful effects of climate change. High school senior Ricky Greene said of the experience, "It gave me a whole new way to look at the way global warming affects us. Now I can explain it better to people who don't understand."

In the face of such challenges, the NPS developed *A Call to Action: Preparing for a Second Century of Stewardship and Engagement*, a document expressing a vision for 2016 and beyond. In it the NPS spells out some priorities in relation to

natural resources: using science as a foundation for park planning; collaborating with other land managers and partners "to create, restore, and maintain landscape-scale connectivity," such as the push to link more of the Yellowstone ecosystem; and increasing resilience to climate change and other stressors.

That third objective—increasing the strength of park resources to withstand rogue forces linked to climate change—exemplifies what one of the latest major reports on the Park Service calls managing for "continuous change that is not yet fully understood." That report, *Revisiting Leopold*, comes from the National Park System Advisory Board and is a new look at the now middle-aged Leopold Report, which had served as the natural

resource managers' beacon since the 1960s. Much of what A. Starker Leopold advised is still relevant, but the fifty-year-old ideal of managing for desired past conditions is no longer feasible. Aside from strapping ice packs to pikas, tossing reflective blankets over glaciers, or building barriers to keep seawater from surging into the Everglades—none of which the Park Service is planning to do—how can natural resources be treated or protected to help them weather tumultuous times ahead?

Dozens of projects being implemented throughout the national park system are part of what NPS chief wildlife biologist Glenn Plumb calls "playing the long game": taking action now to strengthen ecosystems for what lies ahead. In general, species need space, diversity, and time in order to adapt to climate change. Habitat restoration can give species more room to breathe while protecting the park and its neighbors.

One such restoration effort is at the Big Egg Marsh at Gateway National Recreation Area. Gateway is distinguished by its low-lying, intertidal grasslands—feeding grounds for countless wildlife, home to mussels and crabs, nursery for fish and shellfish—that function as a water filter for Jamaica Bay. These grasslands are also the first defense against storm surges and coastal erosion and are critical to the viability and protection of coastal communities. The salt-marsh islands of Jamaica Bay have declined from 2350 acres in 1951 to 800 today. Much of that habitat, seriously degraded by erosion and decay, had become a relatively barren mudflat.

The initial phase of restoration at Big Egg Marsh involved elevating the site with sand, installing natural erosion-control barriers, and then planting 20,000 peat pots of smooth cordgrass, which took park staff and volunteers about six whole weeks. That pilot project, which began with just 2 acres, was small in scale but big in effect. It was so successful that the Park Service went on to restore 60 acres of salt-marsh islands at Elders Point East and West, and restoration is either underway or planned at Yellow Bar, Black Wall, and Rulers Bar marshes. The rate of loss, while still significant, has slowed to roughly 15 to 20 acres per year. The ongoing initiative is led by the NPS with collaborative partners including the US Army Corps of Engineers, state environmental protection and conservation agencies, the Port Authorities of New York and New Jersey, and many others.

With work such as that at Gateway, the NPS must now prepare parks for what may be the most important role in its history: national parks must form the core of a national conservation land- and seascape, says *Revisiting Leopold*. The Park Service has come a long way since 1916, when it shot predators and fed bison; since *Fauna No. 1* condemned its wildlife policy in the 1930s; since Starker Leopold predicted disaster in the 1960s; since the *Vail Agenda* struck a hopeful note in the 1990s; up to the Natural Resource Challenge in 1999, which decisively put science at the helm of that ship that had taken so long to change course.

Much has changed in the past hundred years; parks are now understood to embody some of the last vestiges of untamed terrain. But existence is not ensured, as is plainly seen in the Everglades, those remnants of a shallow sea that struggle still. Awareness and *action* is key, such as the kind embodied by Marjorie Stoneman Douglas, "mother of the Everglades," coiner of the phrase "river of grass," who long ago threw down the gauntlet for park lovers of every era. She was like the saw-grass itself; while it looks easygoing, it's actually a razor-edged sedge. Douglas once remarked, "The Everglades is a test. If we pass it, we may get to keep the planet."

Day's end on the River of Grass

CHAPTER 29

The Next Century of Greatness

BEN CLARK THOUGHT all he'd find was ants when he and other "citizen scientists" went "log busting" in the Jean Lafitte National Historical Park and Preserve in southern Louisiana. They were in the Barataria Preserve, only a few miles south of New Orleans' French Quarter yet light-years away. These 23,000 acres of wild wetlands include swamps, bayous, marshes, and forest hosting species ranging from armadillos and bobcats to water snakes, tree frogs, and, of course, alligators. It was May 2013, and the then-thirteen-year-old was on his first official BioBlitz as a National Park Service biodiversity youth ambassador.

It was warm but not too humid as his group set out with a ranger to document as many species as possible. "You find this rotting log, and you break it open and try to find organisms," says Clark. Sure, there were ants—but also beetles and termites and much more to discover. When he moved on from insects to amphibians, Clark really got excited. "We spent the whole time trekking through mud up to our knees," he says. "It was incredible."

Slogging through muck in southern Louisiana wasn't as inviting to some of Clark's friends, who had come with him from distant Connecticut. "It was *not* what they wanted to do," he says. "But once they got into it, they couldn't get enough." It was a thrilling day, one in which Clark and others from urban areas gained a different perspective. "When you're in the city, you feel superior, like you're on top of everything," he says. "But when you go into a park, you're a small speck. Is that a little scary? Sure, at first, but it's a really amazing experience."

That park is youth ambassador Caleb Ezelle's backyard, where he has made frequent outings with his grandfather. He credits his granddad with teaching him how to look and also to *see*. Now as an intern at Jean Lafitte, Ezelle does the same for visitors on the guided walks he gives. Along the Bayou Coquille Trail, he'll ask people to look for red objects, then other unusual colors. "It gets people to notice that it's not all just green swamp out there, that there's more to it than meets the eye," he says.

In 2010 the NPS began recruiting a corps of biodiversity youth ambassadors in order to connect more kids to science and to parks. The Park Service now has several ambassadors who get in the thick of it, bring that knowledge back to their communities, and make their own creative outreach efforts. In his hometown of Bridgeport, Ben Clark organized his own community species inventory in a nearby estuary, and it was a hit.

When Caleb Ezelle recognized that young people in his area were not particularly interested in going to Jean Lafitte, he tried a different tactic. He sees a "community service" day, for example, as a way to get a cross section of people into parks that might otherwise avoid them. Once they're out there, he knows some like what they see and come back. "I am concerned for the youth in the United States today because people tend to stay indoors all day and not get out and truly see the world for what it really is," he says. "Mainly, my job is to get kids back outside and help them see the world."

High school senior and San Francisco native Lurleen Frazier, who did her first BioBlitz as an

Left: NPS Biodiversity Youth Ambassadors participate in a survey of alpine life during the 2012 NPS and National Geographic Society BioBlitz at Rocky Mountain National Park. *Right*: NPS Biodiversity Youth Ambassadors survey mushrooms at the 2014 BioBlitz at Golden Gate NRA.

SEE AMERICA
UNITED STATES TRAVEL BUREAU

MADE BY WORKS PROGRESS ADMINISTRATION · FEDERAL ART PROJECT NYC

What a difference a century makes: in 1914, geothermal features (like Castle Geyser shown here) in Yellowstone captivated 20,250 visitors; in 2014, overall visitation to the park was 3.5 million.

❁ ❁ ❁

It's not obvious judging by the diverse young crowds congregated in Jean Lafitte or Golden Gate National Recreation Area that the NPS has a problem connecting young people to parks. Yet Sally Plumb, the NPS's biodiversity coordinator who works with the youth ambassadors, says, "One of the greatest challenges we have is relevancy." Visitation trends indicate a rise in the forty-eight- to sixty-six-year-old crowd in parks and a drop in those ages sixteen to thirty. Minority visitation to national parks is low as well, and neither trend reflects the present makeup of the United States or the direction in which those demographics are headed.

NPS youth ambassador in Golden Gate National Recreation Area in 2014, brought along her twenty-year-old brother. Rain dumped from the sky, and as they headed into Muir Woods National Monument to do a mushroom inventory, Frazier's brother turned to her and asked, "Are you sure about this?" Neither had been to Muir Woods before, and they didn't know what to expect. But they were so blown away by the place that they've since returned with their whole family in tow. "I can't believe on the other side of the city there's so much nature and forests that don't look like they do here," Lurleen says. "I wanted [my family] to see it too."

Since school-age children and minorities include present and future explorers, teachers, scientists, voters, CEOs, and policy makers, the Park Service knows it needs a sustainable constituency supporting America's best places. But as population tables turn, the NPS is left wondering—much as it did a hundred years ago—how to attract people of all kinds to parks. Similar to a century ago, maintaining public support for parks requires that all Americans feel linked to them on some level. But how is that possible when many people have never heard of national parks or don't know where they are?

Increasing both awareness and access for city dwellers to national parks in the fifty largest urban areas in the country is a Park Service goal highlighted in *A Call to Action: Preparing for a Second Century of Stewardship and Engagement*, its manifesto for the next century. Providing transportation options has become a priority, such as the free trolley service linking Everglades and Biscayne national parks to the nearby community of Homestead, Florida. Other efforts include bringing rangers into classrooms, either literally or virtually via video chats, so that kids can begin to make a connection to places that initially seem foreign and remote.

In addition to BioBlitzes, another push to reach underrepresented populations includes programs that bring schoolchildren from urban areas to parks. One such program relocates kids for a day from inner city Los Angeles to the Santa Monica Mountains National Recreation Area, the largest urban national park in the nation, with more than 150,000 acres of peaks and coastline. There they get hands-on experience with the natural and cultural resources of the park. For many students, it represents several firsts: first time outside their neighborhood, first visit to a national park, first

Though more than 75 years have passed since this poster was published, ranger-led walks and talks are still a quintessential national park experience.

"wilderness" experience. Plumb remembers one of these outings in which, after the kids piled off the bus at the park, a ranger welcomed and attempted to orient them but quickly realized few were listening. "They were all staring out to the west," says Plumb. "Finally the ranger said,

SIMPLY THE BEST

The familiar phrase describing national parks as "the best idea" America ever had is often credited to Pulitzer Prize–winning writer Wallace Stegner, but it was actually attributed long ago by Stegner to Lord James Bryce. Bryce was the British ambassador to the United States from 1907 to 1913, and he counted President Theodore Roosevelt among his close friends. In a speech at a meeting of the American Civic Association in 1912 (attendees included sitting President William Taft and other political heavyweights), Bryce commended the United States for its conservation work, for having "led the world in the creation of national parks."

He was not solely cheerleading, however; he was imploring the United States to preserve more land: "I beg you to consider that, although your country is vast and has scope of natural beauty far greater than we can boast in little countries . . . even your scenery is not inexhaustible, and, with your great population and the growing desire to enjoy the beauties of nature, you have not any more than you need." In the next breath came a sentiment that speaks to today. "The surface of this little earth of ours is limited, and we cannot add to it," said Bryce. He cautioned that the American people "not find out too late that the beauty and solitude of nature have been snatched from you by private individuals." But it wasn't just quantity the ambassador was interested in. "Let me add that it is not only a question of making more parks, but also of keeping the parks in the best condition," he said.

'OK, what's got all of your attention?' It was then he realized they were looking at the water. Even though they live so close to the coast, most had never seen the ocean."

The NPS Biodiversity Youth Ambassador Program too is increasing park awareness, and in an exponential way, as that handful of young adults introduces entire communities to park resources. The NPS is also seeing young volunteers grow into other positions with the Park Service, including paid internships. That's stewardship the NPS hopes will last a lifetime. "We're introducing people to entirely new concepts that become a core part of their being. It's pretty powerful," says Plumb. "It's something they get really excited about. They find out things about the environment but also about themselves."

Longtime youth ambassador Dara Reyes, who now works at Canaveral National Seashore, wants people, whether they're from the Bronx or Beverly Hills, to know that parks are a shared commodity, owned equally by all citizens. In national parks, economic and ethnic divisions that seem consequential in the outside world are largely irrelevant. The bees and bears—and rangers, for that matter—could not care less what brand of outerwear visitors are sporting or the color of their complexion. "No matter who they are or what their background is, there are so many different kinds of parks, there is something for *everyone*," says Reyes. "It's all of our jobs to tell them that it's just a few steps away." Aside from having an insatiable curiosity that is fed by national parks, what does Reyes get out of it?

"Whenever I'm there, I just have this feeling that I'm at peace," she says.

Despite the many challenges facing the NPS, there's a lot to celebrate on the occasion of its one hundredth birthday. For one, there is much rewilding going on in parks. The Elwha River Restoration Project in Olympic National Park, which included the largest dam removal in history, is bringing back natural processes to that watershed. Freeing the Elwha ultimately took a quarter century of effort by just about everyone under the sun, but now steelhead and all five species of Pacific salmon have more than 70 miles of spawning habitat along that once-again wilderness river.

The Pinnacles Recovery Project has seen the return of the endangered California condor to Pinnacles National Park. When a condor egg hatched there in 2010, it was the first in a century. Twenty-five of the massive birds—their wingspans are more than 9 feet—are now actively managed in the park.

THAT'S A FACT

Established in 1967, the National Park Foundation is still the official nonprofit partner of the National Park Service. Donations to the organization directly support parks; consider a birthday gift for the Park Service at www.nationalparks.org.

In Sequoia, the Giant Forest has been restored. That twenty-year project removed nearly 300 buildings and more than a million square feet of asphalt from the grove and restored soil and vegetation to pre-people patterns; Colonel John White would surely be pleased. A similar project being vetted for Yosemite's Mariposa Grove of Giant Sequoias would remove parking from the forest and shuttle visitors there instead.

Other parks are becoming wilder still under Park Service purview. One of the rarest owls in the Lower 48 was discovered to live and to breed in Glacier National Park. Montana is now one of the few states where the northern hawk owl nests and rears its young. The NPS reintroduced fishers in Olympic National Park. And in Badlands National Park it has brought back four critical species: bison, bighorn sheep, black-footed ferrets, and swift foxes.

There have been many more successes, and there is much potential for other past wounds to be healed. Wildlife biologists are now evaluating whether grizzly bears should be restored to the North Cascades ecosystem. They are also studying the reintroduction of the fisher to Mount Rainier and North Cascades national parks. Whether to introduce additional wolves at Isle Royale National Park has been an ongoing debate; they are not indigenous to the island but crossed an ice bridge from the mainland in the winter of 1949–50. It's been too warm in recent years for an ice bridge to form again, impacting the genetic diversity of the declining wolf population. As climate change continues to shuffle the decks of nature, more complex discussions about the management of biodiversity will no doubt be necessary. But with the commitment of its steadfast guardians, plus old friends and new

YOU'VE GOT A FRIEND

For decades, by raising funds, supplying volunteers, and increasing awareness of park resources and needs, "Friends of . . ." groups have consistently supported National Park Service programs and projects that don't survive budget cuts. More than a hundred groups, such as Friends of Virgin Islands National Park and the Rosie the Riveter Trust, partner with parks. Cooperating associations, which often operate park bookstores and use the profits for park-related projects, are a different kind of philanthropic partner but no less important. Sixty-five such groups working directly with parks include the esteemed Rocky Mountain Conservancy and Voyageurs National Park Association.

ambassadors ready to rise to those challenges, there is cause for optimism.

In the public relations push to establish the National Park Service a hundred years ago, journalist Robert Sterling Yard wrote: "Men return from our mountain tops better shopkeepers and tailors, as well as better teachers, lawyers, and painters." As the Park Service celebrates a century of greatness past, it also peers into the future in a broad campaign to reintroduce the staggering wealth of opportunities for discovery in national parks. The Park Service, like Yard, is urging every person to "Find Your Park" and gently reminding them that they will be the better for it.

At a time when it's as critical as it was a century ago to step back from the industrialized world, the NPS still protects and celebrates our retreats from days filled with pinging and honking, rushing and ringing. It's had 11.7 billion park visitors throughout its history, but it has always been focused on a single mission: "to conserve the scenery and the natural and historic objects and the wild life therein and to provide for the enjoyment of the same in such manner and by such means as will leave them unimpaired for the

enjoyment of future generations." Those resources are the envy of the world.

Though the NPS now faces unprecedented challenges, some of the youngest among us may offer a way forward. With their actions and voices, NPS youth ambassadors are communicating to their friends, neighbors, and local and national leaders that parks are a necessity—ecological, economic, physical, psychological, aesthetic, social, and civic. Through them and the many people who stand with the Park Service, conservation continues to be a core American ethic.

Since youth ambassador Lurleen Frazier began working with the NPS, she's been encouraging her Samoan American family on park adventures. And she's been answering a lot of questions about why she's so passionate about national parks. "The world is really big, but there is a limited amount of these kinds of places," she says. "I say to people, 'Go, give it a chance! Take advantage of what we have.'" High school junior Dara Reyes is less worried than NPS leadership about stewards stepping forward to care for parks in the coming century and more optimistic about parks becoming relevant to kids and to people of color, in time. "I don't

Wolf pups of Yellowstone's 8 Mile Pack rest on a rock; their alpha female first denned in the park in 2011, and the pack now spends most of its time near the park's northern boundary.

know why they're discouraged," she says. "I don't think we're really going to have a problem. We will come and take up the responsibility to protect parks, like the Park Service does today. People are interested, I've seen it."

When youth ambassador Ben Clark, who wants to work for the NPS someday, talks about conservation, he sounds a bit like a young President Theodore Roosevelt, who was inspired by his nation's riches but mindful of their vulnerability.

"We have fallen heirs to the most glorious heritage a people ever received, and each one must do his part if we wish to show that the nation is worthy of its good fortune," said Roosevelt. Clark puts his own spin on it: "Young people have to realize it's important to conserve this. They have to be involved. National parks are the original frontiers. It's important for people to recognize the opportunities there, the diversity we've been given. We have to help the NPS protect that."

PARKS THROUGH TIME

1,000,000

1920
Visitation to national parks surpasses 1 million for first time.

1872
Yellowstone becomes first national park.

1913
Raker Act (Hetch Hetchy Act) passes.

1869
First transcontinental railroad is completed.

1790
National Capital Parks is established.

1864
Yosemite becomes state-run park.

1906
Antiquities Act passes, allowing presidents to declare national monuments.

| 1790 | 1800 | 1810 | 1820 | 1830 | 1840 | 1850 | 1860 | 1870 | 1880 | 1890 | 19 |

1864
George Perkins Marsh's *Man and Nature* is published.

1894
Lacey Act passes; John Meldrum becomes first Yellowstone magistrate.

1871
Hayden Expedition explores Yellowstone.

1907
First automobile enters a national park unit, in Hot Springs, Arkansas.

1916
Organic Act passes, creating the National Park Service.

1929
George Melendez Wright launches first NPS wildlife survey.

1980
Alaska National Interest Lands Conservation Act passes.

1971
NPS creates law enforcement wing.

1964
Wilderness Act passes.

1956
Mission 66 launched; visitation doubles leading up to NPS's fiftieth anniversary.

1933
Reorganization adds dozens of historic sites to NPS.

100 YEARS OF THE NATIONAL PARK SERVICE

2016
NPS turns 100.

2010
NPS Biodiversity Youth Ambassador Program is established.

1992
Vail Agenda is published.

1910 | 1920 | 1930 | 1940 | 1950 | 1960 | 1970 | 1980 | 1990 | 2000 | 2010 | 2016

1933
Civilian Conservation Corps begins work in national and state parks.

1963
Leopold Report is published.

1971
Alaska Native Claims Settlement Act passes.

1972
First "urban" national parks open.

1980
First *State of the Parks* is released.

2013
A Call to Action: Preparing for a Second Century of Stewardship & Engagement is released.

1999
Natural Resource Challenge is launched by NPS Director Robert Stanton.

2014
Annual visitation to national parks hits historic high of 293 million.

293,000,000

APPENDIX

DIRECTORS OF THE NPS

Note: Those with an asterisk (*) are mentioned in this book.

*Stephen T. Mather, May 16, 1917–January 8, 1929

*Horace M. Albright, January 12, 1929–August 9, 1933

*Arno B. Cammerer, August 10, 1933–August 9, 1940

*Newton B. Drury, August 20, 1940–March 31, 1951

*Arthur E. Demaray, April 1, 1951–December 8, 1951

*Conrad L. Wirth, December 9, 1951–January 7, 1964

*George B. Hartzog Jr., January 9, 1964–December 31, 1972

Ronald H. Walker, January 7, 1973–January 3, 1975

Gary Everhardt, January 13, 1975–May 27, 1977

William J. Whalen, July 5, 1977–May 13, 1980

Russell E. Dickenson, May 15, 1980–March 3, 1985

William Penn Mott Jr., May 17, 1985–April 16, 1989

*James M. Ridenour, April 17, 1989–January 20, 1993

Roger G. Kennedy, June 1, 1993–March 29, 1997

*Robert Stanton, August 4, 1997–January 2001

Fran P. Mainella, July 18, 2001–October 16, 2006

Mary Bomar, October 17, 2006–January 20, 2009

*Jonathan B. Jarvis, October 2, 2009–present

SECRETARIES OF THE INTERIOR

Note: Those with an asterisk (*) are mentioned in this book.

*Franklin K. Lane, 1913–1920

John B. Payne, 1920–1921

Albert B. Fall, 1921–1923

Hubert Work, 1923–1928

Roy O. West, 1928–1929

Ray L. Wilbur, 1929–1933

*Harold L. Ickes, 1933–1946

Julius A. Krug, 1946–1949

Oscar L. Chapman, 1949–1953

Douglas McKay, 1953–1956

Fred A. Seaton, 1956–1961

*Stewart L. Udall, 1961–1969

Walter Hickel, 1969–1970

*Rogers C. B. Morton, 1971–1975

Stanley K. Hathaway, 1975

Thomas S. Kleppe, 1975–1977

*Cecil B. Andrus, 1977–1981

*James G. Watt, 1981–1983

William P. Clark, 1983–1985

*Donald P. Hodel, 1985–1989

Manuel Lujan Jr., 1989–1993

Bruce Babbitt, 1993–2001

Gale A. Norton, 2001–2006

Dirk Kempthorne, 2006–2009

Ken Salazar, 2009–2013

*Sally Jewell, 2013–present

PHOTO CREDITS

Photographs are listed by page number and in alphabetical order by the archival source or copyright holder:

Alison Baukney: 351

Creative Commons: 170, photo by Mitch Garrie; 193, photo by Acroterion

Defenseimagery.mil: 180, photo by John Pennell; 182, photo by MC3 Dustin W. Sisco

Heather Hansen: 10, 16, 20, 111, 115, 140, 149, 168, 205, 207, 221, 227, 251, 260, 264, 267, 272, 278, 281, 287, 289, 290, 293, 295

LBJ Presidential Library Photo Archives: 208, White House Photo Office, photo by Robert Knudsen

Library of Congress: 5, Prints and Photographs Division (P&P), Photographer: William Henry Jackson, LC-USZ62-44164; 7, P&P, Carol M. Highsmith's America Project, Carol M. Highsmith Archive, LC-HS503-639, 2011; 11, P&P, Work Projects Administration Poster Collection, Artist Stanley Thomas Clough, LC-USZC2-5415, 1938; 14, George Grantham Bain Collection, LC-USZ62-106746, 1910–1940; 26, Photographer: William Henry Jackson, LC-USZ62-20198, 1871; 31, P&P, photographed by Carleton E. Watkins, LC-USZ62-46914, 1865; 32, P&P, Painting by Thomas Moran, *Lower Yellowstone Range*, LC-USZC4-2114, 1874; 33, P&P, Underwood & Underwood, circa 1912, LC-USZ62-103951; 34, P&P, Underwood & Underwood, circa 1903, LC-USZ62-35722; 36, P&P, photographed by Mathew Brady, Brady-Handy Collection, LC-USZ62-10992, circa 1850; 38, P&P, Artist: Harry Herzog, Work Projects Administration Poster Collection, LC-USZC2-833, 1940; 40, National Photo Company Collection, LC-USZ62-101035, Curtis & Miller, 1911–1920; 42, P&P, Frances Benjamin Johnston Collection, LC-USZ62-136271, 1903; 44, Ingersoll View Company, LC-USZ62-97312, 1905; 46, National Photo Company Collection, LC-USZ62-100874, Curtis & Miller, 1911–1920; 48, P&P, Carol M. Highsmith's America Project, Carol M. Highsmith Archive, LC-DIG-highsm-04260; 50, P&P, Artist: William Allen Rogers, LC-USZ62-122812; 54, left, P&P, Gladstone Collection of African American Photographs, LC-DIG-ppmsca-11406, 1890; 55, Frances Benjamin Johnston Collection, LC-USZ62-98475, 1903; 58, P&P, Theodore Roosevelt Digital Library, Dickinson State University, 1908; 61, P&P, LC-USZ62-135261, 1911; 62, P&P, LC-USZ62-28050, 1906; 66, P&P, Harris & Ewing Collection, LC-DIG-hec-04386, 1914; 69, P&P, HAER CAL,55-MATH.V,1—7; 70, P&P, LC-USZ62-77430, 1906; 72, P&P, LC-USZ62-3863; 77, P&P, LC-USZ62-20305, circa 1880–90; 78, P&P, LC-USZ62-60566, 1919; 79, P&P, HAER CAL,54-THRIV.V,2-18; 80, P&P, panoramic photographs, events no. 107; 86, Frances Benjamin Johnston Collection, LC-USZ62-100864, 1903; 88, LC-USZ62-92911, 1909; 89, P&P, LC-USZ62-40465, circa 1910–20; 92, P&P, LC-DIG-npcc-27642, 1916; 96, P&P, Harris & Ewing Collection, LC-DIG-hec-17013; 107, P&P, LC-DIG-hec-31267, circa 1921–1923; 114, P&P, LC-USZ62-7456; 119, design by J. Hirt, Work Projects Administration Poster Collection, LC-DIG-ppmsca-23061, 1939; 130, P&P, HABS WYO, 20-KEL.V,2-; 143, USGS, Geography and Map Division, 1931; 144, P&P, Photo by Arthur Rothstein, LC-USF33-002170-M3, Farm Security Administration, Office of War Information black-and-white negatives; 148, P&P, LC-DIG-npcc-17662, National Photo Company Collection, 1929; 159, P&P, LC-DIG-ppmsca-13397, Work Projects Administration

New York Public Library: 276, The Miriam and Ira D. Wallach Division of Art, Prints and Photographs: Photography Collection, NYPL Digital Collections, 1876–1877

New York Times: 214, April 23, 1970

Pat Sanders: 234, both, Yukon–Charley Rivers National Preserve

Steven Payne: 198

University of Alaska, Fairbanks: Fairbanks Daily News-Miner Photography Collection, Archives

University of Oregon Libraries, Eugene: 113, Klamath Falls Evening Herald, July 28, 1917, Chronicling America: Historic American Newspapers, Library of Congress

US Army: 270, photo by **Sergeant First Class Al Chang**; 271, photo by Senior Airman Jameel S. Moses; 299, Reserve Specialty photo by Steve Harding

US Department of Agriculture: 216, photo by Jenny Mastanuono

US Geological Survey: 196, USGS Photographic Library, photo by M. F. Meier; 282, photo by Lisa McKeon; 307, top, WC Alden, USGS Photographic Library, 1913; 307, bottom, USGS photo by Kevin Jacks

US National Archives and Records Administration: 144, NPS Photo, ARC Identifier: 286002; 152, Franklin D. Roosevelt (FDR) Library Public Domain Photographs, compiled 1882–1962, ARC Identifier: 195301; 155, Branch of Still and Motion Pictures for the Department of the Interior (DOI), NPS, Ansel Adams Photographs of National Parks and Monuments, compiled 1941–1942, documenting the period ca. 1933–1942, ARC Identifier: 519954; 162, EPA, Project Documerica, photo by Gene Daniels, ARC identifier: 42493; 164, Branch of Still and Motion Pictures for the DOI, NPS, Ansel Adams Photographs of National Parks and Monuments, compiled 1941–1942, documenting the period ca. 1933–1942, ARC Identifier: 519939; 166, Office for Emergency Management, Office of War Information, Domestic Operations Branch, Bureau of Special Services, 1942–45, ARC identifier: 516194; 177, FDR Library and Museum, ARC Identifier: 1184; 178, FDR Library and Museum, National Archives Identifier: 19620; 217, DOI, NPS, Midwest Region, National Archives identifier: 286013, 1961; 242, Branch of Still and Motion Pictures for the DOI, NPS, Ansel Adams Photographs of National Parks and Monuments, compiled 1941–1942, documenting the period circa 1933–1942, ARC identifier: 519830; 243, National Photo Company Collection, LC-USZ62-100919; 245, Branch of Still and Motion Pictures for the DOI, NPS, Ansel Adams Photographs of National Parks and Monuments, compiled 1941–1942, documenting the period circa 1933–1942, ARC identifier: 519851; 250, EPA, Project Documerica, photo by Terry Eiler, National Archives identifier: 412-DA-1865; 266, Mathew Brady Photographs of Civil War–Era Personalities and Scenes, compiled 1921–1940, documenting 1860–1865, ARC identifier: 524418; 277, DOI, Central Photographic File of the War Relocation Authority, 1942–1945, ARC identifier: 536226

US Postal Service: 212

Wikimedia Commons: 146, photo by Jarek Tuszynski

Timeline photos, pages 320–321, credited by their corresponding year: 1864, Marsh portrait, Library of Congress, Prints and Photographs Division, photographed by Mathew Brady, Brady-Handy Collection, LC-USZ62-10992, circa 1850; 1864, Mirror Lake in Yosemite, Library of Congress, Prints and Photographs Division, photographed by Carleton E. Watkins, LC-USZ62-46914, 1865; 1871, Photographer: William Henry Jackson, Library of Congress, LC-USZ62-20198; 1872, Old Faithful, The J. Paul Getty Museum at the Getty Center, photo by William Henry Jackson, 1870; 1907, auto camping, Library of Congress, Prints and Photographs Division, photo by J. E. Hayes, LC-USZ62-41022; 1916, Congress, Library of Congress, Prints and Photographs Division, LC-DIG-npcc-27642, 1916; 1929, George Wright, National Park Service Historic Photograph Collection, photo by Roger Toll, 1936; 1933, CCC workers, US National Archives and Records Administration, Franklin D. Roosevelt Library Public Domain Photographs, compiled 1882–1962, ARC Identifier: 195301; 1956, Mission 66, National Park Service Historic Photograph Collection, 1958; 1972, GGNRA ranger, NPS photo by Richard Frear, circa 1980; 1980, Denali, NPS photo by Kent Miller; 1999, R. Stanton, NPS photo; 2010, NPS photo.

RESOURCES

These sources helped form this book's historical portrait of the National Park Service and, really, 150 years of US conservation. Many are available for free through the Park Service (www.nps.gov /parkhistory) or Library of Congress (www.loc.gov) websites, and they make for riveting reading.

BOOKS AND PRINTED MONOGRAPHS

Abbey, Edward. *Desert Solitaire: A Season in the Wilderness*. New York City: Ballantine Books, 1968.

Adams, Charles C. *Guide to the Study of Animal Ecology*. New York City: The Macmillan Company, 1913.

Albright, Horace M. *Origins of National Park Service Administration of Historic Sites*. Philadelphia: Eastern National Park and Monument Association, 1971.

Albright, Horace M., and Robert Cahn. *The Birth of the National Park Service: The Founding Years, 1913–33*. Salt Lake City: Howe Brothers, 1985.

Albright, Horace M., and Marian Albright Schenck. *Creating the National Park Service: The Missing Years*. Norman: University of Oklahoma Press, 1999.

Albright, Horace M., and Frank J. Taylor. *"Oh, Ranger!"* Stanford University, CA: Stanford University Press, 1928.

Allen, Edward Frank, in cooperation with the Department of the Interior. *Our National Parks*. San Francisco, CA: Wells Fargo & Company, 1917.

Appleman, Roy E. *A History of the National Park Service Mission 66 Program*. Washington, DC: National Park Service, 1958.

Bailey, L. H. *The Holy Earth*. New York City: Charles Scribner's Sons, 1915.

Baillie-Grohman, William A. *Camps in the Rockies*. New York City: Charles Scribner's Sons, 1882.

Bingaman, John W. *Pathways: A Story of Trails and Men*. Lodi, CA: End-Kian Publishing, 1968.

Boerker, Richard H. Douai. *Our National Forests: A Short Popular Account of the Work of the United States Forest Service on the National Forests*. New York City: MacMillan, 1918.

Bryant, William Cullen. *Poems by William Cullen Bryant, Vol. 1*. New York City: D. Appleton, 1854.

Buchholtz, C. W. *Man in Glacier*. West Glacier, MT: Glacier National History Association, 1976.

———. *Rocky Mountain National Park: A History*. Boulder, CO: Colorado Associated University Press, 1983.

Buckley, Rev. J. M. *Two Weeks in Yosemite and Vicinity*. New York City: Phillips and Hunt, 1883.

Burnham, Philip. *Indian Country, God's Country: Native Americans and the National Parks*. Washington, DC: Island Press, 2000.

Burroughs, John. *In the Catskills*. New York City: Houghton Mifflin, 1910.

———. *Our Vacation Days of 1918*. 1921.

———. *The Writings of John Burroughs, Vol 1*. New York City: Houghton Mifflin, 1895.

Carlson, Allen. *Nature and Landscape: An Introduction to Environmental Aesthetics*. New York City: Columbia University Press, 2008.

Carr, Ethan. *Mission 66: Modernism and the National Park Dilemma*. Amherst: University of Massachusetts Press, 2007.

———. *Wilderness by Design: Landscape Architecture and the National Park Service*. Lincoln: University of Nebraska Press, 1998.

Catton, Theodore. *National Park, City Playground: Mount Rainier in the Twentieth Century*. Seattle: University of Washington Press, 2006.

Clark, Galen. *The Big Trees of California*. Redondo Beach, CA: Reflex Publishing, 1907.

———. *The Yosemite Valley*. Redondo Beach, CA: Reflex Publishing, 1910.

Commoner, Barry. *The Closing Circle: Nature, Man, and Technology*. New York City: Bantam Books, 1972.

Dilsaver, Lary M., ed. *America's National Park System: The Critical Documents*. Lanham, MD: Rowman and Littlefield Publishers, 1994.

Dilsaver, Lary M., and William C. Tweed. *Challenge of the Big Trees: A Resources History of the Sequoia and Kings Canyon National Parks*. Three Rivers, CA: Sequoia Natural History Association, 1990.

Dowie, Mark. *Conservation Refugees*. Cambridge, MA: MIT Press, 2009.

Dunraven, Fourth Earl of. *The Great Divide*. London: Chatto and Windus, 1876.

Emerson, Ralph Waldo. *Essays and English Traits*. Edited by Charles W. Eliot. New York City: P. F. Collier and Son, 1909.

Ernst, Joseph W. *Worthwhile Places: Correspondence of John D. Rockefeller Jr. and Horace M. Albright*. New York City: Fordham University Press, 1991.

Everhart, William C. *The National Park Service*. Boulder, CO: Westview Press, 1983.

Fleck, Richard F. *Henry Thoreau and John Muir among the Indians*. Hamden, CT: Archon Books, 1985.

Flint, Linda McClelland. *Building the National Parks: Historic Landscape Design and Construction*. Baltimore, MD: Johns Hopkins University Press, 1998.

Fryxell, Fritiof. *The Tetons: Interpretations of a Mountain Landscape*. Berkeley: University of California Press, 1938.

Gordon-Cumming, C. F. *Granite Crags*. Edinburgh: William Blackwood and Sons, 1884.

Grinnell, Joseph, and Tracy Irwin Storer. *Animal Life in the Yosemite*. Berkeley: University of California Press, 1924.

Hampton, H. Duane. *How the US Cavalry Saved Our National Parks*. Bloomington: Indiana University Press, 1971.

Hartzog, George B., Jr. *Battling for the National Parks*. Mount Kisco, NY: Moyer Bell, 1988.

Hayden, F. V. *The Great West: Its Attractions and Resources*. Bloomington, IN: Charles R. Bordix, 1880.

Hornaday, William T. *Our Vanishing Wild Life: Its Extermination and Preservation*. New York City: Charles Scribner's Sons, 1913.

Ise, John. *Our National Park Policy: A Critical History*. Baltimore, MD: Johns Hopkins Press, 1961.

Jacoby, Karl. *Crimes Against Nature: Squatters, Poachers, Thieves, and the Hidden History of American Conservation*. Berkeley: University of California Press, 2001.

James, G. W. *The Grand Canyon and How to See It*. Boston: Little Brown, 1910.

Jones, Harry. "A London Parson." *To San Francisco and Back*. London: Society for Promoting Christian Knowledge, 1878.

Keiter, Robert B. *To Conserve Unimpaired: The Evolution of the National Park Idea*. Washington, DC: Island Press, 2013.

Keller, Robert H., and Michael F. Turek. *American Indians and National Parks*. Tucson: University of Arizona Press, 1998.

Kephart, Horace. *Our Southern Highlanders*. New York City: Outing Publishing, 1913.

Langford, Nathaniel Pitt. *The Discovery of Yellowstone Park: Journal of the Washburn Expedition to the Yellowstone and Firehole Rivers in the Year 1870*. St. Paul, MN: J. E. Haynes, 1905.

LeConte, Joseph. *A Journal of Ramblings Through the High Sierras of California by the 'University Excursion Party.'* San Francisco: Francis and Valentine, 1875.

Lee, Ronald F. *The Antiquities Act of 1906*. Washington, DC: National Park Service, 1970.

———. *The Origin and Evolution of the National Military Park Idea*. Washington, DC: National Park Service, 1973.

Leopold, Aldo. *A Sand County Almanac*. New York City: Oxford University Press, 1949.

Louter, David. *Windshield Wilderness*. Seattle: University of Washington Press, 2010.

Mackintosh, Barry. *The National Parks: Shaping the System*. Washington, DC: National Park Service, 1991.

Marsh, George P. *Man and Nature; or, Physical Geography*. New York City: Charles Scribner, 1864.

Miles, John C. *Wilderness in National Parks: Playground or Preserve*. Seattle: University of Washington Press, 2009.

Miller, Sally Mae, and Daryl Morrison, eds. *John Muir: Family, Friends, and Adventures*. Albuquerque: University of New Mexico Press, 2005.

Mills, Enos. *The Adventures of a Nature Guide*. New York City: Doubleday, Page, 1920.

———. *Wild Life on the Rockies*. New York City: Houghton Mifflin, 1910.

Muir, John. *My First Summer in the Sierra*. New York City: Houghton Mifflin, 1911.

———. *Travels in Alaska*. New York City: Houghton Mifflin, 1915.

Mumford, Lewis, ed. *Ralph Waldo Emerson: Essays and Journals*. Garden City, NY: Nelson Doubleday, 1968.

Nash, Roderick. *Wilderness and the American Mind.* 4th ed. New Haven, CT: Yale University Press, 2001.

Peterson, Rolf O. *The Wolves of Isle Royale: A Broken Balance.* Ann Arbor: University of Michigan Press, 2007.

Pierce, Daniel S. *The Great Smokies: From Natural Habitat to National Park.* Knoxville: University of Tennessee Press, 2000.

Pinchot, Gifford. *The Fight for Conservation.* New York City: Doubleday, Page, 1910.

Rothman, Hal. *America's National Monuments: The Politics of Preservation.* Lawrence: University Press of Kansas, 1994.

Runte, Alfred. *National Parks: The American Experience.* 3rd ed. Lincoln: University of Nebraska Press, 1997.

———. *Trains of Discovery.* Niwot, CO: Roberts Rinehart Publishers, 1994.

———. *Yosemite: The Embattled Wilderness.* Lincoln: University of Nebraska Press, 1990.

Russell, Carl Parcher. *One Hundred Years in Yosemite.* Berkeley: University of California Press, 1947.

Sax, Joseph L. *Mountains Without Handrails: Reflections on the National Parks.* Ann Arbor: University of Michigan Press, 1980.

Sellars, Richard W. *Preserving Nature in the National Parks: A History.* New Haven, CT: Yale University Press, 1997.

Sontag, William H., ed. *National Park Service: The First 75 Years.* Philadelphia: Eastern National Park and Monument Association, 1990.

Spence, Mark David. *Dispossessing the Wilderness: Indian Removal and the Making of the National Parks.* New York City: Oxford University Press, 2000.

Sumner, Lowell, and Joseph Scattergood Dixon. *Birds and Mammals of the Sierra Nevada: With Records from Sequoia and Kings Canyon National Parks.* Berkeley: University of California Press, 1953.

Thoreau, Henry David. *The Maine Woods.* New York City: Houghton Mifflin, 1906.

Tilden, Freeman. *The National Parks: What They Mean to You and Me.* New York City: Knopf, 1951.

Tweed, William C., Laura E. Soulliere, and Henry G. Law. *Rustic Architecture, 1916–1942.* Washington, DC: National Park Service, Western Regional Office, Division of Cultural Resource Management, February 1977.

Udall, Stewart L. *The Quiet Crisis.* New York City: Hope, Rinehart and Winston, 1967.

Warren, James Perrin. *John Burroughs and the Place of Nature.* Athens: University of Georgia Press, 2006.

Waugh, Frank. *The Natural Style in Landscape Gardening.* Boston: Gorsham Press, 1917.

Wirth, Conrad L. *Parks, Politics, and the People.* Norman: University of Oklahoma Press, 1980.

Yard, Robert Sterling. *Glimpses of Our National Parks.* Washington, DC: Government Printing Office, 1920.

———. *National Parks Portfolio.* Washington, DC: Government Printing Office, 1916.

ARTICLES, REPORTS, STUDIES, AND PAPERS

Adams, Charles C. "Ecological Conditions in National Forests and in National Parks." *Scientific Monthly* 20 (June 1925): 561–593.

Albright, Horace M. "Research in the National Parks." *Scientific Monthly* 36 (June 1933): 483–501.

Anderson, Clinton. "This We Hold Dear." *American Forests*, July 1963.

Annual Report of the Director of the National Park Service to the Secretary of the Interior for the Fiscal Year Ended June 30, 1922 and the Travel Season 1922. Washington, DC: Government Printing Office, 1922.

Annual Report of the Superintendent of National Parks to the Secretary of the Interior. Washington, DC: Government Printing Office, 1916.

Binnewies, Robert, B. J. Griffin, and David Mihalic. "Congress Should Undo the Destructive Raker Act." *San Jose Mercury News*, December 13, 2013.

Brower, David R. "Wilderness—Conflict and Conscience." *Sierra Club Bulletin* 42 (June 1957): 10.

Brown, William E. *A History of the Denali–Mount McKinley Region, Alaska*. Washington, DC: National Park Service, 1991.

Bryant, Harold C., and Wallace W. Atwood Jr. *Research and Education in the National Parks*. Washington, DC: Government Printing Office, 1932.

Buckskin. "Letter from Our Regular Correspondent: Mammoth Hot Springs, Graphic Description of the Wonders of Our Mountains." Bozeman *Avant Courier*, November 2, 1871.

Bureau of Reclamation, Mid-Pacific Region. *Hetch Hetchy: Water and Power Replacement Concepts*. Sacramento, CA: February 1988.

A Call to Action: Preparing for a Second Century of Stewardship and Engagement. Washington, DC: National Park Service, 2013.

Committee on Improving the Science and Technology Programs of the National Park Service, National Research Council. *Science and the National Parks*. Washington, DC: National Academy Press, 1992.

Cook, C. W. "The Valley of the Upper Yellowstone." *Western Monthly Magazine*, July 1870.

Culpin, Mary Shivers. "'For the Benefit and Enjoyment of the People': A History of the Concession Development in Yellowstone National Park, 1872–1966." National Park Service, Yellowstone Center for Resources, Yellowstone National Park, Wyoming, YCR-CR-2003-01.

———. "The History of the Construction of the Road System in Yellowstone National Park, 1872–1966. Historic Resource Study, Volume I." Selections from the Division of Cultural Resources, Rocky Mountain Region, National Park Service. No. 5, 1994.

DeVoto, Bernard. "Let's Close the National Parks." *Harper's Magazine*, October 1953, 49–52.

Dixon, Joseph S. *Fauna of the National Parks of the United States: Birds and Mammals of Mount McKinley National Park*. Washington, DC: National Park Service, Government Printing Office, 1938.

Doane, G. C., Second Lieutenant Second Cavalry. *The Report of Lieut. Gustavus C. Doane upon the So-Called Yellowstone Expedition of 1870 to the Secretary of War*. Washington, DC: August 21, 1870.

Drury, Newton B. "The National Parks in Wartime." *American Forests* 49, August 1943.

Dutton, Clarence E. *Report on the Geology of the High Plateaus of Utah*. Washington, DC: US Geographical and Geological Survey of the Rocky Mountain Region, Government Printing Office, 1880.

———. *Tertiary History of the Grand Canyon District*. Washington, DC: US Geological Survey, Government Printing Office, 1882.

Dykeman, Wilma, and Jim Stokely. *Highland Homeland: The People of the Great Smokies*. Washington, DC: National Park Service History Series, 1978.

Final Report of the Southern Appalachian National Park Commission to the Secretary of the Interior. Washington, DC: Government Printing Office, 1931.

Fleck, Richard F. *Selections from the "Indian Notebooks" (1847–1861) of Henry D. Thoreau*. Lincoln, MA: The Thoreau Institute at Walden Woods, The Walden Woods Project, 2007.

General Accounting Office. *Limited Progress Made in Documenting and Mitigating Threats to the Parks*. Report on Threats to Parks. Washington, DC: 1987.

Grinnell, Joseph, and Tracy Storer. "Animal Life as an Asset of National Parks." *Science* 44 (September 15, 1916): 375, 377.

Grosvenor, Gilbert. "The Land of the Best." *National Geographic Magazine*, April 1916.

Haines, Aubrey L. *The Bannock Indian Trail*. Yellowstone Library and Museum Association in cooperation with the National Park Service, 1964.

Hartzog, George B., Jr. Oral history interview conducted by Janet A. McDonnell. Washington, DC: National Park Service, US Department of the Interior, 2007.

Hayden, Ferdinand V. "The Hot Springs and Geysers of the Yellowstone and Firehole Rivers," *American Journal of Science and the Arts*, 3rd ser., vol. 3, no. 14 (1872): 106–107.

Herrmann, Julie. "Report Highlights Economic Benefits of National Parks in Alaska." *Fairbanks* (Alaska) *Daily News-Miner*, March 9, 2014.

Hill, Craig. "Five National Park Service Workers to Be Added to National Law Enforcement Memorial." *Tacoma News Tribune*, April 23, 2014.

History of the United States Special Naval Hospital. Yosemite National Park: Yosemite Park and Curry Co., January 15, 1946.

Interagency Final Report on Fire Management Policy, Departments of the Interior and Agriculture. Yellowstone National Park, WY: National Park Service, May 5, 1989.

Jackson's Hole Courier. "The Jackson's Hole Courier Raps the 'Courier Dubois.'" March 31, 1921.

Joffe, Joseph. "John W. Meldrum, the Grand Old Man of Yellowstone Park." *Annals of Wyoming* 13, no. 1 (January 1941).

Kieley, James F., ed. *A Brief History of the National Park Service*. Washington, DC: US Department of the Interior, 1940.

Lane, Franklin. *Letter on National Park Management*. Washington, DC: National Park Service, May 13, 1918.

Langford, N. P. *A Report of the Superintendent of the Yellowstone National Park for the Year 1872*. Washington, DC: US Department of the Interior, 1873.

———. "The Wonders of the Yellowstone." *Scribner's Monthly*, 1871.

———. "The Yellowstone Expedition: Interesting Data of the Trip, From Notes Furnished By Hon. N. P. Langford." *Helena* (Montana) *Daily Herald*, September 26, 1870.

Lee, Ronald F. *The Origin and Evolution of the National Military Park Idea*. Washington, DC: Office of Park Historic Preservation, National Park Service, 1973.

Leopold, A. S., S. A. Cain, C. M. Cottam, I. N. Gabrielson, and T. L. Kimball. *Wildlife Management in the National Parks: The Leopold Report*. Washington, DC: Advisory Board on Wildlife Management appointed by Secretary of the Interior Udall, 1963.

Leopold, Aldo. "The Last Stand of the Wilderness." *American Forests and Forest Life* 31, no. 382, October 1925.

Ludlow, Captain William. "Report of a Reconnaissance from Carroll, Montana Territory, on the Upper Missouri, to Yellowstone National Park and Return, Made in the Summer of 1875." War Department, Washington, DC: Government Printing Office, 1876.

Lungren, Dan, and John Van de Kamp. "Restore Yosemite? It Can Be Done." *Los Angeles Times*, December 2, 2013.

Mackintosh, Barry. *Interpretation in the National Park Service: A Historical Perspective*. Washington, DC: National Park Service, 1986.

McClelland, Linda Flint. *Presenting Nature: The Historic Landscape Design of the National Park Service, 1916 to 1942*. Washington, DC: National Park Service, 1993.

McPhee, John. "Ranger." *The New Yorker*. September 11, 1971.

Mech, L. David. *Fauna of the National Parks of the United States: The Wolves of Isle Royale*. Washington, DC: National Park Service, Government Printing Office, 1966.

Monahan, William B., and Nicholas A. Fisichelli. *Climate Exposure of US National Parks in a New Era of Change*. Washington, DC: Natural Resource Stewardship and Science, National Park Service, July 2, 2014.

Muir, John. "Features of the Proposed Yosemite National Park." *The Century Magazine* 40, no. 5 (September 1890).

———. "Let Everyone Help to Save the Famous Hetch-Hetchy Valley and Stop the Commercial Destruction which Threatens Our National Parks: A Brief Statement of the Hetch-Hetchy Case to Date." Pamphlet. San Francisco, CA: Society for the Preservation of National Parks, 1909.

———. Papers. Holt-Atherton Special Collections. University of the Pacific, University Library, Digital Collections. Stockton, CA.

———. "Yosemite Glaciers." *New York Tribune*, December 5, 1871.

Murie, Adolph. *Fauna of the National Parks of the United States: Ecology of the Coyote in the Yellowstone*. Washington, DC: National Park Service, Government Printing Office, 1940.

———. *Fauna of the National Parks of the United States: The Wolves of Mount McKinley*. Washington, DC: National Park Service, Government Printing Office, 1944.

———. *The Grizzlies of Mount McKinley*. Washington, DC: National Park Service, Government Printing Office, 1981.

Musselman, Lloyd K. *Rocky Mountain National Park: Administrative History, 1915–1965*. Washington, DC: National Park Service, 1971.

National Outdoor Recreation Resources Review Commission. *Parks for America, A Survey of Park and Related Resources in the Fifty States and a Preliminary Plan*. Washington, DC: Government Printing Office, 1964.

National Park Service. *State of the Parks*. Washington, DC: Report to Congress, 1980.

———. *A Study of the Parks and Recreation Problem of the United States*. Washington, DC: Government Printing Office, 1941.

National Parks for the 21st Century: The Vail Agenda. Washington, DC: Report and Recommendations to the Director of the National Park Service, 1992.

National Park System Advisory Board Science Committee. *Revisiting Leopold: Resource Stewardship in the National Parks*. Washington, DC: 2012.

"New Parks for the Nation." National Park Service, US Department of the Interior. White House Conference on Conservation, Washington, DC, May 24–25, 1961.

New York Sun. "National Parks as a National Asset." December 26, 1915.

New York Times. "Hetch Hetchy." Editorials, September 4, December 4, and December 9, 1913.

———. "The Hetch Hetchy Steam Roller." Editorial, October 2, 1913.

———. "A National Park Threatened." Editorial, July 12, 1913.

———. "S. T. Mather Dies; Champion of Parks." January 23, 1930.

———. "The Steam Roller Halted." Editorial, October 9, 1913.

1940 Yearbook: Park and Recreation Progress. Washington, DC: Government Printing Office, 1940.

Noe, F. P. *Youth's Perceptions of National Park Service Rangers*. Washington, DC: National Park Service, October 1977.

Norris, P. W. *Report Upon the Yellowstone National Park to the Secretary of the Interior by P. W. Norris, Superintendent for the Year 1877*. Washington, DC: Government Printing Office, 1878.

———. *Report Upon the Yellowstone National Park to the Secretary of the Interior by P. W. Norris, Superintendent for the Year 1878*. Washington, DC: Government Printing Office, 1879.

———. *Report Upon the Yellowstone National Park to the Secretary of the Interior by P. W. Norris, Superintendent for the Year 1879*. Washington, DC: Government Printing Office, 1880.

———. *Annual Report of the Superintendent of the Yellowstone National Park to the Secretary of the Interior for the Year 1880*. Washington, DC: Government Printing Office, 1881.

Ober, Michael J. "The CCC Experience in Glacier National Park." *Montana, the Magazine of Western History* 26 (Summer 1976), 30–39.

Oklahoma City Times. "Former Bandit Lair May Soon Be Park Site." June 7, 1918.

Olmsted, Frederick Law. "Yosemite and the Mariposa Grove: A Preliminary Report, 1865." *Landscape Architecture* 43, no. 1 (October 1952).

Outdoor Recreation Resources Review Commission. *Outdoor Recreation for America—ORRRC Report, 1962*. Report to the president and to Congress by ORRRC, Laurance S. Rockefeller, chairman. Washington, DC: Government Printing Office, January 1962.

Paige, John C. *The Civilian Conservation Corps and the National Park Service, 1933–1942: An Administrative History*. Washington, DC: National Park Service, 1985.

Paige, John C., and Jerome A. Greene. *Administrative History of Chickamauga and Chattanooga National Military Park*. Washington, DC: National Park Service, 1983.

Report of the Director of the National Park Service to the Secretary of the Interior. Washington, DC: Government Printing Office, 1917.

Report of the Director of the National Park Service to the Secretary of the Interior. Washington, DC: Government Printing Office, 1918.

Report of the Director of the National Park Service to the Secretary of the Interior. Washington, DC: Government Printing Office, 1919.

Report of the Director of the National Park Service to the Secretary of the Interior. Washington, DC: Government Printing Office, 1920.

Report of the Director of the National Park Service to the Secretary of the Interior. Washington, DC: Government Printing Office, 1921.

Report of the Director of the National Park Service to the Secretary of the Interior. Washington, DC: Government Printing Office, 1926.

Report of the Director of the National Park Service to the Secretary of the Interior. Washington, DC: Government Printing Office, 1929.

Report upon United States Geographical Surveys West of the 100th Meridian (US). Washington, DC: Government Printing Office, 1889.

Pioneer Press (St. Paul). "An Interview with Former Yellowstone Superintendent, D. W. Wear." September 10, 1886.

Potts, Daniel T. "Early Yellowstone and Western Experiences." *Yellowstone Nature Notes* 21 (September–October 1947): 49–56.

Robbins, W. J., E. A. Ackerman, M. Bates, S. A. Cain, F. D. Darling, J. M. Fogg Jr., T. Gill, J. M. Gillson, E. R. Hall, C. L. Hubbs, and CJS Durham. *National Academy of Sciences Advisory Committee on Research in the National Parks: The Robbins Report*. Washington, DC: National Research Council, August 1, 1963.

Rocky Mountain Weekly Gazette (Helena), "The 'National Park.'" February 19, 1872.

Rydell, Kiki Leigh, and Mary Shivers Culpin. *Managing the 'Matchless Wonders': A History of Administrative Development in Yellowstone National Park, 1872–1965*. Yellowstone National Park, WY: Yellowstone Center for Resources, National Park Service, 2006.

Sax, Joseph L. "America's National Parks: Their Principles, Purposes, and Prospects." *Natural History*, October 1976: 59–87.

Slater, H. D. "A Good Road to Connect All Parks." *El Paso Herald*, August 28, 1920.

Southern Railway Company. "Land of the Sky." Washington, DC: 1903.

Soulliére, Laura E. *Historic Roads in the National Park System*. Washington, DC: National Park Service, 1995.

Stagner, Howard R. "Get the Facts, and Put Them to Work." Comprehensive Natural History Research Program for the National Parks 1962 report, reprinted in *George Wright Forum* 3, no. 4 (1983): 28–38.

Sumner, Lowell. "Biological Research and Management in the National Park Service: A History." *George Wright Forum* 3 (August 1983): 3–27.

"Superintendent's Resolution on Overdevelopment." Prepared at the National Park Service Conference, Yosemite Park, CA, November 13–17, 1922.

Supernaugh, William. "Enigmatic Icon: The Life and Times of Harry Yount." *Annals of Wyoming: Wyoming History Journal* 70, no. 2 (spring 1998).

Unrau, Harlan D., and G. Frank Williss. *Administrative History: Expansion of the National Park Service in the 1930s.* Washington, DC: National Park Service, 1983.

Washington Herald. "National Park Survey Starts." June 16, 1920.

Washington Times. "Uses Private Funds for National Parks: Director of Service Donates Own Money for Improvements Congress Refuses." July 2, 1922.

White, John R. "Letters to the Times: Scare Heads Mislead." *Los Angeles Times.* Letter to editor from superintendent, Sequoia National Park. August 29, 1928.

Williss, G. Frank. *Do Things Right the First Time: Administrative History, The National Park Service and the Alaska National Interest Lands Conservation Act of 1980.* Washington, DC: National Park Service, 1985.

Wright, George M., Joseph S. Dixon, and Ben H. Thompson. *Fauna of the National Parks of the United States: A Preliminary Survey of Faunal Relations in National Parks.* Washington, DC: National Park Service, Government Printing Office, 1933.

Wright, George M., and Ben H. Thompson. *Fauna of the National Parks of the United States: Wildlife Management in the National Parks.* Washington, DC: National Park Service, Government Printing Office, 1934.

SPEECHES, MEETINGS, AND CONGRESSIONAL HEARINGS

Bryce, James, Ambassador of Great Britain. "National Parks—The Need of the Future." Address delivered before the eighth annual convention of the American Civic Association, Baltimore, MD, November 20, 1912.

Cain, Stanley A. "Ecological Islands as Natural Laboratories." Presented at the Sixth Biennial Wilderness Conference, San Francisco, March 20–21, 1959.

Carver, John A., Jr. "Remarks by Assistant Secretary of the Interior John A. Carver Jr." National Park Service Conference of Challenges, Yosemite National Park, October 14, 1963.

McFarland, J. Horace. "The Economic Destiny of the National Parks." Address delivered at the National Parks Conference, Washington, DC, January 3, 1917.

Olson, Sigurd F. "Those Intangible Things." Speech given at the Izaak Walton League of America's national convention, Chicago, 1954.

"Proceedings of the (First) National Park Conference held at Yellowstone National Park September 11 and 12, 1911." Washington, DC: Government Printing Office, 1912.

"Proceedings of the (Second) National Park Conference held at Yosemite National Park October 14, 15 and 16, 1912." Washington, DC: Government Printing Office, 1913.

"Proceedings of the (Third) National Parks Conference held at Berkeley, California, March 11, 12, and 13, 1915." Washington, DC: Government Printing Office, 1915.

"Proceedings of the (Fourth) National Parks Conference Held in the Auditorium of the New National Museum, Washington, DC, January 2, 3, 4, 5 and 6, 1917." Washington, DC: Government Printing Office, 1917.

US Congress. House. Committee on the Public Lands. *Hearing on H. J. Res. 184 Before the Committee on the Public Lands: San Francisco and the Hetch Hetchy Reservoir.* December 16, 1908. Washington, DC: Government Printing Office, 1908.

US Congress. House. Committee on the Public Lands. *Hetch Hetchy Dam Site*, Robert Underwood Johnson letter, 63rd Cong., 1st sess. June 25–28, 1913; July 7, 1913. Washington, DC: Government Printing Office, 1913.

US Congress. Senate. *Mariposa Big Tree Grove, S. 203.* 38th Cong., 1st sess, 1864. Later printed in the *Congressional Globe*, p. 2301.

US Congress. Senate. Subcommittee on National Parks, Committee on Energy and Natural Resources. *Hearing to Consider a Recently Released Report for the National Park Service: A Call to Action: Preparing for a Second Century of Stewardship and Engagement.* 102nd Cong., 1st sess., September 21, 2011.

ORAL HISTORIES AND ARCHIVES

National Park Service: Thousands of NPS pamphlets, handbooks, interpretive displays, visitor center films, maps, and web pages are available thanks to past and present park staff and the adept NPS Harpers Ferry Center, www.nps.gov/hfc. I could not have navigated successfully in more than 150 national park units, or within this book, without these sources. The NPS also has enlightening oral-history projects associated with many parks and makes interviews—some transcripts, some audio—available on parks' web pages. Some of the richest include the I Remember Yosemite project; Civilian Conservation Corps histories at Shenandoah National Park; Rosie the Riveter–World War II Home Front National Historical Park's video series; Gateway National Recreation Area's multifaceted topics; hundreds of interviews related to Lowell National Historical Park; and Project Jukebox, in collaboration with Denali, Katmai, Lake Clark, Sitka, and Yukon–Charley Rivers parks.

Library of Congress: American Memory historical collections, searchable at www.memory.loc .gov, contain the full text of much of the legislation described in this book. Chronicling America, available at www.chroniclingamerica.loc.gov, is a vast historical newspaper archive, a time machine really, into what was going on in the nation and the world during various time periods discussed in the book. The Evolution of the Conservation Movement, 1850–1920, National Digital Library Program, is an archival project consisting of 62 books and pamphlets, 140 federal statutes and congressional resolutions, 34 additional legislative documents, excerpts from the *Congressional Globe* and the *Congressional Record*, 360 presidential proclamations, 170 prints and photographs, 2 historic manuscripts, and 2 motion pictures.

University of California–Berkeley, Bancroft Library: The Regional Oral History Office has some valuable digitized interviews at http://bancroft.berkeley.edu/ROHO/.

Wyoming State Library: The Wyoming Newspaper Project provides digital access to highly entertaining issues (1914–1922) of the *Jackson's Hole Courier* at www.newspapers.wyo.gov.

OTHER AGENCIES AND ORGANIZATIONS
Some historical and current information was gleaned from nonprofit organizations listed below. Useful also were the online archives of other government agencies, as well as those for many scientific organizations and academic institutions.

Aldo Leopold Foundation, www.aldoleopold.org
Appalachian Mountain Club, www.outdoors.org
American Association for the Advancement of Science, www.aaas.org
Bureau of Land Management, www.blm.gov
Cornell Lab of Ornithology, www.birds.cornell.edu
Ecological Society of America, www.esa.org
Environmental Protection Agency, www.epa.gov
Federal Bureau of Investigation, www.fbi.gov
George Wright Society, www.georgewright.org
The Mountaineers, www.mountaineers.org
Museum of Vertebrate Zoology at the University of California–Berkeley, http://mvz.berkeley.edu
National Academy of Sciences, www.nasonline.org
National Audubon Society, www.audubon.org
National Oceanic and Atmospheric Administration, www.noaa.gov
National Parks Conservation Association, www.npca.org
Nature Conservancy, www.nature.org
Save the Redwoods League, www.savetheredwoods.org
Sierra Club, www.sierraclub.org
Smithsonian Institution, www.si.edu
US Army Corps of Engineers, www.usace.army.mil
US Fish and Wildlife Service, www.fws.gov
US Forest Service, www.fs.fed.us
US Geological Survey, www.usgs.gov
Wilderness Society, www.wilderness.org

INDEX

ABOUT THE AUTHOR

HEATHER HANSEN is an independent reporter based in Boulder, Colorado. She has been on staff US and international newspapers and magazines, and her work has appeared in many national publications. Hansen is the coauthor of *Disappearing Destinations*, a critically acclaimed guide to the world's endangered places that received the American Society of Journalists and Authors' general nonfiction prize; the Colorado Authors' League's creative nonfiction prize; and Society of American Travel Writers' Lowell Thomas Award. Learn more about Hansen and the NPS at www.traveltoparks .com and on Twitter @travel2parks.

For this book Hansen logged roughly 20,000 miles in her trusty though filthy hybrid Honda visiting many of America's best places. She ate pounds of campfire mac and cheese while reliving her early days as a junior ranger on Cape Cod National Seashore thirty years ago. Hansen communed with spirits on the Natchez Trace, listened to wolves bay in Yellowstone, relearned everything she'd forgotten about the Civil War, realized how much Steve Jobs had in common with Thomas Edison, and was touched by the fulfilling desolation of Sequoia's wilderness. She'll never tire of the question, "Which park is your favorite?"

recreation • lifestyle • conservation

MOUNTAINEERS BOOKS is a leading publisher of mountaineering literature and guides—including our flagship title, *Mountaineering: The Freedom of the Hills*—as well as adventure narratives, natural history, and general outdoor recreation. Through our two imprints, Skipstone and Braided River, we also publish titles on sustainability and conservation. We are committed to supporting the environmental and educational goals of our organization by providing expert information on human-powered adventure, sustainable practices at home and on the trail, and preservation of wilderness.

The Mountaineers, founded in 1906, is a 501(c)(3) nonprofit outdoor activity and conservation organization whose mission is "to explore, study, preserve, and enjoy the natural beauty of the outdoors." One of the largest such organizations in the United States, it sponsors classes and year-round outdoor activities throughout the Pacific Northwest, including climbing, hiking, backcountry skiing, snowshoeing, bicycling, camping, paddling, and more. The Mountaineers also supports its mission through its publishing division, Mountaineers Books, and promotes environmental education and citizen engagement. For more information, visit The Mountaineers Program Center, 7700 Sand Point Way NE, Seattle, WA 98115-3996; phone 206-521-6001; www.mountaineers.org; or email info@mountaineers.org.

Our publications are made possible through the generosity of donors and through sales of more than 600 titles on outdoor recreation, sustainable lifestyle, and conservation. To donate, purchase books, or learn more, visit us online:

MOUNTAINEERS BOOKS
1001 SW Klickitat Way, Suite 201 • Seattle, WA 98134
800-553-4453 • mbooks@mountaineersbooks.org • www.mountaineersbooks.org

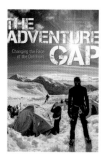
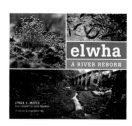

OTHER MOUNTAINEERS BOOKS TITLES YOU MAY ENJOY!